THINKING AND WRITING ABOUT LITERATURE

A Text and Anthology

Resources for Teaching

SECOND EDITION

THINKING AND WRITING ABOUT LITERATURE
A Text and Anthology

Michael Meyer
University of Connecticut

Julie Nash
University of Connecticut

Ellen Darion

Quentin Miller
Gustavus Adolphus College

Anne Phillips
Kansas State University

John Repp
University of Pittsburgh

Robert Spirko
University of North Carolina, Chapel Hill

BEDFORD/ST. MARTIN'S Boston ◆ New York

For information, write: Bedford/St. Martin's, 75 Arlington Street, Boston, MA 02116 (617-399-4000)

ISBN: 0-312-25920-4

Contents

Preface

This instructor's manual is designed to be a resource of commentaries, interpretations, and suggestions for teaching the works included in *Thinking and Writing About Literature*. The entries offer advice about how to approach the literary selections in the text and suggest possible interpretations. Many of the entries also suggest topics for discussion and writing. No attempt has been made to generate definitive readings of the works; the text selections are rich enough to accommodate multiple approaches. Our hope is that the instructors will take what they find useful and leave the rest behind. Inevitably, instructors will disagree with some of the commentaries, but perhaps such disagreements will provide starting points for class discussion.

The format of the entries varies from itemized responses to specific questions to brief essays that present overall views of individual works. This flexibility allows each entry to be more responsive to the nature of a particular work and the questions asked about it in the text. Every entry includes suggestions for further connections. The manual is conveniently arranged by genre and follows the organization of the text. Page references corresponding to the text are included at the top of each page of the manual and after the title of each entry.

This manual also includes tips for teaching the elements of literature, and tips for teaching writing about fiction, poetry, drama, and essays. There are possible approaches to each chapter's student casebook of Writing in Process, with two alternative writing assignments for each casebook. The anthology's final chapters are organized thematically, and the manual contains an introduction to each unit which discusses the connections among several works within the chapter. Entries within these thematically organized chapters often suggest connections to similar works in other chapters as well.

This instructor's manual also contains a number of "Tips from the Field" — class-tested teaching suggestions from instructors who have taught from previous editions. If you have a teaching tip that you would like to submit for the next edition of this instructor's manual, please send it to Aron Keesbury, Editor, at Bedford/St. Martin's, 75 Arlington St., Boston, MA 02116. Your teaching suggestion should be approximately 50 words long and suggest ways of teaching an author or selection that have been particularly effective in your classroom experience. If we use your teaching suggestion, we will be happy to acknowledge you in the manual and pay you an honorarium.

For those instructors who wish to incorporate research into their classes, the Bedford Links to Resources in Literature at www.bedfordstmartins.com/litlinkis.html. are a great resource for merging the research process with the possibilities of the Internet. The links have already been screened and can take students deep into the web and into the world of the author or literary period they are studying.

We hope you and your students enjoy *Thinking and Writing about Literature*, and that you find this instructor's manual a useful complement to the anthology.

THINKING AND WRITING ABOUT LITERATURE

A Text and Anthology

PART I. LITERATURE AND THE WRITING PROCESS

1

Reading and Responding

TIPS FOR TEACHING
RESPONSIVE READING

Teaching students to be responsive readers of literature can be a challenge; of course, all college students know how to read, and most of them have been exposed to literature on their own and in school. Yet although many students have experience reading literature, they sometimes lack the training to get the most out of what they read. Reading actively with an eye for certain details will enable them to better respond to the works in both discussion and writing.

As Chapter 1 points out, "Experience tells us that people respond differently to the same work" (p. 13). You might begin teaching this chapter by acknowledging this fact and asking students to discuss the ways individuals bring their own biases, knowledge, and experience to a work of literature. In many ways, literary interpretation is subjective; there is no single "correct" reading of a short story, poem, play, or essay. Yet opinions about literature must be grounded in careful textual readings.

Call your students' attention to the chapter's section on annotating a text and taking notes (p. 14). As students learn to read literature responsively, they should become able to recognize and discuss certain elements of literature and how these elements unite to create a total effect. You may want to suggest that students take note of and annotate the following elements of literature as they read:

Figurative language: Language that literally means one thing while implying another meaning. Figurative language includes similes, metaphors, and other forms of symbolism. How does this language function in relation to the work as a whole? What patterns exist? Repetitions?

Structure: The way a work of literature is arranged. Is a poem organized into stanzas? A play into acts? A novel into chapters? How does the structure of a work affect your reading of it? Why might an author choose a looser or more formal structure for his or her writing?

Sound and rhythm: The way a work of literature sounds when read aloud has an important effect on the reader. Students should be able to identify the following:

Rhyme — the repetition of similar sounds in the concluding syllables of words

Rhythm — sound stresses at regular intervals

Alliteration — the repetition of the initial sounds in a series of words

Onomatopoeia — words that imitate the sounds they denote

Setting: The physical and social background of a work of literature, especially time and place. How does the setting affect the tone of the work? Are descriptions of setting detailed and descriptive, or minimal? How does an author's attention to setting affect your reading?

Diction: The writer's choice of words and the way they are arranged. Encourage students to circle and look up unfamiliar words. Are certain words or phrases repeated or emphasized? To what effect?

Total effect: Each element of literature cannot exist in a vacuum but must be read in conjunction with the other elements. For example, what words, phrases, or ideas does the writer seem to be emphasizing by using figurative language, rhyme, or alliteration? Are certain terms difficult to reconcile? If so, why might the writer be posing this problem?

WRITING IN PROCESS: READING AND FIRST RESPONSE

The character of Mrs. Mallard in Kate Chopin's "The Story of an Hour" is likely to elicit strong reactions from students. This chapter's casebook builds on this fact and demonstrates the way a student transforms his own personal response to one character into a thoughtful, balanced essay.

KATE CHOPIN, *The Story of an Hour* (p. 18)

Katherine (Kate) Chopin was born in 1851 and was educated in St. Louis. The mother of six children, she produced her first novel, *At Fault,* in 1890. *Bayou Folk* (1894) and *A Night in Acadie* (1897), both collections of short stories, were followed in 1899 by Chopin's most well-known work, *The Awakening,* a work denounced by critics and judged to be "immoral." At the time of her death in 1904, Chopin left unpublished a novel, *Young Dr. Gosse,* and a short story collection, *A Vocation and a Voice,* from which "The Story of an Hour" is taken. Her fiction commonly depicts heroines who attempt to balance personal independence with the demands of marriage, motherhood, and society.

As you begin to consider this story, lead the class into a discussion of Mrs. Mallard's character. What do they think of her? Even for the twenty-first century, this is in certain ways a bold story, and there are likely to be students who will describe the protagonist as callous, selfish, unnatural — even, in Mrs. Mallard's own words, "monstrous" — because of her joyous feeling of freedom after her initial grief and shock. Go through the text with the class, looking for evidence that this radical shift in feeling is genuine. To demonstrate her grief and subsequent numbness, you might point to Mrs. Mallard's weeping with "sudden, wild abandonment" (paragraph 3), the "physical exhaustion that haunted her body . . . and soul" (4), the way she sat "motionless, except when a sob came up into her throat and shook her, as a child who has cried itself to sleep continues to sob in its dreams" (7), and her look, which "indicated a suspension of intelligent thought" (8). Especially important to the defense of Mrs. Mallard's character is her effort to fight off "this thing that was approaching to possess her": "she was striving to beat it back with her will" (9–10).

Ask students to discuss (or write about) what they imagine Mrs. Mallard's marriage to have been like. If her husband "had never looked save with love upon her" (13), what was wrong with the marriage? The answer can be found in the lines "She had loved him — sometimes. Often she had not. . . . What could love, the unsolved mystery, count for in the face of this possession of self-assertion which she suddenly recognized as the strongest impulse of her being!" (15). The surprise ending aside (some readers may find it manipulative), this story is basically about a woman awakening to the idea that all the love and stability in the world can't compensate for her lack of control over her own life.

Ask the class if they can locate any symbols in the story. "The tops of trees that were all aquiver with the new spring life," sparrows "twittering" (5), "patches of blue sky showing...through the clouds" (6), and "the sounds, the scents, the color that filled the air" (9) all suggest the renewal and rebirth that follow.

Students could also write about the ending of the story, specifically the last three paragraphs. What is the tone here? (Ironic. First, Mrs. Mallard suffers a heart attack when she sees her husband, rather than when she learns of his death, which is when everyone originally feared she would have an attack. Second, she does not die of joy, as the doctors claim, but of shock — the shock of having to go back to her old way of life once she has realized there is another way to live.)

For additional background material, see Per Seyersted's *Kate Chopin: A Critical Biography* (Baton Rouge: Louisiana State UP, 1969); Marlene Springer's *Edith Wharton and Kate Chopin: A Reference Guide* (Boston: G. K. Hall, 1976); and Carol P. Christ's *Diving Deep and Surfacing: Women Writers on Spiritual Quest* (Boston: Beacon, 1980).

POSSIBLE CONNECTIONS TO OTHER SELECTIONS

Dagoberto Gilb, "Love in L.A." (text p. 793)
Susan Glaspell, *Trifles* (text p. 496)

RESOURCE FOR TEACHING

Kate Chopin's "The Story of an Hour." 24 min., color, 1982, $1/2''$ open reel (EIAJ), 16-mm film. A dramatization of the story, with an examination of Chopin's life. Distributed by Ishtar.

SUGGESTED TEACHING METHOD

Journal.

Before asking students to read Chopin's story, have them write a journal entry or freewrite about marriage in general. What are their expectations of marriage? What has been their experience with marriage (either their own or that of their parents)? What do they think is the function of marriage? How do they perceive the institution of marriage as changing over time? Then ask them to read "The Story of an Hour," annotating the text as they do so. What is their response to Mrs. Mallard in light of their initial thoughts on marriage? Does Mrs. Mallard's reaction to her husband's "death" violate or confirm their previous opinions about marriage in general? You might also direct students to the "Considerations for Critical Thinking and Writing" (p. 20) and/or the "Questions for Responsive Reading and Writing" (p. 21) to help focus their first responses to the story.

Next, ask students to compare their own textual annotations to those of Wally Villa (p. 22). In general, you can expect students' annotations to be less detailed than Wally's. (Many students have a hard time overcoming a reluctance to write in their book.) Beyond that, ask them what they highlighted that Wally did not and vice versa. What do these similarities and differences say about the different reactions readers might have to the same text?

Similiarly, you might ask students to compare Wally Villa's first response to Mrs. Mallard to the one they generated earlier. Do the different initial responses support Wally's assertion that "readings of Mrs. M[allard] have a lot to do with readers themselves" (p. 24)?

ALTERNATIVE ASSIGNMENTS:

1. In this casebook, you have followed one student's response to a short story, Kate Chopin's "The Story of an Hour." You have seen one way in which a student writer approaches the process of reading, annotating, note-taking, writing a draft, and completing an essay. Write an essay in which you respond to Wally Villa's work in

light of your own responses to literature. What do you admire about the way he responded to the story? How do your own approaches to literature differ? What kind of essay might you have written in response to Chopin's story? What are the strengths and weaknesses of your approach?

2. The assignment to which Wally Villa responded, "Write a three- to four-page discussion of how different readers might interpret Mrs. Mallard's character," elicited from Wally an interesting paper that drew on the ideas of a number of different people in his life. Respond to another work of literature in this text using the same assignment, discussing how different readers might interpret a controversial character. Like Wally, you should annotate the work to which you are responding, take notes, and ask others to read and respond to the work.

Suggested Readings:

T. S. Eliot, "The Love Song of J. Alfred Prufrock" (text p. 1280)
William Faulkner, "A Rose for Emily" (text p. 144)
Lorraine Hansberry, *A Raisin in the Sun* (text p. 636)
Robert Hayden, "Those Winter Sundays" (text p. 214)
David Henry Hwang, *M. Butterfly* (text p. 1296)
Sylvia Plath, "Daddy" (text p. 628)

DISCUSS: Responsive reading #2.
go over page 20 text . for Discussion pts.

2

Writing and Revising

TIPS FOR TEACHING WRITING ABOUT LITERATURE

This chapter describes the process of writing an essay about literature from the earliest stages of choosing a topic to revising the final draft. While many of your students have probably written about literature in the past, teaching a systematic approach to writing like the one demonstrated here can make the process seem less daunting.

Many instructors find it necessary to emphasize the distinction between choosing a topic and developing a thesis; too often students will light on a topic, but have difficulty focusing that topic into a workable thesis. As you teach this section of the book (pp. 29–46), you might develop some sample topics and thesis statements, asking students to determine which ones are more successful and why. Below are some sample topics about Kate Chopin's "The Story of an Hour" (p. 18). Some of these are too narrow, too obvious, or too broad for a short paper. Ask your students to evaluate these topics and determine which ones they find successful and how they might improve the others:

1. Grief in "The Story of an Hour"
2. Marriage in turn-of-the-century America
3. Freedom and imprisonment in "The Story of an Hour"
4. The meaning of the title in "The Story of an Hour"
5. A comparison of Mrs. Mallard and other wives throughout American literature
6. A comparison of Mrs. Mallard and Mrs. Wright from Susan Glaspell's drama *Trifles* (p. 496)

Next, present students with a number of sample thesis statements for their evaluation. Students should be able to identify what makes a thesis statement strong and discuss how a vague or obvious thesis can be improved. Here are some possible thesis statements for a paper on "The Story of an Hour." Which ones are weak? How might students revise them to make them work for a short paper?

1. "The Story of an Hour" is about a woman who is happy when she thinks her husband is dead.
2. Both Mrs. Mallard in "The Story of an Hour," and Mrs. Wright in Susan Glaspell's play *Trifles* are women who see the death of their husbands as their only avenue to freedom.
3. An examination of imagery in "The Story of an Hour" reveals a preoccupation with freedom and imprisonment, but also an ambivalence about them.
4. Mrs. Mallard is a typical oppressed woman from the nineteenth century.
5. Mrs. Mallard's feelings of confusion, fear, and elation upon hearing of her husband's death are normal responses to the new experience of freedom and responsibility that accompanies widowhood.

TYPES OF WRITING ASSIGNMENTS

The book lists several types of essays that are frequently assigned in introductory literature courses. You will of course want to direct your students' attention to the types of assignments that you will be giving your own class and point out that these categories, while useful for the purposes of instruction, are somewhat artificial. In reality, a good essay about literature will demonstrate more than one technique. When introducing each type of assignment, consider the following:

Personal Response: Personal response essays are often very successful because students enjoy the freedom to write about their own ideas, opinions, and even experiences in connection with literature. This kind of assignment helps teach that literature (even the literature of the past!) is relevant to today's readers, and it can involve students in ways that a more formal assignment sometimes cannot. On the other hand, it is important to emphasize that students should still base their responses on the actual language of the text. Direct references, quotations, and well-developed ideas are still an important part of a successful response paper. See the Alternative Assignments in Chapter 1's student casebook (p. 21) for examples of personal response assignments. See also Chapter 1's student casebook (p. 17) for an example of a personal response essay.

Explication: As the text states, "an explication pays careful attention to language — the connotations of words, allusions, figurative language, irony, symbol, rhythm, sound, and so on." A writing assignment that is primarily an explication is an excellent way to teach these terms and to demonstrate how they can work together to achieve a total effect. Most essays about literature use some type of explication, so you may choose to ask students to write an explication prior to assigning other types of essays. Many of the "Considerations for Critical Thinking and Writing" questions in this book ask for explications. See also Chapter 6's student casebook (p. 272) for an example of an explication.

Analysis: Like an explication, an analysis requires that writers pay close attention to textual details. In this case, the writer concentrates on the ways an author uses a single element to create a total effect. Often the biggest challenge student writers face as they write a literary analysis is developing their points and drawing conclusions. Many students may be adept at locating an element — irony, for example — but they may be unsure of how to discuss its contribution to the work as a whole. For this reason, assigning an analysis is a good way to teach the importance of making connections in writing about literature. Ask students, "How does this example of irony (or whatever element they are focusing on) connect to the previous one we discussed? How do both examples affect the way you read the work?" Many of the "Considerations for Critical Thinking and Writing" questions following works in this book ask for analysis. See also Chapter 7's student casebook (p. 494) for an example of a character analysis essay.

Comparison and Contrast: Here is another assignment that asks students to complete close readings of the text(s) and draw conclusions about those readings. Again, your challenge is to encourage students to make connections between these similarities and differences and draw conclusions about them. It's not enough to notice that a theme or symbol is similar (or different) within or between works; students should also be able to discuss the significance of these connections. Ask relevant questions such as, "Why might such similarities be found in otherwise different works?"; "What is the writer trying to emphasize by contrasting these two characters?" The "Connections to Other Selections" questions following works in this book ask for comparison and contrast. See also Chapter 5's student casebook (p. 175) for an example of a comparison and contrast essay.

Applying a Critical Strategy: Many students are intimidated when asked to apply a critical strategy to a work of literature until they are reminded that *all* readings of literature use some kind of critical strategy. When they write this type of essay, make sure students have a good understanding of both the strategy itself (see Chapter 3, "Applying a Critical

Strategy,") and the text with which they are working. Remind them that using a theoretical approach does not eliminate the need for explication and analysis to help support their interpretation of a reading. Many of the "Considerations for Critical Thinking and Writing" questions following works in this book use a critical strategy. See also Chapter 9's student casebook (p. 759) for an example of an essay that applies a critical strategy.

Writing from Sources: Like applying a critical strategy, writing from sources is often an intimidating assignment. (See Chapter 4, "Writing from Sources.") For an introductory course, you might consider spending at least one class period in the library, showing students how to use the resources available to them. Have them locate and read some examples of the type of literary criticism you would like to see them model in their own papers. See the Alternative Assignments in Chapter 4's student casebook (p. 123) for examples of research assignments. See also Chapter 4's student casebook (p. 128) for an example of an essay that incorporates secondary sources.

WRITING IN PROCESS: THE THESIS STATEMENT

This chapter's student casebook focuses on one of the most important and difficult steps in the writing process; revising and honing the thesis. The story itself, David Updike's "Summer," is accessible enough for students to understand and relate to, though they may find it "too obvious." Because the story's characters and events are fairly straightforward, many students may not initially find material on which to write. The processes of writing a first response and brainstorming will likely draw out more than they had initially noticed.

DAVID UPDIKE, *Summer* (p. 47)

"Summer" is a celebration of both a time of year and a time of life. This story of teen protagonist Homer's subtle pursuit of Sandra, his friend Fred's sister, is vitalized by the descriptions of the lake and the characters' youthful energy. From the opening description of the way Homer and Fred pass their time (in athletics, predominantly) to the closing description of the final night at the lake, Updike lavishes description on the images of summer. His story is replete with references to images that evoke all the senses. Students might trace them throughout the story.

Even the characters' names allude to aspects of the summer. "Homer" — as if from home-run — reminds us of one of the boys' favorite activities. (Baseball players are known as "the boys of summer.") Updike's characters play some form of baseball indoors as well as outside, as detailed by the first paragraph: "a variant of baseball adapted to the local geography: two pine trees as foul poles, a broomstick as the bat, the apex of the small, secluded house the dividing line between home runs and outs. On rainy days they swatted bottle tops across the living room floor." Is "Homer" also an indication that the summer — and the adventure — will end in a satisfying way? The name for the female love interest is equally apt: "Sandra" evokes summer; it recalls the lake, the sunshine; it even recalls the female protagonist of the popular 1970s musical and film *Grease*, who sings a duet with the male lead about the romance of "Summer Nights." Finally, the other prominent name contained in Updike's story also emphasizes the theme: here, Thyme equals "time." Not only is summer ending and autumn arriving, but there is the sense that Homer and his friend Fred are at the peak of their vitality. Their sense of indestructibility (drinking for the first time, "wrestl[ing] the car" [11]) and their energy (manifested through their many athletic activities) are relevant indeed. It is during this summer that they become "unofficial [tennis] champions of the lake by trouncing the elder Dewitt boys, unbeaten in several years" (13). It is no coincidence that "glum Billy Dewitt" attributes his loss to the boys' youth. Homer thinks that although Dewitt jests, he also is "hiding some greater sense of loss" (13); indeed, Dewitt's metaphorical "summer," his career as champion, is over.

Although Homer doesn't acknowledge his longing for Sandra until the end of paragraph 9, readers are given many clues that he has a crush on her prior to that point in the story. For instance, Homer lavishes description on Sandra. Instead of saying, "Sandra never tanned," he savors her image: "When she first came in her face was faintly flushed, and there was a pinkish line around the snowy band where her bathing suit strap had been, but the back of her legs remained an endearing, pale white, the color of eggshells, and her back acquired only the softest, brownish blur" (5). The words "endearing" and "softest" indicate his affection for her. He also notes with frustration that she is "strangely indifferent to his heroics" (6).

Of course, there are several hints in the story that Sandra is less oblivious to Homer's crush than he imagines. Although he hopes to impress her by winning the tennis match, she utterly distracts him by leaving at the crucial moment: "Homer watched her as she went down the path, and, impetus suddenly lost, he double faulted, stroked a routine backhand over the back fence, and the match was over" (6). Worst of all, she doesn't even focus on him as he tells her about it afterward. All she says is, "I wish I could go sailing" (7). Coming home from the hike up the mountain, she keeps "his elbow hopelessly held in the warm crook of her arm" (10). Readers must wonder how much of Sandra's summer has been a subtle, friendly campaign to drive Homer to distraction — after all, she's described more than once as appearing in front of him from nowhere, stretching or calling attention to her body in some way, teasing him with her laughter as they cruise home after her shift at the bowling alley. His favorite words for approximating her attraction are "indifference" and "oblivious": "as silently as she arrived, she would leave, walking back through the stones with the same casual sway of indifference" (5); "her life went on its oblivious, happy course without him" (10); "Homer sat at the counter and watched her serve up sloshing cups of coffee, secretly loathing the leering gazes of whiskered truck drivers, and loving her oblivious, vacant stare in answer, hip cocked, hand on counter, gazing up into the neon air above their heads" (12). As the final paragraph of the story reveals, however, Sandra has been anything but indifferent or oblivious throughout Homer's visit to the lake. Looking back on the story after having read it all, students will appreciate the humor and irony of the passages that stress her disregard for Homer.

Homer admits that "to touch her, or kiss her, seemed suddenly incongruous, absurd, contrary to something he could not put his finger on"; "he realized he had never been able to imagine the moment he distantly longed for" (14). Ask students to discuss Homer's motivation here. Why doesn't he kiss Sandra? Why doesn't he need to demonstrate his affection for her in some tangible way? What is there in the story that indicates that longing itself is enough? Is there any connection between his distanced affection for Sandra and his interest in the girl in the canoe who waves to them at the end of the summer? He tells us, "there was something in the way that she raised her arm which, when added to the distant impression of her fullness, beauty, youth, filled him with longing as their boat moved inexorably past, slapping the waves, and she disappeared behind a crop of trees" (15). Is this in some sense a metaphor for the ending of his pursuit of Sandra as the summer comes to a close?

Midway through this story, Homer, the teenage protagonist, reads one of Sir Arthur Conan Doyle's Sherlock Holmes stories (4). In many ways, "Summer" is also a detective story in which Homer discovers that his interpretation of the events at the lake has not been accurate. For an entertaining comparison, students might look up "A Scandal in Bohemia," the one Sherlock Holmes story in which Holmes meets his match, in a woman, Irene Adler. Sandra's outmaneuvering of Homer is in many ways reminiscent of both the mystery and the romance of "A Scandal in Bohemia." One of Holmes's favorite expressions for the thrill of the mystery is "the game's afoot!" Here, the game of teen romance enacted by Sandra and Homer is most satisfyingly, indeed, by the end of the story literally "afoot."

Possible Connections to Other Selections

Dagoberto Gilb, "Love in L.A." (text p. 793)
John Updike, "A & P" (text p. 981)

Suggested Teaching Method

Ask students to read the story and prepare responses to the "Considerations for Critical Thinking and Writing" (p. 51). Either before or after some discussion of "Summer," consider a creative in-class writing assignment to further elicit student responses. You might ask students to write a "sequel" to this story, imitating David Updike's writing style. Despite the narrator's assertion that "this was as far as [their romance] would ever go" (p. 51), do your students see more of a future for Homer and Sandra? What stylistic devices did your students emphasize?

As an alternative, you could ask students to write about the same summer vacation from Sandra's perspective, thereby highlighting the importance of point-of-view in fiction — even in fiction that is written with a third-person narrator. After students have done their own creative writing, ask them to read their work out loud or to share their writing with classmate. Students will probably enjoy the opportunity to write creatively and to compare their own responses to the story's ending or characters with those of their classmates.

Alternative Assignments

1. This assignment can have two or three parts. The shorter version does not include the analysis of the writing process itself, but does include generating a thesis and writing a short paper:

    Generate your own thesis about David Updike's short story, and take that thesis through the same process of revision through which rose Vanderman takes hers, responding to the Questions for Writing (p. 52) and revising the thesis as you do so. Then write a short paper using your new, revised thesis. Finally, write an analysis of the process you used. How did the thesis revision exercise improve the final paper? In retrospect, could you have improved your thesis even more? How important was your thesis to your final paper as a whole?

2. Write an analysis of the relationship between Homer and Sandra, using the questions and descriptions in paragraph 9 (p. 49) of the story to help you focus your ideas and hone your thesis. How much of Homer's attraction to Sandra depends on circumstance and setting? How much is based on the length of their acquaintance? Based on your knowledge of human nature, as well as clues in the text, what is the future of this relationship?

3

Applying a Critical Strategy

Although there is an emphasis on critical strategies for reading throughout *Thinking and Writing about Literature*, this chapter brings into focus an increasing tendency in introductory literature classes to make students aware of critical approaches to literature used by contemporary theorists. The treatment of the eleven major approaches discussed in this chapter — formalist, biographical, psychological, historical (including Marxist, new historicist, and cultural criticism), gender (including feminist and gay and lesbian criticism), mythological, reader-response, and deconstructionist — is designed to supplement the more general Questions for Responsive Reading and Writing that are provided in each genre section. These critical strategies range from long-standing traditional approaches, such as those practiced by biographical and historical critics, to more recent and controversial perspectives represented, for example, by feminist and deconstructionist critics.

By introducing students to competing critical strategies, you can help them to understand that there are varying strategies for talking about literary works. A familiarity with some of the basic assumptions of these strategies and with the types of questions raised by particular ways of reading will aid students in keeping their bearing during class discussions as well as in the deep water of the secondary readings they're likely to encounter for their writing assignments. After studying this chapter, students should have a firmer sense that there can be many valid and interesting readings of the same work. Their recognition should open up some of the interpretive possibilities offered by any given text while simultaneously encouraging students to feel more confident about how their own reading raises particular kinds of questions and leads them into the text. In short, this chapter can empower students to think through their own critical interpretations in relation to a number of critical contexts.

This chapter can be assigned at any point during the course. Some instructors may find it useful to assign the chapter at the start of the course so that students are aware of the range of critical approaches from the beginning. Many students are likely to raise more informed and sophisticated questions about texts as a result of having been exposed to these critical strategies. Instructors who wish to introduce this chapter early in the course may want to take a look at the appendix in this manual entitled "Perspectives by Critical Strategies for Reading," which organizes the perspectives throughout the book by the critical strategy they most exemplify. Other instructors may prefer to lead up to the critical perspectives and assign the chapter later in the course as a means of pulling together the elements of literature taken up during the preceding weeks. When you do assign the chapter, however, remind students to first read Kate Chopin's "The Story of an Hour" (p. 18), since each of the critical approaches is applied to that particular work as well as to other texts.

The purpose of this chapter is not to transform students into Annette Kolodnys or Northrup Fryes (although the chapter's Selected Bibliography might serve to introduce those critics to students); instead, the purpose is to suggest how texts can be variously interpreted by looking through different critical lenses. Despite the intimidating fact that literary criticism is an enormous and complex field, it can be usefully introduced as part of the intellectual landscape to even beginning students.

RESOURCES FOR TEACHING

SELECTED BIBLIOGRAPHY ON THE TEACHING OF LITERATURE

Adler, Mortimer J., and Charles Van Doren. *How to Read a Book*. New York: Simon, 1972.

Bunge, Nancy L. *Finding the Words: Conversations with Writers Who Teach*. Athens: Ohio UP, 1985.

Guerin, Wilfred L., et al. *A Handbook of Critical Approaches to Literature*. New York: Harper, 1979.

Koch, Kenneth. *Rose, Where Did You Get That Red?* New York: Vintage, 1974.

Lipschultz, Geri. "Fishing in the Holy Waters." *College English* 48.1 (1986): 34–39.

Ponsot, Marie, and Rosemary Deen. *Beat Not the Poor Desk*. Upper Montclair: Boynton, 1982. 154–180.

Pound, Ezra. *ABC of Reading*. New York: New Directions, 1960.

Young, Gloria L. "Teaching Poetry: Another Method." *Teaching English in the Two-Year College* (Feb. 1987): 52–56.

TIPS FOR TEACHING CRITICAL STRATEGIES

Many students will be excited about the possibility of applying literature to "real world" ideas, but instructors should be aware that some students will resist what they see as an attempt to "read too much into" the text. Students in introductory classes sometimes resent readings of their favorite works that ask them to be critical of the author's life or to consider his or her positions on race, gender, or politics. Teachers should raise this problem with the class, perhaps in conjunction with a discussion of the canon (p. 5). While we may not agree with some students who think literature should merely be read, understood, and enjoyed, we should remember that theirs is a common view and one that deserves a hearing. The discussion may become heated, but it gets at the heart of why we teach, read, and write about literature. Ask students if it's possible to find fault with, say, an author's perceived sexism and still appreciate his or her use of metaphor. Is it possible to enjoy literature and criticize it at the same time? What is the most important quality of a literary work — its use of language, moral message, character development, historical accuracy? We all have different answers to these questions, and a class discussion or writing assignment on this topic will help students understand why literature is important and why we continue to care about it.

Another challenge for an instructor teaching critical strategies in an introductory course is making the strategies accessible to students without being unnecessarily reductive. For example, psychological criticism has numerous dimensions, but it's not necessary for students to understand every aspect of this critical strategy. At the same time, it's important that they don't reduce this complex school of thought to a mere search for the Oedipus complex in everything they read. As you teach this chapter, you might consider assigning the entire chapter to the class and then breaking the class into small groups to further research or study one strategy per group. Groups can then present to the class their advanced understanding of a strategy.

Here are some more specific suggestions for teaching some of the critical strategies in this chapter:

Formalist Strategies: All good readers and writers about literature should be able to do a formalist reading of a text, noticing the way details work together to create a unified effect. Many students are probably familiar with formalist criticism, though they may not know it by that name. In fact, your biggest challenge in teaching this strategy is to acknowledge that it is *merely a strategy for reading* and writing about literature, not the single "right" way to read. Discuss ways in which other strategies can build on a good formalist textual analysis to yield further insights into a work.

Biographical Strategies: In our "tell-all" society, students tend to enjoy biographical criticism; they find connections between an author's life and works to be an interesting and fruitful way of uncovering new readings. Point out, as the book does, that biographical readings can complicate as well as elucidate our undersanding of a work. For example, knowing that Sylvia Plath committed suicide may help us see the intense pain in some of her poetry, but it may lead us to miss her sometimes playful use of language as well.

Psychological Strategies: Psychological criticism involves a number of complicated ideas and theories that go beyond the scope of an introductory course. Yet students who have an understanding of the power of unconscious motivations will enjoy this type of criticism. Long before Freud elucidated his ideas, writers have known that people often act in ways they don't understand and have desires that they would rather repress. A good character analysis should take these psychological possibilities into account. For example, in Susan Glaspell's short play, *Trifles* (p. 496), Mrs. Wright's alleged murder of her husband could be understood not so much as a conscious, premeditated act of violence but rather as an impulsive act of revenge in response to Mr. Wright's killing of her bird — an animal with whom she had (possibly unconsciously) identified.

Historical Strategies: Historical, political, and cultural critics use materials outside the primary texts to help them understand the work in a larger context. Many students enjoy reading a work in a historical context because this approach often enables them to make sense of puzzling characters and events. Asking students to use these strategies in their own writing poses one major challenge, however: many students lack historical, political, and cultural knowledge. You may have to provide a good amount of background material, or better yet, help students find their own. The extra effort will pay off in more informed class discussions and papers. Knowledge about history, politics, and culture can yield much more sophisticated readings of a text than reading that text in a vacuum can. For example, readers of William Faulkner's "Barn Burning" (p. 84) in this chapter's student casebook will get much more out of the story if they can bring some knowledge of the Reconstruction to their reading.

Gender Strategies: A sometimes controversial approach to literature, gender criticism can open up a text in new ways. Ask students to consider to what degree *gender* is essential to an interpretation of a text and to what degree it is *incidental.* How might a work be different if the characters' genders were changed? Can they detect gender in the voice of the speaker of a poem? Questions like these help students understand that gender is as crucial in literature as it is in life. An examination of a simple story like David Updike's "Summer" (p. 47) can provide a good illustration of these issues. How would the story differ if it were told from the perspective of a young woman instead of a young man? Are the emotions experienced by Homer "universal" coming-of-age longings or are they unique to teenage boys?

Mythological Strategies: Students tend to respond powerfully to archetypal criticism because these mythological symbols are familiar to most of them. You might introduce them to the concept of archetypes by having students read Carl Jung (see the chapter's bibliography, p. 81), as well having them read some actual myths, preferably myths from a cross-section of cultures. Many works respond well to mythological criticism, particularly works from the modernist period. Try illustrating mythological criticism by applying it to a modern poem such as T. S. Eliot's "The Love Song of J. Alfred Prufrock" (p. 1280).

Reader-Response Strategies: Many students like the idea of reader-response criticism though it sometimes seems to be the antithesis of the way they have been taught to read literature. One way to introduce this concept to your class is to provide students with imaginary "readers" of a work. For example, have them compare and contrast the way a teenage girl, a teenage boy, and a middle-aged adult man would read David Updike's short story "Summer" (p. 47), or ask them how a black student, a white student, and a teacher might read Langston Hughes's "Theme for English B" (p. 998). Of course, students' own experiences reading these and other works should be included in this activity.

Deconstructionist Strategies: A difficult strategy, deconstruction is often taught best by emphasizing what (little) it has in common with formalism, namely, that both strategies depend on close textual readings. Ask students to note moments of contradiction or uncertainty in the reading. What possible readings can emerge from those "gaps" in the text? How different are the possible interpretations? What do these differences imply about the possibility of *any* definitive reading?

WRITING IN PROCESS: CRITICAL ANALYSIS

The student casebook for this chapter shows a student, Peter Campion, writing about a familiar text in a possibly unfamiliar way. As in other casebooks, the student writer begins with a personal response that he uses to help develop an examination of the story's larger issues. Peter's first response does not attempt to address every possible detail and element in "Barn Burning," but is rather an emotional reaction to what he does understand — the violence and the "sense of inevitability." The case study shows how Peter builds on this initial reaction to write a strong paper informed by history and politics.

WILLIAM FAULKNER, *Barn Burning* (p. 84)

In William Faulkner's "Barn Burning," a boy is continually placed in situations where he must decide whether to support his family and deny his conscience or to uphold society's conventions and act according to his convictions. Within this plot, Faulkner also reveals the concerns and stylistic traits most characteristic of his fiction by emphasizing the innermost thoughts, impressions, and urges of human beings, or as he identified them in his Nobel Prize acceptance speech, "the problems of the human heart in conflict with itself."

The boy, Colonel Sartoris Snopes, is faced with three distinct moments when he must decide whether to stand with his family or with the society that Abner continually battles. The first trial occurs in a small-town general store, the courtroom where Abner is accused of setting fire to another man's property. The boy's initial response is animal: he convinces himself that he and his father face a mutual enemy in the judge. When he is called forward to testify, he realizes that he is in an impossible position, caught between his father and the judge. "He aims for me to lie, he thought, again with that frantic grief and despair. And I will have to do it" (paragraph 7). He has no practical choice; his psychological and economic security stem from his father's favor. All he knows is that he must fight for his father. Yet when the moment to speak arrives, he cannot lie. Both the judge and his father realize this, and the judge settles the trial without forcing the boy to answer. That night, after the family has left the area, Abner hits Sarty, but the real blow is caused by his words: "You were fixing to tell them. You would have told him. . . . You're getting to be a man. You got to learn. You got to learn to stick to your own blood or you ain't going to have any blood to stick to you" (28–29).

Sarty can only hope that he won't be put in such a situation in the next town, but life there is no simpler. The second trial occurs when Abner sues Major de Spain over the value of the rug that he has spitefully ruined. In that courtroom scene, Sarty is hardly considered one of the family. Although he tries to help, he is banished to the back of the room, where he can watch the proceedings with other strangers. This strengthens his own sense of justice because it releases him from the restricted perception of the family. After this incident, his father addresses him as he might a stranger. His honeyed response to Sarty's attempted reassurance is even more distancing, and dangerous, than his normally harsh treatment of the boy: "His father glanced for an instant down at him, the face absolutely calm, the grizzled eyebrows tangled above the cold eyes, the voice almost pleasant, almost gentle: 'You think so? Well, we'll wait till October anyway' " (81). The father immediately mends the wagon, indicating that the family will be making another move long before harvest. His actions completely contradict the comment he has addressed to the son he no longer trusts.

Sarty's third crisis of conscience occurs in the evening, when he knows that his father is about to burn Major de Spain's barn. Finally, he is able to break free from all of his family loyalties and alert the major. He acts according to his conscience, but he must sacrifice his family ties as a result. As he experiences each psychological ordeal during this short period of time, Sarty matures from a scared, dependent child to a young man capable of making moral distinctions and acting on them.

The conflict between this son and his father is indicative of the clash Faulkner saw between the rising, mechanistic, materialistic "New South" and the receding, chivalric "Old South." Abner Snopes is representative of the new breed of southerner. A scavenger in the Civil War, fighting only for his own gain, he is associated with machines and material gain. Faulkner consistently describes him in industrial terms: "The stiff black back, the stiff and implacable limp of the figure which was not dwarfed by the house . . . that impervious quality of something cut ruthlessly from tin, depthless, as though, sidewise to the sun, it would cast no shadow" (41). Snopes clearly displays animosity toward the wealth and gentility of the fading upper classes. His son, on the other hand, feels an inward loyalty to the upper classes and demonstrates that affinity at the end of the story when he alerts Major de Spain. Named for Colonel Sartoris, an honorable southern warrior, Sarty is of the Old South. His immediate response to seeing the de Spain house is relief that his father cannot reach these people: "They are safe from him. People whose lives are a part of this peace and dignity are beyond his touch" (41). The affluence of the house and its furnishings speaks directly to the boy's soul. "The boy, deluged as though by a warm wave by a suave turn of the carpeted stair and a pendant glitter of chandeliers and a mute gleam of gold frames, heard the swift feet and saw her too, a lady" (43). Nothing else in Sarty's "poor white trash" existence has had this effect on him. At heart, Sarty is more a descendant of Major de Spain (a link indicated as well by their names) than he is of the Snopeses' lineage.

The matter of the de Spain carpet also illustrates this conflict between the Old South and the New South. Abner ruins the valuable rug to show his defiance of de Spain wealth. The major enforces the cleansing, and the penalty for ruining the carpet, not as a genuine response to its destruction but to teach Abner some southern manners: "That won't keep Mrs. de Spain quiet but maybe it will teach you to wipe your feet before you enter her house again" (63).

Does the mechanistic southerner succeed, or does old southern gentility prevail? It may be a mixed solution: Sarty escapes and can finally begin living according to his conscience. On the other hand, a blaze has been set, and there are other Snopeses to continue these acts of arson. If students are interested in reading more about the fortunes of the Snopes family, including Abner's horsetrading career and the effect of the spotted horses on the town in which Sarty has seen them advertised, they should be directed to Faulkner's Snopes trilogy: *The Hamlet*, *The Town*, and *The Mansion*.

Students may find themselves sympathetic to Abner Snopes's instinctual rebellion against an economic system that builds wealth for a few individuals at the expense of black and white labor: "He stood for a moment, planted stiffly on the stiff foot, looking back at the house. 'Pretty and white, ain't it?' he said. 'That's sweat. Nigger sweat. Maybe it ain't white enough yet to suit him. Maybe he wants to mix some white sweat with it' " (46). You might raise the idea of Abner's defiance as socioeconomic protest as a topic for discussion.

POSSIBLE CONNECTIONS TO OTHER SELECTIONS

Andre Dubus, "Killings" (text p. 566)
William Faulkner, "A Rose for Emily" (text p. 144)

RESOURCES FOR TEACHING

Barn Burning. 41 min., color, 1980. Beta, VHS, 16-mm film. With Tommy Lee Jones. Same program available in "The American Short Story II" series. See local retailer.

The Long Hot Summer. 118 min., color, 1958. Beta, VHS. A film adaptation of "Barn Burning." Directed by Martin Ritt. With Paul Newman, Orson Welles, Joanne Woodward, Lee Remick, Anthony Franciosa, Angela Lansbury, and Richard Anderson. See local retailer.

The Long Hot Summer. 172 min., color, 1986. Beta, VHS. A made-for-TV version of "Barn Burning." Directed by Stuart Cooper. With Don Johnson, Cybill Shepherd, Judith Ivey, Jason Robards, and Ava Gardner. See local retailer.

William Faulkner: A Life on Paper. 2 hrs., color, 1980. Beta, VHS, 3/4" U-matic cassette. A documentary biography. With Lauren Bacall, Howard Hawks, Anita Loos, George Plimpton, Tennessee Williams, and Jill Faulkner Summers (the author's daughter). Distributed by Films, Inc.

William Faulkner's Mississippi. 49 min., color and b/w, 1965. Beta, VHS, 3/4" U-matic cassette. Deals with Faulkner's life and works. Distributed by Benchmark Films.

SUGGESTED TEACHING METHODS

Because Faulkner is difficult, students may not be ready to jump into answering the "Questions for Writing" immediately. Emphasize the importance of good textual annotation as they read "Barn Burning." Consider asking each student to come to class with one question for discussion — something they didn't understand or would like to see pursued further. You might then ask students to write in response to the questions they have exchanged with one another, or you could collect all the questions at the beginning of class and go through them together.

Once you feel the class has a better understanding of "Barn Burning," direct them to the "Questions for Writing" (p. 97) that follow the story. Although time-consuming, addressing questions from each strategy will help students put their knowledge of critical strategies into practice. It will also give them a good idea of which strategies will work best for this story and which strategies appeal to them individually.

ALTERNATIVE ASSIGNMENTS

1. Write an essay on "Barn Burning" using one of the critical strategies in the book besides Marxism. Take your writing through the same process that Peter Campion does: first response, brainstorming, and then the paper itself. As you write your first response, consider why the strategy you've chosen appeals to you.

2. Write an essay on a different work of literature using a critical strategy from this chapter. Although you may choose any work in the book, here are some suggestions for texts to consider and strategies which might work with them:

    William Blake, "London" (text p. 237) and "The Chimney Sweeper" (text p. 987): formalist, historicist, Marxist, reader-response
    William Faulkner, "A Rose for Emily" (text p. 144): formalist, historicist, feminist
    Arthur Miller, *Death of a Salesman* (text p. 1007): mythological, Marxist, gender, psychological

4

Writing from Sources

TIPS FOR TEACHING THE RESEARCH PAPER

The experience of teaching students how to write from sources will differ greatly depending on where you are teaching. Some colleges and universities simply have larger libraries and greater opportunities for research than others. Introductory literature classes do not necessarily require top research libraries, but a good undergraduate research paper requires access to some secondary materials, whether those materials be from the library itself or accessed through interlibrary loan. You will obviously be aware of the benefits and drawbacks of your own library and must find a way to work with what you have. Try to get to know the staff at your college library and enlist their assistance in working with your students on their papers. If you are teaching at a college with a small library, you might consider taking a trip with your students to the nearest research library in order to give them a sense of the sheer number of books and journals that are out there.

Whether you are teaching at a large research university or a small community college, you and your students are likely to have access to electronic sources. While these sources can link even the most remote colleges to important literary criticism, students need to be reminded that the World Wide Web can also be a trap. Most Web sites are not referenced by scholars as literary journals are, and many contain inaccurate, inadequate, or outdated information. As with any kind of research, students who use the Internet for research should be prepared to question their sources. The book's section on evaluating sources and taking notes (p. 108) applies to on-line as well as to print research.

Even before they begin the process of choosing a topic and organizing a paper, students (and professional scholars too!) must overcome the heart-stopping fear that they have nothing to contribute about a well-known writer. Faced with shelves of scholarship on Emily Dickinson, Langston Hughes, or Arthur Miller, students might well ask themselves, "What can I possibly add to this body of knowledge?" The fact is, most undergraduate writers will not make a significant contribution to the field, but they should be able to begin to see their ideas as part of a larger "conversation" with other informed and knowledgeable readers.

Even strong writers find it challenging to organize a research paper, often admitting confusion over whether to privilege their own ideas or those of the scholars they are citing. The book notes that "to some degree, developing your thesis and organizing your paper is the same process when you're working on a research paper as it is when you're writing any other kind of assignment" (p. 111). Remind students that the central idea for their paper, the thesis, should still be their own. Their sources can help them make their argument but should not become a substitute for their own thoughts.

Jotting ideas and quotations on notecards, as the book suggests, can help students organize their material and eliminate quotations and sources that are not useful. (It is sometimes difficult to convince students that they don't need to include every source they find.) Another method of organization is to highlight useful passages from photocopied sources and then type them out on their computer. Students can then use the "cut and paste" function on their computer to group ideas and to help them visualize

16

the form their paper might take. If students have also typed out the sources of these quotations in MLA style (see p. 113), they can then cut and paste them alphabetically on the Works Cited page.

WRITING IN PROCESS: THE RESEARCH PAPER

This casebook is a research paper on two of Robert Frost's poems, "Mowing" and "Mending Wall." The writing process illustrated by Stephanie Tobin demonstrates one way to approach the daunting task of researching a topic on an author about whom much has already been written. The final paper, though short, demonstrates how a student can combine her own ideas and thesis with biographical information, literary analysis, explication, and (of course) research.

SUGGESTED TEACHING METHODS

Teaching Frost's poetry is usually a pleasure. Students enjoy his familiar images and are often pleasantly surprised by the levels of ambiguity and complexity in his seemingly simple poems. Have them read both "Mowing" and "Mending Wall" and answer the "Considerations for Critical Thinking and Writing." Stephanie's First Response presents an additional question for your students to consider. She writes, "most everybody seemed to think that the speaker in 'Mowing' was pretty much saying the same thing as the speaker in 'Mending Wall,' that being a farmer is about one guy putting his shoulder to the scythe" (p. 125). What connections do your students see between the two poems? The two narrators? Do they agree with Stephanie that "Mowing" focuses more on the individual and "Mending Wall" focuses more on the larger community?

Frost often uses repetitive words, images, or phrases in his poetry in order to create a total effect. In "Mowing," we see the repeated image of "my long scythe whispering"; in "Mending Wall," we see the repeated phrase "Good fences make good neighbors." An in-class writing or journal entry on the effect of these repetitions might yield some interesting responses to these poems. Can your students find any connections between these phrases? Do your students agree that "Good fences make good neighbors"?

After you have discussed the poems individually and together, follow Stephanie's research methods, observing how her First Response question leads her to relevant sources, a thesis, and ultimately a completed draft. The "Sample of Brainstorming After Research" (p. 126) will be particularly helpful for students who feel overwhelmed if their trip(s) to the library have yielded more material than they can use for a short paper. The paper itself (p. 128) uses the sources well, but in a restrained manner; the sources don't dominate Stephanie's essay and prevent her own ideas from coming through.

ALTERNATIVE ASSIGNMENTS

1. After reading Robert Frost's poems "Mowing" and "Mending Wall," read some more poetry by Robert Frost and write a research paper on a topic of interest to you. Your book includes several: "Acquainted with the Night" (p. 245), "Home Burial" (p. 617), "After Apple-Picking" (p. 991), and "Design" (p. 1163), though of course a visit to any college library will provide many more. Begin by writing a first response like that of Stephanie Tobin that includes a question you have about the readings. Once you've narrowed your topic down and chosen one to three poems, you are ready to begin researching what other critics have said on the subject.

2. One reason why scholars continue to write about an author even when a large body of scholarship already exists is that critical trends change over time. Choose one or two canonical works in this book and trace their critical treatment over the past 50 or 100 years. What changes to do see in the way scholars approach the works? Do

you see certain critical strategies emerging during a certain period only to be replaced by others in the next period? How do you account for these changes? Here are some suggestions of canonical works in this book:

Matthew Arnold, "Dover Beach" (text p. 235)
The poetry of Emily Dickinson
Ernest Hemingway, "Soldier's Home" (text p. 579)
Arthur Miller, *Death of a Salesman* (text p. 1007)
Flannery O'Connor, "Good Country People" (text p. 803)
Sylvia Plath, "Daddy" (text p. 628)
The stories of Edgar Allan Poe
The poetry of William Shakespeare
Jonathan Swift, "A Modest Proposal" (text p. 516)

PART II. LITERATURE AND ITS ELEMENTS

5

Reading and Writing about Fiction

In connection with the introductory material in Chapter 1, it may be useful to engage students in a comparison of the ways in which they read. For instance, how does the text on the back of a cereal box differ from a story in a news magazine? We read differently depending on our interest in the subject, our acceptance of a writer's style and voice, and our environment. Some students may read primarily while they are on the treadmill at the recreation center; others need quiet in which to concentrate. Even students who wouldn't identify themselves as readers might discover that they actually rely on reading skills more than they realize.

After focusing on the reader, students might consider the reading material. Encourage them to consider how reading fiction may be different from reading a newspaper. What different demands are being made on the reader in these contexts? Fiction invites the reader to enter a world that may or may not be familiar to them; it also asks them to think not only about the words on the page but also about their implications. Fiction is, in a sense, not only about what the writer tells the reader, but also what the writer doesn't tell the reader. It's up to the reader to invest the spaces between the words with creative (yet reasonable) meanings.

Finally, students will profit from learning that sharing their interpretations with each other can be intensely rewarding. Because they bring different experiences and values to their readings, they may discover different significant aspects of a given text. To practice building their interpretive skills, students might bring in a letter to the editor in a local newspaper, or a comic strip, or some other reading material, and explain what they think is of interest about their "text." (This may be particularly successful for students in small groups.) Students may be surprised to discover the differences between their readings — or even their similarities. An ironic editorial or a purposely ambiguous (or especially political) cartoon may provide diverse yet reasonable readings. In discussing those readings, students begin to develop the skills that will make their experience with fiction successful and rewarding.

THE ELEMENTS

PLOT

This section explains plot techniques such as flashbacks and foreshadowing. Again, you may wish to invite students to apply these to the "stories" they follow outside of class. It might also be useful to practice in class with texts that most students might already know. Fairy tales, fables, and nursery rhymes are especially fruitful sources for further study of plot. Having "Goldilocks and the Three Bears" begin at the end or in the middle, or investing "Little Red Riding Hood" with foreshadowing in the first paragraph might enable students to discover more meaning both in the original tale and in the retelling.

EDGAR RICE BURROUGHS, *From* **Tarzan of the Apes** (p. 139)

Most of the sixty books Edgar Rice Burroughs wrote recorded bedtime stories he had told his children. In addition to the enormously popular Tarzan series, Burroughs wrote a good deal of science fiction, most notably a series of books that chronicle the adventures of John Carter of Mars. Before making his fortune as a writer, Burroughs was a cowboy, gold miner, policeman, and store manager. His books include *The Princess of Mars* (1917), *Tanar of Pellucidar* (1930), and *Tarzan and the Foreign Legion* (1947). *Tarzan of the Apes* (1914), the first of the Tarzan series, has been translated into more than fifty languages.

Burroughs writes that from Tarzan's "early infancy his survival had depended upon acuteness of eyesight, hearing, smell, touch, and taste far more than upon the more slowly developed organ of reason. The least developed of all in Tarzan was the sense of taste" (paragraphs 29–30). The description in the excerpt relies heavily on physical detail, almost corresponding to this discussion of Tarzan's acute sensory development. Ask students to isolate one paragraph of the Burroughs excerpt and assess the kind of description included in it. What techniques does Burroughs rely on in successfully presenting such heavy — but not excessive — detail?

Much of the plot in this excerpt functions as a device for revealing the characterizations of Tarzan and Terkoz by providing them with occurrences to which they must react. How would the excerpt change if it were altered to reflect primarily Jane's characterization? What details would be emphasized in such a narrative? Would the plot seem in any way diminished in such a representation?

POSSIBLE CONNECTIONS TO OTHER SELECTIONS

Tim O'Brien, "How to Tell a True War Story" (text p. 1149)
Karen van der Zee, From *A Secret Sorrow* (text p. 181)

RESOURCE FOR TEACHING

Tarzan of the Apes [recording]. 6 cassettes (90 min. each). Read by Walter Costello. Distributed by Books on Tape.

WILLIAM FAULKNER, *A Rose for Emily* (p. 144)

The ending of this mystery story is as chillingly gruesome as it is surprising. Just when we think that the discovery of Homer Barron's body ("what was left of him") is the awful revelation that the narrator has been leading up to, we realize in the final climactic paragraph (and particularly in the last three words) that the strand of "iron-gray hair" on the indented pillow belongs to Emily. The details indicate that she has slept with Homer since she murdered him, because we are told in paragraph 48 that her hair hadn't turned gray until after Homer disappeared. The closing paragraph produces a gasp of horror in most readers, but by withholding this information until the very end, Faulkner allows us to develop a sympathetic understanding of Emily before we are revolted by her necrophilia.

The conclusion is skillfully foreshadowed: Emily denies her father's death; she buys arsenic; Homer disappears; and there is a terrible smell around the house. These clues are muted, however, by the narrator's rearrangement of the order of events. We learn about the smell before we know that Emily bought arsenic and that Homer disappeared.

Hence, these details seem less related to one another than they would if they had been presented chronologically. Faulkner's plotting allows him to preserve suspense in a first reading. On subsequent readings we take delight in realizing how all the pieces fit together and point to the conclusion.

The gothic elements provide an appropriate atmosphere of mystery and are directly related to the conflicts in the story. Emily's decrepit house evokes an older, defunct South that resists the change imposed by garages, gasoline pumps, new construction, paved sidewalks, and a Yankee carpetbagger such as Homer. This exposition is essential to the story's theme because it explains Emily's antagonists. Emily rejects newness and change; her house smells of "dust and disuse." Her refusal to let go of the past is indicated by her insistence that her father did not die and by her necrophilia with Homer. She attempts to stop time, and although the narrator's collective "we" suggests the town's tolerance for and sympathy with such an attitude (as a representative of the North, Homer is powerful but vulgar), the story finally makes clear that living in a dead past means living with death. As much as the narrator realizes that Emily's illusions caused her to reject the changing realities of her life, he — like his fellow citizens — admires Emily with "a sort of respectful affection" (paragraph 1). She is like a "fallen monument," a reminder of an Old South that could not survive the new order of Reconstruction. Even though she murders Homer, Emily cannot stop the changes brought by the urbanization associated with him.

This story, minus its concerns about change in the South and its tribute — a rose — to Emily's strong sensibilities (in spite of her illusions and eccentricities), fits into the gothic horror tradition, but it would be a far less intriguing work if the formula were to supersede Faulkner's complex imaginative treatment.

After illustrating the elements of plot with the excerpt from Edgar Rice Burroughs's *Tarzan of the Apes*, ask students to compare the way Faulkner plots his story with the more straightforward narrative of Burroughs. You might ask your students to chart the events in Faulkner's story chronologically, in order to demonstrate the skillful way in which Faulkner withholds and provides important details. How would the total effect of the story be different if Faulkner began his narrative at the beginning and chronicled the events as they happened, leading up to Miss Emily's funeral and the discovery of the body in her bedroom?

Ask your students to identify traditional elements of plot in "A Rose for Emily." What kind of *protagonist* is Emily? Despite (or perhaps because of) her act of murdering her lover, do your students see her as *heroic* in any way? Who do they see as the story's *antagonist*? Homer? Emily's father? The townspeople? How does Faulkner use *foreshadowing* and *rising action* to create suspense? Does the story have a *denouement*?

POSSIBLE CONNECTIONS TO OTHER SELECTIONS

Stephen Crane, "The Bride Comes to Yellow Sky" (text p. 1122)
Ralph Ellison, "Battle Royal" (text p. 931)
William Faulkner, "Barn Burning" (text p. 84)

CHARACTER

Because many students might not be familiar with Dickens's work, it might be fruitful to study characterization in an example or two drawn from popular culture. For instance, students might decide whether the characters in their favorite television shows are static or dynamic, flat or round. They might compare comedies (typically containing stock, static characters) with dramas (often featuring characters who are allowed to change and grow). Ask students whether the title character in *Frasier* is static or dynamic, or whether the doctors on *ER* are predictable or surprising in their choices and actions.

Commonly, the comedy arises from a manipulation of plot in order to force a predictable reaction from a well-established but static character; in contrast, drama's success usually depends on the complexities of characterization. It may be fruitful to discuss why these different "genres" require different manipulations of characterization.

Encourage students to get into the habit of asking themselves a series of questions about characterization after reading a story. First, is the narrator reliable? Is there any reason provided in the text that the narrator may have a particular agenda that causes her or him to alter or slant the telling of the story? (For instance, in "Bartleby, the Scrivener" [p. 944], what is the lawyer's motivation in telling the story? Is it merely that he found Bartleby an interesting character? Or, does he have something to gain from the telling?) Also, to whom is the narrator telling the story? Occasionally, we have a clear sense of audience. (In a poem such as Robert Browning's "My Last Duchess" [p. 827], for example, we know not only the identity of the listener but also his reaction to the tale.) In addition to the narrator, what other characters are significant to the story? Do the characters change in the course of the narration? Are they static or dynamic? (Sometimes, the most effective way to determine this is through a comparison of the characters.) The character's impression on the reader may be based on what the character says, what the character does, and what other characters say about the character or how they react to her or him. Students might envision themselves as private detectives building case files on each character they encounter in a story; they might share their findings in response to a given story as they develop their skills.

CHARLES DICKENS, *From* Hard Times (p. 152)

Charles Dickens (1812–1870) was the author of numerous novels, travel books, and sketches. Many of his most memorable characters are inspired by his memories of childhood, during which time his father was imprisoned for debt. Dickens later acted in amateur theatricals and performed public readings of his work. His novels and other later writings were serialized in both English and American periodicals. Among his works are *Oliver Twist, Bleak House, Great Expectations, A Christmas Carol,* and *A Tale of Two Cities.* He is buried in Poet's Corner, Westminster Abbey.

In this excerpt from *Hard Times,* Dickens's description of "the speaker," Mr. Gradgrind, works to reveal aspects of his character. In addition, other characters' responses to Gradgrind emphasize certain aspects or traits of his character. How does the final paragraph of the excerpt reveal additional information about Gradgrind? How does the information about the other grownups in the room convey a specific impression about the children who are assembled there?

As a means of starting discussion of Dickens's characterization of Mr. Gradgrind, ask students to write a short sketch in which they experience a class taught by him. They might enjoy writing about how he would interact with their actual class.

POSSIBLE CONNECTIONS TO OTHER SELECTIONS

Toni Cade Bambara, "The Lesson" (text p. 925)
Nathaniel Hawthorne, "Young Goodman Brown" (text p. 1246)

RESOURCES FOR TEACHING

Charles Dickens: An Introduction to His Life and Work. 27 min., color, 1979. Beta, VHS, ³/₄″ U-matic cassette, special-order formats. An introduction to Dickens's life and work. Distributed by the International Film Bureau.

The Charles Dickens Show. 52 min., color, 1973. Beta, VHS, ³/₄″ U-matic cassette. Deals with the writer and his times. Includes dramatization from his life and works. Distributed by the International Film Bureau.

Hard Times. 240 min., color, 1977. Beta (text pages) ³/₄" U-matic cassette. A TV adaptation of the novel. Distributed by WNET/Thirteen Non-Broadcast.

Hard Times [recording]. 16 hours, 8 cassettes. Read by Frederick Davison. Distributed by Blackstone Audio.

SYMBOLISM

The story by Colette invites the reader to consider the complexity of symbolism. After reading the introduction, students should be aware of the difference between symbolism and allegory; they should also begin to appreciate the nuances of symbolism. In addition to the common cultural symbols described in the introduction, students might generate a list of other familiar symbols from their daily experience. For instance, what traditional, conventional, or public meanings do students associate with water? (Possible associations range from baptism rites to the territory of the unconscious.) What possible meanings are associated with dragons? In Western cultures, dragons have commonly symbolized danger or obstacles to success. In Eastern cultures, in contrast, they are often perceived to be symbols of good luck. In order to demonstrate the sophistication and breadth of common symbols, instructors might introduce students to reference works such as J. E. Cirlot's *A Dictionary of Symbols* (Philosophical Library, 1971). However, as explained in the introduction, common sense should be a reader's guide in determining the meaning of literary symbols.

COLETTE [Sidonie-Gabrielle Colette], *The Hand* (p. 163)

In "The Hand," Colette's description of one night in the life of a woman and her sleeping husband forces readers to rely for meaning on the imagery associated with the husband's hand and on the wife's limited actions. By contrasting the wife's initial observations of the husband's hand with her later perceptions of it, students can clearly see her changing awareness of her lover. The husband's hand is a microcosm of the whole man, isolated as it is among the sheets. Initially, the wife focuses on its manicure, representative of the man's breeding and elegance: "The flat nails, whose ridges the nail buffer had not smoothed out, gleamed, coated with pink varnish" (paragraph 13). The glazed nails are a symbol of his refinement. However, she is distracted by the color of the nails, a too-feminine touch, which clashes with the size and strength — the masculinity — of the hand. As she discovers this incongruity, her conception of the hand, and of the man, rapidly changes from idealization to realization. She focuses primarily on male qualities of the hand, associating them with uncivilized, inhuman imagery: "The hand suddenly took on a vile, apelike appearance" (15). Her following observations of it are filled with references to its animal qualities: "tensed up in the shape of a crab," "the hand . . . lowered its claws, and became a pliant beast," "red fur" (17, 17, 19). Her husband is no longer a handsome lover; he has become a beast.

The wife's changing awareness of the hand affects her behavior. At the beginning of the story, as she gazes around the bedroom and at her sleeping lover, the hand rests next to her right elbow, and she is content. At the end of her story, her initial response is to shrink from contact with it or with anything it touches, including the piece of toast it has buttered. Her change in attitude toward the hand and its owner is presented in two stages. As she gazes at the hand and its nails, she feels in control: she makes a mental note to convince the husband not to use pink varnish. Then the hand moves, revealing the thumb as "horribly long and spatulate" (15), and she responds with a single word: " 'Oh!' whispered the young woman, as though faced with something slightly indecent" (16). The hand's altered appearance forces her beyond blissful, romantic, honeymoon notions of it and into a more realistic inspection. The setting reinforces this intrusion of reality. As she utters the first "Oh!" she suddenly becomes aware of the world outside the bedroom: "The sound of a passing car pierced the silence with a shrillness that seemed luminous" (17). As she studies the hand, she becomes more aware not only of its appearance, but also of its potential for destruction. It is described in militaristic, warlike terms: "Ready for battle," "It regrouped its forces" (17, 19). These images are reinforced by the association of the hand's power with a criminal act: "Slowly drawing itself in again, [it] grabbed a fistful of the sheet, dug into it with its curved fingers, and squeezed, squeezed with the methodical pleasure of a strangler" (19). The wife's realization of the hand's (and therefore the husband's) absolute power causes her to utter a second "Oh!" Her first whispered response has become a cry of terror. The hand is not only capable of evil and of harming the wife, but it appears to take great pleasure in such acts of cruelty, reinforcing the ultimate representation of the husband as a beast.

At the beginning of "The Hand," the wife is like a character in a fairy tale. A whirlwind romance led to her marrying a man whom she really didn't know well. After her one-night encounter with the hand, representative of her husband in a truly unconscious, natural state, details of the husband's background that previously seemed innocent take on sinister connotations: he is "recently widowed" and her involvement with him "had been little more than a kidnapping" (3). In the end, she is Beauty married to her Beast, legally and eternally. Her expectation of living life "happily ever after" has been defeated; instead, she is preparing for "her life of duplicity, of resignation, and of a lowly, delicate diplomacy" (25). Symbolizing her helplessness, she can only kiss his hand, the "monstrous hand" of the beast to whom she has entrusted her fate.

Ask students to consider the husband's hand as a *literary symbol* in light of the chapter's discussion of symbolism. You might have them freewrite about ways in which hands are symbolic in our culture. Phrases such as "Give me a hand" (assistance or applause), "Hired hand" (a laborer), "She doesn't want to get her hands dirty" (someone from the leisure class), and "He has blood on his hands" (to signify guilt) all suggest more than their literal meaning. How does the husband's hand function as a symbol in this story? Why do you think the wife projects so much meaning into this particular part of his body?

POSSIBLE CONNECTIONS TO OTHER SELECTIONS

Gail Godwin, "A Sorrowful Woman" (text p. 189)
Nathaniel Hawthorne, "The Birthmark" (text p. 1130)
John Updike, "A & P" (text p. 981)

RESOURCES FOR TEACHING

Colette. 13 min., color, 1979. Beta. VHS, $^3/_4''$ U-matic cassette, 16-mm film. A literary biography. Distributed by Coronet/MTI.

Colette. 30 min., b/w, 1950. 16-mm film. Still photos and live footage provide the background for Colette's own narration. In French with English subtitles. Out of print; available through Consortium (see the appendix of Film, Video, and Audiocassette Resources).

Colette Reads Colette [recording]. 1 cassette. The author reads favorite passages, in French. Distributed by Applause Productions.

STYLE, TONE, AND IRONY

Students might experiment individually with style, tone, and irony first by rereading some of their own work and establishing some assessment of their own natural style and tone. Second, they might learn more about these tools by rewriting common fairy tales in different voices. For instance, how might "Goldilocks and the Three Bears" sound as told by a Sam Spade character (from Dashiell Hammett's *The Maltese Falcon*)? A Walter Mitty? A politician? Students might also practice writing excuses why a paper might be late in different modes — both sincere and ironic. You may even want to introduce students to such landmark examples of irony as Jonathan Swift's "A Modest Proposal." Though the irony in literature is rarely as exaggerated as Swift's, it provides the reader with information about the story that might dramatically affect their interpretations. Inventing and practicing their own examples of different styles, tones, and ironic works, and reading other examples embodying them, students will become more confident at recognizing and responding to these literary tools in the work of professional authors.

RAYMOND CARVER, *Popular Mechanics* (p. 169)

Born in 1938 in Clatskanie, Oregon, to working-class parents, Carver grew up in Yakima, Washington, was educated at Humboldt State College in California, and did graduate work at the University of Iowa. He married at age nineteen and during his college years worked at a series of low-paying jobs to help support his family. These difficult years eventually ended in divorce. He taught at a number of universities, among them the University of California at Berkeley, the University of Iowa, the University of Texas at El Paso, and Syracuse University. Carver's collections of stories include *Will You Please Be Quiet, Please?* (1976), *What We Talk About When We Talk About Love* (1981), from which "Popular Mechanics" is taken, *Cathedral* (1984), and *Where I'm Calling From: New and Selected Stories* (1988). Though extremely brief, "Popular Mechanics" describes a stark domestic situation with a startling conclusion.

For an interesting reading of "Popular Mechanics," see "Physical and Social Laws in Ray Carver's *Popular Mechanics*," by Norman German and Jack Bedell, *Critique* 29.4 (Summer 1988): 257–260. This entry incorporates several of their ideas.

What do students think of when they think of the term *popular mechanics*? One possibility is the contemporary "how-to" magazine *Popular Mechanics*, which contains suggestions and instructions for "home improvement" projects. In its form, Carver's story reminds us of such a "how-to." Consisting of a series of very brief paragraphs, or "steps," it contains no complicated instructions or convoluted sentences. It's only when we look beneath the surface and consider the story's implications that we discover its complexities. There is a certain "mechanical" nature to the story as well, as Carver describes the couple's physical grappling over the baby: "in the near-dark he worked on her fisted fingers with one hand and with the other hand he gripped the screaming baby up under an arm near the shoulder" (paragraph 31); "she caught the baby around the wrist and leaned back" (34). As German and Bedell point out, the baby functions as some sort of wishbone during this scuffle (258). Holding him over the stove, and pulling at him from each side, the husband and wife focus solely on their own wishes rather than the baby's safety. Ask students how they interpret the last line: "In this manner, the issue was decided" (36). German and Bedell suggest that "issue" refers both to the argument and to the baby (258). As the last line implies, in this struggle there can only be losers.

Minor details of the story contribute to its effect. In the first paragraph it is "getting dark" both inside and out; the light has faded away by the end of the story. In paragraph 10, the husband looks "around the bedroom before turning off the light"; in paragraph 31, we are told that "the kitchen window gave no light." The scuffle intensifies in proportion to the increasing darkness in the house — and, as German and Bedell note, the sound level rises proportionally to the decreasing light (259). The argument over the baby's picture foreshadows the struggle in the kitchen and reveals the parents' tendency to objectify everything in their attempts to hurt each other. The flowerpot serves as yet another example of this: the symbol of a domestic harmony that has ceased to exist for these people, the pot is knocked off the wall by the parents' mutual efforts. In this story, the baby (often referred to as "it") becomes just one more object.

In class, explain the story of Solomon (1 Kings 3) and ask students to compare its outcome with Carver's conclusion. (Neither of Carver's adult characters is willing to take any responsibility: notice that the wife says, "You're hurting the baby" [29] instead of "We're hurting the baby.") Whereas 1 Kings 3 is ultimately a story about a mother's love and selflessness, "Popular Mechanics" reveals the animosity and selfishness of both parents.

POSSIBLE CONNECTION TO ANOTHER SELECTION

Henrik Ibsen, *A Doll House* (text p. 700)

RESOURCES FOR TEACHING

Interview with Raymond Carver [recording]. 1 cassette (51 min.). Stimulating introduction to Carver's life and work. Distributed by American Audio Prose Library.

Raymond Carver. 50 min., color, 1996. VHS. Fellow writers, Carver's wife, and others discuss his lower-middle-class roots in the Northwest as the source of inspiration for his characters and stories. A BBC Production. From the "Great Writers of the 20th Century" Series. Distributed by Films for the Humanities and Sciences.

Readings [recording]. 1 cassette (51 min.). Distributed by American Audio Prose Library.

Short Cuts. 189 min., color, 1993. Cast: Jennifer Jason Leigh, Tim Robbins, Madeleine Stowe, Frances McDormand, Peter Gallagher, Lily Tomlin, Andie MacDowell, Jack Lemmon, Lyle Lovett, Huey Lewis, Matthew Modine, Lili Taylor, Christopher Penn, Robert Downey Jr. Directed by Robert Altman. Distributed by Columbia Tristar Home Video.

WRITING IN PROCESS: COMPARISON AND CONTRAST

This student casebook provides a good example of the process of writing a comparison and contrast paper; it also offers some material for discussion about formulaic "popular" fiction and more literary, challenging works. Possibly you will have already discussed the literary canon (see Chapter 3, "Applying a Critical Strategy" for a discussion of the literary canon) and tried to define the term "literature" in your class. If not, this casebook might be a good way to introduce this topic. Do your students agree that "A Sorrowful Woman" is a "better" work than *A Secret Sorrow* (regardless of which reading they preferred)? If so, what qualities does Godwin's story possess that van der Zee's does not? If some students argue that neither work is "better," or that van der Zee's is the superior work of literature, ask them to define "good" literature and explain their definition. How much do the elements of fiction highlighted in this chapter contribute to their understanding of what makes a literary work good or great?

As you take your students through the casebook and as you work through this discussion, ask your students to write a First Response along the lines of the one written by Maya Leigh. Have them compare their responses to one another and with Leigh's response on p. 196. Were they equally "irritated" with Faye's histrionics and the wife's complaints in Godwin's story? Did they also experience a split between what satisfied them intellectually and what satisfied them emotionally?

The rest of the casebook moves through the process of writing a comparison and contrast essay. The "Brainstorming" section should be especially helpful in demonstrating the way lists, outlines, and charts can help students see the way such a paper might take shape. Maya's drafts and final paper are good examples of the way a careful reviser picks up on minor details as well as more significant areas for reconsideration.

A Composite of a Romance Tip Sheet (p. 177)

This tip sheet offers an opportunity to begin discussion of the elements of fiction. Reading a romance novel is not a prerequisite for discussion, because most of us have experienced similar formulas in magazines, popular television programs, or films; also, an excerpt from a romance novel begins on text page 181. Students are usually delighted to recognize the patterns prescribed in the tip sheet and have no trouble recalling stories that fit this description. This gets class discussion off to a good start, provided the emphasis is on why readers derive pleasure from romance formulas rather than on a denigration of such reading.

Recent criticism has focused considerable attention on the audience and appeal of romance novels. (See, for example, Tania Modleski's *Loving with a Vengeance: Mass-Produced Fantasies for Women* [New York: Archon, 1982]; Janice A. Radway's *Reading the Romance: Women, Patriarchy, and Popular Literature* [Chapel Hill: University of North Carolina Press, 1984]; and Kay Mussell's *Fantasy and Reconciliation: Contemporary Formulas of Women's Romance Fiction* [Westport, CT: Greenwood, 1984].) Romance readers are typically housewives ranging in age from their twenties to midforties. Not surprisingly, the age of the heroine usually determines the approximate age of the reader, because the protagonists of Harlequin and Silhouette romances — to name only the two most popular series — are created so that consumers will readily identify with the heroines' romantic adventures in exciting settings as a means of escaping the loneliness and tedium of domesticity. (It's worth emphasizing, of course, that male readers engage in similar fantasies; Philip Larkin's "A Study of Reading Habits" on p. 220 suggests some possibilities.) The heroine is "attractive" rather than "glamorous" because she is likely to appeal to more readers who might describe themselves that way.

Romance readers are often treated to a veritable fashion show, with detailed descriptions of the heroine's clothes. This kind of window-shopping is especially apparent in television soap operas, in which the costumes and sets resemble Bloomingdale's displays more than they do real life. In a very real sense, their audience is shopping for images of success, courtship, and marriage. The hero is a man who may initially seem to be cold and cruel but ultimately provides warmth, love, and security. He is as virtuous as the heroine (if he's divorced, his ex-wife is to blame) but stronger. His being "about ten years" older emphasizes male dominance over female submissiveness, a theme that implicitly looms large in many romances.

The use of sex varies in romances, especially recent ones, in which explicitness seems to be more popular. Nevertheless, suspense and tension are produced in all romances by the teasing complications that keep lovers apart until the end. The major requirement in love scenes between the hero and heroine is that they be culminations of romantic feelings — love — rather than merely graphic sexual descriptions.

The simplified writing style of romances is geared for relatively inexperienced, unsophisticated readers. Probably not very many romance readers cross over to *Pride and Prejudice* or *Jane Eyre*, although some of Austen's and Brontë's readers have certainly been known to enjoy romances. Instructors who share their own reading habits with a class might reassure students that popular and high culture aren't necessarily mutually exclusive while simultaneously whetting students' appetites for the stories to come.

KAREN VAN DER ZEE, *From* A Secret Sorrow (p. 181)

Karen van der Zee was born and grew up in Holland. She published a number of short stories there early in her career. Although the United States is her permanent home, she and her husband, a consultant in agriculture to developing countries, often live abroad. The couple was married in Kenya, their first child was born in Ghana, and their second child arrived in the United States. Van der Zee has contributed more than fifteen books so far to the Harlequin line.

The excerpt from *A Secret Sorrow* subscribes to much of the plotting and characterization methods described in the composite tip sheet. Kai and Faye are not definitively brought together until the final chapter, after Faye's secret is revealed and Kai expresses his unconditional love for her. Students should have no difficulty understanding how the heroine's and hero's love for each other inevitably earns them domestic bliss in the "low white ranch house under the blue skies of Texas," where the family "flourished like the crops in the fields" (paragraph 137). Kai is the traditional dominant, protective male who takes charge of their relationship (albeit tenderly). A good many prepackaged phrases describe him: he has a "hard body," and he kisses her with a "hard, desperate passion" when he isn't speaking "huskily" or lifting her face with his "bronzed hand." In contrast, Faye is "like a terrified animal" and no match for his "hot, fuming fury" when he accuses her of jeopardizing their love.

Despite the predictable action, stereotyped characterizations, clichéd language, and flaccid descriptions of lovemaking (108), some students (perhaps many) will prefer *A Secret Sorrow* to Godwin's "A Sorrowful Woman." But that's natural enough. Van der Zee's story is accessible and familiar material, while Godwin's is puzzling and vaguely threatening because "A Sorrowful Woman" raises questions instead of resolving them. Rather than directly challenging students' preferences and forcing them to be defensive, demonstrate how Godwin's story can be reread several times and still be interesting. *A Secret Sorrow* certainly does not stand up to that test because it was written to be consumed on a first reading so that readers will buy the next book in the series.

POSSIBLE CONNECTIONS TO OTHER SELECTIONS

Edgar Rice Burroughs, From *Tarzan of the Apes* (text p. 139)
Gail Godwin, "A Sorrowful Woman" (text p. 189)

GAIL GODWIN, *A Sorrowful Woman* (p. 189)

Gail Godwin traces her beginnings as a writer to her mother, a teacher and writer, who read stories out of a blank address book, "the special book," as Godwin has called it, "a tiny book with no writing at all in it." Although she frequently contributes essays and stories to publications such as *Harper's, Esquire, Cosmopolitan*, and *Ms.* and has written four librettos, Godwin is primarily known as a novelist; her books include *The Perfectionists* (1970), *The Odd Woman* (1974), *Violet Clay* (1978), *A Mother and Two Daughters* (1982), and *The Finishing School* (1985). Born in 1937 in Birmingham, Alabama, Godwin was educated at the University of North Carolina and the University of Iowa. She worked as a reporter for the *Miami Herald* and as a travel consultant with the U.S. Embassy in London before pursuing a career as a full-time writer and teacher of writing. She has received a National Endowment for the Arts grant, a Guggenheim fellowship, and an Award in Literature from the American Institute and Academy of Arts and Letters. She was coeditor of *Best American Short Stories* in 1985 and has had her short stories collected in *Dream Children* (1976), *Real Life* (1981), *and Mr. Bedford and the Muses* (1983).

"A Sorrowful Woman" challenges the assumptions that inform romance novels. The central point of *A Secret Sorrow* is that love conquers all and that marriage and motherhood make women "beautiful, complete, [and] whole." In contrast, Godwin's story begins with an epigraph that suggests a dark fairy tale: "Once upon a time there was a wife and mother one too many times." The story opens with a pleasant description of the woman's husband ("durable, receptive, gentle") and child ("a tender golden three"), but she is saddened and sickened by the sight of them. These unnamed characters (they are offered as types) seem to have the kind of life that allows Kai and Faye to live happily ever after, but in Godwin's world, this domestic arrangement turns out to be a deadly trap for "the woman." The opening paragraph shocks us into wanting to read the rest of the story to find out why the woman is repulsed by her seemingly perfect life.

It may be tempting to accept the husband's assessment that "Mommy is sick." Students might be eager to see her as mad or suffering from a nervous breakdown, but if we settle for one of those explanations, the meaning of the story is flattened. We simply don't know enough about the woman to diagnose her behavior in psychological terms. She is, after all, presented as a type, not as an individual. She does appear mentally ill, and she becomes progressively more unstable until she withdraws from life completely, but Godwin portrays her as desperate, not simply insane, and focuses our attention on the larger question of why the sole role of wife and mother may not be fulfilling.

The woman rejects life on the terms it is offered to her and no one — including her — knows what to make of her refusal. What is clear, however, is that she cannot live in the traditional role that her husband and son (and we) expect of her. She finds that motherhood doesn't fit her and makes her feel absurd (consider the "vertical bra" in paragraph 4). When she retreats from the family, her husband accommodates her with sympathy and an "understanding" that Godwin reveals to be a means of control rather than genuine care. He tells her he wants "to be big enough to contain whatever you must do" (21). And that's the problem. What he cannot comprehend is that she needs an identity that goes beyond being his wife and his child's mother. Instead, he gives her a nightly sleeping draught; his remedy is to anesthetize his Sleeping Beauty rather than to awaken her to some other possibilities.

Neither the husband nor the wife is capable of taking any effective action. The husband can replace his wife with the "perfect girl" to help around the house, and he can even manage quite well on his own, but he has no more sense of what to do about her refusal to go on with her life than she does. Her own understanding of her situation goes no further than her realization that her life did not have to take a defined shape any more than a poem does (22). Her story is a twentieth-century female version of Herman Melville's "Bartleby, the Scrivener" (p. 944); both characters prefer not to live their lives, but neither attempts to change anything or offer alternatives. Instead, they are messengers whose behavior makes us vaguely troubled. The two stories warrant close comparison.

In the end, when spring arrives, the woman uses herself up in a final burst of domestic energy that provides the husband and son with laundry, hand-knitted sweaters, drawings, stories, love sonnets, and a feast that resembles a Thanksgiving dinner. But neither renewal nor thanks is forthcoming. Instead, the boy, unaware of his mother's death, asks, "Can we eat the turkey for supper?" (38). The irony reveals that the woman has been totally consumed by her role.

Ask students why this story appeared in *Esquire,* a magazine for men, rather than, say, *Good Housekeeping.* The discussion can sensitize them to the idea of literary markets and create an awareness of audiences as well as texts. Surely a romance writer for *Good Housekeeping* would have ended this story differently. Students will know what to suggest for such an ending.

For a discussion of Godwin's treatment of traditional role models in the story, see Judith K. Gardiner's " 'A Sorrowful Woman': Gail Godwin's Feminist Parable," *Studies in Short Fiction* 12 (1975): 286–290.

TIP FROM THE FIELD

Because many of my community college students don't understand the distinctions of formulaic writing they are supposed to make between the excerpt from van der Zee's *A Secret Sorrow* and Godwin's "A Sorrowful Woman," I have them focus instead on the similarities and differences between the fairy-tale nature of these two stories. I ask students to consider how each story is a fairy tale or representative of one. Students have little difficulty identifying the fairy-tale elements of Prince Charming rescuing a damsel in distress and living happily ever after in *A Secret Sorrow.* Students have more difficulty recognizing the fairy-tale ("Once upon a time there was a wife and mother one too many times") aspects of "A Sorrowful Woman," but once this heuristic device is in place, good discussion and writing will result. I find this works particularly well with older traditional students who more readily see the invalidity of the first fairy tale and may be all too familiar with the reality of the second.

– JOSEPH ZEPPETELLO, *Ulster Community College*

POSSIBLE CONNECTIONS TO OTHER SELECTIONS

Colette, "The Hand" (text p. 163)
Emily Dickinson, "Much Madness is divinest Sense —" (text p. 1276)
Henrik Ibsen, *A Doll House* (text p. 700)
Herman Melville, "Bartleby, the Scrivener" (text p. 944)

RESOURCE FOR TEACHING

Interview [recording]. 1 cassette (56 min.). Godwin discusses the recurring themes and concerns in her fiction. Distributed by American Audio Prose Library.

ALTERNATIVE ASSIGNMENTS

1. The traditional "romance plot" outlined in the book has been around as long as fiction has. Although numerous stories, books, and movies use this plot — some with better results than others — many writers, like Gail Godwin, have chosen to subvert this traditional narrative in order to call into question its basic assumptions. Find a work of fiction that borrows from the traditional romance plot as it is defined in Chapter 5 and write an essay in which you identify the author's attitude toward romance. Can you identify an explicit or implicit critique of traditional assumptions of love and marriage? Suggested stories:

   Kate Chopin, "The Story of an Hour" (p. 18)
   Nathaniel Hawthorne, "Young Goodman Brown" (p. 1246)
   Flannery O'Connor, "Good Country People" (p. 803)
   Fay Weldon, "IND AFF, or Out of Love in Sarajevo" (p. 817)

2. The behavior of the wife in Gail Godwin's "A Sorrowful Woman" is extreme, to say the least. No doubt you had a strong first response to her withdrawal from her family, her subsequent behavior, and her eventual death. Write a comparison and contrast essay in which you explore the reactions to the story of at least three different readers, one of whom may be yourself. You should try to invite people with different backgrounds to read the story and respond to questions you have provided. You may want to include a married mother, a father, a single person, or a divorced woman in your survey (though not all of these). What kinds of responses did you expect? Were there any surprises? How can you account for the differing responses people have to this story?

6

Reading and Writing about Poetry

READING POETRY RESPONSIVELY

Perhaps the most difficult part of any introductory literature course is convincing the students that they can, in fact, read poetry. Often, students are intimidated by previous experiences, either in high school or other college courses; they have often accepted that they "just don't get it." Thus, it is important to develop students' confidence in themselves as readers. One way to do this is to get the students to articulate what they see actually happening in the poem, to read what is "on the page."

This chapter has several poems that lend themselves to such an application. Robert Hayden's "Those Winter Sundays," John Updike's "Dog's Death," and Wole Soyinka's "Telephone Conversation," among others, are poems that have a clear scene or situation that grounds them: they mean what they say in a concrete way. Students will often "get" this level of the poem, but distrust their reading, figuring that it isn't what the poem is "really about." A good reading, however, is grounded in such particulars. You might want to have students offer a one- or two-sentence summary of the action of such poems: "The speaker in Hayden's poem remembers his father's domestic work, and realizes it was done for love." Students can then be encouraged to build on these readings once their "fear of poetry" has been deflated somewhat.

Even such poems as Robert Morgan's "Mountain Graveyard" can become more accessible; what may seem to some as mere wordplay will be more powerful if students slow down and picture the scene evoked by the title.

There are two strategies you may find effective in working with students' resistance to poetry and helping them understand the poems they are faced with: reading aloud and short writings. On the surface, this sounds obvious, but having to understand a poem well enough to read it or hearing it spoken can make a difference in students' appreciation of poetry.

Similarly, you might want to assign students short, informal writing to help them think through some of the issues you want to cover in class. These writings can be based on questions in the text, questions of your own, or even student-generated questions based on issues that seem to interest them in discussion. Preparing them before class discussion can help students frame ideas to share. You may want to grade these assignments only on a pass/fail basis, to give students the chance to do experimental thinking in a low-stakes environment.

MARGE PIERCY, *The Secretary Chant* (p. 213)

This poem provides an opportunity to discuss point of view in poetry. The secretary's view of herself mirrors the way she is treated. She has become a variety of objects, a list of useful items because she is looked at as an object by people outside her. Her attitude toward herself is framed by other people's perceptions of her, although we must assume that she is aware of her ability to write satire. We get an inkling of her "real" self in the last three lines; the misspelled "wonce" mocks misperceptions of her intellect, while "woman" indicates that there is much more to be learned about the speaker.

31

In a writing assignment, you might ask students to discuss the metaphors in this poem. What assumptions about women and secretaries do the metaphors satirize? How do sound patterns such as "Zing. Tinkle" (line 14) affect the satire?

POSSIBLE CONNECTION TO ANOTHER SELECTION

Katharyn Howd Machan, "Hazel Tells LaVerne" (text p. 1000)

RESOURCE FOR TEACHING

Marge Piercy: At the Core [recording]. 1 cassette (58 min.), 1977. Distributed by Watershed Tapes.

ROBERT HAYDEN, *Those Winter Sundays* (p. 214)

Useful comparisons can be made between any of the poems in this book that speak of love's transcendence or amplitude and any others, like this one and Theodore Roethke's "My Papa's Waltz" (text p. 630), that speak of its difficulty — the time it sometimes takes to recognize love. Hayden's speaker looks back at his father's unappreciated Sunday labor, at last knowing it for what it was and knowing, too, that the chance for gratitude has long since passed. The poem gives a strong sense, especially in its final two lines, that the speaker has tended to "love's austere and lonely offices" (line 14). The repetition of "What did I know?" seems to be a cry into the silence not only of the past but of the poet's present situation as well. The poem plays the music of the father's furnace work, the hard consonant sounds "splintering, breaking" (6) as the poem unfolds and disappearing entirely by the poem's end.

You might begin discussion by asking students to describe the speaker's father in as much detail as possible based on the speaker's spare description. From the poem's second word, "too," the poem reaches beyond itself to suggest something about the man without naming it. What other details contribute to our impression of him? Following that discussion, you could also ask for a description of the speaker. What does his language reveal about his character? And how does this character contrast with his father's character?

POSSIBLE CONNECTIONS TO OTHER SELECTIONS

Margaret Atwood, "Bored" (text p. 613)
Andrew Hudgins, "Elegy for My Father, Who Is Not Dead" (text p. 624)
Theodore Roethke, "My Papa's Waltz" (text p. 630)

JOHN UPDIKE, *Dog's Death* (p. 215)

This narrative poem subtly traces a family's emotional response to the illness and death of their pet dog. Ask students to find the events that lead to the dog's death. How does the speaker relate these events? He tells us the dog's age when he talks about her toilet training and immediately establishes the family's relationship to her by repeating their words: "Good dog! Good dog!" (line 4). Alliteration and assonance soften the story; after they have identified these sound patterns, ask students why the repeated sounds are appropriate to the subject matter. Direct their attention to the enjambment in lines 12–13. Why does the sentence span two stanzas? Might the speaker be reluctant to tell us the dog died?

When he relates his wife's reaction to the death, the speaker describes her voice as "imperious with tears" (14). After they have established a definition of the word *imperious* ask students to determine why it might be used here. The ambiguous "her" and "she" in the final two lines of the stanza make us puzzle out for a moment the pronouns' referent. Is the speaker talking about his wife or the dog? Are both implied? How does this distortion of identity work in a discussion of death?

The final stanza reads as a eulogy; the consonants become harder — "drawing" (18), "dissolution" (18), "diarrhoea" (19), "dragged" (19) — perhaps because the speaker is working at closing off the experience. In a writing assignment, you might ask students to discuss the three uses of "Good dog." How does the last one differ from the first two? How does the poem prepare us for the change?

RESOURCES FOR TEACHING

John Updike, I and II [recording]. 2 cassettes (58 min.), 1987. Distributed by New Letters on the Air.

The Poetry of John Updike [recording]. 1 cassette (47 min.), 1967. Part of YM-YWHA Poetry Center Series. Distributed by Audio-Forum.

THE PLEASURE OF WORDS

WILLIAM HATHAWAY, *Oh, Oh* (p. 217)

The reader's delight in the surprise ending of this poem hinges on the mood set up by the language of the first fifteen lines. Which words create this idyllic mood? What happens to the poem if you replace these words with others? For example, what words could replace "amble" (line 1)? How might one wave besides "gaily" (10)? How could the caboose pass other than with a "chuckle" (15)? How does the poem read with your revisions?

Does the poet give any clues as to what lies ahead? What about the "black window" in line 9, the exact center of the poem? A writing activity dealing with denotation and connotation could develop from a study of this poem. Have students consider a picture (one of an old house works well) and describe it first as though it might be used as a setting for *Nightmare on Elm Street*, then for an episode of the *Brady Bunch*. Discuss the word choices that set the different moods.

POSSIBLE CONNECTION TO ANOTHER SELECTION

Robert Frost, "Design" (text p. 1163)

ROBERT FRANCIS, *Catch* (p. 218)

This poem casts metaphor-making as a game of catch between two boys. If you are using the poem to examine metaphor, you might ask students what is missing from the central metaphor that Francis creates: that is, when two boys are playing catch, they are tossing a ball to one another. If we interpret the two players of this game as the poet and the reader, does the game of catch seem one-sided, as though one player is firing a number of balls at the other one? Once you catch the ball in a game of catch, you throw it back. Does the relationship between reader and poet work the same way?

Encourage students to enjoy listening to this poem. Like a good pitcher, Francis finds various ways of throwing strikes. Consider, for example, line 3, with its "attitudes, latitudes, interludes, altitudes," or "prosy" and "posy" later in the poem.

WOLE SOYINKA, *Telephone Conversation* (p. 219)

"Telephone Conversation" is a narrative poem that takes a satiric look at the emotionally charged issue of racism. One way to approach the topic of racism (and race in general) is to begin discussion of this poem by having your students paraphrase the poem. Student paraphrases will undoubtedly focus on the racial dimensions of the conversation and the racial theme of the poem. In comparing prose paraphrases to the language of the poem, students may notice several things about the poet's style that are lost in a paraphrase: the short sentences and sentence fragments, the unusual syntax of many lines, the terse language, and the fast pace. After identifying some of these characteristics, you may wish to ask students what effects these characteristics have on the tone of the poem. It may also be interesting to talk about the effect the poet achieves by printing the words of the landlady in capital letters. What are the political implications of this shift? By the end of the poem, what do readers know about the speakers based solely on the words that have passed between them?

You may want to ask students to do a Marxist reading of this poem. In addition to race, they should consider issues of class, power, and social injustice in Soyinka's poem. Although the poet's deft handling of the account leaves little doubt as to who got in the last word, given the inevitable outcome of the exchange, who seems to have "won," and how?

POSSIBLE CONNECTIONS TO OTHER SELECTIONS

Chitra Banerjee Divakaruni, "Indian Movie, New Jersey" (text p. 1277)

Gary Soto, "Mexicans Begin Jogging" (text p. 1293)

PHILIP LARKIN, *A Study of Reading Habits* (p. 220)

This poem about a speaker's developing disillusionment with reading is a clever satire of the speaker's attitude. Note the intricate rhyme pattern in the poem. The poet's use of a complex poetic form while having the poem's speaker use slang and trite phrases provides an excellent opportunity to make students aware of the difference between the poet and the speaker of a poem. Does the slang used in Larkin's poem help to identify the speaker with a particular time period? With what current words would your students replace such words as "cool" (line 4), "lark" (8), "dude" (13)? Is any of the slang used in this poem still current?

After your students have read Larkin's poem, you might ask them to discuss their previous (and present) reading habits or have them write a short essay on this subject. What do they expect to gain from reading? Escape? Pleasure? Knowledge?

POSSIBLE CONNECTION TO ANOTHER SELECTION

Langston Hughes, "Theme for English B" (text p. 998)

ROBERT MORGAN, *Mountain Graveyard* (p. 221)

Ask students if they agree with the assertion that "Mountain Graveyard" is "unmistakably poetry." If they think it is poetry, is it a good poem? Meyer's strong argument in the text may be intimidating, but students should be encouraged to develop their own sense of what poetry is as they work through these chapters. Further, this poem and the next afford opportunities (because of their highly unorthodox forms) to lead students into a discussion of the authority of the printed word: Is a piece of literature good because "the book says so"? Is a story "art" because it is anthologized? It might be useful to return to these questions when your class finishes its consideration of poetry.

As a writing activity, have students choose another setting (college campus, supermarket, playground) and develop a set of anagrams for the new locale. Do different arrangements of the anagrams change the overall meaning of the set? Are any of the arrangements poetry?

POSSIBLE CONNECTION TO ANOTHER SELECTION

E. E. Cummings "l(a" (text p. 222)

E. E. CUMMINGS, *l(a* (p. 222)

E. E. Cummings was born in Cambridge, Massachusetts, the son of a Congregationalist minister. He earned a degree from Harvard University and began writing his iconoclastic poems after coming upon the work of Ezra Pound. His experimentation with syntax and punctuation reflects a seriously playful attitude toward language and meaning and a skepticism about institutional authority.

At first glance, "l(a" seems to be a poem spewed out by a closemouthed computer held in solitary confinement. As with Morgan's "Mountain Graveyard," however, the poem comes into its own as the reader not only deciphers but brings meaning to the text. Implied here is a simile between a falling leaf and loneliness. The use of a natural image to suggest an emotion recalls Japanese haiku.

The vertical quality of the poem illustrates the motion of a single leaf falling. Students might also point out the repetition of the digit *one* (indistinguishable in some texts from the letter *l*), along with other "aloneness" words, such as *a* and *one*. If ever a poem's medium enhanced its message, this one surely does.

POSSIBLE CONNECTION TO ANOTHER SELECTION

Robert Morgan, "Mountain Graveyard" (text p. 221)

RESOURCES FOR TEACHING

- **E. E. Cummings Reading His Poetry** [recording]. 1 cassette. Distributed by Caedmon/HarperAudio.
- **E. E. Cummings Reads** [recording]. 1 cassette (60 min.), 1987. From The Poet Anniversary Series. Distributed by Caedmon/HarperAudio.
- **E. E. Cummings Reads His Collected Poetry, 1920–1940, & Prose** [recording]. 2 cassettes (79 min.). Distributed by Caedmon/HarperAudio.
- **E. E. Cummings Reads His Collected Poetry, 1943–1958** [recording]. 2 cassettes. Distributed by Caedmon/HarperAudio.
- **E. E. Cummings: The Making of a Poet.** 24 min., 1978. Beta, VHS, ³/₄″ U-matic cassette. A profile of Cummings told in his own words. Distributed by Films for the Humanities and Sciences.
- **E. E. Cummings: Nonlectures** [recording]. 6 cassettes. 1. "I & My Parents"; 2. "I & Their Son"; 3. "Self-discovery"; 4. "I & You & Is"; 5. "I & Now & Him"; 6. "I & Am & Santa Claus." Distributed by Caedmon/HarperAudio.
- **Poems of E. E. Cummings** [recording]. 1 cassette (60 min.), 1981. Part of Poetic Heritage Series. Distributed by Summer Stream.
- **E. E. Cummings: Twentieth-Century Poetry in English: Recordings of Poets Reading Their Own Poetry, No. 5** [recording]. Distributed by the Library of Congress.
- See also "Poetry for People Who Hate Poetry," "Inner Ear, Parts 5 and 6," and "Caedmon Treasury of Modern Poets Reading Their Own Poetry" in the appendix of Film, Video, and Audiocassette Resources.

ANONYMOUS, *Western Wind* (p. 223)

Students should be aware that, in England, the coming of the west wind signifies the arrival of spring. How is the longing for spring in this lyric connected to the overall sense of longing or to sexual longing? These brief four lines contain examples of several poetic devices worth noting. Ask students to consider the effects of the apostrophe and the alliteration in the first line. Many modern poets would consider these techniques artificial and overdone, but this poet seems to be interested in making a strong statement in just a few words. Does it work? Also, consider the use of the expletive "Christ" (line 3). This word makes the reader feel the intensity of emotion being conveyed and turns the poem into a kind of prayer — it is both sacred and profane.

POSSIBLE CONNECTION TO ANOTHER SELECTION

E. E. Cummings, "in Just-" (text p. 269)

WORD CHOICE, WORD ORDER, AND TONE

Since poetry depends for its effects on the concentrated use of language, word choice can play a pivotal role in determining the meaning of a poem. For instance, in Martín Espada's "Latin Night at the Pawnshop," the choice of the word *apparition* as the first noun in the poem echoes Pound's "In a Station of the Metro." One word sets up an allusion to a key imagist poem, and thus puts Espada's poem in the context of that tradition. Still, students may remain unconvinced that word choice is all that important to a poem.

As an exercise to emphasize the importance of word choice, you might have students type up a short poem or section of a poem on a word processor. Most word processors now come with a thesaurus function that allows the user to replace a word with a synonym provided from a list. Have students replace either a couple of key words in the poem or a word in each line with the synonyms offered, and then read their new poems to the class. For instance, Pound's "In a Station of the Metro" can range from "The mirage of these faces in the throng / petals on a damp black bough" to "The fantasy of these mugs in the bunch / petals on a clammy dire branch." After a few such examples, it should become clear how important word choice is to the overall effect of the poem.

You might try a similar exercise for word order with some of the selections (E. E. Cummings's "in Just-" lends itself to this application). Having students think hypothetically about other options for the poem can help them develop an appreciation for the reasons a poem is the way it is. In general, counterfactuals help sharpen critical thinking skills.

The reasons a poem conveys a certain tone are sometimes hard to pin down, and can initially prove frustrating for students. You might find it helpful to encourage students to look not only at word choice but also other features of the poem, such as imagery, in their discussions of tone.

RANDALL JARRELL, *The Death of the Ball Turret Gunner* (p. 227)

Randall Jarrell attended Vanderbilt University and so became influenced by the Agrarian literary movement, an anti-industrial movement that sought to reinstate the values of an agricultural society. Jarrell's poem probably reflects on personal experience, as he was an air force pilot from 1942 until the end of World War II. However, like most of his poems, it evokes universal human pain and anguish, regardless of its specific circumstances.

The textual discussion of this poem calls attention to Jarrell's intentional use of ambiguity in some of his word choices, but is the overall tone of the poem ambiguous? How would you describe the speaker's attitude toward his subject?

The scene depicted in Jarrell's poem might almost be a synopsis of one of the major story lines in Joseph Heller's novel *Catch-22*. Compare Jarrell's word choices and the mood created by them to Heller's depiction of the gunner in Chapter 5 of *Catch-22*:

> That was where he wanted to be [atop the escape hatch, ready to parachute to safety] if he had to be there at all, instead of hung out there in front like some goddam cantilevered goldfish in some goddam cantilevered goldfish bowl while

the goddam foul black tiers of flak were bursting and billowing and booming all around and above and below him in a climbing, cracking, staggered, banging, phantasmagorical, cosmological wickedness that jarred and tossed and shivered, clattered and pierced, and threatened to annihilate them all in one splinter of a second in one vast flash of fire. (New York: Dell, 1974, p. 50)

POSSIBLE CONNECTION TO ANOTHER SELECTION

Wilfred Owen, "Dulce et Decorum Est" (text p. 1172)

RESOURCES FOR TEACHING

The Poetry of Randall Jarrell [recording]. 1 cassette (67 min.), 1963. Part of YM-YWHA Poetry Center Series. Distributed by Audio-Forum.

Randall Jarrell: The Bat Poet [recording]. 1 cassette. Distributed by Caedmon/HarperAudio.

Randall Jarrell Reads and Discusses His Poems Against War [recording]. 1 cassette. Distributed by Caedmon/HarperAudio.

See also "The Poet's Voice" in the appendix of Film, Video, and Audiocassette Resources.

MARTÍN ESPADA, *Latin Night at the Pawnshop* (p. 230)

This imagist poem describes a scene of a man looking into the window of a pawnshop. In the instruments suspended there, he sees the apparition of a salsa band. The poet compares the instruments to a dead man with a toe tag.

There is nothing apparently "difficult" about this poem, so students may be quick to dismiss it, feeling that they "get the point" instantly. The challenge for discussion then becomes to fill in the considerable space around the poem. The liveliness of a salsa band coupled with the fact that the poem takes place on Christmas, a day of celebration, contribute to the blunt emotional overtones of the poem. What does the speaker's presence at a pawnshop on Christmas suggest? The speaker is implicitly mourning the passage of something vital. Unlike the Christmas ghosts of a character students are familiar with, Dickens's Scrooge, this apparition does not seem to provide any comfort or hope for the future. The apparition is the *absence* of the band, with its instruments apparently sold cheaply. As a way of pointing out what exactly has been lost, emphasize all of the economic allusions in the poem (pawnshop, Liberty Loan, golden, silver, price tags). Does the poem seek to make a broad point about class and culture in contemporary America? Consider the title as a follow-up to this question. Students may think of other examples of the various ways in which immigrants in America must "sell out" their culture for more fundamental survival needs (i.e., money).

When you use this poem to illustrate the elements of word order and tone, emphasize how one contributes to the other. In other words, ask your students to consider how the overall tone would be different if the words were in a different order. An "apparition" and a "dead man's toe" are the first and last images of the poem. In between are the lively, colorful evocations of a "salsa band." How does this order contribute to the poem's tone? Would the tone be different if the more ghostly images were embedded in the interior of the poem?

POSSIBLE CONNECTION TO ANOTHER SELECTION

Wole Soyinka, "Telephone Conversation" (text p. 219)

ANDREW MARVELL, *To His Coy Mistress* (p. 230)

After graduating from Cambridge University in 1639, Andrew Marvell left England to travel in Europe. Almost nothing is known of his life from this time until he became the tutor of the daughter of a powerful Yorkshire nobleman in 1650. Most of his poems seem to have been written during the next seven years. He served for a short time as John Milton's assistant when Milton was Latin secretary for the Commonwealth, and he represented Hull, his hometown, in Parliament from 1659 until he died.

This seduction poem is structured with a flawless logic. Marvell begins with a hypothetical conjecture, "Had we but world enough, and time," which he then disproves with hyperbole, promising his "mistress" that he would devote "an age at least" to praising her every part. Time is, of course, far more limited, and the second section of the poem makes clear time's ravages on beauty. The third section expounds the *carpe diem* theme: if time is limited, then seize the day and triumph over life's difficulties with love.

From his initial tone of teasing hyperbole, the poet modulates to a much more somber tone, employing the metaphysically startling imagery of the grave to underscore human mortality. Lines 31–32 are an example of understatement, calculated to make the listener react and acknowledge this world as the time and place for embracing.

Some classes may need help in recognizing that the verbs in the first part of the poem are in the subjunctive mood, while those in the last are often in the imperative. At any rate, students should easily recognize that the last section contains verbs that all imply a physical vigor that would seize time, mold it to the lovers' uses, and thus "make [time] run" (46) according to the clock of their own desires.

The poem seems far more than a simple celebration of the flesh. It confronts human mortality and suggests a psychological stance that would seize life (and face death) so that fulfilling of one's time would be a strategy of confronting time's passing.

As a writing topic you might ask students to explain the radical and somewhat abrupt change in tone between the opening twenty lines and the rest of the poem. Marvell offers more than one reason to temper his initial levity.

TIP FROM THE FIELD

I use point-of-view writing assignments that ask students to assume a persona in a poem or story and respond to the other characters or situations in the selection accordingly. For example, I have students read Andrew Marvell's "To His Coy Mistress" and then write an essay from the point of view of the wooer or the wooee.

— SANDRA ADICKES, *Winona State University*

POSSIBLE CONNECTIONS TO OTHER SELECTIONS

Diane Ackerman, "A Fine, a Private Place" (text p. 823)
Richard Wilbur, "A Late Aubade" (text p. 843)

RESOURCES FOR TEACHING

Andrew Marvell: Ralph Richardson Reads Andrew Marvell [recording]. 1 cassette. Distributed by Audio-Forum.
See also "Metaphysical and Devotional Poetry" in the appendix of Film, Video, and Audiocassette Resources.

PABLO NERUDA, *Juventud,* with translations by ROBERT BLY and JACK SCHMITT (pp. 233–234)

In this poem, Neruda uses one rolling sentence charged with intense language and studded with images both to capture the power and mystery of adolescence and to reflect elegiacally on youth from a more distant perspective. The erotic imagery in this poem is palpable in any translation, whether it is Bly's "drops of life slipping on the fingertips" (line 4), Schmitt's "sugary kisses on the teeth" (3), or the original's "la dulce pulpa erótica" (5), which even readers who know no Spanish can appreciate, if only for its sounds. As the poem progresses, the perspective seems more distant and the images more general as it is revealed that these images are memories, observed from a distance. The final image of the poem, of a guttering candle flame, yokes the poem's concern with love and youthful sensuality — the flame of passion — with the wiser-if-sadder perspective of the mature observer in whom a flame acts as beacon or guide.

While neither Bly's nor Schmitt's translation veers very far from Neruda's original, neither is exactly literal. Both translators make choices that emphasize different aspects of the Spanish poem. For instance, Bly adds the words "made" (1) and "branches" (2) to the first two lines of his poem — neither appears in the Spanish. By adding words, Bly more closely approximates the lengths and cadences of the Spanish lines, and he holds the reader's attention on the strange opening image. He achieves the same effect in the third line by converting the simpler Spanish metaphor ("los besos del azúcar") into a full-blown simile: "the kisses like sugar in the teeth" (3). Bly seems to opt for reality over mystery, preferring to let the images work by clarifying them. This approach carries him through the rest of the poem: for the Spanish "pulpa," which means pulp or flesh, Bly substitutes "fruit"; for the Spanish "mojándose" Bly chooses "sputtering" — in both instances he's choosing English idiom over absolute faithfulness to the Spanish.

If Bly angles his translation toward maintaining the overall rhythmic shape of the poem, Schmitt leans more toward maintaining a more literal link with the Spanish. Note that, whenever possible, Schmitt uses an English cognate of a Spanish word: "erotic pulp" (5) for "pulpa erótica"; "inciting" (6) for "incitantes"; and "secret" (7) for "secretos." Doing so not only keeps Schmitt's version rigidly close to the literal Spanish; it also forms a sort of linguistic bridge between the English and the Spanish, linking them to their common roots. Schmitt's choice of linguistic over rhythmic faithfulness allows him to compress his lines, making his poem move more quickly than the original. Schmitt gets some of the original's intensity in this way, opting less for an easy reading than for an energetic one.

Be sure to have at least one student who knows Spanish read Neruda's poem aloud; have it read by a few students if several know Spanish. Hearing the poem in a few voices will help students hear the music and the power of the original, which will make the choices that Bly and Schmitt have made more clear.

Students are already very familiar with imagery through advertising. You may find it an interesting exercise to have students compare ads and poems dealing with similar subject matter: a recruitment commercial and Owen's "Dulce et Decorum Est," for instance. This may prove to be a controversial exercise — be prepared for students' resistance. You may instead (or additionally) want to have students focus on several advertisements or television shows and write a short response to the imagery they find there. This exercise can be beneficial because it will show students they already know how to read imagery, and will also help sharpen their critical thinking skills by applying analysis in an area they are unused to.

Still, students can sometimes have trouble with very imagistic poems: such poems may require more effort on the part of students than they suspect. Often, it may help to ask students to consider why it is that a poet focuses so closely on a given scene or object. If students can be helped to see that poets often use images to emphasize significance or preserve a fleeting moment, they may appreciate the poems more.

Another important point in this chapter is that images need not be exclusively visual. Croft's "Home-Baked Bread" and Song's "The White Porch" both employ a variety of imagery to enhance the sensual themes of the poems, whereas Kizer's "Food for Love" uses similar kinds of imagery to darker thematic effect. Blake's "London" is full of auditory images, while Roethke's "The Root Cellar" and Baca's "Green Chile" use smell and taste, respectively. Baca's poem raises an interesting point about the cultural specificity of imagery, particularly when compared to a poem such as Wilbur's "A Late Aubade." Some students may, in fact, be more familiar with the taste of green chile con carne than bleu cheese and wine.

You may find that it helps to have students experiment with their own writing in this chapter: they could be asked to write a descriptive paragraph or poem concretely rendering an object, scene, or activity. This can serve to emphasize ideas raised in class about the significance of detail.

WILLIAM CARLOS WILLIAMS, *Poem* (p. 235)

William Carlos Williams was born and lived most of his life in Rutherford, New Jersey, a town near Paterson, the city that provided the title and much of the subject matter of his "modern epic" poem *Paterson*. He had a thriving medical practice for fifty years, delivering more than 2,000 babies and writing his poems, novels, short stories, and essays at night and in the moments he could snatch between patient visits during the day.

This poem is an imaged motion, but the verse has a certain slant music too. Notice the *t*-sounds that align themselves in the second tercet, the consonance in "hind" (line 8) and "down" (9), the repetitions in "pit of" (10), "empty" (11), and "flowerpot" (12). Sound also helps convey the poem's sense of agility and smoothness.

Students may initially resist this poem because, being apparently simple, it may not conform to their expectations. If this situation arises, or perhaps even if it doesn't, you can use this opportunity to ask the question, "what should poetry do or be?" In all likelihood, you can convince skeptics that Williams's poem does what they don't think it does. In any case, it is an opportunity to refine a definition of poetry while exploring its power to appeal to our imagination.

Possible Connection to Another Selection

E. E. Cummings, "in Just-" (text p. 269)

Resources for Teaching

William Carlos Williams Reads His Poetry [recording]. 1 cassette. Distributed by Caedmon/HarperAudio.
William Carlos Williams, People and the Stones: Selected Poems [recording]. 1 cassette (60 min.). Distributed by Watershed Tapes.
See also "Inner Ear, Part 1," "The Poet's Voice," "Voices and Vision," and "Caedmon Treasury of Modern Poets Reading Their Own Poetry" in the appendix of Film, Video, and Audiocassette Resources.

MATTHEW ARNOLD, *Dover Beach* (p. 235)

Matthew Arnold was born in the English village of Laleham, in the Thames valley. His father was a clergyman and a reformist educator, a powerful personality against whom the young Arnold rebelled in a number of ways, including nearly flunking out of Oxford. After several years as private secretary to a nobleman, in 1851 Arnold became an inspector of schools, a post he held for thirty-five years. For the characteristic jauntiness of his prose style, Walt Whitman once referred to him as "one of the dudes of literature."

Many of us have had the experience of looking out on a landscape and registering its beauty (and possibly its tranquillity) and its undercurrent of something lost or awry. Such is the case for the speaker of "Dover Beach" as he looks out at the shore awash in moonlight. The private moment has its wholeness, for he stands in the "sweetness" of the night air with his beloved. But all the security and peace he could expect to feel are shaken by his concerns beyond the moment and his awareness of the ravages that history brings to bear on the present. We are not fragments of our time alone, the poem seems to say; we are caught in the "turbid ebb and flow / Of human misery" (lines 17–18) that Sophocles heard so long ago.

In the third stanza, Arnold goes beyond commenting on the sadness that seems an inevitable part of the human condition, as his thoughts turn to the malaise of his own time. Faith, which once encircled humanity, is now only the overheard roar of its waters withdrawing to the rock-strewn edges of the world. In short, for whatever happens there is no solace, no consolation or reason to hope for any restoration, justice, or change. Humankind is beyond the tragic condition of Sophocles, and in this poem, Arnold seems to be tipping the balance toward a modernist existential worldview. The tone of the poem barely improves by the final stanza, for the image Arnold leaves us with is that of "ignorant armies" clashing in the night — the sound and fury once again signifying nothing.

The images of Dover Beach or some other imagined seascape work well to evoke the tone that Arnold is trying to convey. In discussion, or perhaps as a writing topic, you might ask the class to review the poem for natural details and images (in lines 9–14 or most of the third stanza, for example) that suggest the dreary, stark, and ominous portrait Arnold is painting here.

General essays on this poem appear in A. Dwight Culler's *Imaginative Reason: The Poetry of Matthew Arnold* (New Haven: Yale UP, 1966) and James Dickey's *Babel to Byzantium* (New York: Farrar, 1968).

POSSIBLE CONNECTION TO ANOTHER SELECTION

Wilfred Owen, "Dulce et Decorum Est" (text p. 1172)

WILLIAM BLAKE, *London* (p. 237)

William Blake's only formal schooling was in art, and he learned engraving as an apprentice to a prominent London engraver. After his seven years' service, Blake made his living as a printer and engraver, writing poetry on the side. The private mythology that came to dominate his poems was worked out in almost total obscurity: at the time of his death Blake had acquired some notice for his art but almost none for his writing.

This poem may seem pessimistic, but is it entirely so? If students would go so far as to call it "apocalyptic," does their knowledge of history help them to discern where the speaker's attitude comes from? The use of "chartered" (line 1) to describe streets and the River Thames makes all the boundaries in the poem seem unnatural and rigid; the cries heard are cries of pain and sadness. Like the rigidities of the chartered streets, the legislation of the "mind-forged manacles" (8) does nothing to promote civil liberty and happiness. Blake implies here that the "manacles" of religion and government that should protect individuals fail miserably to ensure good lives. Children are sold into near slavery as chimney sweeps, their own dark and stunted faces casting a pall (appall) on the benevolent state and the Christian tradition. Soldiers sent off to war die or kill other soldiers. Sexual restrictions invite prostitution and thus promote disease, which may, in turn, afflict marriages and resulting births. Social regulations ("manacles") thus induce societal ills.

The image of the soldier dying for the state, for example, (11–12), is described in a condensed and effective manner that suggests not only his lucklessness (or helplessness) but also the indifference of a government removed from the individual by class ("Palace" [12]), its insularity ("walls" [12]), and the imperturbable security of law.

Comparison of the two versions of the final stanza provides an excellent writing topic. Notice, though, how much more endemic the societal failings and wrongdoings appear in the second (revised) version. Instead of "midnight harlot's curse," the phrase becomes the "midnight streets" (13) (evil as pervasive) and "the youthful Harlot's curse" (14) (a blighting of innocence at an early age). By reversing "marriage hearse" and "infant's tear," Blake suggests not a mere (and societally sanctioned) cause-effect relation between marriage and the birth of afflicted infants but the presence of syphilis in even the youngest members of society and the conditions that would sustain its presence.

How do the urban ills of contemporary society compare with those of Blake's time? It might be an interesting exercise to ask students to write a poem about contemporary social ills, either urban or rural, in Blake's style. What has changed?

Possible Connections to Other Selections

George Eliot, "In a London Drawingroom" (text p. 1280)
Wilfred Owen, "Dulce et Decorum Est" (text p. 1172)

Resources for Teaching

William Blake: The Book of Thel [recording]. 1 cassette. Distributed by Audio-Forum.

Essay on William Blake. 52 min., color, 1969. ³/₄" U-matic cassette, 16-mm film, special-order formats. A profile of the poet. Distributed by Indiana University Instructional Support Services.

William Blake: The Marriage of Heaven and Hell. 30 min., color, 1984. ³/₄" U-matic cassette. Dramatizes the life of Blake and his wife Catherine. With Anne Baxter and George Rose. Distributed by Modern Talking Picture Service.

Poems [recording]. 1 cassette (80 min.). Distributed by HighBridge.

The Poetry of William Blake [recording]. 1 cassette. Distributed by Caedmon/HarperAudio.

Poetry of William Blake [recording]. 1 cassette. Distributed by Spoken Arts.

William Blake. 26 min., color, 1973. 16-mm film. Hosted by Kenneth Clark. Focuses on Blake's drawings and engravings. Distributed by Pyramid Film & Video.

William Blake: Something About Poetry [recording]. 1 cassette (22 min.), 1969. Distributed by Audio-Forum.

William Blake. 30 min., VHS. A dramatization of Blake's inner world. Distributed by Insight Media.

William Blake. 57 min., color, 1976. Beta, VHS, ³/₄" U-matic cassette, special-order formats. A biographical portrait. Distributed by Time-Life Video.

William Blake: Selected Poems [recording]. 2 cassettes (180 min.), 1992. Includes "Tyger! Tyger!" and "A Poison Tree." Distributed by Blackstone Audio Books.

See also "Introduction to English Poetry" and "Romantic Pioneers" in the appendix of Film, Video, and Audiocassette Resources.

FIGURES OF SPEECH

The material in this section can build on issues raised in the previous two: considerations of word choice, tone, and images both influence and reflect choices in figurative speech. You might have your students draw these connections explicitly by having them select a poem from this chapter and analyze it both in terms of its figurative language and also in terms of concepts discussed earlier. Doing so will help them understand how various elements make up the total effect of a poem.

Another possible exercise for this section would be to have students think about and list instances of figurative language used in their everyday speech, working either alone or in small groups..

It is likely that students are already aware of the difference between simile and metaphor; the distinction will become important to them only if they can understand that it has some significance. Similes tend to call attention to the comparison itself. Conversely, metaphors tend to focus on the *content* of the comparison, shifting the focus from the separate entities being compared to the nature of those entities, as in Dickinson's "Presentiment — is that long Shadow — on the lawn —."

Metonymy and synecdoche can be difficult for students to grasp; for some reason, they find it more difficult to remember "metonymy" than "metaphor." You might find it useful to point out (or to have students point out) uses of metonymy in everyday language: "The White House confirms" or "University A beat University B" or "The Chancellor's office responded." This can help students get a grasp of the concepts involved and defuse their anticipation of being unable to understand these terms.

Paradox and oxymoron can be useful tools to encourage students' critical thinking skills. Puzzling out paradoxes and explaining oxymorons often require students to think in unusual ways. Poems that lend themselves to this are Donne's "Death Be Not Proud," as well as nearly any poem by Emily Dickinson.

WILLIAM SHAKESPEARE, *From* Macbeth *(Act V, Scene v)* (p. 239)

After asking students to identify each of the things to which Shakespeare's Macbeth compares life, and to consider how life is like each of them, have them decide which of these figures of speech is the most effective. Does one overpower the others, or does the overall effect depend on the conjunction of all of them?

Have students recall other things to which they have heard life compared. Are these common images examples of strong figurative language, or merely clichés? For example, "Life is a bed of roses" conveys the idea that life is easy and beautiful, but it is such a well-worn phrase that it now lacks the impact it might once have had. As a writing assignment, students could come up with their own similes and metaphors and explain how life is like the image they have created.

See Robert Frost's " 'Out, Out –' " (text p. 992) for one example of how a modern poet has made use of Shakespeare's famous passage. Students familiar with William Faulkner's *The Sound and the Fury* might be able to comment on how another twentieth-century writer has used the reprinted passage from *Macbeth*.

POSSIBLE CONNECTION TO ANOTHER SELECTION

Robert Frost, " 'Out, Out —' " (text p. 992)

EMILY DICKINSON, *Presentiment — is that long Shadow — on the lawn —* (p. 240)

As noted in the text, Dickinson uses richly connotative words such as *shadow* and *darkness* in order to express in a few words the sense of fear and danger inherent in her "Presentiment." You might explore with your students other connotations of the word *presentiment*. Are all premonitions warnings about negative occurrences? Have any of your students had premonitions about good things? What kinds of words might one want to use in order to express — economically — the possibility of pleasant surprise? You could have students, individually or in groups, try to identify specific words and then a controlling metaphor that would be appropriate to express this alternative kind of surprise.

POSSIBLE CONNECTION TO ANOTHER SELECTION

William Shakespeare, from *Macbeth* (Act V, Scene v) (text p. 239)

DYLAN THOMAS, *The Hand That Signed the Paper* (p. 241)

Dylan Thomas's *Eighteen Poems,* published in 1934, when he was twenty, began his career as a poet with a flourish: here, it seemed, was an answer to T. S. Eliot, a return to rhapsody and unembarrassed music. Thomas's poems became more craftsmanlike as he matured, but they never lost their ambition for the grand gesture, the all-embracing, bittersweet melancholy for which the Romantics strove. Thomas lived the role of the poet to the hilt: he was an alcoholic, a philanderer, a wonderful storyteller, a boor, and a justly celebrated reader of his own poems and those of others. Although he never learned to speak Welsh (he was born and grew up in Swansea, Wales), it is said that his poems carry the sounds of that language over into English. He died of alcohol poisoning during his third reading tour of the United States.

Although Thomas seems to be referring to no specific incident in this poem, the date of the poem (1936) indicates a possible concern with the political machinations leading up to the outbreak of World War II. The "five kings [who] did a king to death" (line 4) may even recall the five major powers who signed the Treaty of Versailles to end World War I but in their severe dismantling of Germany set the stage for another war. Some critics suggest that the poem, especially in the last two stanzas, refers to a wrathful God. Which words or phrases would lend credence to this reading? Students may suggest other situations in which a person in power can, by performing a seemingly simple act, adversely affect people at long range.

Discuss the title's allusion to the saying "The hand that rocks the cradle rules the world." Both phrases make observations about the power inherent in the acts of a single person. How are the acts to which they refer alike and different? How does the allusion to motherhood create irony in the poem? (Students familiar with the 1992 horror film *The Hand That Rocks the Cradle* which deals with a deranged babysitter, may have their own associations with this poem.)

POSSIBLE CONNECTION TO ANOTHER SELECTION

Alice Jones, "The Foot" (text p. 1167)

RESOURCES FOR TEACHING

The Days of Dylan Thomas. 21 min., b/w, 1965. Beta, VHS ³/₄″ U-matic cassette, 16-mm film. A biography of the poet. Distributed by CRM Films.

Dylan Thomas [recording]. 4 cassettes. Distributed by Caedmon/HarperAudio.

Dylan Thomas. 25 min., color, 1982. Beta, VHS, ³/₄″ U-matic cassette. A portrait of the poet. Distributed by Films, Inc.

A Dylan Thomas Memoir. 28 min., color, 1972. Beta, VHS, ³/₄" U-matic cassette, 16-mm film. A character study of the poet. Distributed by Pyramid Film and Video.

Dylan Thomas Reading "And Death Shall Have No Dominion" & Other Poems [recording]. 1 cassette. Distributed by Caedmon/HarperAudio.

Dylan Thomas Reading His Poetry [recording]. 2 cassettes. Distributed by Caedmon/HarperAudio.

Dylan Thomas Reading "Quite Early One Morning" & Other Poems [recording]. 1 cassette. Distributed by Caedmon/HarperAudio.

Dylan Thomas Reading "Over Sir John's Hill" & Other Poems [recording]. 1 cassette. Distributed by Caedmon/HarperAudio.

Dylan Thomas Reads a Personal Anthology [recording]. 1 cassette. Distributed by Caedmon/HarperAudio.

An Evening with Dylan Thomas [recording]. 1 cassette. Distributed by Caedmon/HarperAudio.

Dylan Thomas: In Country Heaven — The Evolution of a Poem [recording]. 1 cassette. Distributed by Caedmon/HarperAudio.

Dylan Thomas: A Portrait. 26 min., color, 1989. Beta, VHS, ³/₄" U-matic cassette. A biographical film. Distributed by Films for the Humanities and Sciences.

Dylan Thomas: An Appreciation [recording]. 1 cassette. Distributed by Audio-Forum.

Dylan Thomas Soundbook [recording]. 4 cassettes. Read by the author.

Dylan Thomas: Under Milkwood [recording]. 2 cassettes (90 min.). Distributed by S & S Audio.

The Wales of Dylan Thomas. color, 1989. Images of Wales in Thomas's poetry, prose, and drama. Distributed by Films for the Humanities and Sciences.

JANICE TOWNLEY MOORE, To a Wasp (p. 243)

Discuss with students how an awareness of the intensity and seriousness of purpose that usually accompany the use of apostrophe affect their reading of this poem, which is, after all, about a common insect. In what way is the fist in the last line being waved at both the speaker and the wasp? Whose fist is it? How does the word *chortled* in the first line help us understand the speaker's view of the wasp? Discuss the paradox inherent in the notion of "delicious death" (line 11).

POSSIBLE CONNECTION TO ANOTHER SELECTION

John Donne, "The Flea" (text p. 831)

J. PATRICK LEWIS, *The Unkindest Cut* (p. 244)

Students will enjoy this humorous quatrain that is a play on the saying "the pen is mightier than the sword." To open discussion, ask students to point out the paradox inherent in this simple poem. Discuss also the title of the poem, pointing out that the title is an allusion to Shakespeare's *Julius Caesar* (III.ii.188).

POSSIBLE CONNECTION TO ANOTHER SELECTION

Janice Townley Moore, "To a Wasp" (text p. 243)

SYMBOL, ALLEGORY, AND IRONY

The discussion on symbol and allegory can follow naturally from the discussion of figurative language. In a sense, symbols are metaphors with one term left open, and it is up to the reader to complete them. Many of the poems in the previous section lend themselves well to symbolic readings — a good transition between the sections might have students select a previously covered poem and examine its symbols.

Another exercise that can be useful is to have students brainstorm a list of symbols found in popular culture and articulate the connotations that surround them: what the American flag means, for instance. (This exercise can also illustrate how symbols can have different meanings for different groups.) This can help give students a sense of how symbols work, and how they can be simultaneously specific and general.

Students often seem to believe that every poem is immediately symbolic, which can be simultaneously encouraging and frustrating in their zeal to leap to the "real" meaning of the poem. Alternately, they may be committed to a kind of relativism, in which they believe that some poems can be symbolic of anything. While it is true that some symbols are more loosely focused than others, one of the challenges of discussion in this chapter is to encourage students to offer well-thought-out readings. It is a difficult line to walk between putting pressure on students to read critically and shutting down all discussion because the students come to believe that the teacher has "the right answer," and unless they can provide this they are better off keeping quiet. In fact, students may use silence as a tactic to bring out "the right answer" from the teacher. In this chapter, it is perhaps better to err on the side of caution and try to draw out students' own interpretations, even if these interpretations are initially somewhat off track. You may find it useful to avoid giving your own interpretations at all, relying instead on student input shaped by questions from you and from other students. Students may find this frustrating at first, particularly when they are used to being given answers by authorities, but ultimately it will sharpen their abilities as readers.

Irony can be difficult to explain directly — in this case, examples are a great help. Irony often depends on an understanding of the context, as Janice Mirikitani's "Recipe" illustrates. Without some idea of the "beauty myth," the irony in this poem will not be evident. It may be useful to compare some kinds of irony to an inside joke in that they depend on a shared bit of information before the audience can "get it." Students may in fact be quite familiar with situational irony, as in Jane Kenyon's "Surprise." They may be able to readily call incidents to mind in which all was not as it initially seemed. For an interesting take on irony, you might look at Linda Hutcheon's book *Irony's Edge: The Theory and Politics of Irony*, which is an occasionally dense but well-supported argument about the place of irony in contemporary society.

ROBERT FROST, *Acquainted with the Night* (p. 245)

This poem investigates the mind of a speaker who has seen a part of humanity and of nature that he cannot overlook. His experience has led him to see things that other people have not necessarily seen. The poem invites us to read it on more than one level, as is the case with many of Frost's poems. You might ask the students to discuss in a two-page essay the function of the clock in this poem. How does its presence modify the tone of the poem? Do we read it literally, symbolically, or as a mixture of both?

POSSIBLE CONNECTIONS TO OTHER SELECTIONS

T. S. Eliot, "The Love Song of J. Alfred Prufrock" (text p. 1280)
Octavio Paz, "The Street" (text p. 1290)

EDGAR ALLAN POE, The Haunted Palace (p. 247)

Edgar Allan Poe was born in Boston, the son of itinerant actors. He lived an often harrowing life marked by alcoholism, disease, and misfortune, managing to eke out a rather precarious existence primarily as an editor for a number of newspapers and periodicals in Philadelphia, New York, and Baltimore. Although he was renowned in his lifetime as the author of "The Raven," his most abiding ambition was to be a respected critic. He died after collapsing in a Baltimore street.

Students may have had little exposure to allegory, since it is not frequently used by modern writers. Thus it might be useful to explicate at least one stanza of the poem, discussing how a particular part of the palace corresponds to a particular part of the human body or mind. Notice the two "characters" actually personified by Poe in the poem: Thought (line 5) and Echoes (29). Does there seem to be a particular reason for singling out these two?

What is the purpose of using such archaic expressions as "Porphyrogene" (22) and "red-litten" (42)? What other words in the poem seem especially well chosen for their connotative meanings?

As a short writing assignment or subject for further class discussion, ask your students to contrast the depictions of the "windows" and the "door" of the palace when they first appear in the poem (stanzas III and IV) with their portrayal in the last stanza, after the coming of the "evil things" (33). How do they seem to change?

POSSIBLE CONNECTION TO ANOTHER SELECTION

Thomas Hardy, "The Convergence of the Twain" (p. 1164)

RESOURCES FOR TEACHING

Edgar Allan Poe: "The Raven," "The Bells," and Other Poems [recording]. 1 cassette. Distributed by Spoken Arts.

Edgar Allan Poe: Terror of the Soul. 1 hour, color, 1995. Beta, VHS. A biography revealing Poe's creative genius and personal experiences through dramatic recreations of important scenes from his work and life. Distributed by PBS Video.

Poetry of Edgar Allan Poe [recording]. 2 cassettes (2 hours). Distributed by Dove Audio.

With Poe at Midnight. 60 min., color, 1979, Beta, VHS, $3/4''$ U-matic cassette. Examines the interaction between Poe's life and work. Distributed by Media Concepts, Inc.

See also "Poetry by Americans" in the appendix of Film, Video, and Audiocassette Resources.

EDWIN ARLINGTON ROBINSON, Richard Cory (p. 249)

Edwin Arlington Robinson became a professional poet in the grimmest of circumstances: his father's businesses went bankrupt in 1893, one brother became a drug addict and another an alcoholic, and Robinson could afford to attend Harvard University for just two years. He eked out a livelihood from the contributions of friends and patrons, finally moving to New York City, where his work received more critical attention and public acceptance. He won three Pulitzer Prizes for his gloomy, musical verse narratives.

As the book states, this poem is a good example of situational irony. Ask students to analyze how Robinson achieves the power of the final line of "Richard Cory," paying special attention to the regal language that describes Cory, the repetition of words like "always" and "every," as well as the strong contrasts in the couplets of the final stanza. As a writing assignment you might ask students to place themselves in the position of the "people on the pavement." Is there someone whom they have envied for his or her wealth, success, or achievements? Have they ever been surprised to find that someone who appeared to "have it all" was desperately unhappy? As a creative writing assignment, consider having your students write a poem from the point of view of Richard Cory, comparing his own life to that of "the people on the pavement." Does *he* envy *them*?

POSSIBLE CONNECTION TO ANOTHER SELECTION

M. Carl Holman, "Mr. Z" (text p. 996)

KENNETH FEARING, *AD* (p. 250)

How does the double meaning inherent in the title of the poem — "AD" is an abbreviation for "advertisement" as well as for "in the year of the Lord" — prepare the reader for the satire that follows? Notice how even the type used for this poem contributes to its meaning. The italicized words and phrases might occur in any high-powered advertising campaign. How is the effect of the advertising words undercut by the words in standard type? What is the effect of the reversal of type patterns in the last line?

Students should be aware that the poem alludes, in part, to the Uncle Sam "I want you" Army recruiting posters. Discuss whether the purpose of the satire in "AD" is to expose a situation that exists, to correct it, or both. Is the situation to which the poem refers — the attempt to draw people into a horrifying occupation by making the work sound exciting and rewarding — confined to the pre–World War II era?

POSSIBLE CONNECTION TO ANOTHER SELECTION

Janice Mirikitani, "Recipe" (text p. 1288)

SOUNDS: LISTENING TO POETRY

In this section, encouraging students to read aloud is vital. You may find that you have to lead by example, initially. However, you will probably want to shift the focus onto student readers at some point. In some cases, you may find yourself confronting a considerable degree of resistance, particularly if there has not been much reading aloud previously. Much of this resistance stems from fear of embarrassment, and dealing with it requires either the creation of a "safe space" in which students can read without fear of others snickering, or a slightly raucous classroom environment in which students don't feel as much pressure to be "cool."

If you have a group of particularly shy students, you might find it helpful to assign students poems in advance, so that they have a chance to read the poem through a couple of times before being called on to speak out before the class. If you have a mix of extraverts and introverts, you might schedule the class so that the extraverts read "cold," and announce at the end of class the poems the introverts will read in the next session, to give them fair warning.

In most cases, the addition of student voices to the classroom will help increase involvement and raise the energy level. If the class has not featured student reading much so far, this chapter would be an appropriate time to introduce this feature of the class.

In addition to including student voices in the classroom, this chapter affords an opportunity to include the voices of the poets as well, many of whom have recordings available that will allow students to hear either the voice of the poet or a skilled reader reciting the poems. It is perhaps a judgment call as to whether you should introduce these readings before students have done much reading on their own, in order to provide models of reading for them, or to wait until after students have some experience, to keep from intimidating them into silence. If you have included recordings in previous chapters, this may not be an issue here. In any event, recordings can be very useful in giving students a sense of the reality of the people "behind the page," as it were. You may find it appropriate to do readings or bring in recordings of poems that have been popular with students earlier in the class, and evaluate the poets' use of sound in relation to the students' own preference of these poems.

Thematically, there are some interesting poems in this chapter. If you do not want the focus on reading to overwhelm a discussion of these poems, you could use the reading as a springboard to raise the class's interest and energy, and to give them specific features to discuss when they make connections between the sound of a poem and its "message."

JOHN UPDIKE, *Player Piano* (p. 252)

This poem is a listening exercise in how to translate the sounds poetry can produce to musical analogues we have already heard. From light ditties through more somber 1920s chase-scene music, perhaps, to a medley of chords and light cadences, this poem explores a player piano's repertoire. In doing so, does the poem do anything *besides* impress us with its sounds? Does reading the poem allow us anything beyond the sheer joy of the sounds of words and the way they can be manipulated?

POSSIBLE CONNECTION TO ANOTHER SELECTION

William Carlos Williams, "Poem" (text p. 235)

EMILY DICKINSON, *A Bird came down the Walk* — (p. 252)

Silent reading of this poem, followed by reading it aloud, will reinforce the connection between sound and sense. In particular, students should hear the difference between the irregular movement of the first three stanzas and the smoothness of the last six lines, a difference created visually by punctuation but even more obvious when the poem is heard.

One of the poetic techniques that characterizes Emily Dickinson's poetry is her use of unexpected words and images. Consider her depiction of the bird's eyes and of his flight. How can eyes be "rapid" (line 9)? How can they hurry (10)? How can feathers "unroll" (15)? How is flight like rowing (16)? What is the effect created by the use of unusual language to describe an ordinary creature?

Compare the way the sounds of poetry are used to create a sense of an animal's movement in this poem and in Williams's "Poem" (text p. 235). Are the cat's movements in any way like the bird's?

POSSIBLE CONNECTION TO ANOTHER SELECTION

William Carlos Williams, "Poem" (text p. 235)

ROBERT SOUTHEY, From *The Cataract of Lodore* (p. 255)

Although Robert Southey is now known chiefly for his association with some of the great poets of the Romantic period, such as Wordsworth and Coleridge, he was very popular in his own time and became the poet laureate of England in 1813. He is also credited with the first published version of the children's story *The Three Bears*.

In a twenty-three-line introductory stanza that is not excerpted here, the poet reveals that his son and daughter had requested him to tell them — in verse — about the water at Lodore. He also introduces himself as the poet laureate. Does having this information in any way change your students' response to the poem that follows?

Are any lines in the poem especially memorable? Why is it appropriate that line 68, with its thirteen syllables, is metrically the longest line of the poem?

TIP FROM THE FIELD

One tip I've found helpful in teaching sound in poetry, is to have students stand in a tight circle and recite the excerpt from "The Cataract of Lodore" in round-robin fashion, one after another. Each student reads a line in the order of the poem, repeating the poem several times, faster each time. The results, in terms of student response, are remarkable.

— NANCY VEIGA, *Modesto Junior College*

POSSIBLE CONNECTION TO ANOTHER SELECTION

John Updike, "Player Piano" (text p. 252)

GERARD MANLEY HOPKINS, *God's Grandeur* (p. 258)

Gerard Manley Hopkins was a deeply religious man, a Jesuit ordained in 1877. He had previously graduated from Oxford University and joined the Roman Catholic Church in 1866. He served a number of parishes before being appointed a professor of classics at University College, Dublin. Although he tried to keep his poetic vocation from interfering with his spiritual one, he wasn't successful, and he suffered greatly because of this conflict, once burning all his finished work and another time forsaking poetry for seven years.

Although this poem follows sonnet form and an exact rhyme scheme, the first eight lines still read very roughly. How does the poet achieve this effect? Note the disruptions in rhythm as well as the use of cacophonic sounds. Have students try reading line 4 aloud to better appreciate its difficulty. Is there any change in the level of disruption or the level of cacophony in the last six lines? What is the effect of the inserted "ah!" in the last line?

Compare the halting beginning and smooth ending of this poem to the similar transition that occurs in Emily Dickinson's "A Bird came down the Walk —" (text p. 252). How does Dickinson's bird compare to the bird image Hopkins evokes in the last two lines?

POSSIBLE CONNECTIONS TO OTHER SELECTIONS

William Blake, "The Lamb" (text p. 1160)
William Blake, "The Tyger" (text p. 1161)

RESOURCES FOR TEACHING

The Poetry of Gerard Manley Hopkins [recording]. 1 cassette. Distributed by Caedmon/HarperAudio.
Gerard Manley Hopkins: The Wreck of the Deutschland [recording]. 1 cassette. Distributed by Audio-Forum.
See also "Romantics and Realists" and "Victorian Poetry" [recording] in the appendix of Film, Video, and Audiocassette Resources.

Rhythm and Meter

Reading aloud can be of great benefit here. Abstract discussions of prosody will almost certainly turn students off. However, if students can understand how rhythm contributes to the overall impression a poem makes, they will be more likely to show interest in questions of meter. One way to emphasize this impression is to have students read these poems out loud.

These readings will also show that even the strictest metrical forms are not absolute — no one really reads iambic meter da-dum da-dum da-dum, and students will find attempts to do so unnatural (and perhaps humorous). There are variations in rhythm built into the language, and often into the meter of the poems themselves. Once students understand this, they can approach prosody as a descriptive rather than prescriptive activity, and can see scansion as a way of understanding effects rather than as an end in itself.

You may want to encourage this perception in the kinds of writing you have students do in this chapter. Critics almost never use exclusively prosody-based arguments about poems; students would be well advised to do the same. You might craft the writing assignments to have students talk about prosody among other features of a poem that contribute to its overall effect or meaning. This kind of assignment has the added advantage of keeping skills students have developed in previous chapters alive by continued use.

This section also lends itself well to the inclusion of popular culture — rap music, for instance, can be very sophisticated metrically. Students will probably immediately understand the difference in feeling between songs with a heavy beat and ones where the rhythms are lighter and more trippingly phrased. Depending on the tastes of your class, the students themselves may be able to provide current examples.

Another exercise you might try would be to have students look for patterns of rhythm in other kinds of language — Martin Luther King, Jr.'s "I Have a Dream" speech lends itself particularly well to this application, and can be compared in structure to the selection from Whitman's "Song of the Open Road."

From Chapter 9, Philip Larkin's "This Be the Verse" is a particularly good example of the use of rhythm to help the overall impact of the poem. The rhythms Larkin employs create a cadence that emphasizes certain words and brings out a certain tone, at once flippant and cynical. In fact, in this poem the rhythms and the content work somewhat at cross purposes to produce this effect: the rhythms are light and almost singsong in places, the content dark and ultimately despairing about the human project.

WILLIAM WORDSWORTH, *My Heart Leaps Up* (p. 263)

The text discusses the enjambment in lines 8–9. What is the effect of the enjambment in the first two lines? Note that all the lines between are end-stopped. Is there a thematic connection between the pairs of enjambed lines? Between the end-stopped lines?

Ask students to discuss what they think Wordsworth means by "the child is father of the Man" (line 7). Do any current songs or other elements of popular culture reflect this same sentiment, or is it dismissable as a nineteenth-century Romantic impulse?

POSSIBLE CONNECTION TO ANOTHER SELECTION

Gerard Manley Hopkins, "Pied Beauty" (text p. 1167)

TIMOTHY STEELE, *Waiting for the Storm* (p. 264)

The text thoroughly discusses the poem's metrics and how they contribute to its meaning. In addition, you may wish to discuss word choices in the poem. How can darkness be "wrinkling," as stated in line 1? Why do you suppose Steele uses such a prosaic title for a poem so full of poetic images? You might have students examine the individual images and discuss the senses to which they appeal. Is the poem mostly auditory, visual, tactile, or does it touch all of the senses? Why does Steele start and end with the images he does? Can your students suggest other prestorm sensations the poet might have included? Would their inclusion alter the mood of the poem? You might have students decide on a topic for description and brainstorm to produce images that draw on each of the senses. Are some senses harder to utilize than others?

POSSIBLE CONNECTION TO ANOTHER SELECTION

Robert Southby, From "The Cataract of Lodore" (text p. 255)

SOME COMMON POETIC FORMS

There is some degree of controversy over the role of form in poetry. The movement calling itself New Formalism advocates a widespread return to form, and criticizes what it calls the status quo of open form. (A possible introduction to this position is in Dana Gioia's "Notes on the New Formalism" in the Autumn 1987 *Hudson Review,* reprinted in *Can Poetry Matter?* Also, see Timothy Steele's *Missing Measures.*) There are also, however, several defenses of open form (perhaps the best of which is Stanley Plumly's "Chapter and Verse" from *American Poetry Review.*) You might find it interesting to introduce your students to this controversy and have them find their own positions on the matter. This exercise can help students understand that there are reasons for the choice to write in or out of traditional forms, and that traditional forms are not always or necessarily conservative. In addition, it emphasizes the idea that poetry is a dynamic genre, full of conflict and contradiction.

As in previous sections, this material will likely be most appealing to students in terms of its relation to the overall impact of a poem — form only takes on meaning when married to content and presented in context. Quizzes that ask students to give the structure of a Petrarchan sonnet tend not to work as well as those that ask students to explain how the form of a particular sonnet contributes to its overall effect. (Some historical notes might be useful in this chapter, since the importance of traditional forms has as much to do with the history of those forms as with each current instance of the form.)

SONNET

JOHN KEATS, *On First Looking into Chapman's Homer* (p. 267)

The principal theme of Keats's sonnet is discovery; he uses the sudden and unexpected discovery of the Pacific Ocean by early explorers of the Americas as a metaphor for those moments in life when we feel that a previously held view has been radically shaken.

You might ask students whether they have experienced a moment of discovery similar to that which Keats describes. After they have read Keats's poem, give them a few minutes to write about a moment when they felt a sense of revelation similar to that felt by "stout Cortez" and his men, and then discuss the results.

A comparison of Keats's sonnets provides ample evidence of the poet's continual experimentation with form during his brief career. In "Chapman's Homer," Keats utilizes the characteristic division of the Italian sonnet into octave and sestet, with the opening eight lines setting up a situation or argument and the remaining six resolving it. You may wish to compare Keats's use of the sonnet form in "Chapman's Homer" with his use of the form in other poems in the book.

POSSIBLE CONNECTION TO ANOTHER SELECTION

John Donne, "Death Be Not Proud" (text p. 273)

VILLANELLE

DYLAN THOMAS, *Do not go gentle into that good night* (p. 268)

This poem is a villanelle, a French verse form ordinarily treating light topics, whose five tercets and concluding quatrain employ only two end rhymes. The first and third lines of the poem must alternatively conclude the tercets and form a couplet for the quatrain. Despite these formal restrictions, Thomas's poem sounds remarkably unforced and reflects quite adequately the feeling of a man who does not want his father to die.

Just as remarkable is the poem's rich figurative language; this villanelle could be used as a summary example of almost all the points outlined in this chapter. Variety is achieved through the metonymies for death, such as "close of day" (line 2), "dark" (4), "dying of the light" (9). The overall effect is to describe death metaphorically as the end of a day and thus, in some sense, to familiarize death and lessen its threat. Even to describe death as "that good night" (1) reduces it to a gesture of good-bye. Other figures of speech include a pun on "grave" men (13) (both solemn and mortal), an oxymoron in "who see with blinding sight" (13), various similes, such as "blaze like meteors" (14), and the overall form of the apostrophe.

Thomas introduces several examples of people who might be expected to acquiesce to death gently but who, nonetheless, resist it. "Wise men" (philosophers, perhaps) want more time because so far their wisdom has not created any radical change ("forked no lightning"). Men who do good works (theologians, possibly) look back and realize that the sum total of their efforts was "frail" and if they had devoted more time to a fertile field ("green bay"), their deeds might have been more effective. "Wild men" (inspired artists, writers) know their words have caught and held time, but they know too how in various ways — with their relations with others or perhaps with alcohol and drugs — they have "grieved" the sun. Grave men at the end of their lives realize too late that joy is one means of transcending time. All these groups experience some form of knowledge that makes them wish they could prolong life and live it according to their new insights.

As a writing assignment you might ask students to analyze a character or group of people that they have read about in a short story who seem to fit into one of the categories Thomas describes. What advice would he give them? How otherwise could they lead their lives?

Possible Connection to Another Selection

Sylvia Plath, "Daddy" (text p. 628)

OPEN FORM

Whereas traditional forms depend on the interplay of the poet's current speech and an established form, open form hinges on the poet's (and the reader's) ability to discover a form that works toward the overall effect the poet wishes to produce. Just as in the previous chapter, each of the poems here can form the basis of a rewarding discussion about how form relates to content. With open form, the poet theoretically has absolute control over the form chosen, although some may choose a fairly constraining pattern to guide the poem. As a result of this freedom, the poem must actually withstand closer and more critical reading, as each formal choice takes on greater significance.

Poems like E. E. Cummings's "in Just-" obviously foreground the layout of the poem on the page as a formal technique. In fact, some of Cummings's poems cannot be read aloud because of their formal experimentation. Cummings's poems, like those of William Carlos Williams, tend toward spareness and intense focus on the medium of language. By contrast, a poet like Whitman uses repetition, catalog, and long rhythmic units to create a sense of plenitude and richness, a spilling over of language onto the page.

For some students, a poem like Galway Kinnell's "After Making Love We Hear Footsteps" (p. 625) may seem to be formless. This results from Kinnell's "plain speech" style and the seeming randomness of the line breaks. You may find it productive to push students to examine the breaks and rhythms in the poem more closely. The breaks serve to create units of meaning and to insert very slight pauses in the reading, which help create rhythms that add to the overall mood of the poem. You might ask students why Kinnell chooses to put a stanza break between lines 18 and 19. Why not run the whole poem together? In both traditional and open forms, stanza breaks create a pause in which ideas can shift, focuses can change, or previous statements can be reassessed. Line breaks can do this on a much smaller scale. In either event, the white space on the page can be as telling as what is said in words.

As an exercise, you might have your students experiment with line breaks by taking a poem from the book and redoing the breaks. They might then give that poem to another student and have that student evaluate the new poem, asking themselves "Has the meaning of the poem (or parts of the poem) changed?" This exercise may help to emphasize felicitous or infelicitous choices in poetic structure. A related exercise might have students create found poems by taking a piece of prose and inserting line breaks. Students could again evaluate the results, looking for meanings that have been altered or significances that have been added by the change in form.

E. E. CUMMINGS, *in Just-* (p. 269)

Exactly how poems operate as a graphic medium on our visual sense is not well understood by critics. The open-endedness of the question provides a good occasion for students to make their own guesses. Notice, for example, that the most important thematic word in this poem, *spring*, either is set off from the line (as in line 2) or appears by itself, as in lines 9 and 18. In fact, the placement of *spring* at approximately the beginning, middle, and end of the poem is almost an organizational motif. Another repeated phrase, "whistles far and wee," also is placed first on one line (5) with "whistles" later receiving separational emphasis, over two lines (12 and 13), with "far and wee" receiving space — like long pulses on the whistle — and, at the close of the poem, on separate lines, as though the sound of the whistle were still present but moving away.

The whistle is, of course, united with spring as a modern rendition of Pan's pipes drawing Persephone from the underworld and awakening the calls of birds and the sounds of wildlife. In response to the "goat-footed" (Pan) balloon man's pipes, "bettyand-isbel" come running — the elision of their names mimicking the pronunciation, the swift movement, even the perception patterns of children.

Many other word patterns offer themselves for discussion in this poem. These comments are only a beginning, and an enthusiastic class can discover much more.

Many poems written in open form are more accessible to students than some of the more formal poetical styles; thus some students might conclude that this form is easier to write in as well. It may well be, depending on the poem, but emphasize to your students that each individual word choice and its placement on the page remains essential, even in the more "free" poetical forms. To demonstrate this point, you might ask them to write a poem in imitation of E. E. Cummings's "in Just-." You could ask them to choose a different season, or to find another topic altogether. After they have written their poems, go over some of them as a class, noting what effect the placement and choice of words has on the poem's total effect. Which poems are the best imitations of Cummings's? Are they also the most successful in other ways? (These last two questions may need to be tailored to avoid hurt feelings.)

POSSIBLE CONNECTION TO ANOTHER SELECTION

Emily Dickinson, "A Light exists in Spring" (text p. 1163)

WALT WHITMAN, From *I Sing the Body Electric* (p. 270)

Whitman's outpouring is an homage to the body, the soul, and poetry all at once. In a word, Whitman offers here an anatomy of wonder.

The rhythm of this portion of the poem is striking. Notice how many of the lines begin with a trochee or a spondee. The initial heavy stresses lend a kind of relentless thoroughness to Whitman's catalog of the human body. You might have the class scan a portion of the poem, say from line 25 to line 30. The lines change from heavily accented to a lighter, roughly iambic rhythm that suggests "the continual changes of the flex of the mouth."

The chief difficulty is, of course, discerning the exact relationship between these things. We tend to think of them as separate from each other. Does Whitman's poem help us to unify them in our minds? The poem lists a number of body parts: do any of them tend to stand out or to form any sort of unexpected patterns?

POSSIBLE CONNECTION TO ANOTHER SELECTION

Marge Piercy, "The Secretary Chant" (p. 213)

WRITING IN PROCESS: EXPLICATION

In her explication of John Donne's "Death Be Not Proud," Rose Bostwick explores Donne's use of metaphor as a way of unifying his ideas about death. Her final essay is a good example of an explication that is carefully structured and pays close attention to detail but isn't bogged down with the "line by line" analysis that makes some explications very dull reading.

Donne's is one of many poems about death in this anthology and this casebook might be a good place to explore some of the "universal" subjects of poetry. While some poems, like Marge Piercy's "The Secretary Chant," feature unusual topics, many poems throughout literature focus on such universal themes as love, death, nature, and religion. Ask your students which "universal" themes they associate with poetry and why they think these topics have been revisited by poets so many times. Are your students more drawn to poetry that explores these common subjects, or do they prefer poems like Martín Espada's "Latin Night at the Pawnshop," which surprises the reader with new subjects?

Studying this chapter's casebook will enable students to examine the specific ways in which a large topic like death can be treated. Though death is a vague and unknown terror, Donne uses metaphors to make the idea more concrete; he compares death to sleep, to a slave, and ultimately, to human beings, who he says are not vulnerable to the permanent effects of death as death itself is. As an exercise or a writing assignment (see Alternative Assignments, question 1), take a look at ways another poem about death approaches the same subject. What metaphors do the two poems have in common? What attitudes do the speakers have toward death? Many of your students will have had their own experiences with death. How does "Death Be Not Proud" speak to their beliefs about death? Are other poems about the subject more or less satisfying on the personal level?

JOHN DONNE, *Death Be Not Proud* (p. 273)

Many students will have read this sonnet in high school. It should serve as a reminder that the logic of a poem can be as tightly constructed as that of any other form of rhetorical argument. In the frame of Donne's religious belief, which promises life after death, death is a very brief moment and is, furthermore, slave to the darker dealings of fate. As usual Donne has a sense of the rhythmic force of words. Notice the quarter of heavy-stressed beats in his opening injunction; the sonnet concludes with another group of four stressed syllables.

Ask students to compare in a brief essay the attitude toward death taken by Donne in this poem and by Dylan Thomas in "Do not go gentle into that good night" (text p. 268).

ALTERNATIVE ASSIGNMENTS

1. Choose another poem in this anthology that explores the issue of death, and write a paper comparing and contrasting it to John Donne's "Death Be Not Proud." Your essay should contain some explication of both poems, focusing on the way the two poems use a poetical element (or elements) to explore the problem of death as the casebook focused on metaphor. Suggested poems:

   Robert Frost, "Home Burial" (text p. 617)
   Robert Frost, " 'Out, Out —' " (text p. 992)
   Randall Jarrell, "Death of the Ball Turret Gunner" (text p. 227)
   William Shakespeare, from *Macbeth* (Act V, scene v) (text p. 239)
   Dylan Thomas, "Do not go gentle into that good night" (text p. 268)
   John Updike, "Dog's Death" (text p. 215)

2. Choose another poem in this anthology that you think uses metaphor effectively and write an explication of your own. Your process should imitate Rose Bostwick's, with a first response and informal outline. Use the "Questions for Writing about Poetry" (p. 274) to help you narrow your focus and find a thesis for your paper. Suggested poems:

   John Donne, "The Flea" (text p. 831)
   Robert Frost, "Mending Wall" (text p. 121)
   Andrew Marvell, "To His Coy Mistress" (text p. 230)
   Marge Piercy, "The Secretary Chant" (text p. 213)

7

Reading and Writing about Drama

READING DRAMA RESPONSIVELY

Before beginning a class unit on drama, you may want to find out if many of your students have seen a play performed. Most of them will probably have had some exposure to drama on stage, but for many that exposure may have been limited to a school or church play during childhood. If possible, arrange for your students to view a play live while they study drama. Many colleges have theater departments that produce a show every semester. If live drama is not available, try showing a video of a play to your class. (This manual suggests several.) Seeing a show as a class will give you the opportunity to discuss certain theatrical conventions, staging challenges, casting, and other elements of drama which cannot be represented in a written script.

This unit's opening section, "Reading Drama Responsively" (p. 282) highlights the benefits of reading drama instead of (or in addition to) viewing it. Ask your students about their experiences reading drama. Do they agree that there are some advantages to reading a play over watching one? Discuss the role of imagination. How does their imagination affect the way they read a play they haven't seen?

SOPHOCLES AND GREEK DRAMA

Students (and their teachers) may be surprised at how much they enjoy studying classical Greek drama. Despite the significant barriers of time and place that separate contemporary audiences from Sophocles, these plays continue to hold our fascination. Robert Fagles's accessible translation of *Oedipus the King* should pose no language difficulties for students, and the complex characterizations will draw readers in. Nonetheless, there are important conventions of classical Greek drama that may be puzzling. Have your students read and discuss the chapter's section on "Theatrical Conventions of Greek Drama" (p. 287) before beginning the plays. Many of them may be familiar with Aristotle's definition of "tragedy," but it bears going over in detail. As this section notes, it is important not to reduce tragic characters to a single "fatal flaw," but to see the "hamartia" of Oedipus in a larger context.

In order to emphasize the difference between the conventional and the literary use of the term "tragedy," you might ask students to bring in newspaper articles and discuss them in light of the classic definition. Using concrete and familiar examples, students can then determine, for example, that a car accident is less classically "tragic" than the downfall of a successful politician whose political greatness is overshadowed by a personal flaw or a bad decision.

Many of your students will have read *Oedipus the King* (p. 293) in the past, and those who have not will certainly be familiar with the story through Freud's "Oedipus Complex." No doubt there will be vigorous debate about Freud's interpretation of the play. Do students really see Oedipus's actions as "the fulfillment of our childhood wishes," as Freud claims? In today's talk-show culture, we are all armchair psychologists to some degree, and students should be encouraged to "analyze" the play in light of Freud's assessment.

SOPHOCLES, *Oedipus the King* (p. 293)

Student discussions of this play are likely to center on Oedipus's powerful character and the fate that has been prophesied for him. The two compete for our attention, and the ironies associated with each raise intriguing questions about human freedom and fate. For a broad range of critical responses to the play see *Oedipus Tyrannus,* edited by Luci Berkowitz and Theodore F. Brunner (New York: Norton, 1970).

Consider using this classic drama as a way of teaching the chapter's elements as well. The play's *setting* is crucial to the outcome of the drama. If Oedipus had stayed in his home town and not ended up as king of Thebes, obviously there would be no story at all. The play contains a number of complex and interesting *characters:* Oedipus himself, of course, but also Jocasta and Creon, less important characters who nonetheless wrestle with conflicting emotions and moral dilemmas. Ask your students who they think the play's *antagonist* is — Oedipus himself? How does Sophocles' characterization contribute to the play's central *conflict*? The *plot* of the play, in addition to presenting a fascinating dilemma, is interesting in that most of the play's action has occurred before the drama opens. We don't witness Oedipus's murder of Laius, his marriage to Jocasta, or his years as a successful king. We are left to witness his fall from this position during the play's *rising action* as Oedipus gradually learns the truth about himself. Ask your students to write a brief in-class essay about the play's theme or *themes.* They may identify a number of possible themes including a quest for identity, the arrogance of power, or incest. How do these elements work together to create the play's overall effect?

CONSIDERATIONS FOR CRITICAL THINKING AND WRITING

2. The opening scene presents Oedipus as a powerful king who has defeated the Sphinx and ruled successfully for many years. The priest's speech (lines 16–69) offers this exposition and characterizes Oedipus as the "first of men" (41) and the "best of men" (57). The city turns to heroic Oedipus to save it once again.

3–5. Oedipus's fury at Tiresias for initially refusing to tell his "dreadful secrets" (374) establishes Oedipus's fierce determination to discover the truth. His quick temper and unreasonableness are also revealed when he accuses Tiresias of conspiring with Creon to usurp the throne (431–459). Oedipus's rage renders him, in a sense, blind (the ironies abound) to the information Tiresias directly tells him: "I say you are the murderer you hunt" (413).

   When Oedipus also accuses Creon of treason, Creon correctly assesses a significant element — an error or frailty — of Oedipus's personality as a "crude, mindless stubbornness" that has caused Oedipus to lose his "sense of balance" (615–616). Oedipus's absolute insistence on learning who murdered Laius shows him to be a decisive leader while simultaneously exposing him to the consequences of making public the message from Delphi and his cursing of the murderer of Laius.

   Oedipus's self-confidence, determination, and disregard for consequences propel him toward his goal and his destruction. His downfall is not brought about solely by the gods or fate but by the nature of his own remarkable character. The gods may know what will inevitably happen, but it is Oedipus's personality — especially his proud temper — that causes it to happen. As much as he is responsible for the suffering in the play, he is the victim of it. His virtues as well as his vices contribute to his horror and shame.

6. Irony is pervasive in the play, but the greatest irony is that the murderer Oedipus seeks is himself. He sets out to save the city, to appease the gods, and to see that justice is done, but all his altruistic efforts bring ruin on himself. Ignorant of the

truth, Oedipus is consistently used as a vehicle for dramatic irony because we know more than he does; this strategy allows Sophocles to charge Oedipus's speeches with additional meanings that the protagonist only gradually comes to perceive. A review of Oedipus's early speeches will yield numerous instances of dramatic irony, as when he declares that if anyone knows about the murder of Laius that person must report to Oedipus "even if he must denounce himself" (257). His curse on the murderer (280–314) is especially rich in ironic foreshadowings.

7. The Chorus voices community values of reason, order, and moderation. It knows better than to defy the gods, and it firmly condemns human pride (for instance, in lines 963–980). It reacts to and comments on the action and also links scenes. In contrast to Jocasta's rejection of the oracles, the Chorus worries about the irreverence it observes. Its final words confirm the unpredictable ironies that we must endure: "Count no man happy till he dies, free of pain at last."

8. Tiresias's blindness does not prevent him from seeing the truth of Oedipus's past. His insight is in ironic contrast to Oedipus, who sees physically but is blind to the pattern of events that defines his life. Once Oedipus does see the truth, he blinds himself, a fitting punishment that will not allow him to escape his suffering. Oedipus does not choose suicide because to live is even more painful; he takes complete responsibility for what has happened and accepts his suffering as his destiny.

1, 9. Students should be encouraged to examine both Oedipus's irrational willfulness — which his behavior demonstrates and the Chorus comments on — and prophecies, coincidences, and actions that transform a powerful, bold man into a tragic figure whose only remaining dignity is in complete suffering. What happens to Oedipus raises questions concerning human guilt and innocence and cosmic justice. Students are likely to recognize that though Oedipus's circumstances are specific to himself, the larger issues he encounters are relevant to them too.

10. In *The Interpretation of Dreams*, Sigmund Freud reads the play as a manifestation of men's unconscious desire to replace their fathers and have sexual relations with their mothers. In healthy personalities this jealousy and sexual impulse are overcome and suppressed. Jocasta urges Oedipus not to worry that this has happened to him (1074–1078). Certainly Oedipus had no conscious design to marry his mother; he is appalled by the possibility. But Freud would argue that a significant part of our fascination with this play is our identification with Oedipus's fears. Students with some background in psychology will probably be eager to pursue the question; others are likely to be wary and skeptical.

Possible Connections to Other Selections

Susan Glaspell, *Trifles* (text p. 496)
David Henry Hwang, *M. Butterfly* (text p. 1296)
Henrik Ibsen, *A Doll House* (text p. 700)
William Shakespeare, *Hamlet, Prince of Denmark* (text p. 345)
Tennessee Williams, *The Glass Menagerie* (text p. 448)

Resources for Teaching

SELECTED BIBLIOGRAPHY

Bloom, Harold. *Sophocles' Oedipus Rex*. New York: Chelsea, 1988.
Edmonds, Lowell. *Oedipus: The Ancient Legend and Its Later Analogues*. Baltimore: Johns Hopkins UP, 1985.

Fergusson, Francis. *The Idea of a Theater*. Princeton: Princeton UP, 1949. 14–53.
Knox, Bernard M. *Oedipus at Thebes: Sophocles' Tragic Hero and His Time*. New York: Norton, 1971.

AUDIOVISUAL RESOURCES

Oedipus Rex. 20 min., color, 1957. Beta, VHS, $^3/_4''$ U-matic cassette. A performance by deaf actors. Distributed by Gallaudet University Library.

Oedipus Rex. 87 min., color, 1957. VHS, 16-mm film. With Douglas Campbell, Douglas Rain, Eric House, and Eleanor Stuart. Based on William Yeats's translation. Directed by Tyrone Guthrie. Contained and highly structured rendering by the Stratford (Ontario) Festival Players. Distributed by Water Bearer Films. Available for rental from member institutions of the Consortium of College and University Media Centers.

Oedipus the King. 97 min., color, 1967. VHS. With Donald Sutherland, Christopher Plummer, Lilli Palmer, Orson Welles, Cyril Cusack, Richard Johnson, and Roger Livesey. Directed by Philip Saville. Simplified film version of the play, filmed in Greece using an old amphitheater to serve as the background for much of the action. Distributed by Crossroads Video.

Oedipus the King. 45 min., color, 1975. Beta, VHS, $^3/_4''$ U-matic cassette, 16-mm film. With Anthony Quayle, James Mason, Claire Bloom, and Ian Richardson. A production by the Athens Classical Theatre Company, with an English soundtrack. Distributed by Films for the Humanities and Sciences. Available for rental from member institutions of the Consortium of College and University Media Centers.

Oedipus Tyrannus. 60 min., color, 1978. Beta, VHS, $^3/_4''$ U-matic cassette. Hosted by Jose Ferrer. Shown from the point where Oedipus is informed of the death of his father. Expository portion shows scenes of Greek theaters and recounts Aristotle's definition of tragedy. Distributed by Films, Inc.

Oedipus the King. 120 min., color, 1987. VHS. With John Gielgud, Michael Pennington, and Claire Bloom. Distributed by Films for the Humanities and Sciences.

Oedipus Rex [recording]. 2 cassettes. Translated by William Butler Yeats. Performed by Douglas Campbell and Eric House. Dramatization. Distributed by Caedmon/HarperAudio.

Oedipus Rex: Age of Sophocles, I. 31 min., color and b/w, 1959. Beta, VHS, $^3/_4''$ U-matic cassette, 16-mm film. Discusses Greek civilization, the classic Greek theater, and the theme of man's fundamental nature. Distributed by Britannica Films. Available for rental from member institutions of the Consortium of College and University Media Centers.

Oedipus Rex: The Character of Oedipus, II. 31 min., color and b/w, 1959. Beta, VHS, $^3/_4''$ U-matic cassette, 16-mm film. Debates whether Oedipus's trouble is a result of character flaws or of fate. Distributed by Britannica Films. Available for rental from member institutions of the Consortium of College and University Media Centers.

Oedipus Rex: Man and God, III. 30 min., color and b/w, 1959. Beta, VHS, $^3/_4''$ U-matic cassette, 16-mm film. Deals with the idea that Oedipus, although a worldly ruler, cannot overcome the gods and his destiny. Distributed by Britannica Films. Available for rental from member institutions of the Consortium of College and University Media Centers.

Oedipus Rex: Recovery of Oedipus, IV. 30 min., color and b/w, 1959. Beta, VHS, $^3/_4''$ U-matic cassette, 16-mm film. Deals with man's existence between God and beast. Distributed by Britannica Films. Available for rental from member institutions of the Consortium of College and University Media Centers.

SHAKESPEARE AND ELIZABETHAN DRAMA

Most college students have read at least one William Shakespeare play in high school, usually *Romeo and Juliet* or *Julius Caesar.* Recent mainstream movie versions of *Hamlet, Much Ado about Nothing, Richard III,* and *Romeo and Juliet* may have exposed more people to his works, so few students will approach *Hamlet* as true Shakespeare novices. You may want to begin your introduction by asking your students to write about or discuss what they already know about Shakespeare and his writings. Many of them will be familiar with his life as a London actor and playwright, his association with the Globe Theatre, and the three basic categories of history plays, comedies, and tragedies into which his works fall. Invite students to contribute their own knowledge to your initial discussion about Shakespeare, then fill in the gaps by reading and discussing the chapter's introduction, which provides important background. Students may be surprised at how much they already know.

Nonetheless, many of them are likely to be intimidated by the prospect of reading Shakespeare's plays. Much of this intimidation stems from Shakespeare's reputation as the "greatest" writer in English as well as the daunting language of his plays. Believing that they need years of schooling and expertise to truly understand Shakespeare's greatness, students may shy away from reading his works. These apprehensions should be discussed openly. You may even want to lead a discussion "translating" some passages into "hip," contemporary English to highlight the universal themes that the plays included here encompass. Once students feel they have permission to "read Shakespeare's work as best [as they] can" (p. 344), they will be more open to the pleasure that a study of William Shakespeare has to offer.

WILLIAM SHAKESPEARE, *Hamlet, Prince of Denmark* (p. 345)

Many of your students will already have read *Hamlet* or at least seen one of the film versions. This familiarity can work for you since reading Shakespeare can be intimidating for many students inexperienced in Elizabethan drama. Once they become familiar with the language and the conventions, however, students (like the rest of the world) will no doubt enjoy studying this multifaceted work.

The possible approaches for teaching Shakespeare are numerous. The drama can certainly benefit from any number of theoretical readings. You might divide your class into groups of three or four and have each group write a paper to present to the class in which they read *Hamlet* through the lens of one critical strategy. What kinds of questions might a formalist ask about the text? Which characters would a feminist critic examine? How does historical criticism shed light on the events of the play? As a class, consider which approaches best help open up a new understanding of the play.

Two standard sources for the study of *Hamlet* are A. C. Bradley's *Shakespearean Tragedy* (1904; rpt. New York: St. Martin's, 1965) and Harley Granville-Barker's "Preface to *Hamlet,*" in his *Prefaces to Shakespeare,* vol. I (Princeton: Princeton UP, 1946). Both discuss character and motivation in detail. A useful study of the relation of imagery to character is Maynard Mack's "The World of *Hamlet,*" *Yale Review* 41 (1952): 502–523, reprinted in *Shakespeare: Modern Essays in Criticism,* rev. ed., edited by Leonard F. Dean (New York: Oxford UP, 1967), 242-262. Useful too is Harold Jenkins's introduction in the 1982 Arden edition. He sorts through the criticism and offers a sensible, adaptable reading.

TIP FROM THE FIELD

I have students see videotapes of the famous "To be, or not to be" soliloquy from three different productions of *Hamlet*. I then ask them to write an essay comparing the version they like best to the text and explain why they prefer it over the other two.

— RICHARD STONER, *Broome Community College*

CONSIDERATIONS FOR CRITICAL THINKING AND WRITING

1. (See also question 5.) Hamlet's attempts to define his own character in a corrupt world, his fear of death (apparently resulting from his new view of the world's corruption), the fact that death is an inevitable consequence of revenge, the fact that his image of the world is so wrapped up in his now-horrible image of his mother, even his legitimate desire (at least in a revenge-play world) to send Claudius to hell — all cause delay.

2. Insofar as Claudius's advice generalizes from the traditional Boethian consolation, it is sensible. But if we look back at this advice after we hear of Claudius's crime, his speech's sensibility is undercut by his lurking suspicion of Hamlet. Hamlet cannot heed the advice because it does not address his particular grief, deeply felt because he remembers his father as "Hyperion" (see his first soliloquy, I.ii.129–159). Nor can the advice smooth over other complications in Hamlet's mood arising from his hatred of the "satyr" Claudius and his revulsion at his mother's incestuous "frailty."

3. Polonius's advice to Laertes is sound, albeit in its political content rather than its moral or ethical content. It thus reflects Polonius's political role in court as well as the delicate, sometimes finicky care with which a courtier must conduct himself. Polonius's political view of life is asserted more clearly when he sends Reynaldo to spy on Laertes (II.i.3–72).

4. When Horatio first tells him of the ghost's appearance, Hamlet immediately offers an interpretation that hints at prophecy: "I doubt some foul play" (I.ii.255), and later, when the ghost beckons him, he says, "My fate cries out" (I.iv.81). So there is evidence of Hamlet's foreboding early on. And the fact that the ghost's revelation of the crime (I.v.60–76) nearly repeats Hamlet's first soliloquy makes the suggestion of prophetic insight more plausible. The ghost's principal demand is that Hamlet "revenge his foul and most unnatural murder" (I.v.25); three secondary demands are

    > Let not the royal bed of Denmark be
    > A couch for . . . damned incest. . . .
    > Taint not thy mind, nor let thy soul contrive
    > Against thy mother aught. (I.v.82–86)

    Hamlet has difficulty fulfilling all of these.

5. What we know of Hamlet before his father's death comes in snippets from other characters. Claudius identifies him as a student (I.ii.113). Laertes and Ophelia (and Hamlet himself) speak of his love for Ophelia (I.iii.14–16, III.i.113–141, V.i.237–239). Laertes and Ophelia remark on his greatness as a prince (I.iii.17, III.i.142–146). Claudius too recognizes and fears his popularity (IV.iii.1–5) and power (III.i.158–159). And Fortinbras says, in the end, that Hamlet would have "proved most royal" (V.ii.368). We also see him actively fearless in pursuing the ghost (I.v.1–32); we hear him speak knowledgeably on the theater (II.ii.393–485, III.ii.1–36); and he proves himself an expert swordsman. In addition we are given subtler indications of his former character. Hamlet's friendship with Horatio is evidence of his gentle nature.

His language is richly imaginative. Even the stability he shows after his return from sea and his "readiness" to face his task and his death bespeak a personality that was the "rose of the fair state" (III.i.144).

The initial change in Hamlet occurs before the play begins: with his father's death and his mother's hasty remarriage, the ideas upon which he based his life and his view of the world have been severely shaken. His references to his father as Hyperion and to his mother's doting love for his father, coupled with his pained speech to Rosencrantz and Guildenstern about the earth, the heavens, and humanity all gone to corruption (II.ii.277–290), suggest that his former image of the world was somewhat idealistic. That Hamlet has been robbed of the crown, that the world is now rank, humanity a "quintessence of dust," the king a satyr, and the queen an incestuous beast point to the utter destruction of Hamlet's ideological basis for living. With this sudden demolition comes near madness. Upon receiving news of the murder, Hamlet barely avoids total distraction (I.v.92–112), but he never, apparently, falls into true madness. His verbal antics are usually contrived, such as those with which he fends off Polonius. When his verbal violence is aimed at Ophelia, particularly in III.i, or at Gertrude in the closet scene (III.iv), he seems closer to madness. But uncontrolled passion is probably a better way to describe these expressions of Hamlet's mental condition. In general we might say that in exchanges with the women in the play, Hamlet tends toward passionate distraction.

But intermingled with these shifts between feigned madness and violent passion are the soliloquies. While each contains the conflict between reason and passion, between action and inaction, and each ends with a determination to act that remains unfulfilled, there is also from the first soliloquy to the last a traceable development toward logical and rhetorical control. The first (I.ii.129–159) shifts topics frantically, apparently by rapid associations. The second major soliloquy (II.ii.499–557) progresses emotionally, but each topic is more clearly separated, as if Hamlet were becoming aware of and beginning to control his distraction. The third (III.i.56–90), following hard upon the second, flows smoothly but maintains a delicate tension, only seemingly resolved, between the personal fear of death and the general fear. Its conclusive "Thus conscience does make cowards of us all" is a statement both individual and communal. The last major soliloquy (IV.iv.32–66) is clearly logical, moving from controlled personal reflection, to the contrary example, to the particular application of the contrary to Hamlet himself.

This various, sometimes contradictory mental activity creates for us a character unlike any other. Our sense of Hamlet as a tragic hero depends largely on his (and our) endurance through this chaotic progress toward the courageous stability we see in Acts IV and V.

6. The dramatic purpose of the play within the play is to verify the ghost's story and to trap Claudius into revealing his guilt. Its themes refer to Gertrude's inconstancy in love. (She, however, as the closet scene will show, is deaf to all this.) One other interesting feature is the player king's speech (III.ii.165–194) on the changeability of human affection; its tone suggests acceptance of human frailty.

7. Ophelia is only indirectly connected with the crime. Because Hamlet feels that the world, including himself, has become sinfully corrupt (see his soliloquy and the nunnery scene, III.i.56–141) and because he sees women as being a source of corruption in two senses — as lusting beasts and as bearers of children — he feels that Ophelia must necessarily be corrupt. In III.i, Hamlet's vehemence comes from

this view of the world and Ophelia's place in it. (In III.ii, however, Hamlet's crudities are aimed through Ophelia at Gertrude and Claudius.) Ophelia's fall into madness mirrors Hamlet's. Having lived, it seems, solely according to the guidance of Polonius, Laertes, and perhaps Hamlet, she has no strength to bear up when her supports collapse. With Polonius dead, Hamlet, whom she loved, a murderer and madman, and Laertes absent, she crumbles.

8. Hamlet's words to Gertrude after she calls the killing of Polonius "a rash and bloody deed" — "almost as bad, good mother / As kill a king and marry with his brother" (III.iv.28–30) — are a slip that reveals Hamlet's belief that she is deeply, conspiratorially guilty. Her crime, however, seems to be one of omission as well as commission. In setting up a "glass" wherein she will see her soul, Hamlet hits on an image appropriate to his mother's failure to perceive what has occurred. In presenting the pictures of his father and Claudius and returning to an analogy to the gods in describing his father, Hamlet indicates that he feels compelled to reveal to his mother what he has seen and learned. His words must call up the same torment in her that he has felt.

9. The two questions will probably give rise to opposing responses. The likelihood of sympathy for Claudius depends to a great extent on the reader because Claudius expresses remorse for his crime and unwillingness to make reparation. One particular source of sympathy will be the speech's closeness logically, rhetorically, and thematically to Hamlet's soliloquies. But sympathy in whatever degree survives only as long as Claudius is on his knees. The safest answer to why Hamlet does not kill Claudius is Hamlet's own: perfect revenge requires that Claudius suffer as much as or more than Hamlet's father did. Perhaps, too, Hamlet wishes Claudius to feel torment equal to his own — the idea of infernal or purgatorial punishment has been strong in Hamlet since the ghost's revelation.

10. This question addresses one of the central complexities of the play — Hamlet finds himself bound by external command to act on a situation that is, in one sense, outside himself and, in another, deeply personal. Because of his complex emotional involvements, he is slow to act. His various perceptions of corruption combine to retard the fulfillment of a seemingly simple command. From the closet scene on, we watch Hamlet come to terms with these ideas of corruption. Cathartic images occupy his mind — the dead Polonius (Hamlet is now an active agent in dealing death), the stricken mother, the ghost again, the planned destruction of Rosencrantz and Guildenstern, Fortinbras's army marching to death for an "eggshell," the graveyard, Yorick's skull, foul-smelling, and Ophelia's corpse.

Through this process of images and actions, Hamlet also comes to terms with corruption and death, including his own, and reaches a spiritual stability, a conception of humanity and the universe, that frees him to act and die. Because we share with him this movement and conclude with him, however unconsciously, that there has been some "special providence" at work, we can have little or no sense of his moral culpability.

11. Fortinbras is the foil toward which Hamlet seems to move. In structural terms, he is Hamlet's most important foil. His situation as described by Horatio (I.i.80–107) parallels Hamlet's before we meet Hamlet, and Fortinbras's action serves twice as a contrast to Hamlet's inaction (I.ii.17–33, IV.iv.32–66). His appearance in the final scene concludes the play on a note of order and stability. His armor (he is the only living character to be seen prepared for battle) finally opens the play to a world of action beyond the confines of Denmark.

12. The humor of the play is remarkable for its poignant commentary on the central themes. Hamlet's joke about the "funeral baked meats" (I.ii.180), his satiric assaults on Polonius (II.ii.173–214), his initial quips with Rosencrantz and Guildenstern (II.ii.215–256), his bitter sexual jibes at Ophelia's expense (III.ii.97–118), his dark humor regarding Polonius's body and death (III.iv.214–216, IV.iii.18–35), the gravedigger's callous joking, and Hamlet's thoughts on the deaths of ladies and great men (V.i.65–184) — all reflect on the many forms of corruption that Hamlet contemplates. Often the humor reveals the pain inherent in his thoughts and a desire to be released from them. In the gravedigger scene, there is a nice shift toward a more pathetic although resolved opinion of death and corruption. Such humor, one of the many mirrors of Hamlet's evolution, differs from the humor in the comedies because of its dark tones and its tragic import.

POSSIBLE CONNECTIONS TO OTHER SELECTIONS

T. S. Eliot, "The Love Song of J. Alfred Prufrock" (text p. 1280)
David Henry Hwang, *M. Butterfly* (text p. 1296)
Henrik Ibsen, *A Doll House* (text p. 700)
Jane Martin, *Rodeo* (text p. 1004)
Arthur Miller, *Death of a Salesman* (text p. 1007)
William Shakespeare, *A Midsummer Night's Dream* (text p. 852)
Sophocles, *Oedipus the King* (text p. 293)

RESOURCES FOR TEACHING

SELECTED BIBLIOGRAPHY

Bloom, Harold, ed. *William Shakespeare's Hamlet*. New York: Chelsea, 1986.
Mack, Maynard. "The World of Hamlet." *Yale Review* 41 (1952): 502–523.
Prosser, Eleanor. *Hamlet and Revenge*. Stanford: Stanford UP, 1967.
Wilson, John Dover. *What Happens in* Hamlet. Cambridge: Cambridge UP, 1967.

AUDIOVISUAL RESOURCES

Approaches to Hamlet. 45 min., color, 1979. Beta, VHS, ³/₄" U-matic cassette, 16-mm film. Includes footage of the four greatest Hamlets of this century: John Barrymore, Laurence Olivier, John Gielgud, and Nicol Williamson. Shows a young actor learning the role. Narrated by Gielgud. Distributed by Films for the Humanities and Sciences. Available for rental from member institutions of the Consortium of College and University Media Centers.
Discovering Hamlet. 53 min., color, 1990. VHS, ³/₄" U-matic cassette. An exposition of the play, hosted by Patrick Stewart, including a behind-the-scenes look at a production by the Birmingham Repertory Theatre. Distributed by PBS Video.
Hamlet. 242 min., color, 1996. VHS. Directed by Kenneth Branagh. Starring Kenneth Branagh, Kate Winslet, John Gielgud, Jack Lemmon, Julie Christie, Gerard Depardieu, Judy Dench, and others. Distributed by Columbia Tristar Home Video.
Hamlet. 153 min., b/w, 1948. VHS and 16-mm film. With Laurence Olivier, Basil Sydney, Felix Aylmer, Jean Simmons, Stanley Holloway, Peter Cushing, and Christopher Lee. Voice of John Gielgud. Directed by Olivier. Photographed in Denmark. Cut scenes include all of Rosencrantz and Guildenstern. Emphasizes Oedipal implications in the play. Video: see local retailer. Film: Learning Corporation of America. Available for rental from member institutions of the Consortium of College and University Media Centers.

Hamlet. 115 min., color, 1969. Beta, VHS, 16-mm film. With Nicol Williamson. Directed by Tony Richardson. Distributed by Learning Corporation of America. Available for rental from member institutions of the Consortium of College and University Media Centers.

Hamlet. 150 min., color, 1979. Beta, VHS, $^3/_4''$ U-matic cassette, other formats by special arrangement. Directed by Derek Jacobi. Distributed by Time-Life Video.

Hamlet. 135 min., color, 1990. VHS. With Mel Gibson, Glenn Close, Alan Bates, Paul Scofield, Ian Holm, and Helena Bonham Carter. Directed by Franco Zeffirelli. See local retailer.

Hamlet [recording]. 3 cassettes (210 min.), 1993. Performed by Kenneth Branagh. Distributed by Bantam Audio Publishers.

Hamlet [recording]. 4 cassettes. Dramatization performed by Paul Scofield and Diana Wynyard. Distributed by Caedmon/HarperAudio.

Hamlet [recording]. 1 cassette (60 min.), 1985. Dramatization performed by Michael Redgrave. Living Shakespeare Series. Distributed by Crown Publishers.

Hamlet [recording]. 2 cassettes (120 min.). With John Gielgud and Old Vic Company. Distributed by Durkin Hayes Publishing.

Hamlet [recording]. 1 cassette (51 min.). Performed by Dublin Gate Theatre. Using key scenes and bridges, a complete telling of *Hamlet*. Distributed by Spoken Arts.

Hamlet: The Age of Elizabeth, I. 30 min., color, 1959. Beta, VHS, $^3/_4''$ U-matic cassette, 16-mm film. An introduction to Elizabethan theater. Distributed by Britannica Films. Available for rental from member institutions of the Consortium of College and University Media Centers.

Hamlet: What Happens in Hamlet, II. 30 min., color and b/w, 1959. Beta, VHS, $^3/_4''$ U-matic cassette, 16-mm film. Analyzes the play as a ghost story, a detective story, and a revenge story. Uses scenes from Acts I, III, and V to introduce the principal characters and present the structure of each substory. Distributed by Britannica Films. Available for rental from member institutions of the Consortium of College and University Media Centers.

Hamlet: The Poisoned Kingdom, III. 30 min., color, 1959. Beta, VHS, $^3/_4''$ U-matic cassette, 16-mm film. Observes that poisoning in the play, both literal and figurative, affects all the characters. Distributed by Britannica Films. Available for rental from member institutions of the Consortium of College and University Media Centers.

Hamlet: The Readiness Is All, IV. 30 min., color, 1959. Beta, VHS, $^3/_4''$ U-matic cassette, 16-mm film. *Hamlet* is presented as a coming-of-age story. Distributed by Britannica Films. Available for rental from member institutions of the Consortium of College and University Media Centers.

Hamlet: The Trouble with Hamlet. 23 min., color, 1969. 16-mm film. Emphasizes Hamlet's existentialist dilemma. Distributed by the National Broadcasting Company. Available for rental from member institutions of the Consortium of College and University Media Centers.

The Tragedy of Hamlet: Prince of Denmark. 22 min., color, 1988. VHS. Actors depict Shakespeare and his contemporary, Richard Burbage, rehearsing the play. "Shakespeare" gives a line-by-line analysis of scenes from the play along with insight into plot and character. Part of the Shakespeare in Rehearsal Series. Distributed by Coronet/MTI Film & Video. Available for rental from member institutions of the Consortium of College and University Media Centers.

TENNESSEE WILLIAMS AND MODERN DRAMA

TENNESSEE WILLIAMS, *The Glass Menagerie* (p. 448)

Williams depicts a fragile world founded on illusions. Amanda, Laura, Tom, and Jim indulge their own illusions, but so does the world at large as it rushes toward the devastation of total war. Instead of sensing danger, society steeps itself in drink, dance, music, movies, sex, and anything else that pushes reality aside. This tendency characterizes the general tenor of things both inside and outside the family. The play dramatizes a family and a culture that are trapped in its dreams of self-fulfillment.

In his drama, Tennessee Williams often plays with point of view. His use of fantasy and illusion allows him to depict a character's interior viewpoint as well as "objective" reality. When discussing point of view in this play, you might ask the students to choose a scene that is clearly presented through one character's point of view and rewrite it through that of a different character. This exercise will open up a discussion of Williams's use of subjective reality to comment on the way we experience our lives.

TIPS FROM THE FIELD

With any selection, I find it useful to elicit discussion by posing a specific interpretive problem. For example, when teaching *The Glass Menagerie* I ask students why Tennessee Williams ends the play with Laura blowing out the candles. Once directed to something so specific, students tend to examine the text carefully as they try to answer the question. Because it is also interpretive, an answer that "works" leads them to a deeper understanding of the selection.

— ROBERT M. ST. JOHN, *DePaul University*

After my students read *The Glass Menagerie*, I have them read E. E. Cummings's poem "somewhere I have never traveled, gladly beyond." In class, we analyze the images of power and frailty in the poem. This serves as an excellent prelude to a discussion of the themes of the play. I then ask students to consider why Williams chose to precede his play with the line from Cummings's poem.

— THOMAS S. EDWARDS, *Westbrook College*

POSSIBLE CONNECTIONS TO OTHER SELECTIONS

Lorraine Hansberry, *A Raisin in the Sun* (text p. 636)
David Henry Hwang, *M. Butterfly* (text p. 1296)
Arthur Miller, *Death of a Salesman* (text p. 1007)
Sophocles, *Oedipus the King* (text p. 293)

RESOURCES FOR TEACHING

The Glass Menagerie. 134 min., color, 1987. Beta, VHS. With Joanne Woodward, Karen Allen, John Malkovich, and James Naughton. Directed by Paul Newman. See local retailer.

The Glass Menagerie [recording]. 2 cassettes. 1 hour, 49 min., unabridged. Dramatization performed by Montgomery Clift and Julie Harris. Distributed by Caedmon/HarperAudio.

The Glass Menagerie [recording]. Read by Tennessee Williams. Includes "The Yellow Bird" (short story) and poems. Distributed by the American Audio Prose Library.

In the Country of Tennessee Williams. 30 min., color, 1977. Beta, VHS, 1/2" reel, 3/4" U-matic cassette, 2" Quad. A one-act play about how Williams developed as a writer. Distributed by the New York State Education Department.

Tennessee Williams Reads *The Glass Menagerie* **and Others** [recording]. 1 cassette. 45 min. Complete selections. Read by Tennessee Williams. Includes *The Glass Menagerie* (opening monologue and closing scene), "Cried the Fox" "The Eyes," "The Summer Belvedere," "Some Poems Meant for Music: Little Horse," "Which Is My Little Boy," "Little One," "Gold-Tooth Blues," "Kitchen-Door Blues," "Heavenly Grass," and "The Yellow Bird." Distributed by Caedmon/HarperAudio.

WRITING IN PROCESS: CHARACTER ANALYSIS

Student writer William Dean's response to Susan Glaspell's *Trifles* uses close reading and attention to detail to analyze of one of the play's most important characters. His first response, that Mrs. Hale "made all of the most vital discoveries about the murder" (p. 507), is really not much more than an initial impression, but his brainstorming, in which he charts Mrs. Hale's actions in the play and analyzes what these actions reveal about her character, yields some fresh insights. As your own students try to generate ideas for a character analysis, have them try this approach — list the character's most important actions or speeches, looking for patterns that reveal the way the character functions in relation to the play.

SUSAN GLASPELL, *Trifles* (p. 496)

In this play, the stark, gloomy setting evokes the hard life Mr. Wright imposed on his wife. Within this cold environment, the relationship between the Wrights is immediately and subtly recapitulated in the opening scene by Glaspell's having the men dominate the room as they stand by the stove, while the two women remain timidly near the door. The sympathy that we increasingly feel for Mrs. Peters and Mrs. Hale will eventually be extended to Mrs. Wright, despite the fact that she murdered her husband.

Exposition is used throughout to characterize Mr. and Mrs. Wright; Glaspell makes us feel as if we know the essential qualities of this couple even though we never actually see them. Just as the dialogue reveals their characters, it displays the insensitivity of the men, whose self-importance blinds them to the clues woven into the domestic setting, which they dismiss as mere "trifles." The women understand what these details reveal, for example, that the bird cage and dead bird offer evidence concerning Mrs. Wright's motive for murdering her husband. The cage (now broken) symbolizes the lifeless, joyless, confining marriage Mrs. Wright had to endure, and the bird (strangled) suggests both the husband and the wife, Minnie Foster, who used to sing in the choir. Although the women recognize the significance of these objects as well as of the identical knots Mrs. Wright used on her husband and on her sewing, they will not give this evidence to the men because, as women, they empathize with Mrs. Wright's circumstances.

Trifles is packed with irony. On a second reading, the dialogue takes on a strong ironic flavor, for example when the sheriff says there's "nothing here but kitchen things" (p. 498) or when the county attorney sarcastically asks, "What would we do without the ladies?" (p. 498) and expresses mild surprise to Mrs. Hale about her being "loyal to her sex" (p. 498).

The play's title comments on the kind of evidence that *could* be used to convict Mrs. Wright if the men were not so smugly certain of their powers of observation. What appears to be unimportant in the play — the domestic details and the two women — turns out to be powerfully significant. In the final line, Mrs. Hale answers the county attorney's condescending question about Mrs. Wright's sewing. She is standing center stage, he by the door so that their positions are the reverse of what they were in the opening scene. She has the dead canary in her pocket and Mrs. Wright's fate on her lips, but she chooses to exonerate her.

Mrs. Wright is tried by "A Jury of Her Peers" (the short story title); Mrs. Hale and Mrs. Peters penetrate the meaning of what appears only trifling to the men and go beyond conventional, shallow perceptions to discover and empathize with Mrs. Wright's reasons for killing her husband. *Trifles,* although written in 1916, has a distinctly contemporary quality because its feminist perspectives make a convincing case for women stepping outside general attitudes and oppressive values to be true to their own experience. This play is well worth comparing with Henrik Ibsen's *A Doll House* (p. 700), especially in terms of characterization and theme.

TIP FROM THE FIELD

When teaching the play *Trifles,* I divide my class in half and have one half write a final act determining the fate of Mrs. Wright in accordance with the time period of the play. The other half writes a final act in accordance with today's social and legal mores.
— OLGA LYLES, *University of Nevada*

ALTERNATIVE ASSIGNMENTS

1. Compare and contrast the play's two female characters. On the surface, both Mrs. Hale and Mrs. Peters have much in common: they are small-town wives of "important" men, leading conventional domestic lives. Yet a close examination of their exchanges reveals some important differences between the two. Write an essay in which you examine their characters closely, and draw conclusions about their similarities and differences. Why does Glaspell make a point of contrasting the two women in these specific ways? How do these differences contribute to the play's themes?

2. Two of the play's most important characters never appear on stage at all. Mr. and Mrs. Wright's character traits are crucial to why Mrs. Hale and Mrs. Peters make the decision they do. By the time the play is over, we know more about Mr. and Mrs. Wright than we do about any of the characters who actually appear on stage. Write an essay in which you analyze these two important characters and speculate as to why Glaspell chooses never to introduce us to them. How might our reading of the play be different if she had included a scene (in the beginning, in a flashback, etc.) in which the audience sees the Wrights interacting with one another?

POSSIBLE CONNECTIONS TO OTHER SELECTIONS

Kate Chopin, "The Story of an Hour" (text p. 18)
Andre Dubus, "Killings" (text p. 566)
Henrik Ibsen, *A Doll House* (text p. 700)
David Ives, *Sure Thing* (text p. 844)
Sophocles, *Oedipus the King* (text p. 293)

RESOURCES FOR TEACHING

Trifles. 21 min., color, 1979. Beta, VHS. Distributed by Phoenix/BFA Films.
Trifles. 22 min., b/w, 1981. Beta, VHS, 3/4″ U-matic cassette. Distributed by Centre Communications.

8

Reading and Writing about the Essay

Some of your students may be surprised to find the genre of the essay included in this literature anthology. While good essays require strong creative talents, we tend to think of essays as more "practical," less "literary," than the other genres. You might begin this unit by raising this very question with your students. Would they include a unit about the essay in a literature textbook? If so, would they limit their coverage to a certain kind of essay — the memoir but not the argumentative, for example? As they read the essays in this unit and throughout the text, ask them which ones they feel are more literary. How valuable is it to study essays alongside other forms of literature?

The chapter defines the most common essay classifications and gives examples. Most students have experience with each of these writing forms, especially if they have taken a composition course in high school or college. Ask them which of the categories — narration, description, exposition, or argumentation — they enjoy reading the most. In which form are they most comfortable writing? To what degree does their own writing overlap these categories? Students will be familiar with the elements of writing from the book's previous chapters. Ask them why they think voice and tone, style, structure, and theme are the elements emphasized for this particular chapter. Do they think that an examination of other elements — such as setting, character, figures of speech, or point of view — is useful in a study of the essay?

JONATHAN SWIFT, *A Modest Proposal* (p. 516)

Jonathan Swift's "A Modest Proposal" is neither modest, nor a real proposal, which is perhaps why this essay has emerged as one of the most famous in the English language. The speaker's detached voice of reason is juxtaposed sharply with his gruesome proposition that the wealthy Anglo-Irish landlords raise the children of the poor to be slaughtered and eaten. Call your students' attention to moments in the text in which the speaker seems especially detached and objective (such as when he argues for using the skin of dead children to make gloves and boots). These are often the essay's more shocking moments, and of course, they serve as great examples of Swift's irony. Note Swift's use of "objective" numbers and statistics to back up his claims, as well as his use of the word "breeders" and other comparisons between the Irish peasants and animals that are raised for food. Also examine the irony of the positive tone adopted by the speaker, such as when he describes the inevitable death by starvation of Ireland's numerous young laborers as a "hopeful condition" (para. 19). Ask your students to note other examples of the speaker's incongruously cheerful attitude.

Contrast the speaker's views with those of Swift himself. Presumably your students did not make the mistake that many of Swift's original readers made and assume that his proposal was legitimate. How did they know that Swift had adopted an ironic voice? What clues does the text provide? Embedded in Swift's satire are some serious suggestions for reform that the speaker quickly rejects but that Swift is clearly trying to advance (29). How does Swift manage to include serious views in such an outrageously satirical essay?

Teaching this essay can be a lot of fun and can lead to some interesting student papers. Ask students to write a Swiftian argument about an issue that they care about.

What shocking or radical proposal might they put forth to call attention to this issue? Ask students to imbed a more serious solution to the problem within their essay, as Swift does.

POSSIBLE CONNECTION TO ANOTHER TEXT

William Seebring, *The Original Last Wish Baby* (text p. 1178).

BERNARD COOPER, *A Clack of Tiny Sparks: Remembrances of a Gay Boyhood* (p. 523)

This essay both is and is not a typical coming-of-age story. Cooper's experiences are typical of those of many adolescents in that he feels insecure and alienated from his peers, he experiences unrequited desire, and he senses that his parents are unable to understand or help him. Of course, the fact that Cooper is coming to terms with the knowledge that he is gay makes his story unusual and adds another dimension to the typical pain of growing up. Students will probably identify with Cooper at times. Many of them will recall admiring other students who seemed more sophisticated than they did, as Cooper admires Theresa Sanchez. They may also have experienced awkward sexual rites of passage, like Debbie Coburn's party. Certainly many of your students will remember conversations with their parents in which it became clear that honest communication between the two generations was impossible.

Yet some of your students may also find themselves in an uncomfortable position as they read this essay. While they may sympathize with Cooper, they may also recall times in which they were the ones ridiculing other students or calling them "fags." Chances are that your students will not feel comfortable admitting this in class, but you might want to ask them to write a private first response to this essay in which they honestly assess their own feelings about homosexuality and their own behavior toward people known or suspected to be gay. This first response can lead to a discussion of Cooper's style. How does he describe his somewhat unusual experience as a gay teenager in such a way as to make the heterosexual reader identify with him? Although this essay is primarily a narrative, Cooper's vivid use of description accomplishes much: "my arms and legs would sometimes act of their own accord, knocking over a glass at dinner or flinching at an oncoming pitch" (para. 9) or "My father sat there chomping with gusto, emitting a couple of hearty grunts to dramatize his satisfaction" (18). Ask your students to locate and analyze descriptive passages that help make Cooper's narrative compelling.

Cooper tries a number of different methods to try to understand who he is and to change his sexual orientation. For example, he tries kissing girls and seeks self-knowledge by reading a dictionary. What do these methods tell us about him? Why do they ultimately fail? As the essay comes to an end, we learn that Cooper has "few regrets," that eventually he makes peace with himself and finds happiness in a relationship with a man. Yet we never learn how he reaches this acceptance of himself, whether his secret is discovered in high school, or how his parents feel about his homosexuality. Is the essay more successful because it leaves these issues unexplained?

Call your students' attention to the abrupt conclusion. Why do they think Cooper chose to end his story in this way? How would their impression of the essay be different if Cooper had concluded his essay at the end of paragraph 38 with the lines "The two of us flailed, pretended to drown. Beneath the heavy press of water, Grady's hair wavered, a flame that couldn't be doused"?

POSSIBLE CONNECTION TO ANOTHER SELECTION

David Updike, "Summer" (text p. 47)

E. B. WHITE, *Once More to the Lake* (p. 532)

"Once More to the Lake" is a narrative essay, but one that is less intent on telling a story than on making a point about the cycles of life and death, a point that is not fully realized until the last line. The essay is carefully structured to contrast its light beginning with its serious ending. As the essay opens, White humorously describes the "ideal" family vacation in which "[w]e all got ringworm from some kittens and had to rub Pond's Extract on our arms and legs night and morning, and my father rolled over in a canoe with all his clothes on; but outside of that the vacation was a success" (para. 1). The ironic voice implies that the narrator is assuming a somewhat detached tone — nostalgic but realistic about his childhood vacations. This tone never fully disappears from the essay, as White later explains that he decided to bring his son to the lake to give him the experience of "fresh water up his nose" (2), but the voice jostles with other voices as the essay progresses. Memories of past vacations are compared with White's vacation with his own son, and descriptive passages interrupt the narrative in order to bring the lakeshore of Maine to the reader's mind. Ask your students to write about or discuss the way that White interweaves narration and description to create a total effect.

We may not anticipate the somewhat shocking final line in which the narrator confesses that he "felt the chill of death" while watching his son put on his wet bathing suit, but a close rereading of the essay reveals some thematic links. Ask your students to identify moments in the essay in which the cycle of life and death seem to be haunting the narrator. In paragraph 4, he writes of the "creepy" sensation that "I was my father," and later he writes about the feeling that time is standing still, that the waitresses at the diner "were the same country girls" (7) who served him in his youth. Given this illusion of time standing still, evidence of change seems especially disconcerting, such as when White describes the effect of hearing outboard motors. Of course, he is not his father; his son is not him, and that is the most disturbing illusion of all.

If any of your students are parents themselves, ask them if they have ever experienced this sense of *deja vu*, of seeing their youth relived in their children, of finding themselves surprised to be the generation that plans vacations, issues the rules, and initiates the children into the family traditions. You might ask other students to show this essay to their parents or to other parents that they know. How do readings of this essay differ based on whether the readers have children themselves?

POSSIBLE CONNECTION TO ANOTHER SELECTION

Dylan Thomas, "Do not go gentle into that good night" (text p. 268)

K. C. COLE, *Calculated Risks* (p. 538)

Before asking your students to read "Calculated Risks," have a class discussion about risk. Ask your students to brainstorm or freewrite about the risks that they perceive to themselves, to the people they love, and to Americans in general. Write these risks on the board and ask students why they have the fears they do and why they believe certain risks to be more dangerous than others. Do they see themselves as risk takers? After students have read "Calculated Risks" revisit your class discussion. Do they still feel the way they did about the risks they cited? Do they agree with Cole's themes, that "people are notoriously bad at risk assessment" (para. 5) and that "[o]ur perceptual apparatus is geared toward threats that are exotic, personal, erratic, and dramatic" (6)?

Cole's essay is not a narrative, and it may seem less "literary" than the other essays in this chapter. It uses statistics and numbers rather than poetic description or figures of speech. Do your students consider this essay a work of literature? Why or why not? Despite her scientific evidence, Cole acknowledges that "[n]umbers are clearly not enough to make sense of risk assessment" (11). What techniques besides facts and figures does Cole use to illustrate her essay's themes? How successful is she? How does Cole combine a scientific with a conversational style to convey that she is knowledgeable about her topic without being out of touch with the average person? (Contrast the writing styles in paragraphs 22 and 24, for example.)

Ask your students to locate places in the reading in which they recognize themselves. For example, do they, like the "average person," believe "they will enjoy longer lives, healthier lives, and longer marriages than the 'average' person" (36), or "believe it won't happen to us if it hasn't happened yet" (38)?

POSSIBLE CONNECTION TO ANOTHER SELECTION

Regina Barreca, "Envy" (text p. 1073)

WRITING IN PROCESS: ARGUMENT

This chapter's student casebook should provoke some good class discussion about the problems and advantages of multiculturalism. April Bovet's student essay contains a well-written summary of Linda Chavez's essay "Demystifying Multiculturalism." April's paper, however, concentrates less on critiquing Chavez's essay than explaining it, reserving most of her own personal views on the issue until the final paragraph. This imbalance is fairly common in writing by students, many of whom feel more grounded when discussing the work of an "expert" but feel somewhat insecure contradicting or criticizing an author and establishing themselves as the "expert." It might be useful to use April's essay for a revision exercise in your class. Ask your students to imagine that April is a classmate seeking advice on how best to improve her paper. Where would your students encourage her to expand her ideas? Would they ask her to restructure her paper in any way? Reduce the summary of the Chavez essay? Move back and forth between Chavez's views and her own? April's paper is a good draft that could be improved through a number of strategies. Asking your students to help think about ways to work with April's paper will help them to ask the same questions about their own work.

LINDA CHAVEZ, *Demystifying Multiculturalism* (p. 546)

"Multiculturalism" is one of those words, like "feminism" and "traditional," which mean different things to different people. Before beginning a discussion of Linda Chavez's essay, ask your students to define "multiculturalism," arriving at both denotative and connotative definitions. After they have finished the reading, establish whether they think Chavez is working with the same definition they are. If not, how is Chavez defining "multiculturalism"? What does she define it against?

Depending on the makeup of your class, your students may or may not feel they have benefited from the multicultural movement. Once they have established Chavez's main point and their own opinion of that main point, ask them how much of their opinion is founded on their own experience and how much on the reading. Several of Chavez's arguments may surprise them. Ask your students which of her ideas struck them most forcibly. They may point to some of the following statements: "[T]he problem is not culture — or race, or ethnicity — but education" (para. 5); "Indeed the multiculturalists seem to believe that a person's character is determined by the color of his skin and by his ancestry" (6); "The proponents [of multiculturalism] are most often the elite" (10).

Regardless of their opinion of Chavez's views, ask your students to assess her argument *as* an argument (see Alternative Assignments, question 2). Does she define her terms, expand on her ideas, give examples, avoid sweeping generalizations? Does she acknowledge and address opposing viewpoints? Which parts of her argument are the strongest?

ALTERNATIVE ASSIGNMENTS

1. Look around your campus for evidence of "multiculturalism." Are there any political or social clubs based on ethnic background? Is there an "office of diversity" or similar institution? Are ethnic holidays celebrated? Investigate one or more of these examples and write a paper in which you argue for or against its inclusion on your campus. Using Chavez's essay to help you frame your argument, describe the multicultural group or event on your campus, explain its purpose, and argue whether it is beneficial to the campus as a whole or to the ethnic group it represents.

2. Reread the chapter's discussion of the argumentative essay (p. 513) and write an analysis of Chavez's essay as an argument. Rather than discussing her ideas, write about the way she presents those ideas. Your own essay will have a thesis that establishes whether (or to what degree) "Demystifying Multiculturalism" is a successful argument. The rest of your paper will be an argumentative essay explaining, with quotations and analysis, why you take the position you do.

PART III. LITERATURE AND LIFE

9

Home and Family

FICTION

When most of us pick up a novel we want to read, it isn't primarily because we are intrigued by the way the author sets an ironic tone, or by her use of extended metaphor and dynamic characters; most people read because good literature is interesting: it speaks about subjects people can relate to, or it takes us out of our present situation and into a world and mindset more wonderful or more terrible than our own. The third part of this anthology is organized into topics that students (and nearly everyone else) care about and have experience with. This is not to say that students should "relate" to every work in this section of the book. On the contrary, it is hoped that many of the works will introduce students to places, situations, and characters quite different from any they have encountered.

Nonetheless, the broad topics of "Home and Family," "Love and Its Complications," "Lessons from Life," "The Natural and Unnatural," and "Culture and Identity" are ones everyone has had to consider at some point in his or her life. By grouping works with similar themes and topics, instructors can draw connections between genres, times, and places to see ways in which the human experience is both universal and individual.

Knowledge of the elements of literature will still serve students well as they confront these readings. An understanding of the importance of setting in Nathaniel Hawthorne's "Young Goodman Brown" or of tone in Gary Soto's "Mexicans Begin Jogging," for example, is crucial to a good understanding of these works as a whole. As we've already seen, a work's elements cannot be divorced from its subject or meaning. This unit will help you drive home that important point.

Before beginning a discussion of this chapter's theme, consider this in-class activity: have students write two anonymous entries on separate index cards — one entry about the ideal home and family and one about their own home and family. They should not use titles to show which card is about the ideal family and which is about the real family. Collect the cards and shuffle them, and then hand them out to the class, two to each student. Ask students to read the cards they've been given and discuss whether they think they are reading an "ideal" entry or a "real" entry. As discussion unfolds, you will raise a number of issues that are explored in this chapter. Barbara Kingsolver's essay "Stone Soup" addresses the disparity between the ideal family, which she calls the "Family of Dolls," and the reality of most people's lives. This essay might be a good starting point in teaching this chapter, because it provides some theoretical background, statistics, and a vocabulary for discussing family.

The chapter's texts contain few, if any, examples of "ideal" families, but instead reflect a number of families struggling to do the best they can in difficult circumstances. In "A Slave's Family Life," Frederick Douglass comments that he barely knew his absent mother, but tells of her sneaking away from her master to visit him on several occasions. Several of the works tell of family members coping with tragedy and loss: Gwendolyn Brooks's poem "The Mother" reflects on the speaker's abortions, and Robert Frost's "Home Burial" narrates the struggle of a couple to cope with their child's death. Some works, like John Cheever's story "Reunion", and Bharati Mukherjee's "A Father," relate the failure of family members to come together even if they try.

Students may or may not recognize their own families in these pages, but they will certainly recognize some of the struggles, triumphs, and moments of despair that are present in every family. Encourage them to bring their own experiences into a discussion of the families in these pages.

JOHN CHEEVER, *Reunion* (p. 563)

"Reunion" is one of those stories in which nothing really happens and everything happens. The plot is unremarkable: a father meets his son at a train station for a quick lunch. They attempt to eat at several restaurants, but only manage to have drinks before the father's rudeness forces them to leave. Before long, the son says good-bye to his father and catches his train.

Yet these seemingly ordinary (if awkward) events clearly have an enormous significance to the son, who is on the verge of adulthood and seeking some connection with a father whom he barely knows. Traumatized by his father's behavior, he chooses never to see the man again, but when he first encounters his handsome father, the boy immediately views him as an extension of himself: "my flesh and blood, my future and my doom" (p. 563). The narrator tells us, "I was terribly happy to see him again" (p. 563). Interestingly, this first paragraph is the last one in which we are given any information about the narrator's feelings. As you teach this story, ask your students about this unusual use of point of view. "Reunion" is told in the first person, but the point of view is objective throughout most of the story. Ask your students why they think Cheever withholds the boy's reactions to his father's rudeness. What do they imagine he is thinking as the "lunch date" progresses?

The boy is clearly the protagonist in this work and the more sympathetic of the story's two characters, but the father's situation is difficult as well. Ask your students if they have any sympathy for this man who has an hour and half in which to impress his growing son. Consider having them write their own version of this story from the father's perspective. Would they paint him as a self-centered villain, or ˜as a more pathetic man who is at a loss to relate to the stranger before him?

A number of works in this chapter address the relationships of fathers and their children. Ask your students what they think the particular challenges of fatherhood are. If any of your students are fathers themselves, ask them what they think of this story. Are they more or less likely to be sympathetic with the father in "Reunion"?

POSSIBLE CONNECTION TO OTHER SELECTIONS

E. B. White, "Once More to the Lake" (text p. 532)
Robert Hayden, "Those Winter Sundays" (text p. 214)

ANDRE DUBUS, *Killings* (p. 566)

At the heart of "Killings" is the issue of the justice of the legal system — a system of arrest, bail, trial, and sentencing — versus the ancient concept of justice known as "an eye for an eye." When Willis and Matt are discussing the matter, Willis argues that the established American legal system will prove unsatisfactory: "Know what he'll do? Five at the most" (paragraph 16). In the flashback, when Frank returns home after Strout has assaulted him, Matt wants him to press charges, but Frank refuses (38–39). The laws are simply inadequate in many respects for the circumstances surrounding the events of the story; as Matt tells his wife when she objects to Frank's seeing Mary Ann before her divorce is final, "Massachusetts has crazy laws" (58). Later in the story, as Matt forces Strout to pack his belongings, Strout attempts to defend his actions: "I wanted to try to get together with her again. . . . I couldn't even talk to her. He was always with her. I'm going to jail for it; if I ever get out I'll be an old man. Isn't that enough?" (120). In this mock trial, Matt becomes both judge and jury: "You're not going to jail" (121). Matt knows that no system of justice will deny Strout what Strout's action has denied Frank, and the thought of Strout living in freedom at any time in the future is intolerable for Matt: "just thinking of Strout in Montana or whatever place lay at the end of the lie he had told, thinking of him walking the streets there, loving a girl there . . . would be enough to slowly rot the rest of his days" (135). In the end, Matt ensures that Strout's punishment is appropriate to his crime: as Strout shot Frank, so Matt shoots Strout. In the last paragraph, Matt seems to find justice in the knowledge that both Frank and Strout will be covered by the "red and yellow leaves falling on the earth" (169).

Neither Matt nor Strout is really a "killer" (hence the title — "Killings," not "Killers"). By means of the flashbacks and the sequence in which we see Strout's house and hear his "defense," we realize that each of the murders is committed out of love. Matt cannot live with Ruth's daily pain on encountering Strout in town. He is also motivated by the love he continues to feel for his dead son. Remembering how he would stand beneath the tree behind his house as one of his children climbed it, "poised to catch the small body before it hit the earth" (77), Matt carries an undeniable burden of guilt that he could not save his son. After Frank's death, Matt feels "that all the fears he had borne while they [the children] were growing up, and all the grief he had been afraid of, had backed up like a huge wave and struck him on the beach and swept him out to sea" (77). His response to this metaphorical assault is to punish Strout. Matt is constantly reminded of that "huge wave"; as he forces Strout into the car, he recognizes "the smacking curling white at the breakwater" (87). Later, we are told that "over the engine Matt could hear through his open window the water rushing inland under the bridge" (91). Matt uses his awareness of the wave's presence to bolster his courage during his interaction with Strout. Significantly, after he has buried Strout, he throws the gun into a nearby pond (152) and the keys to Strout's car into the Merrimack River (153). In a sense, the water — the force that can drown him in grief and fear unless he opposes it in some way — represents the senseless violence that has destroyed his peaceful existence; his actions serve as defiant gestures against what he feels has "struck him on the beach and swept him out to sea."

As we learn from the interaction between Strout and Matt, Strout has also acted out of love. He attempts to explain to Matt that he wanted Mary Ann and his children back; as the earlier flashback reveals, although his life has been violent and unsuccessful in some aspects, he has not previously demonstrated that he is a "killer." Although Dubus offers these occasional insights into Strout's character, the distance between readers and Strout remains. We have a much greater understanding of Matt's thoughts and feelings than Strout's, and while other characters are referred to throughout the story by their first names, Strout is almost always referred to by his last name only.

How important is the setting? You might ask students what time and place they associate with Frank. When Matt thinks of Frank, he thinks of Frank's job as a lifeguard, of the way he smells of the beach when he comes home, of his tan. Toward the end of the story, Matt and Strout drive past "the Dairy Queen closed until spring, and the two lobster restaurants that faced each other and were crowded all summer and were now also closed" (91). Ask students why this is a significant passage. Certainly the busy summer season, replete with tourists, is associated in Matt's mind with Frank. It is appropriate that the emptiness of the fall season follows Frank's death.

Even though Matt commits a murder in this story, readers may feel tremendous sympathy for him. He is a victim who takes action against the man who caused his grief; he is also portrayed as a man of humanity who takes pains to understand other people's perspectives and the complexities of a situation. Watching his son with Mary Ann, Matt tries to imagine what Frank feels and wants Frank to find the kind of intimacy with Mary Ann that he has established with Ruth. Later, as Matt and Strout go through Strout's house, Matt attempts to understand the situation from Strout's perspective. When he is in bed with Ruth at the end of the story, Matt sees both "Frank and Mary Ann making love in her bed" (169) and Strout's lover: "The other girl was faceless, bodiless, but he felt her sleeping now" (169). Because he is such a finely drawn character, readers may find it difficult to condemn Matt for his actions in "Killings."

POSSIBLE CONNECTIONS TO OTHER SELECTIONS

Isabel Allende, "The Judge's Wife" (text p. 1226)
Alison Baker, "Better Be Ready 'Bout Half Past Eight" (text p. 1232)
William Faulkner, "Barn Burning" (text p. 84)
Susan Glaspell, *Trifles* (text p. 496)

RESOURCES FOR TEACHING

Andre Dubus: Reading [recording]. 1 cassette (51 min.). The writer reads his work and discusses the writing process. Distributed by American Audio Prose Library.
Andre Dubus: Interview [recording]. 1 cassette (50 min.). The writer reads his work and discusses the writing process. Distributed by American Audio Prose Library.

ERNEST HEMINGWAY, *Soldier's Home* (p. 579)

This is a war story that includes no physical violence because Hemingway focuses on the war's psychological effects on the protagonist. A truce ended the wholesale butchery of youth fighting during World War I, but the painful memory of it has made Krebs a prisoner of war. Although the story's setting is a peaceful small town in Oklahoma, Hemingway evokes the horrors that Krebs endured and brought back home with him. In a sense the real setting of this story is Belleau Wood as well as the sites of the other bloody battles Krebs experienced. (A brief student report summarizing the nature of these battles and the casualties they produced can provide a vivid context for class discussion of the story.)

Krebs cannot talk about his experiences at home because people in town have "heard too many atrocity stories to be thrilled by actualities" (paragraph 4). He has been affected as a result of his experiences in a way they'll never be, and therein lies the story's conflict. The fraternity brother who went off to war in 1917 with romantic expectations returns knowing what the real picture is (consider the ironic deflation produced by the two photographs in paragraphs 1 and 2). Krebs knows that popular visions of the glory of war are illusions and that the reality consists more typically of sickening fear. An inadvertent hint of that comes from his sister, who calls him "Hare," a nickname that suggests fright and flight. (For a poem with a similar theme see Wilfred Owen's "Dulce et Decorum Est," p. 1172.) Krebs prefers silence to lying.

Krebs refuses to engage in the familiar domestic patterns of life expected of him. He also rejects the "complicated" world of the young girls in town. Nothing really matters very much to him; he appears numb and unwilling to commit himself to what he regards as meaningless, trivial games. He feels more at home remembering Germany and France than living in his parents' house. Reading a history of the battles he's been in gives him a feeling of something more real than his life at home, which strikes him as petty, repressive, and blind. His father's permission to use the family car, for example, is neither wanted nor needed.

Krebs's mother brings the conflict to a climax. She speaks for the family and the community, urging Krebs to get back to a normal life of work, marriage, and "being really a credit to the community." Krebs finds his mother's values little more than sentimental presuppositions that in no way relate to the person he has become. The only solution to the suffocating unreality imposed on him by his family and town is to leave home. He can neither love nor pray; he's no longer in "his Kingdom" (63). There's no going back to that prewar identity as an innocent fraternity brother from a Methodist college. The story's title, then, is ironic, for Krebs cannot go home again, because home seems to be either a lie or a place stunningly ignorant of what he discovered in the war.

A writing assignment based on a comparison of how settings are used in "Soldier's Home" and Tim O'Brien's "How to Tell a True War Story" will encourage students to relate the characters and themes to each story's setting. The landscape of home in each story is equally important but radically different in its significance.

POSSIBLE CONNECTIONS TO OTHER SELECTIONS

Tim O'Brien, "How to Tell a True War Story" (text p. 1149)
Flannery O'Connor, "Good Country People" (text p. 803)
John Updike, "A & P" (text p. 981)

RESOURCES FOR TEACHING

Ernest Hemingway. 53 min., color, 1983. VHS. This program explores Hemingway's life and literary psyche through the eyes of those who knew him. A BBC Production. Part of the "Great Writers of the 20th Century" series. Distributed by Films for the Humanities and Sciences.

Ernest Hemingway: A Life Story [recording]. Part 1, 11 cassettes; Part 2, 10 cassettes (1 hr., 30 min., per cassette). Read by Christopher Hunt. Draws from Hemingway's diaries, letters, and unpublished writing, as well as personal testimony from the people who played a part in the author's life. Distributed by Blackstone Audio Books.

BHARATI MUKHERJEE, *A Father* (p. 585)

You might begin your discussion of this story by focusing on its title. Bharati Mukherjee chose to call it "*A Father*" rather than "*The Father*," or just "Father" (or something else entirely). Her decision to use the indefinite article implies that this is the story of a father, one among many, whose struggles are typical of fathers everywhere. Of course, Mr. Bhowmick's struggles *are* those of any father trying to support his family and understand his incomprehensible daughter, but his status as an Indian immigrant trying to make "small trade-offs between new-world reasonableness and old-world beliefs" (p. 587) adds another dimension to the tale. Ask your students what they think some of these trade-offs are. Do they think Mr. Bhowmick is successful at making them?

His daughter Babli is a young woman from a different generation and a different culture. This fact becomes painfully obvious when we learn that she has chosen to become pregnant by artificial insemination, but evidence of her different values appears earlier in the story as well. Babli extols the virtues of a microwave oven while drinking Slim-Fast as her mother struggles to make "French Sandwich Toast with complicated filling" (p. 586) for her husband's breakfast. Ask your students to discuss the way Mukherjee sets up the cultural and generational conflicts in that first scene.

Mr. Bhowmick's feelings for his daughter are ambivalent, and your students' opinions of her may be as well. He believes that she lacks femininity and that she is too serious, and he notes that he would not have chosen her "as his only heir" (p. 587). Nonetheless, he tries to understand that she has to negotiate living in a country that "was both native to her, and alien" (p. 588). Although not entirely likable himself, Mr. Bhowmick does have a sympathetic side. Your students may have a mixed response to his thoughts and behaviors prior to the story's final scene. Ask them if they see him as the protagonist. Clearly he commits an inexcusable act of violence in the end. Do your students think that Mukherjee has adequately prepared us for this action? In other words, is Mr. Bhowmick's character consistent? What about his wife's fierce anger at the end? As a woman who had prided herself on being a progressive American, she is unable to accept the idea that her daughter was artificially impregnated. Why is this method of conceiving a child so horrifying to the parents?

After you've discussed the events and characters in this tragic story, you might want to address the story's tone, which is actually far from tragic. The opening scene at breakfast is rather humorous; the Bhowmick family seems slightly ridiculous but hardly destined for tragedy. Mr. Bhowmick's inept attempts to understand his daughter, his fantasies about her pregnancy, and his imagined life as a grandfather of a "chubby baby boy" (p. 589) all belie a seriously repressed man (and family) for whom open conflict is practically unknown. The final scene — hysterical, violent, and stomach-turning — seems completely out of place in this world that Mukherjee has created, making the ending all the more powerful and shocking.

POSSIBLE CONNECTION TO ANOTHER SELECTION

Raymond Carver, "Popular Mechanics" (text p. 169)

ALICE MUNRO, *An Ounce of Cure* (p. 593)

Part of the charm of "An Ounce of Cure" is Munro's humorous characterization of many aspects of adolescent life. She recalls nearly universal teenage experiences, and her wry tendencies toward both understatement and exaggeration serve her well here. Many traditional students (who would be only a year or two beyond the kind of experiences detailed in this story) will find it easy to relate to aspects of this story.

Although the plot — the narrator's recollection of her first crush, her senior year in high school, and her first experience with alcohol — will be enough to attract readers' attention, the rich characterization should also be a source for discussion. Students should realize that the strong narrative voice benefits from perspective on the events described in "An Ounce of Cure": the narrator is looking back on this story with far more wisdom, experience, and humor than she could have mustered right after it happened. In a key passage, she alludes to this added perspective and to the striking difference time makes: "Why is it a temptation to refer to this sort of thing lightly, with irony, with amazement even, at finding oneself involved with such preposterous emotions in the unaccountable past? That is what we are apt to do, speaking of love; with adolescent love, of course, it's practically obligatory" (paragraph 5). Students might identify passages that ring with irony throughout the story. They might also consider writing passages of their own that feature the same narrator telling her story the morning after her adventure at the Berrymans', or at graduation, or even at the end of her college career. It might be interesting to discover how different amounts of time affect our perspectives on the past.

One of the strengths of "An Ounce of Cure" is its strong characterization. The narrator, her mother, and even fairly minor characters are fully developed; we understand and appreciate their predicaments. For instance, the narrator's friend Joyce is the quintessential best friend — the kind of person who calls the narrator the morning after the prom to suitably denigrate the date who attended with the narrator's former boyfriend: "yes, M.C. *had* been there with M.B., and she had on a formal that must have been made out of somebody's old lace tablecloth, it just *hung*'" (7). Kay Stringer, whom the narrator meets as a result of her brush with the alcohol, turns out to have "a great female instinct to manage, comfort, and control" (20) — nurselike assets that the narrator recognizes years later in a maternity ward (24). We also find an insightful perspective on Mr. Berryman's probable state of mind as he drives the narrator home: "I suppose that besides being angry and disgusted with *me*, he was worried about taking me home in this condition to my straitlaced parents, who could always say I got the liquor in his house. Plenty of Temperance people would think that enough to hold him responsible, and the town was full of Temperance people. Good relations with the town were very important to him from a business point of view" (31). Not only do we perceive an individual character's motivation here, but we also have a broader sense of the community. In keeping with the information that the narrator took a temperance pledge in seventh grade, and that her mother had to take the bus to the next town to acquire a new bottle of scotch to replace the one the narrator filled with water, we have a clear sense of a time and a place that might be nearly unrecognizable otherwise to students in the 1990s.

Munro's use of description is strikingly original. Consider, for instance, the narrator's (academic) expectation of the effects of alcohol: "I had thought of some sweeping emotional change, an upsurge of gaiety and irresponsibility, a feeling of lawlessness and escape, accompanied by a little dizziness and perhaps a tendency to giggle out loud" (13) — in part a splendid foreshadowing of some of her behavior a few hours later. The matter-of-fact sentence "I reached up and turned on a floor lamp beside the chair, and the room jumped on me" (12) eloquently and visually depicts the way the narrator felt as the alcohol worked its way into her system. Encourage students to examine the story for other moments when the description evokes a significant reader response.

On her way to disaster at the Berrymans', the narrator acknowledges, "My approach [to the alcohol] could not have been less casual if I had been the Little Mermaid drinking the witch's crystal potion" (11). It might be fruitful for students to reread the original Hans Christian Andersen fairy tale and develop an analogy between the situations of the Little Mermaid and Munro's narrator. Each heroine drinks because of great romantic longing for an unattainable boy. Considered together, these stories might lead to an especially fruitful discussion of fantasy and reality in connection with adolescence, gender, and culture.

POSSIBLE CONNECTIONS TO OTHER SELECTIONS

Susan Minot, "Lust" (text p. 796)
David Updike, "Summer" (text p. 47)

FAE MYENNE NG, *A Red Sweater* (p. 601)

Students may not fully understand the symbolism of the red sweater until they comprehend some of the complexity of characterization in Ng's story. The narrator's deep ambivalence about her family and her ethnic heritage fuel her desire to give her sister this special gift; its meaning evolves as we obtain more of an understanding of the family's history and interpersonal dynamics.

The narrator is filled with conflicting emotions about her family. It is, she tells us, a "failed family" (paragraph 3); after the suicide of her middle sister (who remains nameless), "the family just sort of fell apart" (18). In addition, her parents' relationship has caused the narrator to look for a means of escape; she explains that her pregnancy and ensuing abortion became her "opportunity" (13) to leave her family behind. But she is unable to make a complete break from them; thus, she meets her elder sister, Lisa, for dinner in an annual ritual. The sisters are ambivalent about talking to each other as well: Lisa's "voice is sullen. She doesn't look at me. Once a year, I come in, asking questions. She's got the answers, but she hates them. For me, I think she's got the peace of heart, knowing that she's done her share for Mah and Deh. She thinks I have the peace, not caring. Her life is full of questions, too, but I have no answers" (29). Listening to her sister's stories, the narrator thinks, "I tell myself not to come back next year. I tell myself to apply for another transfer, to the East Coast" (68). But she still wants to hear the stories. The narrator demonstrates bitterness toward her parents, recalling their attacks on each other and their treatment of their daughters: "The stories themselves mean little. It was how hot and furious they could become. Is there no end to it? What makes their ugliness so alive, so thick and impossible to let go of?" (86–87). She also uses irony to summarize her parents' rejection of her: "My parents always had a special way of saying things" (17).

Nonetheless, she also reveals a sense of duty, love, and compassion toward them. She acknowledges, "the folks still won't see me, but I try to keep in touch with them through Lisa" (18). Her drink, Johnny Walker, "reminds me of Deh" (33), and looking into Lisa's eyes, she sees "Mah's eyes. Eyes that make you want to talk" (37). She tells us of Mah's kindness toward Deh: "Even though it was nonstop for Mah — rushing to the sweatshop in the morning, out to shop on break, and then home to cook by evening — she did this for him" (57), and she also defends her father: "his work was hard, too" (74). She sums up her attitude by saying, "their lives weren't easy. So is their discontent without reason?" (78).

She also would like to reject her Chinese heritage, particularly the misogynistic aspects of Chinese culture. She refers to the "failure" of her parents to produce a male heir at the beginning of the story, but at the end, she writes of "the bondmaids growing up in service, or the newborn daughters whose mouths were stuffed with ashes. Courtesans with the three-inch feet, . . . the frightened child-brides" (105). When the waiter asks her whether she and her sister are Chinese, she denies it (99); instead, she offers, "we're two sisters" (100). She establishes a contrast between what is Chinese and what is American: "at the Chinatown places, you have nothing to talk about except the bare issues"; there, "the food is good and the living hard. You eat a steaming rice plate, and then you feel like rushing home to sew garments or assemble radio parts or something" (22). In contrast, "in American restaurants, the atmosphere helps you along. I want nice light and a view and handsome waiters" (22). The narrator's choice of a fork over chopsticks ("The only chopsticks I own, I wear in my hair" [24]) signifies her ambivalence about her ethnicity.

And yet, she is unable to break with her heritage in the same way that she is unable to break with her family. Significantly, the time of year when the narrator and her sister meet, "January, New Year's, and February, New Year's again, double luckiness with our birthdays in between" (19), involves both American and Chinese celebrations. In addition, she acknowledges, "sometimes I get very hungry for Chinese flavors: black beans, garlic and ginger, shrimp paste and sesame oil. These are tastes we grew up with, still dream about. Crave" (50). During dinner, she suggests that maybe they should have gone to Chinatown after all (92).

Having established the narrator's family's history and patterns, ask students to compare the narrator's description of Lisa with her description of the red sweater. In the course of the evening, Lisa announces, "I don't want to think about [the family violence] anymore" (88). Though the narrator tells us, "for a long time Lisa's wanted out" (103), she also tells us that Lisa "can stay at that point of endurance forever" (103). According to the narrator, "Lisa is reed-thin and tall. She's got a body that clothes look good on. My sister slips something on, and it wraps her like skin. Fabric has pulse on her" (37). Hence, the narrator selects as Lisa's special gift the "lucky" red angora sweater.

What is the connection between the narrator's description of the sweater as "Hand Wash Only. Worn Once" (109) and the fact that Lisa "grabs at things out of despair, out of fear. Gifts grow old for her. Emotions never ripen, they sour. Everything slips away from her. Nothing sustains her. Her beauty has made her fragile" (91)? In addition, what is the narrator wishing for Lisa in giving her this gift? The narrator acknowledges, "I want her beauty to buy her out" (106), and she adds "time is what I would like to give her" (107); she also notices the dark, attractive waiter's evident interest in Lisa. Will this particular sweater be enough to help Lisa find love? Will Lisa be able to escape the dynamics of her parents' violence if she can devote herself to a love of her own? Can Lisa ultimately benefit from the sacrifices of her parents? As the narrator emphasizes, "we're the lucky generation" (105); "the idea is that the next generation can marry for love" (71). Neither the narrator nor the middle sister achieved this goal; perhaps Lisa will achieve it. Do students believe Lisa will be able to achieve this goal? Students might list the descriptions of the sweater at the beginning and the end of the story and discuss the ways in which Ng endows each description with meaning as she tells her story. For instance, understanding more of the intensity of the parents' relationship to each other, and to their daughters, we might begin to understand the narrator's choice of "fierce" and "dark red" and "made in Hong Kong" (1) in describing her gift to her sister.

Finally, students should examine Mah's philosophy: "Bones are sweeter than you know" (48). In what way does this sum up not only Mah and Deh's relationship but the narrator's relationship to her family as well? In addition, in what way is the story about Deh waiting in line at the bank four times significant? Can it apply metaphorically to Lisa as well as Deh? Studying these aspects of the story, students may understand that the narrator's gift involves not only a change of clothing but a change of life.

POSSIBLE CONNECTION TO ANOTHER SELECTION

Toni Cade Bambara, "The Lesson" (text p. 925)

TOBIAS WOLFF, *Powder* (p. 609)

"Powder" is a story about a significant moment in a relationship between a father and his son. The first-person narrator's parents are separated at the time of the events described in this story, and the narrator, who is young enough not to have gotten a driver's license yet, tells us, "my mother was still angry with [my father] for sneaking me into a nightclub during our last visit, to see Thelonious Monk" (paragraph 1). Though he tells us that his father eventually did get him home for Christmas Eve dinner, "buying a little more time before my mother decided to make the split final" (34), there is evident tension between the father and son, particularly at the beginning of the story and leading up to when the state trooper tells the father that the road is closed. The boy seems nervous; he knows that the mother is going to be angry; and he himself seems irritated that his father has dawdled so long: "as we were checking out of the lodge that morning it began to snow, and in this snow he observed some quality that made it necessary for us to get in one last run. We got in several last runs. He was indifferent to my fretting" (2). The father's dialogue with his son at the beginning of the story signals the difficulties in their relationship. The father says "Right, doctor?" (4). The son, who is supposed to respond by saying, "Right, doctor" (5), remains silent. A little later, he reproaches his father: "We should have left before, . . . Doctor" (12); significantly, the father fails to respond according to their ritual.

The turn in the story comes when the son can relinquish his criticism of his father and admire him for who he is. This comes in part when the father insists on driving past the barricades, despite the possible penalties. In contrast with the earlier dialogue, once they have committed themselves to making the trip together (father driving, son becoming "an accomplice" [19] by moving the barricades), they both participate in their routine. When the father says, "Joke, doctor" (19), the son replies, "Funny, doctor" (20).

Students should decide whether these characters are static or dynamic. The father remains consistent throughout the story: he savors the adventure, despite the possible penalties. (Though he cannot please his son's mother, he does wheedle his way out of any trouble with the state troopers.) The son is a more dynamic character: he has to move past his inflexible opinions into an appreciation of his father's talents. He characterizes himself for the reader: "I always thought ahead. I was a boy who kept his clothes on numbered hangers to ensure proper rotation. I bothered my teachers for homework assignments far ahead of their due dates so I could make up schedules" (34). However, he finally relaxes and accepts his father for the free spirit that he is: a persuasive, appealing man, a great driver, a loving father who is committed to making sure his son experiences exhilaration and joy in his life, despite his parents' problems. Though earlier in the story, the narrator manifests anxiety about traveling over the closed road ("to keep my hands from shaking I clamped them between my knees" [21]), he now notes, as his father deftly drives through the fresh snow, "I actually trusted him" (35). He also describes his father as "rumpled, kind, bankrupt of honor, flushed with certainty" (35). Compare this statement with the son's responses to and thoughts about his father earlier in the story. In addition, direct students to reread paragraph 3. The son and father have been skiing during the snowfall, and the son acknowledges his dependence on his father's skill: "By now I couldn't see the trail. There was no point in trying. I stuck to him like white on rice and did what he did and somehow made it to the bottom without sailing off a cliff." This passage foreshadows the drive down the closed road later in the day; however, the tone is quite different. Ask students to explain the ways in which the narrator changes his attitude between this journey down the mountain and the one made later on in the "purring" Austin-Healy.

In what way is this drive down the mountain a metaphor for the future of the boy's relationship with his father? The narrator describes the setting: "Down the first long stretch I watched the road behind us, to see if the trooper was on our tail. The barricade vanished. Then there was nothing but snow: snow on the road, snow kicking up from the chains, snow on the trees, snow in the sky; and our trail in the snow. I faced around and had a shock. The lie of the road behind us had been marked by our own tracks, but there were no tracks ahead of us. My father was breaking virgin snow between a line of tall trees. He was humming 'Stars Fell on Alabama' " (21). We know that the narrator's mother will eventually decide to leave his father. We also know that the father is deeply committed to being with his son. Though there are no clear solutions or easy answers, readers may get the feeling from this passage that the father will continue to find ways of loving his son.

POSSIBLE CONNECTIONS TO OTHER SELECTIONS

Margaret Atwood, "Bored" (text p. 613)
William Faulkner, "Barn Burning" (text p. 84)
David Updike, "Summer" (text p. 47)

POETRY

ELIZABETH ALEXANDER, *Harlem Birthday Party* (p. 612)

This poem reads like a prose narrative that serves both as a description of the speaker's grandfather's life and of his ninetieth birthday party. Students may wonder why this poem is written in verse as opposed to prose. It is a valid question. A good place to start discussion might be with the question of selection: what are some of the details that the speaker includes that do not seem to "fit in" with a simple prose narrative? A good example is the detail about the speaker and her boyfriend Gustavo buying pillows before they return from New York to Philadelphia. Why is that detail included? How does it compare to the description of Harlem in the first two stanzas? Do the characters in the poem besides the speaker and her grandfather fit into some pattern? Perhaps not; perhaps that is what makes this poem unique. Our attempts to analyze it as we would analyze another poem are frustrated. Yet there is something resonant about the dichotomy the poem sets up between special events and everyday details. The poem contains famous people on one side and ordinary people on the other; it describes the details of a menu and the way someone's life was changed as a result of talking to the speaker's grandfather. Does the poem attempt to reconcile the ordinary and the extraordinary?

POSSIBLE CONNECTION TO ANOTHER SELECTION

M. Carl Holman, "Mr. Z" (text p. 996)

MARGARET ATWOOD, *Bored* (p. 613)

This adult speaker reflects on her boredom as a young girl spending time with her father. She recounts their activities together, and ultimately realizes that her mature perceptions differ greatly from her childhood perceptions. She ends with the wistful realization, "Now I would know." Careful readers will notice that the relationship between the speaker and the "he" of the poem is likely that of a daughter and father; she sits in the back seat, helps him to build a garden, and learns about nature from him. It might be interesting to discuss why no one else exists in the poem. Is it primarily about him or about her? If the daughter is sitting in the back seat, it is likely that her mother is sitting in the front seat; why is her mother never mentioned?

The poem's single stanza doesn't help to identify points at which the speaker's attitude, point of view, or definition of boredom shift. It may be productive to have students identify and discuss these points: when boredom transmutes into "looking hard and up close at the small / details" (lines 13–14), or when her activity merges with "what / the animals spend most of their time at" (25). How does the meaning of the word "bored" change from the title through line 37? Students might be more likely to recognize the pun with "board" (4) — an object that almost seems an extension of the speaker in the early lines. However, the more elusive pun on boring as digging or burrowing represents a crucial turn in the speaker's perspective, as it allows the speaker to connect her activities with those of the animals her father "pointed . . . out" (27–28). "Boring" — a negative word to any child — becomes a positive word from the speaker's adult perspective since it connotes digging deeper in order to find meaning, resulting in a mature appreciation of her father.

POSSIBLE CONNECTION TO ANOTHER SELECTION

Robert Hayden, "Those Winter Sundays" (text p. 214)

REGINA BARRECA, *Nighttime Fires* (p. 614)

This narrative poem has a recurrent theme, indicated by the repetitions of the word *smoke*. Smoke is the end of the father's quest, but what, exactly, is he looking for? His daughter, the speaker, provides a clue when she tells us that her father lost his job, so he had time to pursue fires. Smoke is the father's assurance that there is justice in the world because fires destroy rich and poor people alike. Ask students to look at the images the speaker uses to describe her father: What kind of man is he? How would they characterize the daughter's relationship to him? Does the mother also think of these drives as "festival, carnival" (line 15)? In some respect, the carnival is the father's performance before his family, in which the "wolf whine of the siren" (9) is matched by his "mad" (8) expression.

In a writing assignment, you might ask students to examine the metaphors describing the father. What do these figures tell us about his life? For example, in the final image of the father, his eyes are compared to "hallways filled with smoke" (31). Why is he likened to a house? What might this image tell us about his life?

POSSIBLE CONNECTION TO ANOTHER SELECTION

Robert Hayden, "Those Winter Sundays" (text p. 214)

ROBERT BLY, *The Man Who Didn't Know What Was His* (p. 615)

This poem considers the personality of a man who, as a child, was given mixed signals as to what was truly his. The gist of the argument is that a child who is told to finish what is on *his* plate or to go to *his* room will begin to feel as though nothing is truly his. Since he has no freedom as a child, he has no imagination as an adult, and as a result, becomes "helpful and hostile in the same moment" (line 11). This person both "leans toward you and leans away"; the speaker concludes ambiguously.

Some students may relish the opportunity to complain about how they were brought up. Bly describes too much control as a "demon" in line 2; could too much freedom also be considered a "demon"? Which is worse? Ask students to consider the symbolism of dinner, the assumption that a child's parents are commanding him to finish what's on his plate or sit on his chair. This rhetoric is no doubt familiar to students, and they might offer other examples of it from their own childhood. Be prepared, if you go this route, to monitor a debate about the proper means of child rearing: how much freedom can children handle? Where is the line between parental guidance and excessive control? Or, in connection with Heitzman's poem (see "Possible Connections," below), when does an adult's need for order interfere with or damage a child's sense of self?

A more difficult concept is the idea behind line 1: "There was a man who didn't know what was his." How do students interpret that line? What, as an adult, belongs to you? Students are likely to recognize that Bly is speaking in terms beyond material possession, but they might find it difficult to articulate exactly what he means. It might help to have them write about what they think is theirs, excluding material possessions, before discussing the poem, and to extrapolate by asking them how they think such things could be lost.

POSSIBLE CONNECTION TO ANOTHER SELECTION

Judy Page Heitzman, "The Schoolroom on the Second Floor of the Knitting Mill" (text p. 995)

GWENDOLYN BROOKS, *The Mother* (p. 616)

This poem discusses a controversial issue in very contradictory images. The difference between the title and the first word points out this contradiction immediately. Isn't an abortion about *not* being a mother? Students may tend to simplify this poem because abortion is a heated moral and ethical issue. Urge them to consider the way the poem talks about the experience. They might begin by noting the matter-of-factness of the first stanza: the perfect rhymed couplets, the direct statements. This directness breaks down in the second stanza, as "You" shifts to "I."

Ask students to compare the first and second stanzas. How, for example, does *sweet,* a word that appears in both stanzas, mean something different each time? The rhyme scheme changes in the second stanza. How does this change affect the speaker's attitude toward her experience? She speaks of "I" and "you" in the second stanza. Is this poem directed to her unborn children, or to herself? Why does she list the events of her children's lost lives in lines 15–20? How does this listing affect the reader? Does the speaker effectively separate herself from her lost children, or is she somewhat confused about their loss? She returns to the direct statement at the end of the stanza, perhaps trying to regain control over herself. In the third stanza, the speaker admits that she is unsure of how to describe her experience in order to say "the truth" (line 28). Ask students to identify possible meanings for this truth. Is it definable? Finally, you might consider why the last stanza is separated from the rest.

A writing assignment might ask students to discuss at length the form of the poem. How does the structure illustrate the speaker's feelings or change of feeling?

Raymond Carver, "Popular Mechanics" (text p. 169)

EMILY DICKINSON, *The Bustle in a House* (p. 617)

The images in this poem suggest that getting on with mundane, everyday activities helps us to move beyond the pain of death. Look closely at the diction in line 7. The phrase "We shall not want" echoes the Twenty-third Psalm, a hymn of comfort and confidence in God's support at the time of death. But does the expression also imply that even though we don't want to deal with any thought other than being reunited with the loved one in eternity, the reality may not be so simple?

In *Literary Women* (Garden City: Doubleday, 1976), Ellen Moers claims that "Emily Dickinson was self-consciously female in poetic voice, and more boldly so than is often recognized" (61). Does the imagery in this poem confirm or repudiate Moers's assertion? Ask your students to consider the many speakers they have encountered in Dickinson's poems. Is her poetic voice generally identifiable as female? If so, how? If not, how would you characterize her poetic voice(s)?

Donald Hall, "Letter with No Address" (text p. 621)

ROBERT FROST, *Home Burial* (p. 617)

"Home Burial" is a dialogue in blank verse between a husband and wife who have recently lost their child and who have different ways of coping with loss. One way to begin discussion is to consider the form of the poem: does it seem more like a poem or a miniature play? How does the rhythm of the poem affect its theme? The haunting repetition of the word "don't" in line 31, for example, is realistic dialogue when we consider the tension behind the situation, but it also serves to mark a turning point in the poem. At what other points in the poem do similar repetitions occur, and do they also mark turning points in the dramatic situation, or do they reveal something about the psychological state of the characters?

Biographical criticism is beginning to come back into fashion, and you might remind the class of some of the introductory notes on Frost in this chapter before discussing the poem. Clearly the speaker is more matter-of-fact than his wife, and there is decidedly a communication problem between them. Note how Frost splits their dialogue in the interrupted iambic lines. But doesn't the husband deserve some special commendation for possessing the courage and integrity to initiate a confrontation with his wife? Discussion of the poem might also consider the value that ancients and moderns alike ascribe to a catharsis of emotions.

You might, if the class seems at all responsive, examine the speaker's claim that "a man must partly give up being a man / With women-folk" (lines 52–53). What does this statement mean? Has feminism done anything to challenge what are uniquely man's and uniquely woman's provinces of concern?

Robert Frost, " 'Out, Out' " (text p. 992)

RACHEL HADAS, *The Red Hat* (p. 620)

The child of the speaker of this poem has recently begun to walk to school alone. The speaker and her husband take turns secretly following the boy most of the way toward school. She finds this change toward maturity unsettling; rather than feeling joy at her child's newfound independence, she and her husband feel "empty, unanchored, perilously light" (line 21). The title of the poem, and its post-Christmas setting, emphasize the youth of the boy and the irrevocable loss of childlike innocence that is the basis for the poem's core emotion.

The poem is written in heroic couplets, but the poet prevents the rhythm from sounding singsongy with enjambment, punctuating the lines unevenly, ending a sentence midline; or often by altering the meter with a semicolon or colon. Ask students how this rhythm affects the poem's tone: Would it have been as poignant if the poet hadn't interrupted the rhythm with punctuation? If the rhymes had been end-stopped and full? Does the uneven meter have something to do with the theme of the poem? This theme is obviously related to the sometimes painful passage from childhood into adulthood, the "pull / of something more powerful than school" (lines 15–16), less commonly presented from the parent's point of view than from a child's. Who do students sympathize with? Do they better understand the child's need to be independent, or the parent's need to follow him at a distance?

POSSIBLE CONNECTIONS TO OTHER SELECTIONS

Robert Bly, "The Man Who Didn't Know What Was His" (text p. 615)

Sharon Olds, "Rite of Passage" (text p. 627)

DONALD HALL, *Letter with No Address* (p. 621)

The speaker of this poem, grief-stricken over the death of his wife, writes her a letter in which he describes both the events of his day-to-day life and his lingering emotions over her death. It is a devastatingly honest poem, hiding nothing from the reader. Much of the real heartbreak comes from the speaker's need to share even the most mundane details of his life with his wife. This is not a highflown "poetic" love, but a very deep, real, everyday love. The truly heart-rending irony is that the speaker especially needs his wife now, after, and because of, her death. You might begin by asking how students feel when they read something so personal. It is, after all, a "letter with no address"; do they feel as though they have stumbled upon someone's mail or diary? Is the speaker's purpose in writing the poem part of the way he deals with grief, or does the poem also serve another purpose, perhaps to connect his soul with that of his wife? In either case, where does the reader fit in?

The poem is also noteworthy for its vivid imagery. Much of this imagery serves to connect the world of the living and the world of the dead, or to show how these two worlds overlap. One way of opening up discussion is to have students locate two images in the poem, one that defines the poem's overall tone and another that seems to clash with this tone, then to work through the poet's reasoning for including both images. (For example, how do students reconcile the opening image of dying daffodils with the final image of automobiles as a symbol of lewd sexuality?)

POSSIBLE CONNECTIONS TO OTHER SELECTIONS

Emily Dickinson, "The Bustle in a House" (text p. 617)

Robert Frost, "Home Burial" (text p. 617)

Andrew Hudgins, "Elegy for My Father, Who Is Not Dead" (text p. 624)

ANDREW HUDGINS, *Elegy for My Father, Who Is Not Dead* (p. 624)

The speaker of this poem, unlike his father who is "ready" (line 2) to die, is not convinced "about the world beyond this world" (4). His father seems ready to die, happy "in the sureness of his faith" (3) that his journey into the afterlife will be like a vacation to a place where he will wait for his son to join him. The speaker is skeptical; he "can't / just say good-bye as cheerfully / as if he were embarking on a trip" (14–16). The difference in their attitudes is represented in terms of a ship; the speaker is convinced only that his father's "ship's gone down" (19) while the father is convinced that he will eventually wave and shout "welcome back" (21) to his son when his son's time comes.

The poem raises a crucial question: will the son adopt his father's attitude when he himself is closer to death, or is he simply more skeptical than his father? Both options are raised; the speaker acknowledges, "He's ready. I am not" (14), but he also says "I do not think he is right" (13). Does our attitude toward death change as we get older because we have accepted our mortality, or is belief in the afterlife a defense mechanism? This question is central to the poem's interpretation, as is the speaker's focus: is he more concerned about his father's death or his own? The poem is rather self-involved for an "elegy." Is the poet playing with two senses of the term "elegy" — a poem of mourning and a meditation on death?

POSSIBLE CONNECTIONS TO OTHER SELECTIONS

Donald Hall, "Letter with No Address" (text p. 621)
Dylan Thomas, "Do not go gentle into that good night" (text p. 268)

LANGSTON HUGHES, *doorknobs* (p. 625)

You might begin discussion of this poem by offering some historical context to your students. Ask them what they know about the social and political climate of the early 1960s in America. The civil rights movement was gaining momentum when this poem was published, and the nation was facing an important turning point. In this context, ask your students what the "doorknob on a door / that turns to let in life" (lines 2-3) might represent. Ask them to explain what might be so terrifying about a metaphorical doorknob turning and opening the door to "life."

Students might also consider the uncertainty and fear that the speaker feels toward whoever might be behind that door, waiting to enter. Ask them to examine the implications of the description that the "life / on two feet standing" (3-4) may be male or female, drunk or sober, happy or terrified. Ask your students to characterize the speaker in this poem. What details in the poem contribute to the readers' understanding of the speaker's persona?

Stylistically, this poem is very different from the other Hughes poems in this collection. One unusual detail is that "doorknobs" is one long sentence that may be read both literally and symbolically. You might ask students to examine the final three lines. Why might the "yesterday" (24) that is "not of our own doing" (25) be so terrifying to the speaker?

POSSIBLE CONNECTION TO ANOTHER SELECTION

Theodore Roethke, "My Papa's Walz" (p. 630)

GALWAY KINNELL, *After Making Love We Hear Footsteps* (p. 625)

Kinnell's poetry is known for its directness, precision, and carefully controlled idiom. In his *Book of Nightmares*, from which this poem is taken, he explores the difficult project of explaining human mortality to our children. Love is his answer in many of the poems, but it requires confronting physical as well as emotional issues.

This is a popular poem with students because it vividly presents a scene that is familiar to many of them. Ask them to describe the speaker. What does his language tell us about his character?

In an essay, you might ask students to explore the poem's auditory appeal. How do the various sounds create a mood for the speaker's discussion of his relationship to his child and his wife?

Robert Frost, "Home Burial" (text p. 617)

PHILIP LARKIN, *This Be the Verse* (p. 626)

At once indicting and absolving parenthood for the faults and woes of the world, this poem's depth goes beyond the humor and unexpectedness of its blunt first line. Students are likely to find some humor here because, or in spite of, Larkin's particularly "non-poetic" diction. But this poem is more than a simple cynical witticism.

Larkin builds a funny tone by inverting the syntax of the first line (which places the shocking "fuck" as the poem's second word), by lightening the tone with mocking language such as "just for you" in line 4, and by using childish words like "mum and dad" (line 1). Furthermore, readers may not expect this kind of "talk" from a poet — especially one who is espousing as serious a point as "man hands misery to man" (9). The contrast in the speaker's two levels of diction is, itself, funny, but at the same time, calls greater attention to the more serious, if not beautiful lines: "It deepens like a coastal shelf" (10). The glib ending, in particular, both humorously undermines the more serious message and enhances it by contrast.

You may want to begin a discussion by trying to characterize the speaker. Apart from the techniques of the poet, why would this speaker be funny when there is such a sad message sitting there in the middle of his diatribe? Is the speaker sad?

POSSIBLE CONNECTION TO ANOTHER SELECTION

Robert Bly, "The Man Who Didn't Know What Was His" (text p. 615)

SHARON OLDS, *Rite of Passage* (p. 627)

Olds's work is often focused on gender distinctions and characteristics. In "Rite of Passage," Olds emphasizes the highly masculine qualities inherent in males of any age. The title refers not only to the birthday party — a ritual by which we celebrate milestones in the maturation process — but also the boys' transition from child to adult behavior. Even six- and seven-year-olds demonstrate adult male characteristics: "Hands in pockets, they stand around / jostling, jockeying for place, small fights / breaking out and calming" (lines 5–7). They also emulate adult male behavior by comparing themselves to each other and by valuing power, force, assertiveness: "They eye each other, seeing themselves / tiny in the other's pupils. They clear their / throats a lot, a room of small bankers, / they fold their arms and frown" (11–12). The final lines, in which "they clear their throats / like Generals, they relax and get down to / playing war" (24–26), provide an overt context for much of the preceding covert activity. Socializing is akin to war: at this party, even the cake — "round and heavy as a / turret" (13–14) — is evocative of combat.

The power in Olds's poem lies in her insistence in the final lines, where the birthday boy assures his guests, *"We could easily kill a two-year-old"* (22), that this transition occurs much earlier than we might commonly expect. The "clear voice" of this child contrasts sharply with the thoughts he expresses, indicating dissonance between the image of a child and the reality of that image. Ultimately, the "rite of passage" refers less to the son's celebrating a birthday than to our own recognition that these children contain and manifest even at this early age the energy and the desire for brutality.

POSSIBLE CONNECTIONS TO OTHER SELECTIONS

Carolyn Forché, "The Colonel" (text p. 1285)
Wilfred Owen, "Dulce et Decorum Est" (text p. 1172)
Gary Soto, "Behind Grandma's House" (text p. 633)

SYLVIA PLATH, *Daddy* (p. 628)

Read this poem aloud before you begin teaching it. That way the class will hear some of the insistent and bizarre nursery-rhyme repetitions of sound that hammer their way through it. The critic A. Alvarez describes "Daddy" as a love poem. That idea, given the tone and imagery, might surprise some students, but it can be related to Plath's own comment on her father's early death and her attempt to cut through the entanglements of a relationship that never had a chance to mature.

The person we need most to love but are unable to is the one most likely to be projected in an effigy of hatred. One wants to exorcise what one cannot embrace. The most memorable feature of this poem is the string of transformations Plath projects on the father. From the inorganic statue to the mythical vampire (killed by a stake "in" the heart), the transforming range could not be wider. In this imaginative process Plath begins to think that she is a Jew and that her father is with the German Luftwaffe and then with the armored tank division ("panzer-man"). She eventually connects him with Fascism and the sadomasochism of male aggression against women. The real picture of Otto Plath as teacher is suddenly rendered in Plath's mind as surreal — father as devil. The crescendo of memories and images reaches its peak when Plath recalls an earlier suicide attempt (one she described, in fact, in her novel *The Bell Jar*). She also seems to implicate her husband, the British poet Ted Hughes, in this memory, as she portrays him in the roles of torturer and vampire.

Plath is often described as a "confessional poet." Despite the highly idiosyncratic nature of this poem, what in it allows for a sharing of this personal experience with a wide and impersonal audience? What, if any, are the universal themes touched on here? You might develop one of these questions into a writing assignment.

POSSIBLE CONNECTIONS TO OTHER SELECTIONS

Philip Larkin, "This Be the Verse" (text p. 626)
Dylan Thomas, "Do not go gentle into that good night" (text p. 268)

THEODORE ROETHKE, *My Papa's Waltz* (p. 630)

From the perspective of a man looking back at his childhood, the speaker recollects the drunken lurchings of his working-class father as he waltzed around the room. The remembrance is one of those strong early memories that, years later, one sifts through. The rhythm of the poem reflects well those moments the speaker recalls with some pain. Notice the spondees, for example, in "My right ear scraped a buckle" (line 12) or in "You beat time on my head / With a palm caked hard by dirt" (13–14). The title, with its use of *Papa,* seems to indicate a memory from early childhood — as does line 12. It also connotes a certain gentle affection for "Papa," despite all the other memories.

POSSIBLE CONNECTIONS TO OTHER SELECTIONS

Regina Barreca, "Nighttime Fires" (text p. 614)
Dylan Thomas, "Do not go gentle into that good night" (text p. 268)

INDIRA SANT, *Household Fires* (p. 631)

This poem delineates the roles (or "jobs") of four children in an Indian household. The father's role is only suggested, but the poem's final focus is on the mother, who seems to be caving in as a result of the demands placed on her. You might explore in discussion the effect of the way this poem is arranged: where are our sympathies? And would they be different if the poem were ordered differently? The poem categorizes the roles of the children in terms of gender, but also in terms of age. Is there a clear-cut hierarchy based on these criteria? If there were a sixth stanza about the father's "job," what would it be like and where would it most effectively be placed?

POSSIBLE CONNECTIONS TO OTHER SELECTIONS

Julia Alvarez, "Woman's Work" (text p. 986)

Chitra Banerjee Divakaruni, "Indian Movie, New Jersey" (text p. 1277)

Sylvia Plath, "Daddy" (text p. 628)

CATHY SONG, The Youngest Daughter (p. 632)

Essentially a recollection of the afternoons spent with her aging mother, this poem recounts several specific incidents that serve as emblems of the speaker's relationship with her mother. In the meantime, the speaker's psychological state is revealed through a number of telling details. Beginning with a description of her skin as "pale as rice paper" the speaker hints at her own physical (if not psychological) delicacy which, throughout ("aspirin colored" skin in line 12 that "tingles with migraine" in line 13, for example) are contrasted with the mother's relative ruggedness. Though old and presumably frail, the speaker's first recollection of her mother is of her skin drying in the fields. Later, her "breathing was gravelled" (line 18), "her voice gruff" (line 20), and her breasts are likened to "whiskered" "walruses" (lines 25 and 24, respectively).

You may want to have your students trace other images of delicacy throughout the poem, mapping out which characters are associated with which—and, importantly, when. Directly after the speaker's revulsion with her mother's breasts, she feels a tenderness considering her bruises. And, indeed, their relationship seems to be based on a sort of give and take of tenderness. After students have traced the images of delicacy, have them consider how it relates to the dynamics of tenderness that characterize this relationship. What does this have to do with the "thousand cranes" of the last line?

GARY SOTO, *Behind Grandma's House* (p. 633)

In this poem, Soto captures a moment that almost every individual experiences in growing up — the trying on of different identities to discover one that "fits." Ultimately, the grandma in the poem helps the speaker along in the process by showing him how the identity he is trying cannot work. Students may connect the episode described in this poem to times in their own lives when they've searched for an identity or tried too hard to prove something to themselves or others.

You might begin the class discussion by suggesting that the real "happening" of the poem is the arrival of the grandma, who, with total nonchalance, sets the speaker straight on what it means to be tough. Ask students why Soto limited his description of the grandma to simply "her apron flapping in a breeze, / her hair mussed" (lines 19–20). She seems a fairly "typical" grandma in appearance — clearly she's not looking for a fight — yet her simple "Let me help you" followed by a well-aimed punch teaches the speaker more about toughness than he learned through an entire alley's worth of vandalism.

POSSIBLE CONNECTION TO ANOTHER SELECTION

Sharon Olds, "Rite of Passage" (text p. 627)

MITSUYE YAMADA, *A Bedtime Story* (p. 634)

Irony is this poem's most striking feature. A father tells his child an ancient story from his culture (we presume), and his daughter, the speaker, is unable to understand the story's message. To figure out the speaker's inability to grasp this message, we must look into the way the story is framed. At the beginning of the poem, the time is nonspecific; the father begins his story as many stories begin: "Once upon a time" (line

1). At the end of the story, the speaker describes where the story is told, "In the comfort of our / hilltop home in Seattle / overlooking the valley" (40–42). This tension between the timeless and the present indicate a gap between father and daughter that goes beyond a typical generation gap. The daughter cannot grasp the moral of her father's story because she is safe and comfortable, and, presumably, privileged. The irony is that she cannot identify with the woman in the story who is turned away from houses in town, identifying instead with the townspeople who turn the old woman away. The speaker can no more see the message of the story than the people in that town can see the beauty of the moon. As readers of the poem, we are put in a similar position: what are we to take away from the story, frame-tale and all? Do students identify with the daughter (who wants a fuller story with a more exciting plot), with the father (who wants to pass on a piece of his culture), with both, with neither, or with the woman in the story? One way to enter such a discussion is to ask students how they read the poem's tone; is it meant to be humorous or instructive? Compare the poem's tone with that of the legend recounted.

POSSIBLE CONNECTIONS TO OTHER SELECTIONS

Julia Alvarez, "Woman's Work" (text p. 986)

Margaret Atwood, "Bored" (text p. 613)

Jimmy Santiago Baca, "Green Chile" (text p. 1274)

DRAMA

LORRAINE HANSBERRY, *A Raisin in the Sun* (p. 635)

Like the characters in Williams's and Miller's plays, the members of the Younger family in Hansberry's play are caught up in their dreams of a better future. However, their situation is complicated by the fact that they are an African American family living in a racist society. At first, a life insurance check seems to promise the answer to their dreams, but as they come to understand that they have conflicting ambitions, they must struggle to find a way to move into the future as a family without sacrificing their individual goals.

As you teach this play, you might compare it to other selections in this chapter. Which works have similar conflicts or themes? To what degree is this a play about family, and to what degree is it a play about race? Is it possible, or even desirable, to separate these two issues in this case?

How important is the American Dream to this play? Do your students agree with Walter that the American Dream essentially boils down to the attitude that "there ain't nothing but taking in this world, and he who takes most is smartest — and it don't make a damn bit of difference *how*" (Act III)? How critical are your students of Walter's willingness to achieve financial success at the cost of being "dead inside" (to use Mama's phrase)? Do these two attitudes represent a generational difference or just a personal one?

POSSIBLE CONNECTIONS TO OTHER SELECTIONS

Arthur Miller, *Death of a Salesman* (text p. 1007)

Tennessee Williams, *The Glass Menagerie* (text p. 448)

RESOURCES FOR TEACHING

> **A Raisin in the Sun.** 128 min., b/w, 1961. Beta, VHS. With Sidney Poitier, Claudia McNeil, and Ruby Dee. Directed by Daniel Petrie. See local retailer. Available for rental from member institutions of the Consortium of College and University Media Centers.

A Raisin in the Sun. 171 min., color, 1989. Beta, VHS. With Danny Glover, Esther Rolle, and Starletta DuPois. Directed by Bill Duke. An "American Playhouse," made-for-television production. See local retailer.

A Raisin in the Sun [recording]. 2 cassettes, 2 hr., 21 min. Dramatization performed by Ossie Davis and Ruby Dee. Distributed by Caedmon/HarperAudio.

Black Theatre Movement from A Raisin in the Sun to the Present. 130 min., color, 1979, 16-mm film. Traces the Black Theatre Movement from its roots in Hansberry's play to the current black plays and musicals on Broadway. Includes interviews with performers, writers, and directors, as well as footage from plays and theatre pieces from around the country. Available for rental from member institutions of the Consortium of College and University Media Centers.

Lorraine Hansberry: The Black Experience in the Creation of Drama. 35 min., color, 1975. Beta, VHS, 3/4" U-matic cassette. With Sidney Poitier, Ruby Dee, and Al Freeman, Jr. Narrated by Claudia McNeil. A profile of the playwright's life and work. Distributed by Films for the Humanities and Sciences.

Lorraine Hansberry Speaks Out: Art and the Black Revolution [recording]. 1 cassette. By Lorraine Hansberry, edited by Robert Nemiroff. Distributed by Caedmon/HarperAudio.

To Be Young, Gifted, and Black. 90 min., color, 1981. Beta, VHS 1/2" open reel (EIAJ), 3/4" U-matic cassette, 16-mm film. With Ruby Dee, Al Freeman, Jr., Claudia McNeil, Barbara Barrie, Lauren Jones, Roy Scheider, and Blythe Danner. A play about the life of Lorraine Hansberry. Distributed by Monterey Home Video. Available for rental from member institutions of the Consortium of College and University Media Centers.

HENRIK IBSEN, *A Doll House* (p. 700)

In the final scene of this play, just before Nora walks out on Helmer, he instructs her that she is "before all else . . . a wife and mother." Ever since the play was first performed in 1879, Nora's reply has inspired feminists: "I don't believe in that any more. I believe that, before all else, I'm a human being, no less than you — or anyway, that I ought to try to become one." As a social problem play, *A Doll House* dramatizes Nora's growth from Helmer's little pet and doll to an autonomous adult who refuses to obey rules imposed on her by a male-dominated society.

Ibsen, however, preferred to see Nora's decision in a larger context. In a speech before a Norwegian women's rights group that honored him in 1898, he insisted that

> I have been more of a poet and less of a social philosopher than most people have been inclined to think. I am grateful for your toast, but I can't claim the honor of ever having worked consciously for women's rights. I'm not even sure what women's rights are. To me it has seemed a matter of human rights.

Ibsen is being more than simply coy here. He conceives of Nora's problems in broad human terms, not in polemical reformist ones. The play invites both readings, and students should be encouraged to keep each in focus.

Ibsen deliberately leaves the ending of the play ambiguous. Undeniably, Nora leaves her family, but she allows Torvald the slight hope that "the greatest miracle of all" might occur and they could have a "true marriage" (Act III). The play's last lines are delivered by Torvald, who hopefully repeats her phrase, "The greatest miracle —?" In contrast, the final stage direction is "the sound of a door slamming shut" (Act III). Ask your students how they interpret this ending. If they were directing this play, would they emphasize Torvald's question or Nora's slam? As a creative writing exercise, you might have your students write an additional scene in which they depict Nora's future. Does she return to her family? Does she ever see her husband and children again? Is she happy?

TIPS FROM THE FIELD

When I teach *A Doll House*, I have students choose a character from the play. You may find it best to assign a group of three or four students to each of the main characters and have the remaining students assume the roles of the children and the nanny. You might also want one or two students to assume the role of Ibsen. At the following class, I group the students together by role and have them discuss their character. I also have them prepare at least one question directed toward another character about any aspect of the play. The class then comes together in a circle with everyone wearing a name tag of their character. Discussion follows with all students "in character" for the rest of the class meeting.

— CATHERINE RUSCO, *Muskegon Community College*

After they read Ibsen's *A Doll House*, I have my students write an entry in Nora's diary. They may choose to date the entry before, during, or after the action of the play takes place. My students especially enjoy tracing Nora's thought process as she decides whether or not she should abandon her children.

— ELIZABETH KLEINFELD, *Red Rocks Community College*

CONSIDERATIONS FOR CRITICAL THINKING AND WRITING (p. 747)

1. The title points to the Helmers' unreal domestic arrangement. Nora chooses to stop this game when she realizes that she can no longer play her assigned role.

2. Nora lies about trivial matters, such as the macaroons, and she deceives her husband about the source of the money that helped restore him to health, but these lies are not to be seen as moral lapses because the trivial lies are inconsequential and her deception about the money is selfless. What is significant is that Nora's *life* is a lie because Helmer has no real idea who she is as a human being.

3. Helmer expects Nora to be a submissive helpmate who leaves all the important matters to the man of the house. He treats her more like a child than a wife. His affectionate terms for her are condescending, perhaps even dehumanizing.

4. The confident expectations of security and happiness that Nora has expressed to Mrs. Linde have been miserably deflated by the end of Act I. Nora worries that Helmer will regard her with the same contempt he heaps on Krogstad, and worse, she fears that her husband will judge her to be a destructive influence on their children. The Christmas tree — a symbol of domestic well-being and happiness in Act I — is stripped and ragged at the beginning of Act II, when Nora's world is threatened by both Krogstad's possible betrayal and Helmer's possible harsh judgment. Other symbols include Nora's desperately wild dance, Dr. Rank's fatal illness (the sins of the fathers), and Nora's removal of her masquerade costume as she moves closer to the truth of her circumstances.

5. Although Dr. Rank's characterization has been referred to as unimportant because he is not directly related to advancing the plot, his interest in talking with Nora and understanding her character provides a contrast with Helmer's behavior. Moreover, like Nora, Dr. Rank has been adversely affected by his father's corruption.

6. Krogstad and Mrs. Linde are reunited in what appears to be an honest, lasting relationship just as the Helmers are splitting up.

7. Krogstad's decision not to expose Nora's secret is motivated by his love for Mrs. Linde. Many readers find this abrupt romantic reconstruction of his character unconvincing.

8. Nora rejects Helmer's attempts to start over because she realizes that she's never been truly happy as his "doll-wife." Helmer's character is to some degree sympathetic if only because he is thoroughly bewildered and incapable of understanding the transformation his little "squirrel" has undergone.

9. We don't know what will become of Nora after she leaves her husband. Although she arrives at a mature understanding of herself as an adult woman, that recognition shatters the pattern of her life and forces her to confront her new freedom on her own. Even if we imagine her as fulfilled and happy in the future, her life at the close of the play takes on tragic proportions because she is thrown completely back on herself. A discussion of this topic will help bring students to the heart of the play.

10. This alternate ending is a "barbaric outrage" because it undercuts the seriousness of Nora's plight and the significance of her discovery about her life. Moreover, it represents a calculated sentimentalization of the issues raised in the play.

11. Ibsen proposes no solutions to the problems he depicts concerning Nora's individualism and the repressive social conventions and responsibilities she rejects. If we imagine the inclusion of solutions, we can also imagine the play turning oppressively didactic. Ibsen knew what he was doing in leaving the solutions to his audience.

12. The play certainly reflects the kinds of problems we might encounter in our everyday lives. The characters look and sound real. Less true to life are Krogstad's transformation from villain to generous lover, the two forgeries, and the fairly obvious use of symbols such as the Christmas tree and Nora's dance.

POSSIBLE CONNECTIONS TO OTHER SELECTIONS

Susan Glaspell, *Trifles* (text p. 496)
Gail Godwin, "A Sorrowful Woman" (text p. 189)
William Shakespeare, *Hamlet, Prince of Denmark* (text p. 345)
_____. *A Midsummer Night's Dream* (text p. 852)
Sophocles, *Oedipus the King* (text p. 293)

RESOURCES FOR TEACHING

A Doll's House. 89 min., b/w, 1959. Beta, VHS, ³/₄″ U-matic cassette. With Julie Harris, Christopher Plummer, Jason Robards, Hume Cronyn, Eileen Heckart, and Richard Thomas. An original television production. See local retailer.

A Doll's House. 98 min., color, 1973. VHS, 16-mm film. With Jane Fonda, Edward Fox, Trevor Howard, and David Warner. Screenplay by Christopher Hampton. Video: see local retailer. Distributed by Prism Entertainment. Available for rental from member institutions of the Consortium of College and University Media Centers.

A Doll's House. 39 min., color, 1977. Beta, VHS, ³/₄″ U-matic cassette. With Claire Bloom. Distributed by AIMS Multimedia.

A Doll's House. 96 min., color, 1989. Beta, VHS. With Claire Bloom, Anthony Hopkins, Ralph Richardson, Denholm Elliott, Anna Massey, and Edith Evans. Directed by Patrick Garland. Distributed by Hemdale Home Video.

A Doll's House [recording]. 3 cassettes (180 min.), 1993. Read by Flo Gibson. Distributed by Audio Book Contractors.

A **Doll's House** [recording]. 3 cassettes. Translated by Christopher Hampton. Dramatization performed by Claire Bloom and Donald Madden. Distributed by Caedmon/HarperAudio.

A **Doll's House, Part I.** 34 min., color, 1968. Beta, VHS, ¾" U-matic cassette, 16-mm film. "The Destruction of Illusion." Norris Houghton discusses the subsurface tensions that make up the play. Distributed by Britannica Films. Available for rental from member institutions of the Consortium of College and University Media Centers.

A **Doll's House, Part II.** 29 min., color, 1968. Beta, VHS, ¾" U-matic cassette, 16-mm film. "Ibsen's Themes." Norris Houghton examines the cast of characters and the themes in the play. Distributed by Britannica Films. Available for rental from member institutions of the Consortium of College and University Media Centers.

Ibsen's Life and Times, Part I: Youth and Self-Imposed Exile. 28 min., color. VHS. The conflict between individual and society is illustrated in scenes from *Ghosts,* featuring Beatrice Straight as Mrs. Alving. Includes a biographical segment on the playwright. Distributed by Insight Media.

Ibsen's Life and Times, Part II: The Later Years. 24 min., color. VHS. Includes scenes from *The Master Builder* and *Lady from the Sea,* emphasizing the realism in Ibsen's plays. A biographical segment includes on-location footage. Distributed by Insight Media.

ESSAYS

FREDERICK DOUGLASS, *"A Slave's Family Life"* (p. 749)

Students usually respond powerfully to this essay that illustrates the incompatibility of family life and the institution of slavery. Douglass's opening paragraphs about his parentage are particularly painful. He describes seeing his mother only a few times before she died, a death that felt to him like "the death of a stranger" (p. 750). Perhaps more disturbing is Douglass's discussion of his father, whom he never knew, but whom rumors ascribed to be his mother's master. Douglass writes almost matter-of-factly about the common practice of white masters fathering children with their slaves, resulting in the unnatural situation of a man forced to choose between selling his own children or "whip[ping] them himself." So perverted are natural family relationships under slavery that often "one white son [of a slave owner must] tie up his brother, of but a few shades darker than himself, and ply the gory lash to his naked back" (p. 750). You might begin teaching this essay by asking your students how the concepts of home and family must be different under slavery than under any other circumstances.

Douglass's description of his cruel master and that master's treatment of his Aunt Hester are particularly graphic, and students may want to discuss the way Douglass's vivid descriptions show the reality of torture endured by slaves. You might address the fact that not all slave owners were so abusive. This selection is a good opportunity to discuss the terrible implications of being owned by another human being, regardless of how that human being treats his "property." Although the circumstances are different, ask your students to consider the situation of Nora in *A Doll House* as a comparison. In some ways she is like the well-treated slave, working to entertain and please her husband, who is kind to her but who cannot see her as a complete human being. Do your students think this is a valid comparison? They may point out (rightly) that though Nora can and does exercise her choice to leave Torvald, a slave obviously lacks that option.

Consider Douglass's audience as you discuss this essay. He is writing to convince his mainly white readers about the evils of slavery in order to inspire reaction against the institution. In light of this audience and purpose, ask students why Douglass chose to address the issues and incidents he does. Which ones are most effective and why?

POSSIBLE CONNECTION TO ANOTHER SELECTION

Henrik Ibsen, *A Doll House* (text p. 700)

BARBARA KINGSOLVER, *Stone Soup* (p. 752)

Note the date of this essay's original publication: 1995. Point out to your students that the 1990s were a decade of redefining, embracing, and manipulating the concept of "family" for personal, political, and religious reasons. In this essay, Barbara Kingsolver adds her voice to the debate and argues for broadening the definitions of *home* and *family* to reflect the realities of contemporary life. Before they read this essay, you might ask your students to write a brief essay in class in which they define and give examples of the term *family*. When they have finished reading and discussing Kingsolver's essay, they could compare and contrast their own definitions of *family* with hers. This short assignment could be expanded and revised into a more formal essay.

Kingsolver uses a number of examples, outside sources, and extended metaphors to make her argument. Examine the way this anecdotal and statistical "evidence" works to create a writer's voice that is at once personal and objective. Look at Kingsolver's use of symbolism and metaphor. Do your students recognize the power of the "Family of Dolls" in shaping one's expectations of family life? How does Kingsolver substitute the idea of "Stone Soup" for the "Family of Dolls"? Which metaphor do your students think better represents the contemporary American family? Do they celebrate the change in the traditional family make-up as Kingsolver does, or do they mourn it? How has their own experience with family informed their reading of this text?

Kingsolver's methods of argument could be usefully compared with other arguments in this anthology (see "Possible Connections," below). How do these different arguments compare with one another in their approach, voice, and use of outside sources and examples?

POSSIBLE CONNECTIONS TO OTHER SELECTIONS

Linda Chavez, "Demistifying Multiculturalism" (text p. 546)
K. C. Cole, "Calculated Risks" (text p. 538)
Frederick Douglass, "A Slave's Family Life" (text p. 749)
Jonathan Swift, "A Modest Proposal" (text p. 516)

WRITING IN PROCESS: FEMINIST ANALYSIS

For students (and teachers) who enjoyed Ibsen's *A Doll House*, this student casebook will provide more readings for discussion and a student essay that demonstrates how critical strategies can be used to shed light on the controversial aspects of a work of literature. Have students read the casebook's readings, all of which provide additional contexts for the play. The letter by Marcus Ulrike may be of particular interest to students who question why Nora's decision to leave her family was so controversial. Ask students if they think Ulrike and his wife appear to be real-life parallels to Torvald and Nora. Are your students surprised by the conditions of Ulrike's letter? The casebook's student writer, Kathy Atner, reads Ibsen's play through a feminist lens. If your students primarily see Ibsen's play in terms of feminism, they may find the chapter's other theoretical approaches enlightening, a good reminder that rich works of literature can be read on many levels. Kathy's own essay is a good example of how a student can move from a strong first response to a measured argument. Her comments that *A Doll House* is "obviously about women's rights!" (p. 769) is not supported or thought out in her early notes and writings, but her strong belief in this thesis leads her to seek support for her ideas within the play and in external sources. This is a good model of the writing process.

ALTERNATIVE ASSIGNMENTS

1. Kathy Atner's paper is a good example of the way feminist and historical criticism can be combined to support a thesis about a work of literature. This assignment asks you to combine two approaches in a similar way, but this time use Ulrike's letter in connection to Marxist criticism, specifically the entry by Witham and Lutterbie in the casebook. After writing a first response, write a paper in which you analyze *A Doll House* in light of those sources. Here are some questions to consider as you brainstorm to generate a thesis: What kinds of assumptions about class does Ulrike make in his letter to his wife? How does the presence of servants in the play (and in Ulrike's letter) affect the lives of the characters and outcome of the drama? Do you agree with Witham and Lutterbie that "financial enslavement is symptomatic of other forms of enslavement" (p. 763)? Finally, how essential is a Marxist approach to a thorough understanding of the play?

2. Consider *A Doll House* in a different historical context — that of today. After a careful examination of the play, write an essay in which you argue whether the play's problems — about money, women's rights, honesty, or personal freedom — are relevant to our time. Would it be possible to stage this play in a contemporary setting? As you write your essay, include examples both from the play and from contemporary life. Newspaper articles and current events are good sources to support your discussion of life today.

10

Love and Its Complications

Most of your students do not have to be told that love is complicated, but this chapter will convince even the most devoted romantics of that fact. Students, even those with little or no romantic experience themselves, have certainly been exposed to ideas and myths of romantic love through television, books, movies, and magazines. Before beginning this chapter, you might assign Chapter 5's student casebook, which compares and contrasts an excerpt from a romance novel with a more complicated story by Gail Godwin. Keep the conventions of romance in mind as you work your way through Chapter 10. To what degree do the authors in your text defy or surrender to the expectations of romance?

The chapter contains a number of works in which characters manipulate the idea of romance for selfish and even dangerous purposes, such as those in Flannery O'Connor's "Good Country People" and Robert Browning's "My Last Duchess." Other characters, such as those in David Ives's *Sure Thing* and William Shakespeare's *A Midsummer Night's Dream,* are struggling more honestly to find happiness in love despite communication difficulties and other obstacles. Deborah Tannen's essay "Sex, Lies, and Conversation" takes up the issue of communication more directly as she argues for better understanding about the ways men and women speak to one another. Other selections in the chapter — such as Susan Minot's "Lust," Emily Dickinson's "Wild Nights — Wild Nights!," John Donne's "The Flea,"and Sharon Olds's "Sex Without Love" — address the way sexual desire can complicate or enhance love.

Regardless of their own experience with romantic love, most of your students probably have an ideal in mind (you might have them write about this early on). How do they reconcile the type of love they are reading about with this ideal? Which authors come closest for them? The chapter proves a wide selection range of possibilities for heterosexual love.

FICTION

ANTON CHEKHOV, *The Lady with the Pet Dog* (p. 776)

The story is told from Gurov's point of view, which Chekhov refuses to comment on, morally or otherwise. His aim is simply to portray Gurov as accurately as he can; here is a man who does certain things, feels certain feelings, and so on. It is by this constant exposure to Gurov's thoughts and actions that we get to know, and eventually care about, the protagonist. Initially, he is not a sympathetic character; he speaks ill of his wife and of women in general. He considers women inferior because of "bitter experience" with them (paragraph 5), but later thoughts reveal that it is he who has treated them badly. For evidence of this, direct the class to paragraph 28: "From the past he preserved the memory of carefree, good-natured women whom love made gay and who were grateful to him for the happiness he gave them . . . and of women like his wife who loved without sincerity . . . and of very beautiful, frigid women, across whose faces would suddenly flit a rapacious expression — an obstinate desire to take more from life than it could give . . .

and when Gurov grew cold to them their beauty aroused his hatred, and the lace on their lingerie seemed to him to resemble scales."

The fact is that he is afraid of women, afraid of their power over him. (See the end of paragraph 5: "Some force seemed to draw him to them [the women], too.") Gurov calls women inferior to empower himself against them, so that he can control them, instead of the other way around. Yalta's atmosphere, which is deceptively festive, is the perfect place for Gurov to play his games with women and himself. It is a resort town, a place people visit for vacations, or as in Anna's case, to escape their daily lives. Since everyone is there on a temporary basis, nothing that happens there is permanent or matters in the "real" world to which the vacationers must all eventually return.

Chekhov sticks to Gurov's consciousness so closely that while we may or may not sympathize with him, we cannot help but begin to understand him. For instance, many readers will not be kindly disposed to Gurov when he becomes annoyed by Anna's distressed reaction to committing adultery (37), but even then we can comprehend what is going on in his mind. (All the other women he has had affairs with were old hands at the game; he is not used to a woman like Anna, who is genuinely disturbed by what she has done.) But in the story's third section, we see Gurov changing; he realizes that Anna is different (63), that he is unable to forget her the way he forgot the others, and that she is "the only happiness that he now desired for himself" (84). Finally, he realizes that "only now when his head was gray he had fallen in love, really, truly — for the first time in his life" (115). If the story had been told from Anna's perspective, we would miss the crucial insights and transitions Gurov experiences in the last two sections.

Chekhov's objectivity makes it possible for us to understand Gurov and Anna; his presentation of his characters is so compassionate it is clear he sympathizes with them and their situation. This is not to say he condones their actions; he is simply able to see (and to make us see) how this relationship has come about and why these characters behave the way they do. Both married young, perhaps too young to know any better, and apparently neither of their marriages is based on love. This information helps explain the characters' motivations as well as their plight at the end of the story. Living in a society where divorce was not considered an acceptable alternative, and having recognized their love for each other as too powerful to deny, they can have no resolution to this conflict. For as long as Anna and Gurov love each other, life will remain "complicated and difficult."

POSSIBLE CONNECTION TO ANOTHER SELECTION

Fay Weldon, "IND AFF, or Out of Love in Sarajevo" (text p. 817)

RESOUCES FOR TEACHING

Anton Chekhov: A Writer's Life. 37 min., color and b/w, 1974. Beta, VHS, ³/₄″ U-matic cassette, 16-mm film. A biographical portrait of the writer. Distributed by Films for the Humanities and Sciences.

Gielgud's Chekhov. 52 min., color, 1981. Beta, VHS. Three programs: (1) "The Fugitive," "Desire for Sleep," and "Rothschild's Violin"; (2) "Volodya" and "The Boarding House"; (3) "Revenge" and "The Wallet." Distributed by Mastervision.

The Lady with the Pet Dog. 86 min., b/w, 1960. Beta, VHS. In Russian, with English subtitles. Distributed by Facets Multimedia.

LOUISE ERDRICH, *I'm a Mad Dog Biting Myself for Sympathy,* (p. 788)

This may seem an odd selection for a chapter titled "Love and Its Complications," so consider asking your students what the story says about love. You might begin by noting that the speaker's crime spree starts from an innocent wish to purchase a Christmas gift for his girlfriend, Dawn. A close reading reveals that at the beginning of the story the narrator describes himself as "almost rehabilitated," implying that he had been in some kind of trouble in the past. His girlfriend's name, Dawn, connotes a new day or a new beginning, something the narrator was presumably looking forward to before he steals the toucan. Examine the brief references to the narrator's relationship with Dawn. Ask your students what they think is significant about the fact that the narrator wishes he had been to a country fair with Dawn. What kind of couple is implied in the image of a man winning stuffed animals for his girlfriend at the fair? Contrast that implied couple with one in which the stuffed animal is stolen by the man at a Walgreens in Fargo. Like many characters in this chapter, this narrator is trapped by the disparity between ideal romance and real life.

As you discuss the story, note the humorous tone. How does Erdrich make the reader laugh at and with the narrator even as we wince at his stupidity and callousness? How does the tone of the story's final paragraphs differ from that of the rest of the story? How much self-awareness does the narrator have? What do we see as readers that the narrator does not see about himself? As you teach this story ask your students what they think about the narrator's assessment that "people will leave you, no matter what you say" (p. 792). Does that statement hold true for other texts in this chapter?

POSSIBLE CONNECTION TO ANOTHER SELECTION

Bharati Mukherjee, "A Father" (text p. 585)

DAGOBERTO GILB, *Love in L.A.* (p. 793)

"Love in L.A." might be interpreted as "California Dreamin'." Set in the shadow of the Hollywood Freeway, it is all about pretending to be someone different and attempting to attract an audience. Although Jake drives a '58 Buick (without insurance), he dreams of "something better": a "crushed velvet interior with electric controls for the L.A. summer, a nice warm heater and defroster for the winter drives at the beach, a cruise control for those longer trips, mellow speakers front and rear of course, windows that hum closed, snuffing out that nasty exterior noise of freeways" (paragraph 1). Given the centrality of cars and freeways in southern California, this is an apt metaphor for the kind of life of wealth and status that Jake would like to lead, the person he'd be if only the reality of his situation lived up to his imagination. Instead of sitting in "a clot of near motionless traffic" (1), he'd be cruising through life. Tellingly, the "green light" (2) of his imagination is more real than the actual traffic in front of him. Lost in his fantasy, he rear-ends the car ahead of him.

Jake is conscious of "performance" throughout his encounter with Mariana. He stalls for time while he prepares lines based on both his inability (and unwillingness) to make financial reparation and his attraction to her. He also considers at least two options for escaping the situation. Students can deduce from this significant information about his character that Jake is not the upstanding individual he appears to be at the start of his conversation with Mariana. Jake's performance is further undermined by the information that emphasizes Jake's scam in action. For instance, Jake tells Mariana, "I really am sorry about hitting you like that" (12), but the text following this ("he sounded genuine" [12]) implies that he is trying to pull some sort of scam. His deception becomes more obvious throughout the exchange. After acting sincere, Jake "exaggerated greatly" (20) about his lack of identification and his vocation as a musician; later, "he lied" about whether he had insurance (28). He might think he's been convincing ("back in his car he took a moment or two to feel both proud and sad about his performance" [38]). Ask students to consider whether or not Jake feels guilty for his deceitful actions. Exactly what might he feel sad about?

Ask students to characterize the cars featured in "Love in L.A." Jake's aging Buick is big and sturdy and mechanically reliable, and he regards its lack of nicks or dents as "one of his few clearcut accomplishments over the years" (3). Mariana's car is a newer Toyota with Florida plates. As Jake puts it, these cars are "so soft they might replace waterbeds soon" (12). There are unmistakable parallels between the cars and their owners' personalities. Jake dresses in "less than new but not unhip clothes" (6), and while he appears to be having a conversation about the damage to Mariana's car, he's really more interested in whether he can get her into bed. It's no accident that while Jake talks, he "fondle[s] the wide dimple" (12) in Mariana's (car's) rear end.

Although he seems to think he won over Mariana because she gives him her phone number, the final paragraph reveals that she hasn't been influenced by his act. It won't do her any good to trace the license number that she copies off the plate on his car, but then, he's not going to drive off thinking that his deception worked. In fact, one could argue that each character has attempted to scam the other. Jake plays his "genuine" act to escape from responsibility, while Mariana may have relied on her beauty in order to coerce him into giving her the information she needs. Neither character will be satisfied. Love, in this story, is less about genuine affection and attraction than it is about running (and deflecting) a scam. Ultimately, Jack is yet another kind of used-car salesman, and his encounter with Mariana will be only another hit-and-run statistic.

POSSIBLE CONNECTION TO ANOTHER SELECTION

Tennessee Williams, *The Glass Managerie* (text p. 448)

SUSAN MINOT, *Lust* (p. 796)

Beginning their study of this story, students might look up the meaning of "lust" in the dictionary. Definitions of the term range from "pleasure, delight" to "intense sexual desire: lasciviousness." Ask the students whether these denotations really apply to Minot's story. (They might wonder *whose* lust is referred to here.) Though they might initially be overwhelmed by the numerous sexual encounters described by the narrator, they should examine in particular the narrator's selection of metaphors and similes to come to some conclusions about the meaning of the story. Studying the narrator's analogies, readers become aware of the irony inherent in the title.

Trace the narrator's references to her encounters throughout the story. Describing her initial sexual experience, she claims that she "flipped" (paragraph 1), implying a certain exhilaration about discovering her sexuality. Being sexually active is for her a way of asserting her independence and maturity, particularly when she compares herself to her mother: the narrator "kept the dial [of birth control pills] in my top drawer like my mother and thought of her each time I tipped out the yellow tablets in the morning before chapel" (31). However, her sexual experiences don't enhance her self-confidence; rather, they steadily diminish her. She later tells us that during and after sex, she felt like "a body waiting on the rug" (6), that she was "filled absolutely with air, or with a sadness that wouldn't stop" (28). Elsewhere, she tells us, "you wonder how long you can keep it up. You begin to feel as if you're showing through, like a bathroom window that only lets in grey light, the kind you can't see out of" (64). In many of her analogies, she compares herself to a piece of meat (recalling derogatory terms for the body): "Then you start to get tired. You begin to feel diluted, like watered-down stew" (44); "you wonder about things feeling a little off-kilter. You begin to feel like a piece of pounded veal" (72); "after sex, you curl up like a shrimp, something deep inside you ruined, slammed in a place that sickens at slamming, and slowly you fill up with an overwhelming sadness, an elusive gaping worry" (79). It's evident that the narrator's encounters with these young men increasingly make her feel more like an object than a person. It is significant that she is an unnamed narrator, that none of her partners (not lovers) ever calls her by her name. The structure of the story, fragmented by her experiences with different men, also illustrates her fragmentation of self.

In addition to revealing her personal feelings through her analogies, the narrator provides some sense of the larger, cultural assumptions about gender. She asserts that there are different "rules" of behavior for young men and young women: "The more girls a boy has, the better. He has a bright look, having reaped fruits, blooming. He stalks around, sure-shouldered, and you have the feeling he's got more in him, a fatter heart, more stories to tell. For a girl, with each boy it's as though a petal gets plucked each time" (43). You may want to ask students to compare the language of these descriptions, and examine the description in paragraph 48. Here, the narrator explains the typical roles for boys and girls:

> On weekends they play touch football while we sit on the sidelines, picking blades of grass to chew on, and watch. We're always watching them run around. We shiver in the stands, knocking our boots together to keep our toes warm, and they whizz across the ice, chopping their sticks around the puck. When they're in the rink, they refuse to look at you, only eyeing each other beneath low helmets. You cheer for them, but they don't look up, even if it's a face-off when nothing's happening, even if they're doing drills before any game has started at all.

In other words, men are those who act; women are those who observe. Men have the authority in their interaction with women. The narrator describes the way her partners take the initiative: " 'come here,' he says on the porch. . . . He kisses my palm then directs my hand to his fly" (12–15); they focus on their own needs and interests rather than on hers: ". . . trying to be reasonable, in a regular voice, 'Listen I just want to have a good time.' So I'd go because I couldn't think of something to say back that wouldn't be obvious, and if you go out with them, you sort of have to do something" (25–26). The narrator uses words such as "surrender" (28) to describe the way she feels about these encounters. She doesn't demonstrate any sense of personal authority in dealing with men: "I thought the worst thing anyone could call you was a cock-teaser. So, if you flirted, you had to be prepared to go through with it" (38). The one time she tries to achieve more of a relationship with the boy she's sleeping with, his response is " 'What the hell are you talking about?' " (60). Ask students to explain the irony in the narrator's comment, "I hate those girls who push away a boy's face as if she were made out of Ivory soap, as if she's that much greater than he is" (68).

Students might discuss the way the girls in this story interact with each other. What are their value systems? We get two glimpses of the narrator with her friends Giddy and Jill. In the first, the other girls cannot imagine that the narrator is unhappy, because she "always [has] a boyfriend" (36). (Students might explain the narrator's reaction to her friends' comments here.) In the second, all three are talking with the housemother, Mrs. Gunther, whose own life history doesn't promise anything more for these young women. Having married her first boyfriend (because she was pregnant, we wonder?), she affirms for Jill, Giddy, and the narrator the passiveness of women and the centrality of male attention. Students might discuss the circumstances of the narrator's school and family life — there are certainly very few adults who seem aware of her experiences or their ramifications. In this predominantly upper-class setting, in which the narrator and her companions attend prep schools, go on ski trips, and stay at family apartments and summer houses, there is surprisingly little positive, constructive interaction with adults. The few adults who take notice of her sexual activity — the school doctor, Mrs. Gunther, the headmaster — never offer her any constructive alternative choices.

In connection with "Lust," students might consider whether the narrator's assertions about the gender roles described in Minot's story reflect their experience. In this context, it might be useful to discuss the roles of male and female characters in popular fairy tales. Compare, for instance, the roles of Prince Charming and the Sleeping Beauty, or even those of the characters in "Little Red Riding Hood." Can students think of a fairy tale in which the female character takes an authoritative stance? Two excellent essays on the subject might be relevant to such a discussion: Marcia K. Lieberman's " 'Some Day My Prince Will Come': Female Acculturation through the Fairy Tale," and Karen E. Rowe's "Feminism and Fairy Tales," both reprinted in Jack Zipes's *Don't Bet on the Prince: Contemporary Feminist Fairy Tales in North America and England* (Methuen, 1986).

Minot's story also seems relevant to recent studies about Mary Pipher's *Reviving Ophelia* and other studies about girls' loss of confidence during their teenage years. Significantly, the narrator tells us, "I could do some things well. Some things I was good at, like math or painting or even sports, but the second a boy put his arm around me, I forgot about wanting to do anything else, which felt like a relief at first until it became like sinking into a muck" (19).

POSSIBLE CONNECTIONS TO OTHER SELECTIONS

Alice Munro, "An Ounce of Cure" (text p. 593)
David Updike, "Summer" (text p. 47)

FLANNERY O'CONNOR, *Good Country People* (p. 803)

The central conflict in this story is between Hulga, who believes herself to be vastly superior to everyone around her, and the Bible salesman, Manley Pointer, whom Hulga and her mother at first take to be simple, naive, "good country people." Hulga wants to seduce Pointer to shatter his alleged innocence, both physical and spiritual. She wants him to believe in nothing, as she does. Her initial impulse is meanspirited, but even her first thoughts of seducing him include a fantasy of being with him once she has enlightened him about her version of the truth. "She imagined that she took his remorse in hand and changed it into a deeper understanding of life. She took all his shame away and turned it into something useful" (paragraph 91). Despite her façade of nastiness, which she uses as a sort of defense mechanism, Hulga really does want warmth, respect, admiration, and even love. She begins to recognize these feelings in herself, ironically, as Pointer is convincing her to show him her artificial leg. She is moved by what she perceives to be his innocence, which has enabled him (she thinks) to see the truth about her: that she "ain't like anybody else" (128).

But the joke is on Hulga. No sooner does Pointer get his hands on her leg than all his apparent innocence and tenderness disappear. It was the leg he wanted all along, for his collection; the sexual activity would have been a nice fringe benefit, but he is perfectly willing to leave without it. When Hulga asks him, in paragraph 136, "aren't you just good country people?" she is, ironically, clinging to the very values that she previously denounced and satirized. She is forced to acknowledge that civility and common decency (which Pointer has flouted by taking her leg) do matter. She has been deceiving herself by pretending that these things are dispensable, that she does not need affection, and that she does not believe in, or need to believe in, anything. It has taken someone more cynical and evil than herself to make her aware of the truth.

Hulga now realizes that, compared with Pointer, she is the innocent one. O'Connor's suggestion is that Hulga will soon get the same message we do from Pointer's last words: the result of "believing in nothing" is the kind of depravity of spirit Pointer exhibits, and if she wants to save herself from that she'd better start believing.

Hulga's two names represent her inner conflict between everything she is and everything she is repressing. The name "Joy," of course, is just another of her mother's empty clichés, so she changes it to Hulga (which suggests some combination of the words *ugly, huge,* and *hulk.* By denying the "nice" name her mother gave her, she can deny the "niceness" in herself. She can, in fact, create a new self: hostile, angry, and abusive — all to hide the pain she feels because of what she is repressing. Mrs. Hopewell's name emphasizes the shallowness of her beliefs that "nothing is perfect" (11) and that "people who looked on the bright side of things would be beautiful even if they were not" (17).

And Mrs. Freeman's name suggests that she is free in a way that both Joy and her mother are not.

Mrs. Freeman sees through Hulga as her mother can't; direct the class to paragraph 16, where we learn that Mrs. Freeman calls the girl "Hulga" rather than "Joy." "Mrs. Freeman's relish for using the name only irritated [Hulga]. It was as if Mrs. Freeman's beady steel-pointed eyes had penetrated far enough behind her face to reach some secret fact." This secret fact is that, as the author says "there is a wooden part of [Hulga's] soul that corresponds to her wooden leg." Mrs. Freeman's statement at the story's end, "Some can't be that simple," suggests that she has seen through the Bible salesman as well. That Mrs. Hopewell repeatedly refers to Mrs. Freeman with condescension as "good country people" becomes increasingly ironic in light of the fact that Mrs. Freeman is much smarter and a much better judge of human nature than either her employer or her employer's daughter.

The older women are introduced before Hulga so that her character can be developed in relation to theirs. By the time Hulga appears, we are as alienated by her mother's insipid thoughts and conversation as Hulga is, so we can empathize with the girl somewhat. The last two paragraphs of the story depict an unchanged, vapidly optimistic Mrs. Hopewell, who knows nothing of what has gone on between Hulga and Pointer in the barn. Her cheerful ignorance contrasts sharply with Hulga's "churning face" and emotions in the preceding paragraph; it is Mrs. Hopewell who has the most to learn.

The limited omniscient point of view lets O'Connor alternate between Mrs. Hopewell's and Hulga's perspectives, giving us access to the actions and thoughts of both characters and allowing us to make informed judgments that we would not be able to make if we were limited to Hulga's point of view.

POSSIBLE CONNECTION TO ANOTHER SELECTION

Ernest Hemingway, "Soldier's Home" (text p. 579)

FAY WELDON, *IND AFF, or Out of Love in Sarajevo* (p. 817)

In this brief cautionary tale, Weldon manages to question the nature of fate and individual will, desire, and imagination, as well as question the relationship between the apparently political and the apparently personal. It is not so much the "sad story" promised by the first line as it is a fable about taking responsibility for one's actions and understanding the essentially interconnected nature of all events.

When the twenty-five-year-old unnamed narrator fell in love with her forty-six-year-old thesis director (who was already married and the father of three children), she fell in love with her idea of him rather than with him as a man. The narrator, who tells her story from the perspective of one who has learned her lesson and is now simply imparting it, has come to understand that she had confused "mere passing academic ambition with love" (48), believing this man's assessment of the world and of herself ("He said I had a good mind but not a first-class mind and somehow I didn't take it as an insult" [4]) when she should have been coming up with her own conclusions. Weldon comments in another story concerned with a young woman's infatuation with a much older man that "it was not her desire that was stirred, it was her imagination. But how is she to know this?" What the narrator wishes to believe about her lover — that this is "not just any old professor-student romance" — and what she actually feels about him are two different things.

Peter Piper (the name itself should indicate a certain lack of respect on the part of the author for such characters), the Cambridge professor who has been married to a swimming coach for twenty-four years, likes to "luxuriate in guilt and indecision" and has taken his student/mistress with him on a holiday to see whether they are "really, truly suited," to make sure that it is "the Real Thing" before they "shack up, as he put it."

The narrator is desperately drawn to her teacher because he represents much more than he actually offers. To maintain her affection for Peter, she overlooks his stinginess ("Peter felt it was less confusing if we each paid our own way" [44]), his whining ("I noticed I had become used to his complaining. I supposed that when you had been married a little you simply wouldn't hear it" [12]), the fact that often when she spoke "he wasn't listening," the fact that he might not want her to go topless at the beach ("this might be the area where the age difference showed"), and his "thinning hair" because he seems authoritative (speaking in "quasi-Serbo-Croatian") and powerful. He "liked to be asked questions" and obviously adores the adoration of his student. She loves him with "inordinate Affection," she claims. "Your Ind Aff is my wife's sorrow" (27), Peter moans, blaming a girl who was born the first year of his marriage for his wife's unhappiness, absolving himself from any blame.

The question of whether particular events happen because of the inevitable buildup of insurmountable forces or, instead, because of a series of particular moments that might have been avoided with care, caution, or consideration is brought to bear not only on the narrator's relationship with Peter but on the question of World War I. With the background material effortlessly supplied by Weldon, even readers unfamiliar with the story of Princip's assassination of the archduke will be able to see the way Princip's tale parallels that of the narrator. Was the war inevitable? Was it, as Peter Piper claims, bound to "start sooner or later," because of the "social and economic tensions" that had to find "some release"? Along the same lines of reasoning, is the twenty-four-year marriage between Peter and the woman who is known only as Mrs. Piper doomed to failure, or is it instead pressured into failure by the husband's infidelity? Is it, as the narrator's sister Clare (herself married to a much older professor) claims, a fact that "if you can unhinge a marriage, it's ripe for unhinging, it would happen sooner or later, it might as well be you" (36)? Is it, in other words, the narrator who is assassinating the Piper marriage?

The climax of the story occurs when the narrator and Peter are waiting to be served wild boar in a private restaurant. She notices a waiter whom she describes as being "about my age" (showing her keenly felt awareness of the difference in age between herself and Peter). She has felt desire for Peter in her mind, and has learned to feel "a pain in her heart" as an "erotic sensation," but in looking at the virile, handsome man her own age she feels "quite violently, an associated yet different pang which got my lower stomach." She describes this desire as the "true, the real pain of Ind Aff!" Her desire for the waiter has nothing to do with his position, his authority, or his power. It has to do with his "flashing eyes, hooked nose, luxuriant black hair, sensuous mouth" (38). She asks herself in a moment of clear vision, "What was I doing with this man with thinning hair?" (41). She thinks to herself, when she automatically tells Peter that she loves him, "How much I lied." She has freed herself from the confines of his authority and declares in opposition to him that "if Princip hadn't shot the archduke, something else, some undisclosed, unsuspected variable, might have come along and defused the whole political/military situation, and neither World War I nor II ever happened" (43). She then gets up to go "home."

"This is how I fell out of love with my professor," declares the narrator, describing their affair as "a silly, sad episode, which I regret." She sees herself as silly for having confused her career ambitions with desire and silly for trying to "outdo my sister Clare," who has married her professor (but has to live in Brussels as a sort of cosmic penance). Piper eventually proves spiteful and tries to refuse the narrator's thesis, but she wins her appeal and, delightfully, can confirm for herself that she does indeed have a "first-class mind." She feels, finally, a connection to poor Princip, who should have "hung on a bit, there in Sarajevo" because he might have "come to his senses. People do, sometimes quite quickly" (48).

Mark Halliday, "Graded Paper" (text p. 994)
Nathaniel Hawthorne, "The Birthmark" (text p. 1130)
Katherine Mansfield, "Miss Brill" (text p. 1270)

POETRY

DIANE ACKERMAN, *A Fine, a Private Place* (p. 823)

Ackerman's poem might serve as sequel to Marvell's "To His Coy Mistress" (text p. 230) because it focuses less on the man's pursuit of his love (the subject of the speaker's rhetorical assault in Marvell's poem) than on the actual act of intercourse. The title of this poem is an allusion to the following lines from "To His Coy Mistress": "The grave's a fine and private place, / But none, I think, do there embrace" (lines 31–32). Ackerman depicts a grave of sorts — below the surface of the ocean — where the lovers in her poem, referred to at different times as "a pirate vessel" (48) and "a Spanish Galleon" (60), do embrace. Underwater, the man can phrase his desire only in physical gestures. Beginning with the description of his erection, when the woman notices "the octopus / in his swimsuit / stretch one tentacle / and ripple its silky bag" (15–18), Ackerman constructs an elaborate extended metaphor in which the lovers' bodies and their actions are construed in the highly specific imagery of the underwater world.

While Ackerman devotes significant and elaborate description to the couple and their lovemaking, enacting Marvell's speaker's plea to "tear our pleasures with rough strife" (43), there are instances in the poem in which, like Marvell, she seems to regard the woman as a commodity, as a "sea-geisha" (24). The lovers return to the surface only after the male is satisfied, and after he gives the signal. We are told that he leads the woman to safety (80). Throughout this process, even the ocean pets the woman, "cell by cell, murmuring / along her legs and neck, / caressing her / with pale, endless arms" (85–88). How does she seem to regard this?

It is only at the end of the poem that Ackerman delves into the woman's response to her experience. Whereas Marvell focuses solely on the male's perspective, Ackerman remedies this in the final lines of her poem, in which the woman continues to envision the surface world in marine terminology. She sees the snowflakes as "minnows" (109) and savors "holding a sponge / idly under tap-gush" (110–111) as it reminds her of her underwater tryst. The final stanza would seem to suggest that the woman treasures her experience underwater. Ask students to identify the poem's tone. Are we to regard the relationship portrayed in the poem as an ideal encounter?

Andrew Marvell, "To His Coy Mistress" (text p. 230)

KATERINA ANGHELÁKI-ROOKE, Jealousy (p. 826)

Ask students to consider what the speaker knows about the couple in the poem and how she knows it. Is this simply a poem of speculation? Does the speaker admit anything that she *doesn't* know about the couple's relationship?

Discuss the role of landscape in this poem. Throughout the poem, the poet moves between describing the surroundings and describing the couple. Ask your students how the landscape connects to the individuals described in the poem. Note the transformation of images that occurs as the poem progresses. Early on, "the rural / landscapes [are] in ruins" (line 3) and the earth "is still mute / and alone before it becomes a butterfly" (9–10); later, "the dry branches retreat / in memory" (25–26); and at the end of the poem "the landscape starts anew within them / in full spring" (27–28). What might such a transformation indicate? At what point in the poem does the transformation begin to occur? In a writing assignment, you might ask students to discuss who or what is symbolically changing in this poem.

Ask students to consider what the speaker's attitude toward love is. Explore how the details the speaker includes make her at times seem to be a vicarious participant in the romantic encounter.

POSSIBLE CONNECTION TO ANOTHER SELECTION

Regina Barreca, "Envy" (text p. 1073)

ROBERT BROWNING, *My Last Duchess* (p. 827)

Robert Browning lived with his parents in a London suburb until he married Elizabeth Barrett at age 34; he had previously left home only to attend boarding school and for short trips abroad. He and his wife lived in Italy for fifteen years, a period in which he produced some of his first memorable poems. *Men and Women,* published in 1855, gained Browning the initial intimations of his later fame. The poet returned to England after his wife died in 1861. His work continued to elicit increasing public (if not always critical) acclaim.

Ironically, the speaker is talking about the portrait of his last duchess (how many went before?) to the marriage broker, who is handling the current arrangement between the duke and the broker's "master," father of the bride-to-be.

The last wife's principal fault was that she was too democratic in her smiles; she did not reserve them for the duke alone. The duke holds no regard for kindness and thoughtfulness; he thinks only of money, rank, and name. He treats women as objects and possessions.

The visitor seems to want to leave early, perhaps to warn his master of the unfeeling tyrant who would marry the master's daughter at a cut rate (cf. lines 47–54).

Students may have already read this dramatic monologue in high school. The second time around they should appreciate the irony even more as the duke reveals so much of his own character while ostensibly controlling the situation.

POSSIBLE CONNECTIONS TO OTHER SELECTIONS

Mark Halliday, "Graded Paper" (text p. 994)
Katharyn Howd Machan, "Hazel Tells LaVerne" (text p. 1000)

SALLY CROFT, *Home-Baked Bread* (p. 829)

This poem describes a seduction by way of cooking, cleverly departing from the title of the source of the epigraph, *The Joy of Cooking,* into another popular text from the 1970s, *The Joy of Sex.* The great-aunt of the second stanza is an interesting inroad. Great-aunts are generally associated more with cooking than with seduction; is this one figured into the poem as a contrast to the amorous speaker, or does she reinforce the idea that all women have their "cunning triumphs" (line 2), which are sometimes hidden or only suggested?

"Cunning triumphs," appearing amid the measured dryness of a cookbook text, certainly has the potential to arrest someone's poetic sensibilities. *Cunning* seems more appropriately applied to the feats of Odysseus than to the food in *The Joy of Cooking.* At any rate, "cunning triumphs" rises, as it were, beyond the limits of technical discourse. It shines, it sparkles, it almost titillates the kitchen soul.

"Insinuation" (3), too, is a pivotal word in the poem. It looks back on the questioning attitude of the opening lines and points toward the wily, winding seductiveness of what will follow.

At first we hear the speaker reading and questioning the cookbook. Then we hear the speaker transformed into a new identity — of Lady Who Works Cunning Triumphs. She is addressing someone she would charm and seduce.

The poem achieves a unity through the repetition of certain images, such as the room that recalls the great-aunt's bedroom as well as the other reiterated images, of honey, sweet seductiveness, warmth, and open air.

POSSIBLE CONNECTION TO ANOTHER SELECTION

Cathy Song, "The White Porch" (text p. 841)

E. E. CUMMINGS, *since feeling is first* (p. 830)

Once again in the head-heart debate, the heart comes out the winner in this poem. The eliding of the syntax supports the value of feeling over rational thought. Students will probably enjoy the syntactical turn of line 3, which can either complete line 2 or be the subject of line 4. Considering the mention of death and its prominent position in the poem, you might explore with the class — or use as a writing assignment — a defense of this as a *carpe diem* poem.

POSSIBLE CONNECTION TO ANOTHER SELECTION

John Donne, "The Flea" (text p. 831)

EMILY DICKINSON, *Wild Nights — Wild Nights!* (p. 830)

A class discussion of this poem could focus on a few well-chosen words. Researching the etymology of *luxury* (line 4) will leave no room for doubt as to the intended eroticism of the poem; it comes from the Latin *luxuria,* which was used to express lust as well as extravagant pleasures of a more general sort, which it has now come to mean. You might also discuss the use of natural imagery in the second and third stanzas. The heart in stanza two has no more need of compass or chart. Ask your students what these images mean to them. They seem to imply attention to order, rules, and laws. These images are set aside in the third stanza in favor of Eden and the sea.

A study of "Wild Nights" provides an excellent opportunity to discuss the possibility of disparity between the author of a work and the created narrator who speaks within the work. Students may wish to dismiss the eroticism of this poem if they have stereotyped Dickinson as a pure spinster in a white dress. However, the speaker of this poem cannot be specifically identified as Dickinson. Indeed, it is debatable whether the speaker is male or female.

POSSIBLE CONNECTION TO ANOTHER SELECTION

Walt Whitman, From "I Sing the Body Electric" (text p. 270)

JOHN DONNE, The Flea (p. 831)

An interesting discussion or writing topic could be organized around the tradition of the *carpe diem* poem and how this poem both accommodates and alters that tradition.

The wit here is ingenious, and after the individual sections of the poem are explained, more time might be needed to review the parts and give the class a sense of the total effect of the poem's operations.

The reason the speaker even bothers to comment on the flea stems from his belief that a commingling of blood during intercourse (here, admittedly, by the agency of the flea) may result in conception. Hence his belief that the lovers must be "yea more than" united and that the flea's body has become a kind of "marriage temple." For the woman to crush the flea (which she does) is a multiple crime because in so doing she commits murder, suicide, and sacrilege (of the temple) and figuratively destroys the possible progeny. The flea in its death, though, also stands as logical emblem for why this courtship should be consummated. The reasoning is that little if any innocence or honor is spent in killing the flea, then, likewise, neither of those commodities would be spent "when thou yield'st to me."

One way to begin discussion is to consider the poem as an exercise in the making of meaning: what does the flea represent to the speaker, and how does its meaning change as the poem progresses? What, in effect, is the relation between the flea and the poem?

POSSIBLE CONNECTION TO ANOTHER SELECTION

Sally Croft, "Home-Baked Bread" (text p. 829)

ROBERT HASS, *A Story about the Body* (p. 832)

As the title indicates, this poem is indeed a story about the body. You might want to begin by discussing in what ways bodies appear in the poem: What is it that the young composer loves about the Japanese woman? How does he respond when she tells him about her double mastectomy?

It's obvious that the body of the Japanese woman is central to this poem. However, you might ask students to explore in writing how this piece is about the young man's body as well: What is the symbolism of the gift of rose petals that cover dead bees (lines 13–17)? What is the woman trying to tell the young man through this gift? You may also want to ask your students to consider what they think the poet is saying about beauty, desire, and love.

POSSIBLE CONNECTION TO ANOTHER SELECTION

Joan Murray, "Play-by-Play" (text p. 837)

ROBERT HERRICK, *To the Virgins, to Make Much of Time* (p. 832)

Robert Herrick, son of a well-to-do London goldsmith, rather halfheartedly became an Anglican clergyman assigned to Dean Prior in Devonshire, in the west of England. He wrote poems secretly, making up for many of them alluring, exotic, phantom mistresses. After losing his position when the Puritans rose to power, Herrick published his only book, containing some 1,200 poems, in 1648.

This is one of the better-known poems of the *carpe diem* (seize the day) tradition. Here, Herrick is advising young women in a tone of straightforward urging to make the most of their opportunities for pleasure while they are in the prime of youth and beauty. These "virgins," Herrick implies, are like the sun at its zenith or a flower in full bloom; they will soon begin to decline and may never have the same opportunities for marriage again. The word *virgins,* rather than *women,* accommodates the advice in the last stanza to "go marry" and carries with it as well the connotation of sought-for sexual fulfillment. Some of your students might point out how a young woman's situation is much more complex today than it apparently was in Herrick's time, since "seizing the day" can and often does mean pursuing opportunities for career over those for marriage.

One possible way to enter a discussion of the poem is to consider the arrangement of the argument. The speaker has a definite intent: to communicate bits of wisdom to the "virgins" of the title. What effect does the order of his points of argument have on the way the poem reads? What would happen if we were to rearrange the first three stanzas: Would the message of the poem remain exactly the same?

POSSIBLE CONNECTIONS TO OTHER SELECTIONS

Andrew Marvell, "To His Coy Mistress" (text p. 230)
Richard Wilbur, "A Late Aubade" (text p. 843)

RESOURCE FOR TEACHING

See "Palgrave's Golden Treasury of English Poetry" in the appendix of Film, Video, and Audiocassette Resources.

LANGSTON HUGHES, *Rent-Party Shout: For a Lady Dancer* (p. 833)

This poem sounds as much like a song lyric as it does a poem; the short lines make the tempo fast and sharp, like the words themselves. You may wish to ask students to consider this "shout" as a story; ask them to describe the speaker's situation and her feelings toward her "man." Ask your students if they see any humor in this "shout." Responses might include the speaker's declaration that "I knows I can find him / When he's in de ground — (lines 15–16) her jealousy is taken to a bitingly satirical extreme.

Ask students to describe the setting of this poem. Point out that the backdrop to this piece is desperate poverty, where friends and neighbors have to help raise a person's rent money. So the music played at such a party would need to be energetic, entertaining, and cathartic enough to distract the partyers from their own personal troubles. In this way, "Rent-Party Shout" can be interpreted simultaneously as a threat to the wayward man and as a necessary release for the singer herself. Ask students to discuss what might be considered "therapeutic" about this woman's singing about her troubles.

POSSIBLE CONNECTION TO ANOTHER SELECTION

Martín Espada, "Latin Night at the Pawnshop" (text p. 230)

JOHN KEATS, *La Belle Dame sans Merci* (p. 834)

You might read this ballad in connection with other ballads in this book. How is it that ballads have stood the test of time and continued to appeal to many generations of listeners and readers? Is this ballad any different from medieval ballads? Is it more suggestive, perhaps, of a state of mind?

The opening three stanzas hold a descriptive value for the reader, for they present the knight as pale, ill, possibly aging and dying. The stanzas possess a rhetorical value as well, for they whet our curiosity. Just why is the knight trapped in this withered landscape?

The femme fatale figure goes back at least to Homeric legend and the wiles of Circe. Note how the "belle dame" appeals here to several senses — with her appearance, her voice, the foods she offers, the physical comforts of sleep. Above all else, though, she seems otherworldly, and Keats here seems to insist in her elfin qualities, her wild eyes, and her strange language.

Words change meaning and grow in and out of popularity over generations (even decades). Contrast the way we might use *enthrall* today (with what subjects) and what Keats intends by "La Belle Dame sans Merci / Hath thee in Thrall!" (lines 39–40). Note how the shortened line of each quatrain gives both a sense of closure and the chill of an inescapable doom.

In his well-known essay on the poem, Earl R. Wasserman begins by remarking, "It would be difficult in any reading of Keats's ballad not to be enthralled by the haunting power of its rhythm, by its delicate intermingling of the fragile and the grotesque, the tender and the weird, and by the perfect economy with which these effects are achieved" (from "La Belle Dame sans Merci," in his *The Finer Tone: Keats's Major Poems* [Baltimore: Johns Hopkins UP, 1953, 1967], 65–83, and reprinted in *English Romantic Poets: Modern Essays in Criticism,* edited by M. H. Abrams [New York: Oxford UP, 1960], 365–380). In a writing assignment you might ask students to select any one of these elements and discuss it with several examples to show how it shapes the tone and mood of the poem.

Other studies of this poem include Jane Cohen's "Keats's Humor in 'La Belle Dame sans Merci,' " *Keats-Shelley Journal* 17 (1968): 10–13, and Bernice Slote's "The Climate of Keats's 'La Belle Dame sans Merci,' " *Modern Language Quarterly* 21 (1960): 195–207.

JANE KENYON, *Surprise* (p. 835)

From the perspective of the woman "surprised," this poem encompasses many of the conflicting emotions of a surprise party in spare, deliberate imagery. Distracted by the unnamed male, and oblivious to the gathering elsewhere, the speaker notes all of the changes around her as a result the onset of spring. The last three lines of the poem reverse the mood, suggesting that the speaker's surprise comes at the ease with which her husband/lover has deceived her, opening up the possibility that there is something wrong with their relationship.

It might be useful to begin by asking students if they have ever been involved in a surprise party — either as the victim or as the scheming organizer. A discussion of what a surprise party intends to do leads naturally into a discussion of what it often actually does. Similarly, the poem leads us from the mundane — "pancakes at the local diner" (line 1), "casseroles" (4) — to the surprising renewal of nature in springtime, to the woman's astounding realization that the man has had such an easy time lying to her. The word "astound," with its connotations of bewilderment, direct our attention away from the surprise party and into speculation about the relationship between them. The irony centers around the renewal of the spring birthday juxtaposed against some almost funereal undertones (consider "spectral" in line 8, and "ash" in line 9, for example). The tension between images enables us to interpret their relationship in a novel, surprising way.

POSSIBLE CONNECTION TO ANOTHER SELECTION

Sharon Olds, "Rite of Passage" (text p. 627)

CHRISTOPHER MARLOWE, *The Passionate Shepherd to His Love* (p. 836)

Marlowe was the first English dramatist to use blank verse in his plays. He completed a master of arts at Cambridge in 1587 and was stabbed to death six years later, having lived an eventful, though somewhat mysterious, life.

Anyone with an ounce of romance will respond favorably to this pastoral lyric, whose speaker pledges to do the impossible (yet how inviting to entertain the vision of "a thousand fragrant posies" on demand!) if only his beloved will be his love. What lovers have not believed, for a time at least, that they could "all the pleasures prove," that all the pleasure the world offered was there for the taking?

It's significant, of course, that his song is sung in May, the month when spring takes firm hold (in England, at least) and when the end of winter was (and still is) celebrated with great exuberance.

POSSIBLE CONNECTION TO ANOTHER SELECTION

Richard Wilbur, "A Late Aubade" (text p. 843)

Christopher Marlowe: Elizabethan Love Poems [recording]. 1 cassette (50 min.). Unabridged edition. Distributed by Spoken Arts.

See also "Medieval and Elizabethan Poetry" and "Palgrave's Golden Treasury of English Poetry" in the appendix of Film, Video, and Audiocassette Resources.

JOAN MURRAY, *Play-By-Play* (p. 837)

This series of hypothetical questions makes us consider the effect of older women gazing at and admiring the bodies of young men. One way to begin discussion is to try to answer each of the questions, read exactly as it is written, as a way to try to determine the speaker's intent in raising the questions. That is, are there implicit answers to the questions? It is a very different thing to ask "I wonder how men would react if they knew that women occasionally scrutinized their bodies" than it is to phrase the questions as the speaker of this poem does, in careful detail with a definite setting. Consider the word "caress" (line 16). If discussion strays too far into general questions of the effect of the female gaze, you might need to bring students back to the specific nature of this poem. It is all about perception, as the final lines make clear. One possible assignment is to have students write a poem from the perspective of these young men, either how they see themselves or how they see the women who are gazing at them. Try to encourage students to recognize the fine line between appreciation of beauty and sexual desire in this poem; how might the poem be different if the poem did not take place at an artist's colony with "marble Naiads" (21) as part of the background?

POSSIBLE CONNECTIONS TO OTHER SELECTIONS

Diane Ackerman, "A Fine, a Private Place" (text p. 823)

Robert Herrick, "To the Virgins, to Make Much of Time" (text p. 832)

SHARON OLDS, *Sex without Love* (p. 838)

The word *beautiful,* which begins the second sentence of this poem, may puzzle students at first. Coupled with the ambiguity of the initial question (which may indicate either the speaker's envy or her disdain), the appeal of the lovers as performing artists may signal a positive view of them. But students will soon recognize that the beautiful images of the poem are surface images only; they are also empty and somewhat violent. The textural imagery — "ice" (line 3), "hooked" (4), and even "red as steak" (6) — suggests an undertone of danger in this act. As an artist, the poet must show the lovers as beautiful forms, but as an artist with a social consciousness, she must also explore the vacuum beneath the forms.

A discussion of the poem's imagery may begin with an exploration of all the possible meanings of its initial question. The speaker examines not only the moral implications of this self-centered experience but also the mechanics of the physical act: *how* as well as *why* they do it. Discuss the shift in tone from the portrayal of the lovers as ice skaters and dancers in the initial lines to their likeness to great runners. This last metaphor solidifies the coldness of the speaker's assessment. Like great runners, the lovers concentrate only on the movement of their bodies, surrendering their mental and emotional health to the physical act. Students will see that the energy and concentration of runners are essential to a track event but not to an act of mutual communication. It is essential for the couple to think of themselves as athletes in order to escape the negative moral and potentially painful emotional implications of their act.

The religious images of the poem contrast with its athletic metaphors. Beginning with "God" (line 9) and moving into "light / rising slowly as steam off their joined / skin" (11–13), the speaker subtly distinguishes between the false, body-bound vision of the lovers and the "true religion" that is implied through their negation. Ask students to identify the speaker's tone in these lines: is she really talking about a religious experience, or is she pointing out the lovers' self-absorption? The mathematical language with which the speaker imagines her subjects talking about themselves, "just factors" (21), is undercut by her derogatory tone. Although *they* may act as if they are God, if we are searching for truth, we know that we can never really be single bodies alone in the universe. The implied "truth" here is a communal one, just the opposite of what is described.

In a writing assignment, you might ask students to explore what is not said in the poem. What is the alternative? Why would the speaker not state her idea of truth directly?

POSSIBLE CONNECTIONS TO OTHER SELECTIONS

Alberto Ríos, "Seniors" (text p. 840)

Richard Wilbur, "A Late Aubade" (text p. 843)

REBECCA BARBARA, *Junior Year Abroad* (p. 839)

In this reminiscence, the speaker employs a string of metaphors to explain the dynamics of her relationship with an unwelcome visitor and her own state of mind throughout the visit. Emotionally-even morally-this poem is anything but simple and might engender some interesting discussions among students. While the speaker is clearly bothered by her visitor's presence, she nonetheless acknowledges more than once that he can't be blamed for the intrusion: we can infer, for example, that his ticket was bought around the same time as her promise was made; in line 9, she calls him "the invited man;" and in the second-to-last line, she acknowledges that she "offered a welcome." Ask your students how the speaker reconciles her unwelcoming feelings with her visitors relative ignorance. How do your students reconcile the two viewpoints? You may want to first ask them what the tone-and in particular, the last line-suggests about the speaker's attitude towards her visitor, and then consider how much the visitor is responsible for the speaker's feelings.

One interesting in-road would be to compare the many images of covering in the poem (the cocoon in line 7, the "snake under the evergreen" in line 14, the "sheet against/ [her]self" in line 0). What do these images suggest about how the speaker feels in the situation? How do they resemble the primary image of the boy she has recently met, kissing the "inside of [the speaker's] palm?" And what does such a resemblance reveal about her relationships with the two men?

It may even be interesting to hold a mock trial for the visitor to determine his culpability in the speaker's displeasure. If, as in a real trial, there first must be a determination if any laws have been broken, a mock Grand Jury might be an excellent place to start: what is the man accused of?

POSSIBLE CONNECTIONS TO ANOTHER SELECTION

Theodore Roethke, "My Papa's Waltz" (text p. 630)

ALBERTO RÍOS, *Seniors* (p. 840)

You might begin your discussion of this poem by asking students to talk about its use of slang, particularly in the first stanza. The slang establishes the speaker's environment as well as his conversational tone. As the poem progresses, it focuses on the speaker, and the tone becomes more meditative. Although they modify his relationship to other people, the images of cavities, flat walls, and water (particularly in stanza III) distance the speaker from the social realm, until he is left "on the desert" in the last stanza.

Students might write an essay on these images. How does their evocation of sexual experience prepare us for the last line of the poem? What is the speaker trying to say about sex, about life? How does the language of the final stanza compare with that of the first stanza? What might this changed diction indicate in the speaker's attitude toward himself and the world?

POSSIBLE CONNECTIONS TO OTHER SELECTIONS

T. S. Eliot, "The Love Song of J. Alfred Prufrock" (text p. 1280)
Sharon Olds, "Sex without Love" (text p. 838)

RESOURCES FOR TEACHING

Alberto A. Ríos: Reading His Poetry [recording]. 1 cassette. Distributed by Sound Photosynthesis.
See also "Birthright: Growing Up Hispanic" in the appendix of Film, Video, and Audiocassette Resources.

WILLIAM SHAKESPEARE, *My mistress' eyes are nothing like the sun* (p. 841)

Students may have read this sonnet in high school, and you might begin by asking them what they think the mistress looks like. Some clarification of Shakespeare's use of the term *mistress* (beloved or chosen one) may be in order. This sonnet plays with the conventions and clichés of the Petrarchan sonnet, which elaborated on the extraordinary qualities of the maiden's eyes as compared to the splendor of the sun. But Shakespeare refuses to do this and thus argues for a poetry that avoids cliché and the excess metaphor that tries to outdo reality. He is, in fact, asserting the beauty of his beloved in the last line. She is as attractive as any other woman who has been "belied" (made to seem more beautiful) by false comparison.

POSSIBLE CONNECTION TO ANOTHER SELECTION

John Donne, "The Flea" (text p. 831)

CATHY SONG, *The White Porch* (p. 841)

The speaker in this poem establishes a conversation with her listener in the first stanza: "your" (line 10), "think" (12). She projects her listener into the future even as she captures the present moment through the description of her newly washed hair. The second stanza moves the conversation toward sexual innuendo, comparing the speaker's arousal to a flower, a flock of birds, and a sponge cake with peaches. Ask students to determine how these images give us a sense of what the speaker is like. What is her relationship to the listener? The final stanza returns us to the initial image of hair, but whereas the first stanza moves toward the future, the third plunges us back into the past. Students will enjoy comparing the images describing the mother to those describing the lover in the final lines. Like the rope ladder (an allusion to Rapunzel?), the poem is column-shaped, inviting its listener into the experience of reading it as it talks about a sexual relationship.

In a writing assignment, ask students to examine the concrete nouns and participial verbs in the poem. How do they evoke the speaker's message? How do images of domestic life summon the speaker's more "philosophical" side?

POSSIBLE CONNECTION TO ANOTHER SELECTION

Sally Croft, "Home-Baked Bread" (text p. 829)

RICHARD WILBUR, *A Late Aubade* (p. 843)

A prolific poet, critic, translator, and editor, Richard Wilbur (b. 1921) studied at Amherst and Harvard and was awarded the Pulitzer Prize and the National Book Award in 1957 for *Things of This World*. Influenced by the works of the Metaphysical Poets and Wallace Stevens, Wilbur's poetry has been described by poet and critic John Ciardi as often concerned with "the central driving intention of finding that artifice which will most include the most of life."

It is difficult to translate the forms of Renaissance charm and wit into the more hurried, less mannered tones of the twentieth century. So Wilbur seems to find as he writes his "late" aubade ("late," one supposes, as in "late Corinthian," as well as late in the day), in which going means staying and seizing the day dictates staying in bed. Despite the turnabout in manners and customs, this poem achieves its own special charm. You might begin discussion, though, by asking the class to evaluate the speaker here as rhetorician or persuader. Does he keep to the rules of logic, or does he beg some questions and employ loaded language in other instances? Obviously, he has no admiration for women who spend hours in either libraries or shopping malls, and with deadpan doggerel he sets up a rhyme in stanza 1 between "carrel" (line 1) and "Ladies' Apparel" (4) that devalues both activities. Likewise, he colors the attitude of the person being addressed by talking of planting a "raucous" (5) bed of salvia (which yield bright blue or red flowers) or lunching through a "screed" (7) (the archaism is deliberate here) of someone's loves.

The poem is an appeal to the assumed and presumed sensuality of both the speaker and the woman he addresses. Thus the Matisselike still life of chilled white wine, blue cheese, and ruddy-skinned pears with which Wilbur concludes the poem is a fitting tricolor tribute to the senses, even though the woman here is still the one who serves and waits.

A writing assignment could be organized around a comparison of Herrick's "To the Virgins, to Make Much of Time" (text p. 832), Marvell's "To His Coy Mistress" (text p. 230), and this poem. Wilbur's poem is more conversational and relaxed, reflecting a commonality of spirit between the lovers. The speaker here dwells more on the prolonged moment than on the bleak foreknowledge of death.

POSSIBLE CONNECTIONS TO OTHER SELECTIONS

Robert Herrick, "To the Virgins, to Make Much of Time" (text p. 832)
Sharon Olds, "Sex without Love" (text p. 838)

D R A M A

DAVID IVES, *Sure Thing* (p. 844)

This short drama appeals to all of us who have ever wished we could go back and redo a conversation (especially with a potential romantic partner) until we get it right. Students will probably identify with the play's two characters who are both trying to impress the other but who cannot do so by being themselves. Ask your students if they think Bill and Betty are a genuinely well-matched couple or if they are simply the product of good self-revision.

When teaching this play, emphasize the importance of a close reading. Ask your students to note what types of lines precede the bell. What comments require another try before the speaker can move on in the courtship? Bill and Betty cover nearly every conventional small-talk topic — from reading material to politics — and find that even most "safe" subjects have the potential to disrupt a connection between two people.

Of course, the rest of us don't have the good (or bad) fortune to be followed around through life by a bell that will let us start over when we don't do well. Ask your students to rewrite a scene from their own lives in which such a bell would have been useful. How would they rewrite the event in question?

CONSIDERATIONS FOR CRITICAL THINKING AND WRITING (p. 850)

1. Even though Ives provides us with very little information about the setting of the play, we understand that the action takes place in a relatively busy place (indicated both by one of Bill's early pick-up lines and the fact that he cannot seem to get a waiter's attention). Yet the anonymity of the place also suggests that the setting is not really important; Ives is satirizing any sort of "pick-up scene" between two strangers.

2. The ringing bell, which relentlessly interrupts the dialogue throughout the play, indicates moments where the characters can go back in time and have the opportunity to revise their words. Students may note that the ringing bell divides the play into dozens of miniscenes, as the conversation between Bill and Betty is continually reworked and the characters, in a sense, "start over."

3. Students might consider Betty to be the antagonist and Bill to be the protagonist of the play, insofar as Betty is the character with most of the power to terminate their conversation and Bill is the character who is constantly struggling to say the right thing. Conflicts arise throughout the conversation, as one or the other says something offensive, ridiculous, or merely bizarre. Yet the overall conflict is an internal one, resulting from the struggle of individuals to create public identities that others will find acceptable, attractive, and interesting.

4. The characters' struggles to create acceptable identities complicate the formulaic "boy-meets-girl" plotline, since we are inclined to think that when two people are attracted to each other it is because they are "destined" to be together, and not because they invent clever and highly idealized versions of themselves in order to get past their first impressions. The climax of the play seems to occur at the ringing of the final bell; after this point, Bill and Betty get along so well that there is no further need for them to "back up" and start over. They reach a more comfortable level of conversation and discover that they have some similar likes and dislikes, which leads to their decision to stay together.

5. The play is farcical; nevertheless its theme may be described as the difficulties of really knowing other people and of knowing oneself. Bill and Betty try to mold themselves to fit what they think are the expectations of others. For example, Bill disregards his true sense of identity and invents colleges, grade-point averages, political leanings, anything at all in order to keep Betty interested. One might say that they succeed in their endeavors; they are together at the end of the conversation. But students should consider what Ives suggests are the implications of beginning a relationship based on the false impressions that preceded that final ringing bell.

6. The title of the play is ironic because at no particular point during Bill and Betty's conversation is their future together a "sure thing" — only through backpedaling and revising their conversation are they able to connect. Their relationship can be considered a "sure thing" only in the sense that in the world that Ives created they can redo their conversation as many times as they want, until they get it right.

7. Just as Bill explains that it is important to "hit these things at the right moment or it's no good" (p. 846), Ives inserts the ringing bell at precisely the moments when the conversation goes out of control and one person is ready to dismiss the other.

Ives's sense of timing also extends to the length and shape of the conversation; in spite of the humor, Bill and Betty's first encounter couldn't go on forever. Ives brings his audience just to the point when it seems doubtful that the two characters will *ever* "connect," and then he lets them connect with a comic intensity that pokes fun at all romantic "pick-ups."

POSSIBLE CONNECTION TO OTHER SELECTIONS

Henrik Ibsen, *A Doll House* (text p. 700)

Deborah Tannen, "Sex, Lies, and Conversation" (text p. 913)

WILLIAM SHAKESPEARE, *A Midsummer Night's Dream* (p. 852)

If you have already taught *Hamlet* from Chapter 7, reading one of Shakespeare's comedies will be both familiar and unfamiliar to your students. The language and some of the stage conventions (like soliloquies and asides) are the same in nearly all Elizabethan dramas, but *A Midsummer Night's Dream* is surprisingly playful, even silly — a fact that may come as a surprise to students who view Shakespeare as the representative of "serious" literature. Your students will probably enjoy reading this play and may be eager to discuss the play's more irrational moments. You might initiate a discussion about the role of this silliness in the play. Ask your students to discuss how the romantic complications of the play's clownish characters (like Bottom) parallel the romantic complications of the play's romantic characters.

In addition to considering the problems of love and its complications, this play invites discussion of character. The two female and the two male leads in the play seem almost interchangeable. Do your students see them as flat romantic types or as dynamic characters? You might break your class into four groups, assigning each group one of the four characters. Have each group locate a speech or scene within the play that exemplifies that character. How distinct is that character's personality?

Although much has changed since Shakespeare's time, the experience of falling in love, of being disoriented, jealous, and irrational remains with us. This play invites students to think about the universality of romantic love.

For a comprehensive annotated bibliography of criticism on the play, see *A Midsummer Night's Dream: An Annotated Bibliography,* edited by D. Allen Carroll (New York: Garland, 1986). There have been several attempts to associate the play with a specific wedding, among them E. K. Chambers's essay. Chambers argues that the play was written to be performed at the wedding of William Stanley, Earl of Derby, to Lady Elizabeth Vere on January 26, 1595. The reading of the play by G. Wilson Knight in *The Shakespearean Tempest* (1932; rpt. Methuen, 1953) discusses the interplay of imagery and thus emphasizes the play's formal properties over its historical context. C. L. Barber's highly influential *Shakespeare's Festive Comedy* (1959; rpt. Princeton UP, 1972) takes a sociological approach . by considering many of Shakespeare's romantic comedies, including *A Midsummer Night's Dream*, in light of their relation to English holiday traditions.

CONSIDERATIONS FOR CRITICAL THINKING AND WRITING (p. 906)

1. The title of *A Midsummer Night's Dream* creates at least two immediate expectations. First, the relationship between dreams and reality is a prominent theme in the play. Shakespeare recognized that dreams are expressions of our profoundest longings and desires; he also understood that we often dismiss them as trifles that are not to be taken too seriously. In *Midsummer,* he explores deep human longings, the desire to fall in love and marry, and encourages us to see the play as trivial entertainment, "No more yielding but a dream," as Puck says in the epilogue. Dreams and references

to dreams occur throughout the play: for example, Hermia awakens from a nightmare (one with interesting Freudian implications) in Act II, Scene ii, to discover Lysander is missing, while Bottom believes his transformation into an ass was a dream. Theseus's opening speech in Act V is worth examining as an exploration of the relation between illusion and reality.

The play's title also draws our attention to the time of year when the action occurs; it is a *midsummer* night's dream. In Shakespeare's England, the summer solstice, the longest day of the year, was commonly associated with madness and with fertility rituals whose origins were rooted in pre-Christian antiquity. Shakespeare's title would thus have connoted an atmosphere of celebration and sexual license for an Elizabethan audience.

2. Shakespeare's removal of the action in *A Midsummer Night's Dream* from the city of Athens to the forest signals a loosening of the restraints that threaten to prevent the young lovers from freely selecting their own mates. In Shakespeare's day, ancient Athens was associated with the highest level of civilization humankind had ever achieved, and the playwright strengthens this connotation by making Theseus, who is traditionally portrayed as the strongest and wisest of rulers, the chief human authority figure in the play. For Shakespeare's audiences, Athens would have represented civilization, order, and social stability.

The forest represents Athens's opposite, a world in which disorder and confusion reign. While the strong patriarchal ruler Theseus has a nominal counterpart in Oberon, the true spirit of the forest is represented by the mischievous Puck. Puck represents *misrule*, the inversion of normal social restrictions. When the four young lovers cross the boundary that separates urban, civilized Athens from the wild world of the forest, they enter a topsy-turvy world in which lovers switch allegiance at a moment's notice, the girls chase the boys rather than the other way around, and Titania, the queen of the fairies, falls in love with an ass.

In the end, however, the social rules represented by Theseus and Athens have not only been reasserted, they have clearly been strengthened by their temporary suspension. When the four lovers waken from their "dream" at the end of Act IV, they are reintegrated into society by Theseus, an assimilation symbolized by the group marriage of Act V. Similarly, the dissension in the fairy world is healed by the play's end when the marital spat between Oberon and Titania is amicably resolved.

3. In Shakespearean comedy, marriage commonly functions as a symbol of order restored. The marriage of Theseus and Hippolyta brackets the main action of *A Midsummer Night's Dream*. The play opens with Theseus announcing his impending wedding to Hippolyta, the queen of the Amazons, whom he has conquered in battle. The marriage thus connotes not only the natural harmony of male-female bonding but also a political alliance designed to prevent further warfare between two peoples.

The harmony represented by Theseus and Hippolyta's wedding is disrupted, however, by Egeus's desire to force Hermia to marry Demetrius against her will. While Hippolyta is Theseus's prisoner, there is no suggestion that she is averse to the marriage. Egeus's extreme patriarchalism contrasts unfavorably with the more benign rule of Theseus.

Egeus's unreasonably domineering attitude results in the flight of the young lovers into the forest, where, with the aid of the fairies, they work out their relationships. Tellingly, it is precisely when the lovers waken from their "dream" that Theseus and

Hippolyta reappear in the play near the end of Act IV. In keeping with the general symbolism of marriage in comedy, the reintegration of Hermia, Lysander, Helena, and Demetrius into society as adults is symbolized by their inclusion in Theseus and Hippolyta's nuptials.

4. *A Midsummer Night's Dream* is one of Shakespeare's earlier comedies, and the play's four young lovers lack the brilliant delineation of individual character that the playwright would achieve in subsequent comedies. Indeed, Lysander and Demetrius are virtually interchangeable; they possess the virtues and defects of male youth. Both are spirited and courageous; they are also stubborn and hot-headed. Both also seem somewhat opportunistic: Demetrius, we learn early on, "Made love to Nedar's daughter, Helena, / And won her soul" (I.i.107–108) before switching his affections to Hermia. Similarly, Lysander shows no squeamishness about running away with Hermia after Theseus rules against him in Act I.

The two young women in the play, while scarcely displaying the brilliantly captivating personalities of a Rosalind or a Viola, are considerably more individuated than their boyfriends. Their differing temperaments are related to the differing physical characteristics we may deduce from the insults Lysander and Demetrius hurl at Hermia and that Hermia flings at Helena in Act III, Scene ii. Hermia is described, and has traditionally been cast, as small and dark, with a sharp tongue and a hot temper. By contrast, Helena is fair, tall, and timid; she is "a right maid for [her] cowardice" (III.ii.303). Interestingly, it is Helena who displays perhaps the most growth of any of the four young lovers. When she pursues Demetrius into the woods, her lack of self-esteem is appalling even for a farce: she literally is willing to be treated like a dog. When she imagines that her friends have united to make her the butt of their jokes, however, she responds with some spirit, and her tone is one of genuine hurt. Hermia, too, may experience some emotional growth in Act III, Scene ii, as she realizes that she has gone from being avidly pursued by two young men to having been rejected by them both. For a headstrong girl accustomed to having her way, suddenly to find herself spurned by both her lovers is sobering.

5. The essence of Bottom's comic appeal is his complete absence of self-awareness. The oafish, ignorant weaver sees himself as a splendid actor; not only does he see no reason he should not be cast as Pyramus in the artisans' play, he wishes to play all the other parts as well. He also displays no surprise whatever when the beautiful fairy queen, Titania, falls passionately in love with him. To the audience, however, Bottom's shortcomings as both an actor and a lover are patently obvious. He is, literally and figuratively, an ass.

Yet Bottom is not the only character in the play who suffers from a lack of self-awareness. A lack of reflectiveness is evident in the four young lovers, who are as doggedly bent on having their own ways as Nick Bottom is on playing all the parts in the artisan's play. We must wonder why Hermia and Helena feel they will die if they cannot have the men of their choice, for Demetrius and Lysander seem interchangeable. Oberon's desire for the changeling boy is rooted in a similar lack of self-awareness; it is clearly as much a consequence of his personal vanity and need for ascendancy over Titania as it is a product of concern for the boy's welfare. Thus, other characters besides Bottom suffer from self-delusion; the difference is that they do not have the excuse of stupidity.

6. The opening scene of *A Midsummer Night's Dream* makes it clear from the outset that we are in a male-dominated world. Theseus begins the play by anticipating his

marriage to Hippolyta, the Amazon warrior queen whom he has captured by force of arms. Almost immediately, Egeus enters and demands the death penalty for the disobedient Hermia. Lysander's revelation that Demetrius had previously wooed Helena is reproved by Theseus but is clearly not regarded as any impediment to Demetrius's marriage to Hermia, since that is what her father desires. Although he mitigates the Athenian death penalty for Hermia to a lifetime in a nunnery, Theseus does not question Egeus's fundamental right to dictate Hermia's choice of a mate, as his speech to her in lines 46–52 makes clear.

This tone of patriarchal domination also extends to the world of the fairies. Oberon's ire results from Titania's disobedience, and in the end he gets his way. While a modern audience might look askance on the ease with which the fairy king reestablishes his authority, most members of Shakespeare's audience would have regarded the patriarchalism of the play's "real" and fairy worlds as normative.

The play's four female characters are drawn with varying degrees of distinctiveness. Hippolyta has little depth; she says almost nothing until the last act, and even then her lines seem chiefly designed to give Theseus an opportunity to display his wisdom (in his famous speech of lines 2–22) and sense of *noblesse oblige* toward the artisans' wretched play. Titania possesses more substance; her speech to Oberon in II.i.121–137 shows genuine concern about the changeling's welfare, and most of us probably feel she has gotten a bit of a raw deal by the play's end. Hermia and Helena, unlike Lysander and Demetrius, are different from each other both in appearance and temperament. They also relate to their men differently. Hermia is more assertive — some might say domineering. She is accustomed to having her own way, and when she realizes that Lysander and Demetrius are pursuing Helena, she is first incredulous and then aggressive. Helena's behavior, on the other hand, when she invites Demetrius to treat her as he would his dog, constitutes a parody of female passiveness. Both young women undergo changes during the course of the play. By Scene iv Hermia seems somewhat chastened, Helena a little more self-confident. Shakespeare seems to suggest that such moderation is a necessary prelude to each woman's making a mature commitment to marriage.

7. Puck's remark to Oberon (III.ii.115) ostensibly refers to the foolish conduct of Lysander and Demetrius under the spell of Oberon's potion. In a larger thematic sense, however, *A Midsummer Night's Dream* is filled with foolishness on the part of many of the characters, mortal and fairy. Egeus is foolish in his unreasoning paternalism; Lysander and Hermia in their precipitate flight from Athens; Demetrius in his fickle rejection of Helena and his unmanly abuse of her continued affection. Oberon's insistence on having his way is almost childish, and Titania's refusal to negotiate on the subject of custody of the changeling violates the spirit of compromise that characterizes most healthy marriages.

8. Puck directs the barely controlled chaos of the lovers' "fond pageant," and at times we must wonder if even Oberon has control over this mischievous sprite. Indeed, Oberon seems to wonder about this himself: "This is thy negligence. Still thou mistak'st," he tells Puck, "Or else thou committ'st thy knaveries willfully" (III.ii.346–347). Puck's explanation for his error is plausible; nevertheless, he makes no bones about the fact that he is delighted with the consequences of his mistake. This is the pattern throughout the play; while Oberon represents a nominal authority figure in the fairy kingdom, it is Puck who controls the action. It is fitting that the actor who plays Puck speaks the play's epilogue, which reminds the audience that what they have just seen should be given no more importance than a dream. Throughout

the play we have seen Puck as a director of sorts. In the epilogue, when he promises to "mend" those parts of the play that do not please, he is identified with the role of author. We are reminded by Puck's speech that at the original production of this play he spoke on behalf of a living author who could conceivably "mend" those parts of the production that the audience found unsatisfactory.

9. In Act V, the four groups of characters are brought together by means of the symbolic harmony of the marriage ritual. Theseus and Hippolyta, who represent rational authority and stability, are married along with Hermia, Lysander, Demetrius, and Helena. This triple wedding signals the reacceptance of the young people into Athenian society, and the royal wedding is blessed by the royalty of the fairy world, Oberon and Titania. Even the artisans' silly play has symbolic significance. It represents a gift offered, as Theseus observes to Hippolyta, in "simpleness and duty" (V.i.83).

    A Midsummer Night's Dream resembles modern television situation comedies in that all its complex conflicts are satisfactorily resolved in the end — at least on the surface. In the conventional television situation comedy, an initially stable situation is complicated by some sort of conflict so that order has to be restored. As in Shakespeare's play, this complication often stems from thwarted desire. In a typical *I Love Lucy* episode, for example, the stable domesticity of the Ricardo's middle-class life is disrupted when Lucy embarks on some crazy scheme. Chaos invariably ensues, but by the end of the show order has been restored. Students should be encouraged to apply this basic comic movement from order, to disruption, and back to order to an episode of their own favorite sitcom.

10. *A Midsummer Night's Dream* provides a wealth of comic scenes for analysis, ranging from the verbal comedy of Helena's exchange with Demetrius in II.i to the outrageous slapstick of the *Pyramus and Thisbe* play. Many scenes combine both verbal and physical humor. For example, the encounter between the four young lovers in III.ii depends for its comic effect partly on the verbal barbs the lovers toss at each other. Equally important, however, is the scene's physical comedy as Lysander tries to shake off Hermia as he would a burr, and he and Demetrius try to prevent her from attacking Helena.

11. The *Pyramus and Thisbe* play in *A Midsummer Night's Dream* is Shakespeare's parody of the early Elizabethan interludes he knew from his youth and may, perhaps, have performed in as a young actor in London. It is a comic exaggeration of such crude works as Thomas Preston's *Cambises, King of Persia* — although, as anyone who has read the latter play can attest, it is not much of an exaggeration. The artisans' incompetence as actors, of course, further intensifies the humor already inherent in the play's clumsy verse.

    Thematically, however, the play-within-the-play constitutes a sophisticated comment on the relationship of illusion to reality. Theseus opens the fifth act of the play with a lengthy speech on the power of the imagination, and when Hippolyta complains of the silliness of the play after hearing its first few lines, her husband comments, "The best of this kind are but shadows; and the worst are no worse, if imagination amend them," adding, "If we imagine no worse of [the actors] than they of themselves, they may pass for excellent men" (V.i.205–206, 208–209). In other words, if the three newly married couples are willing to utilize their imaginations to compensate for the deficiencies of the play's script and acting, it will be the equal of a well-written, skillfully presented production. Since Bottom and his companions present the play "with good will" (V.i.110), the aristocrats ought to receive it in the same spirit and use their superior imaginations to "amend" its deficiencies. By appealing to the sense of *noblesse oblige* on the part of his original aristocratic audience, Shakespeare invites them to accept his play, *A Midsummer Night's Dream*, in the same charitable spirit as that with which Theseus and his court accept the artisans' inept interlude.

The plot of *Pyramus and Thisbe* is also significant. It is a tragedy of star-crossed lovers — the sort of play *A Midsummer Night's Dream* might have become had it not been for the benign intervention of Oberon and Puck in the young lovers' affairs.

Finally, the plot of the play may be something of an inside joke for Shakespeare and his audience, since many scholars believe that the play he had written directly before *A Midsummer Night's Dream* was *Romeo and Juliet*, another tale of star-crossed lovers who "kill [themselves] most gallant for love."

12. There are several points in the play at which we are aware that the action might take a tragic turn. First, Hermia faces a possible death penalty for resisting her father's will, although Theseus does commute this penalty to life imprisonment in a nunnery. The fighting match between Hermia and Helena in the woods has decidedly nasty and even violent overtones, and when Lysander and Demetrius withdraw to fight, they might actually hurt each other if Puck does not intervene.

On the whole, however, the edge of danger in *A Midsummer Night's Dream* is not so pronounced as in some of Shakespeare's later comedies, especially the so-called problem comedies, such as *All's Well That Ends Well* and *Measure for Measure*. The Athenian marriage law with which Egeus threatens his daughter is so draconian that we are probably not meant to take it very seriously, and the conflict between the young couples is obviously adolescent in tone. It is conceivable that the play could be transformed into a tragedy, but it would be more like the artisans' *Pyramus and Thisbe* play than like *Romeo and Juliet*.

POSSIBLE CONNECTIONS TO OTHER SELECTIONS

Henrik Ibsen, *A Doll House* (text p. 700)
Jane Martin, *Rodeo* (text p. 1004)
Tim O'Brien, "How to Tell a True War Story" (text p. 1149)
William Shakespeare, *Hamlet, Prince of Denmark* (text p. 345)

RESOURCES FOR TEACHING

SELECTED BIBLIOGRAPHY

Chambers, E. K. "The Occasion of *A Midsummer Night's Dream.*" *A Book of Homage to Shakespeare*. Ed. Israel Gollancz. London: Oxford UP, 1916. 154–160.

Dent, R. W. "Imagination in *A Midsummer Night's Dream.*" *Studies in English Literature* 35 (1964): 115–129.

Leggatt, Alexander. *Shakespeare's Comedy of Love*. London: Methuen, 1974.

Price, Anthony, ed. *Shakespeare's* A Midsummer Night's Dream: *A Casebook*. London: Macmillan, 1983.

Warren, Roger. A Midsummer Night's Dream: *Text and Performance*. London: Macmillan, 1983.

AUDIOVISUAL RESOURCES

A Midsummer Night's Dream. 117 min., b/w, 1935. VHS. With James Cagney, Mickey Rooney, Olivia de Havilland, Dick Powell, and Joe E. Brown. Directed by William Dieterle and Max Reinhardt. See local retailer.

A **Midsummer Night's Dream.** 111 min., b/w, 1963. Beta, VHS. With Patrick Allen, Eira Heath, Cyril Luckham, Tony Bateman, Jill Bennett. A Live BBC-TV performance, with Mendelssohn's incidental music. Distributed by Video Yesteryear.

A **Midsummer Night's Dream.** 120 min., 1968. Beta, VHS, 16-mm film. With Diana Rigg and David Warner. Directed by Peter Hall. A Royal Shakespeare Company performance. Distributed by Drama Classics Video. Available for rental from member institutions of the Consortium of College and University Media Centers.

A **Midsummer Night's Dream.** 120 min., color, 1982. Beta, VHS. With Helen Mirren, Peter McEnry, and Brian Clover. See local retailer. Available for rental from member institutions of the Consortium of College and University Media Centers.

A **Midsummer Night's Dream.** 165 min., color, 1983. Beta, VHS, ³/₄″ U-matic cassette. With William Hurt and Michelle Shay. A lively interpretation by Joseph Papp. Distributed by Films for the Humanities and Sciences. Available for rental from member institutions of the Consortium of College and University Media Centers.

A **Midsummer Night's Dream.** 194 min., color, 1987. Beta, VHS. With Ileana Cotrubas, James Bowman, and Curt Appelgren. Directed by Peter Hall. A performance of the Benjamin Britten opera, taped at the Glyndebourne Festival Opera. Distributed by Films, Inc.

A **Midsummer Night's Dream** [recording]. 1 cassette. Dramatization performed by the Folio Theatre Players. Distributed by Spoken Arts.

A **Midsummer Night's Dream** [recording]. 3 cassettes (text included). Dramatization performed by Paul Scofield and Joy Parker. Distributed by Caedmon/HarperAudio.

A **Midsummer Night's Dream** [recording]. 1 cassette (60 min.), 1985. Dramatization performed by Stanley Holloway and Sarah Churchill. Living in Shakespeare Series. Distributed by Crown Publishers.

A **Midsummer Night's Dream** [recording]. 2 cassettes (120 min.). Performed by Robert Helpmann and Moira Shearer. An Old Vic production. Distributed by Durkin Hayes Publishing.

A **Midsummer Night's Dream: Introduction to the Play.** 26 min., color, 1970. Introduction to famous scenes and characters. Distributed by Phoenix/BFA Films and Video.

ESSAYS

KATIE ROIPHE, *The Independent Woman (and Other Lies)* (p. 907)

A good place to begin discussion of this essay is with the title. Ask your students what kinds of expectations the title sets up for readers. Does the essay meet these expectations? The title implies that the notion of an independent woman is a lie, yet the essay itself is more ambivalent. What kind of tone does the title have? Is this tone found in the rest of the essay?

Roiphe asserts that the attraction which she and other successful women have for financially successful men is not about their money, as much as it is about "the reassuring feeling of being protected and provided for, a feeling that mingles with love and attraction on the deepest level" (p. 909). Although this statement is arguable, ask your students if they recognize some truth about relationships in these words. Do they think that most women still long to be financially provided for?

Roiphe voices the objections that many of your students will share: "What about love? Love isn't supposed to be about dollars and cents and who puts their Visa card down" (p. 910). Yet a closer examination of many of the works in this anthology (and throughout literature) will demonstrate that in many ways love is about dollars and cents. From the tale of Cinderella to Ibsen's *A Doll House*, a woman's financial dependence on her mate has been an attraction on both sides. Ask your students if they can think of other examples in which a female character struggles between a desire to be taken care of and a desire to be independent.

Ask your students their opinion of the somewhat brief and undeveloped conclusion. Roiphe claims that she continues to date men who who lack financial means, but that she still longs for the Man in the Gray Flannel Suit (a metaphor for the 1950s image of the successful male). What do your students think of this inconsistency? Do they dismiss Roiphe as a materialist and a hypocrite, or do they recognize her "dark and unsettling truth" (p. 912)?

POSSIBLE CONNECTIONS TO OTHER SELECTIONS

Robert Browning, "My Last Duchess" (text p. 827)

Henrik Ibsen, *A Doll House* (text p. 700)

Arthur Miller, *Death of a Salesman* (text p. 1007)

DEBORAH TANNEN, Sex, Lies, and Conversation (p. 913)

This essay gets at the heart of why most relationships are complicated: people, men and women in particular, have a hard time making themselves understood and understanding one another. In this essay, Tannen makes sweeping generalizations about the way males and females behave that she backs up with evidence and examples. Many of your students will intuitively recognize some of the conversational patterns that Tannen describes. You might ask them to write an in-class essay in which they choose one of Tannen's statements about male-female communication and argue why or why not their experience supports the same conclusion. Which ideas does your class seem to find most compelling? Do they agree with Tannen that these communication differences are the result of socialization? Do they agree that neither gender is more or less to blame for these problems, or do they think that one type of communication is genuinely preferable to another?

As an essay assignment, either brief or extended, have your students apply Tannen's ideas to a work in this anthology in which men and women are in conversation (see Possible Connections, below). Do literary examples support Tannen's thesis? Would the characters in the work benefit from a sociolinguistic approach to their problems? Why or why not?

POSSIBLE CONNECTIONS TO OTHER SELECTIONS

John Cheever, "Reunion" (text p. 563)

Susan Glaspell, *Trifles* (text p. 496)

David Henry Hwang, *M. Butterfly* (text p. 1296)

Henrik Ibsen, *A Doll House* (text p. 700)

WRITING IN PROCESS: PERSONAL RESPONSE

Eric Hoffbauer's student essay on Katie Roiphe's "The Independent Woman (and Other Lies)" is a well-written argument based on a personal response. In his first response and his brainstorming, Eric continues to come back to the issue of class, pointing out that the women about whom Roiphe generalizes in her essay are all members of the upper middle class. Ask your students if they considered the issue of class when they read Roiphe's essay. Do they agree with Eric that Roiphe's assumptions about class represent a flaw in her argument? How do your students respond to Eric's use of examples from his own life and those of his friends? Many of your students may be uncomfortable personalizing their own writing in this way, but you might point out to them that published essayists (including Roiphe) do this all the time.

ALTERNATIVE ASSIGNMENTS

1. Student writer Eric Hoffbauer claims that "[w]omen have the desire to be safe and secure, but so do men." Do you agree that women and men both long for security and protection? Do you think Roiphe's claims about women's ambivalence about independence apply to men as well? If so, is there a difference in the way men and women long to be taken care of? If not, why do you think men lack the desire for protection? Generate a thesis and write an essay in which you address these issues, using your own experiences for support.

2. (This assignment is a good exercise in learning how to develop and expand paragraphs as you revise drafts of your papers.) Eric Hoffbauer's essay, though short, is a good personal response to Katie Roiphe's essay. Choose a paragraph or an idea in Eric's essay that you think could be developed further and expand on that idea in a paper of your own.

11

Lessons from Life

As the works in this chapter demonstrate, life's lessons do not end with one's childhood. This chapter includes several coming-of-age stories such as John Updike's "A & P" and Gary Soto's "The Childhood Worries, or Why I Became a Writer," but it also demonstrates that people continue to struggle with growth and identity throughout their lives. Mark Halliday's "Young Man on Sixth Avenue" and Arthur Miller's *Death of a Salesman* both depict older men learning about themselves and confronting the illusions they had lived by in their youth.

Life's lesson's can be especially painful if one is a member of a racial or ethnic minority. Ralph Ellison's "Battle Royal," Langston Hughes's "Theme for English B," Saundra Sharp's "It's the Law: A Rap Poem," Patricia Smith's "What It's Like to Be a Black Girl (For Those of You Who Aren't)," and Gloria Naylor's "Taking Possession of a Word" all reflect the obstacles and contradictions that minorities face in American life.

You may wish to teach the works in the chapter in the order in which they are printed; if so, connections will emerge as you move through the readings. Ask your students to come to class each day with connections drawn between that day's reading and the ones that preceded it. You might also choose to narrow the theme to reflect genre or content (poetry, race, or childhood, for example). Either way, this chapter provides some canonical and some new writers that students may bring together.

FICTION

TONI CADE BAMBARA, *The Lesson* (p. 925)

"So I deal in straight-up fiction myself, 'cause I value my family and friends, and mostly 'cause I lie a lot anyway." Toni Cade Bambara's "straight-up fiction" has been collected in *Gorilla, My Love* (1972) and *The Sea Birds Are Still Alive* (1977), and in 1980 she published her first novel, *The Salt Eaters*. A number of her screenplays have been produced, including "Zora" (1971), "The Johnson Girls" (1972), "Epitaph for Willie" (1982), "Tar Baby" (1984), "The Bombing of Osage" (winner of the 1986 Best Documentary Award from the Pennsylvania Association of Broadcasters and a Documentary Award from the National Black Programming Consortium), and "Cecil B. Moore: Master Tactician of Direct Action" (1987). Born in New York City in 1939, Bambara graduated from Queens College in 1959, studied at the University of Florence and the École de Mme. Étienne Decroux in Paris and New York between 1961 and 1963, and earned her M.A. from City College, New York, in 1964. She has also studied dance, linguistics, and filmmaking. Her working life demonstrates similar variety: Bambara has been employed by the New York State Department of Welfare, directed recreation programs in the psychiatry department of Metropolitan Hospital, New York City, served as program director of Colony House Community Center, New York City, and taught at various colleges and universities, including Rutgers University and Spelman College.

The title is a good way to start discussion of this story: what is the lesson Miss Moore is trying to teach Sylvia (the narrator) and her friends? Is she successful?

Miss Moore is trying to get her charges to see that they live in a "society . . . in which some people can spend on a toy what it would cost to feed a family of six or seven" (paragraph 50) and that, in Sylvia's words, "Poor people have to wake up and demand their share of the pie" (44). But despite Sylvia's ability to paraphrase Miss Moore's lecture, it is clear she hasn't completely taken it in when she goes on to say, "Don't none of us know what kind of pie she talking about in the first damn place." Miss Moore has, however, had some success: Sugar provides her with precisely the answer she was hoping to hear: "You know, Miss Moore, I don't think all of us here put together eat in a year what that sailboat costs. . . . This is not much of a democracy if you ask me. Equal chance to pursue happiness means an equal crack at the dough, don't it?" (49 and 51).

Still, the fact that Miss Moore can sense Sylvia's anger assures her that at least some of her point has gotten across. We (the readers) can sense it too, when Sylvia thinks things such as "I sure want to punch somebody in the mouth" (41), "Who are these people that spend that much for performing clowns and $1,000 for toy sailboats? What kinda work they do and how they live and how come we ain't in on it?" (44), and finally "I'm going . . . to think this day through. . . . Ain't nobody gonna beat me at nuthin" (58).

Ask the class what they think the last line of the story means. Does Sylvia think Sugar is smarter than she is because Sugar knew the answer to Miss Moore's question and she didn't? Could the "nobody" in that line refer to anyone other than Sugar?

Sylvia is annoyed and feels betrayed partly because Sugar is suddenly playing into the student/teacher game Miss Moore creates on these occasions, which the kids all usually hate; Sylvia feels Sugar shouldn't be giving Miss Moore the time of day. But Sylvia is also unhappy because to identify the problem (the unequal distribution of wealth), as Sugar has done, is to admit that there is a problem — and this is something Sylvia hasn't come to terms with. We know this from her earlier comments about Miss Moore's lecture: "And then she gets to the part about we all poor and live in the slums, which I don't feature" (3). So the last line of the story refers not only to Sugar but to Sylvia's position (and that of black people in general) in society.

Clearly Bambara intends this story to be instructive to her readers as well as to the children in Miss Moore's charge. It is not easy to make a social comment of this nature without sounding preachy; ask the class how she manages it.

Humor is one of the hallmarks of Bambara's style, and the accuracy with which she renders her characters' speech is marvelous. Her language is charged with enough energy to snare even the most lethargic reader, and she captures the rhythm and idioms of her characters' dialect precisely, brilliantly contrasting the children's "street" talk against Miss Moore's "proper speech."

Possible Connections to Other Selections

Ralph Ellison, "Battle Royal" (text p. 931)
Katherine Mansfield, "Miss Brill" (text p. 1270)

Resource for Teaching

Interview with Toni Cade Bambara [recording]. 1 cassette (58 min.). Discussion of Bambara's origins, work habits, publishing, and writing. Distributed by American Audio Prose Library.

RALPH ELLISON, *Battle Royal* (p. 931)

The opening paragraph of this story is fairly abstract and may be difficult for some students to grasp on first reading. But by the story's end the narrator's comments in this paragraph should have become very clear. Throughout this story Ellison is concerned with the masks, roles, and labels people impose on one another in this society. The narrator is invisible because the town's white citizens don't see him (or anyone else black) for what he is — which is, simply, a human being. What they see is a black man, or, in their vocabulary, a "nigger," "coon," or "shine." And "niggers," to their minds, are to be treated a certain way; mainly, they are to be publicly humiliated and abused. It is bitterly ironic that these men can bestow a great honor on this boy (the college scholarship) and simultaneously treat him worse than they would treat their dogs. It is equally ironic that, despite the brutal treatment the narrator receives at the hands of these men, he still wants to give his speech and is still proud to receive their gift.

The horrifying battle royal can be seen as a metaphor for the society the narrator lives in, in which nothing makes sense. Ten black boys are viciously used by some of the most important men of the town; they are forced to provide a freak show — first in the boxing ring, later on the electrified rug. In both cases they are jerked around like puppets on a string. They are, in fact, puppets; the white men are the puppeteers. If the boys refuse to fight one another, or to grab for the money with sufficient enthusiasm, it is clear the drunken white mob will hurt them much worse than they will hurt one another. White men have the power and make the decisions in this society, so the boys do as they are told. And not once do any white men — the very source of all this angry violence and confusion — get hurt.

The boys are brought in front of the naked blonde in an attempt to make them feel as uncomfortable as possible; they are not supposed to look at white women, and, left to their own devices, they wouldn't, especially in a room full of drunken white men. The blonde, with her ironic American flag tattoo, suggests all the things the boys (who are supposed to be Americans too) can't have simply because they are black: dignity, self-respect, freedom of choice, the freedom not to beat each other up or be beaten up by the white citizens present.

The blonde also serves another, very different function: at the same time that she is supposedly superior to the boys by virtue of the color of her skin, she is being used by the men; she too is a puppet. In paragraph 9, when she is being tossed into the air, the narrator sees the same "terror and disgust in her eyes" that he and the other boys are feeling.

As a high-school graduate, the narrator is extremely naive and believes that these men really respect him as he gives his speech after the battle, barely able to talk because he is choking on his own blood. In retrospect, as an educated adult, he realizes that he could not possibly have gotten an ounce of respect from any of them, and that, if he had known better at the time, he would not have respected himself. He realizes now that he was a laughing stock and that the white men were sending him the very message he read in his dream: "Keep This Nigger-Boy Running." In retrospect, too, he is able to understand his grandfather's dying words. His grandfather meant that a black man in this society didn't stand a chance by fighting racism openly. Instead, he believed blacks should pretend to play the game; white people had so much power that it was only by working within their system (by receiving scholarships to black colleges, for example, and then leading black people "in the proper paths") that blacks could hope to accomplish anything in the fight for equality. Dignity and self-respect, meanwhile, could come from within, since you would know you were agreeing them "to death and destruction" (2).

POSSIBLE CONNECTIONS TO OTHER SELECTIONS

Toni Cade Bambara, "The Lesson" (text p. 925)
Paul Laurence Dunbar, "We Wear the Mask" (text p. 1279)
William Faulkner, "A Rose for Emily" (text p. 144)
M. Carl Holman, "Mr. Z" (text p. 996)

MARK HALLIDAY, *Young Man on Sixth Avenue* (p. 942)

It is difficult to estimate how students might identify with the young man described in Halliday's story. Their reaction may be dictated by their age, their experience, and their ability to empathize with others. Traditional college students might prefer the ambitious, confident man characterized in the first three paragraphs of the story to the older, more settled figure described in the three final paragraphs of the story. However, nontraditional students might identify more closely with — or appreciate the perspective of — the older man.

Ask the students how they might characterize the time and setting of this story. In 1938, for instance, America was coming out of the Great Depression. Manhattan was then, as it is now, in many ways the center of American business and culture: as Halliday notes, it is "the biggest, the most overwhelming city" (paragraph 1). In addition, the story includes numerous references not only to the year but also to such public figures as Rita Hayworth, Theodore Dreiser, Thomas Wolfe, and John O'Hara. Students might benefit from studying standard bibliographic entries about these figures, but at the least, they should know that these references enforce the theme of the story — that a person's confidence and expectations of success in youth are too often balanced by the reality of a later life that may be, at best, mundane. Consider how the reference to Rita Hayworth informs the story: in 1938, Hayworth had recently married Edward Judson, a businessman who furthered his wife's career in significant ways, in part by renaming her and transforming her from a dancer of Hispanic origin into a red-haired, much-admired American star. However, Hayworth is also significant because although she made such a vivid impression in films such as *Gilda* (1946), her potential was never realized. She ended her career a pathetic figure unable to remember lines or manage her own assets. She was eventually diagnosed as a victim of Alzheimer's disease. The distance between her youthful success and the reality of her later life parallels the experiences of the protagonist in Halliday's story.

The literary references also reinforce the theme of unrealized potential. Perhaps the most fruitful comparison that may be made is between Halliday's protagonist and Dreiser's George Hurstwood, from *Sister Carrie* (1900). Hurstwood is portrayed at the beginning of the novel as an ambitious, reasonably successful Midwestern resort manager. After leaving his position and his family to move to New York with a young woman to whom he is not married, he experiences a dramatic decline of fortune. By the end of the novel, he has succumbed to despair.

The protagonist of "Young Man on Sixth Avenue" is supremely confident at the beginning of the story. Halliday characterizes his abundant energy: "His legs were long and his legs were strong; there was no question about his legs; they were unmistakable in their length and strength; they were as bold and dependable as any American machine . . ." (paragraph 1). In addition, this man is confident that he conveys evident cachet; others on the street, he is sure, will notice him. When he dines with his friend John at a "witty" late lunch, "Everything was — the whole lunch was good. It was right. And what they said was both hilarious and notably well-informed" (5). All in all, this man has intelligence, style, ambition, and potential. However, in the very next paragraph, and throughout the remainder of the story, his energy has been replaced by lethargy; readers may be shocked to discover that the up-and-coming young man has become someone who dozes off "in the blue chair, with his work on his lapboard, after a pleasant dinner of macaroni and sausage and salad" (6). Not only is the man's sedentary life-style surprising, but his prosaic dinner is in sharp contrast to the earlier reference to the man's appreciation for "the right restaurant for red roast beef, not too expensive" (3), or the Seventh Avenue lunch described in paragraph five.

The narrative structure of this story emphasizes the way in which the man is surprised by the relentless march of time. In the space of three sentences, the better part of this man's life — his business success, his marriage, and his fatherhood — passes. Just as he is shocked to discover that much of his life is over, so the reader is shocked by the sudden transition from youth to middle age. In essence, Halliday elides the climax in order to enable readers to appreciate some of the confusion and surprise the man must be feeling about the passing of his own life.

Halliday provides some foreshadowing of the man's later life in paragraph four when the man encounters "an unexpected zone of deep shade." Though his future is, he thinks, quite bright, the shadow makes him shiver and pause (4). This is in striking contrast to his energetic, almost mechanized pace one block earlier. Ask students to identify what the "deep shade" represents. In addition, invite them to envision the experience of being surrounded — and dwarfed — by the tall buildings and the enclosed space of midtown New York City. For a man who conceives of his potential through metaphors of height ("he moved visibly tall with the tall potential of the not-finite twentieth-century getting that would be his inheritance" [1]), this sudden recognition of his limitations is daunting.

Finally, you may want to call students' attention to the man's different attitudes toward women at the beginning of his life and at the end. (In fact, the final paragraph details his posthumous awareness.) In the beginning, he regards women in the same way that he regards his career: "He knew they knew he would *get* some of them" (1). He's supremely confident in his effect on them: "They felt that they or their sisters would have to take him into account, and they touched their scarves a little nervously" (1). In the end, however, he has lost his confidence (or his arrogance): "Women see past him on the street in this pseudo-present and he feels they are so stupid and walks fierce for a minute . . ." (8). What makes this character worth a second, more sympathetic evaluation is his immediate adjustment of his attitude: "his shoulders settle closer to his skeleton with the truth about these women: not especially stupid; only young" (8). It is evident in this passage that although the man may never have accomplished his early goals (something "that would have made people say 'Yes that's why you matter so much'" [7]), he has nonetheless achieved some sense of humanity and sympathy in his life.

Ask students to interpret the final sentence of the story. What does the man's memory of himself as a young man add to the story as a whole? What is the significance of the young man stepping back onto the curb in that final line? Is this more a reflection of the older man's wistful yearning for the energy of his youth, or some form of regret about the way he once approached life?

POSSIBLE CONNECTIONS TO OTHER SELECTIONS

T. S. Eliot, "The Love Song of J. Alfred Prufrock" (text p. 1280)
Herman Melville, "Bartleby, the Scrivener" (text p. 944)

HERMAN MELVILLE, *Bartleby, the Scrivener* (p. 944)

Although students are usually intrigued by Bartleby's bizarre behavior, they are likely to respond to the "inscrutable scrivener" in much the same way that Ginger Nut assesses him: "I think, sir, he's a little *luny*" (paragraph 49). But to dismiss Bartleby as, say, a catatonic schizophrenic reduces the story to merely a prescient case study and tends to ignore the narrator-lawyer, the other major character. Besides, we don't learn enough about Bartleby to make anything approaching a clinical judgment because, as the lawyer tells us in the first paragraph, "No materials exist, for a full and satisfactory biography of this man." He is as disturbingly mysterious as Godwin's protagonist in "A Sorrowful Woman" (p. 189).

Before you begin your discussion of "Bartleby, the Scrivener," consider asking students to write a first response in which they describe their reactions to the story's title character. Like the narrator, many students find him infuriating, while others admire his determination, sometimes in spite of themselves. As they write, they should consider some of the terms relating to character introduced in this chapter. One difficult question concerns Bartleby's *motivation*. Your students may speculate about his motives for his peculiar behavior, but Melville never provides one. Does this fact make him a less *plausible* character for them? Certainly he is a *consistent* one; do they think the narrator's character is *consistent* as well? To what degree is he *plausible*? Which characters, if any, are *dynamic*, and which are *static*? Which characters, if any, are *flat*, and which are *round*? Have your students compare their answers. You may find that they have very different readings of these characters.

What makes the story so weird — a term that nearly always comes up in discussions of Bartleby — is that the lawyer and the scrivener occupy two radically different fictional worlds. We recognize the lawyer as a character from the kind of fictions that convey at least some of the realistic textures of life, but Bartleby seems to be an allegorical or symbolic intruder in that world. Melville uses Bartleby to disrupt the lawyer's assumptions about life. It's as if a Kafka character suddenly turned up in a novel by Dickens or James. Melville makes us, as much as the lawyer, feel that Bartleby is somehow out of place.

The protagonist is the lawyer. (Some critics, however, see Bartleby as the story's central character. For alternative readings see the article by Stern cited at the end of this discussion.) Melville has the lawyer characterize himself in the first few paragraphs so that we understand the point of view from which we will see Bartleby. No champion of truth and justice, the lawyer makes his living doing a "snug business among rich men's bonds, and mortgages, and title-deeds" (2). He is convinced that "the easiest way of life is best"; he is an "eminently safe man" who takes pride in his "prudence," "method," and status (signified by his reference three times in the second paragraph to John Jacob Astor). His other employees, Turkey, Nippers, and Ginger Nut, are introduced to the reader before Bartleby in order to make credible the lawyer's tolerance for eccentric behavior. So long as the lawyer gets some work out of these human copying machines, he'll put up with just about everything — provided they don't publicly embarrass him or jeopardize his reputation. It is significant that he is a lawyer rather than simply a businessman because the law is founded on precedents and assumptions; Bartleby, however, is "more a man of preferences than assumptions" (149). Because Bartleby is beyond the lawyer's experience, the lawyer does not know how to respond to the scrivener's passive refusal to "come forth" and do "his duty."

Despite the title, the story is the lawyer's, because his sense of humanity enlarges as a result of his experience with Bartleby. "The bond of a common humanity" creates "presentiments of strange discoveries [that] hover[ed] round me" (91). The lawyer moves beyond his initial incredulity, confusion, anger, and frustration and begins to understand that Bartleby represents a challenge to all his assumptions about life. Finally, he invests meaning in Bartleby instead of dismissing him as eccentric or mad. Melville expects the reader to puzzle out his meaning too.

Bartleby's physical characteristics foreshadow his death. When we first meet him (17), he already seems to have withdrawn from life. He is "motionless" and "pallidly neat, pitiably respectable, incurably forlorn!" He seems scarcely alive and is described as "cadaverous." With nearly all the life gone out of him, he is capable of nothing more than "silently, palely, mechanically" (20) copying until he prefers not to — a refusal that marks the beginning of his increasing insistence on not living.

Bartleby's "I would prefer not to" confuses and enrages the lawyer and his employees. This simple declaration takes on more power and significance as the story progresses (not unlike Edgar Allan Poe's use of "nevermore" in "The Raven"). Bartleby's seemingly mild statement carries with it considerable heft, because "some paramount consideration prevailed with him to reply as he did!" (39). His declaration is both humorous and deadly serious.

The Dead Letter Office is essential to understanding what motivates Bartleby's behavior. Although Melville is not specific, he suggests enough about the nature of the thwarted hopes and desires that the scrivener daily encountered in the Dead Letter Office to account for Bartleby's rejection of life. Somehow it was all too painful for him and rendered life barren and meaningless — hence his "dead-wall reveries." The lawyer makes the connection between this experience and Bartleby. But Melville has him withhold that information so that we focus on the effect Bartleby has on the narrator rather than on the causes of Bartleby's rejection of life. By the end of the story, the lawyer has a chastened view of life that challenges his assumption that "the easiest way of life is best."

You may want to ask students to identify the different walls that comprise the various settings of this story. (In addition to those in the office, the walls of the prison at the end of the story are significant.) Melville's story is subtitled "A Story of Wall Street" because Bartleby's "dead-wall reveries" represent a rejection of the materialistic values that inform the center of American financial interests. Business and money mean nothing to Bartleby, but they essentially constitute the sum total of the lawyer's life until his encounter with him. Melville sympathizes with the characters while rejecting their responses to life. He clearly does not endorse the lawyer's smug materialism, but neither does he offer Bartleby's unrelenting vision of death as an answer to the dehumanizing, mechanical meaninglessness that walls the characters in. In this story Melville presents issues, not solutions; it is exploratory rather than definitive.

This story can be usefully regarded as a kind of sit-in protest — at least on a metaphysical level — with nonnegotiable demands. Bartleby is a stubborn reminder that the lawyer's world is driven by expediency rather than principle — that the lawyer's satisfaction with life has been based on his previous avoidance of the big issues. Surprisingly, there is some delightful humor in the story as the characters' exasperation with Bartleby's behavior develops. We know that the scrivener is going to get a rise out of them. There is also humor in Bartleby's reply to the lawyer that he is "sitting upon the banister" (195) when the lawyer asks him what he's doing in his office building on a Sunday. And consider the lawyer's suggestions that Bartleby be a bartender, a bill collector, or a traveling companion "to entertain some young gentleman with your conversation" (199–210). A student once suggested that a dramatization of the story should feature Richard Nixon as the lawyer and Woody Allen as Bartleby. Ask students for their own suggestions on who might play these roles; the question encourages them to think of what goes into a characterization.

Students might be asked to trace their reactions to Bartleby while they read, then to compare them with how they respond to him after class discussion of his character.

For an excellent survey of the many varied critical approaches to the story, see Milton R. Stern's "Towards 'Bartleby the Scrivener,' " in *The Stoic Strain in American Literature,* ed. Duane J. MacMillan (Toronto: U of Toronto P, 1979), 19–41.

POSSIBLE CONNECTIONS TO OTHER SELECTIONS

Robert Frost, "Mending Wall" (text p. 121)
Gail Godwin, "A Sorrowful Woman" (text p. 189)
Nathaniel Hawthorne, "Young Goodman Brown" (text p. 1246)

RESOURCES FOR TEACHING

Herman Melville. 22 min., color, 1978. Beta, VHS, $^3/_4$" U-matic cassette, 16-mm film. Ancillary materials available. Part of the "Authors" series of biographies. Distributed by Journal Films, Inc. Available for rental from member institutions of the Consortium of College and University Media Centers.

Herman Melville: Consider the Sea. 28 min., color, 1982. Beta, VHS, $^3/_4$" U-matic cassette, 16-mm film, special-order formats. Deals with the author and his relationship with the sea. Major works discussed include *Moby-Dick, Billy Budd,* and "Bartleby, the Scrivener." Distributed by the International Film Bureau. Available for rental from member institutions of the Consortium of College and University Media Centers.

Melville: Six Short Novels [recording]. 8 cassettes (60 min. each). Read by Dan Lazar. Includes "Bartleby, the Scrivener," "The Apple Tree Table," "My Chimney," and "The Happy Failure." Distributed by Books on Tape.

Herman Melville: Damned in Paradise. 90 min., color, 1986. Beta, VHS, ³/₄" U-matic cassette. Documents Melville's personal and intellectual history. Distributed by Pyramid Film and Video. 8 cassettes (60 min. each). Available for rental from member institutions of the Consortium of College and University Media Centers.

Bartleby. 79 min., color, 1970. VHS. Cast: Paul Scofield, John McEnery. Directed by Anthony Friedman. Distributed by: White Star.

Bartleby. 28 min., color, 1969. VHS. Distributed by Britannica Films.

Bartleby. 29 min., b/w, 1965. VHS. Videotape from the "American Story Classics" series. Distributed by Film Video Library.

Bartleby, the Scrivener [recording]. 1 cassette (90 min.). Read by Walter Zimmerman. Distributed by Jimcin Recordings.

JOYCE CAROL OATES, *The Night Nurse* (p. 969)

In this story, Oates effectively creates a terrifying situation for her protagonist; she also invests the story with surprising compassion. The reader's initial expectations of both protagonist and antagonist are transformed; both women discover depth of character within themselves that is surprising. Grace Burkhardt's self-satisfied assumptions about herself are challenged and dramatically altered in the course of the story; in addition, though Harriet Zink might at first remind us of a stereotypical Stephen King character (perhaps Annie, the woman who entraps and tortures the writer in *Misery*), she, too, is a surprisingly dynamic character.

"The Night Nurse" contains all the elements of a thoroughly frightening story. A hospital would seem to be a place of safety and security, well-staffed with knowledgeable, caring people. However, even before night falls, there are several suggestions that the setting might be more ambiguous than the reader initially imagines. Grace thinks of a former lover, "an intelligent man, a reasonable man, yet, on the subject of hospitals, adamantly irrational" (paragraph 33). In addition, her potential for anxiety is intensified, albeit inadvertently, by the stories she hears: "her sister, meaning well, had told her alarming tales of negligent and even hostile nurses and attendants at big-city hospitals as a way of assuring Grace that here, by contrast, in this suburban hospital, she would receive better treatment" (46). Left alone for the night, she cannot help but imagine the worst. She is also in intense physical pain. In addition, after visiting hours are over, she feels completely alone and helpless. She is immobilized; she is shivering; she cannot seem to get any help from the staff at the hospital. The "sharp smell of urine" (36), even after the bedpan has been taken away, intensifies the unpleasant impression of this setting. In addition, the eeriness of the setting is enhanced by the consistent references to the time.

What is most alarming to Grace is her lack of control. She envisions herself as a smart, capable, kind, successful woman: "Her name was Grace Burkhardt and she was forty-four years old and she was a woman accustomed, as the chief administrator of a state arts council, to exercising authority" (6). As she deals with friends and business matters on the phone after her surgery, it is most important to her to regain some authority over her own life: "Nothing meant more to her than to take back the control she'd lost back there in the pedestrian mall, to tell her story as if it were her own" (11). In the night, without anyone there, she succumbs to panic (15). She also turns, uncharacteristically, to prayer (17), a gesture that will be increasingly significant by the end of the story. Until this point in her life, she has always regarded herself as a kind person: "Hadn't she overheard, to her embarrassment, just the other day, two young women staff members at the arts council speaking of Grace Burkhardt warmly, comparing her favorably to her male predecessor" (74). This passage is ultimately ironic: Grace will leave the hospital with a much clearer sense of her pride, selfishness, and lack of charity. After her encounter with Harriet Zink, Grace is particularly aware of her spiritual shortcomings. (Her name is especially apt in this context.) She recognizes that she was far more unkind to Harriet than she has ever acknowledged; in addition, Grace recognizes, *"I am not that strong. I am not evil, but I am not that strong. In [Harriet's] place, I could not forgive"* (111). Thus, by the end of the story, we have a deeper, richer understanding of this flawed but sympathetic character.

When we first encounter Harriet, surprisingly early in the story, long before she and Grace have their revealing conversation, she is a nameless, ominous impression: "a face floated near, a stranger's face that was at the same time familiar as a lost sister's" (8). (Given their history together and their similarities — they are both scholarship girls, from farming families — this is especially significant.) The physical description of Harriet is also ominous: "The features were indistinct but the skin was strangely flushed and shiny, like something not quite fully hatched. There was a smile, thin-lipped and tentative. No-color eyes" (10). In the phrases "not quite fully hatched" and "no-color," Oates establishes readers' initial impression of the nurse as something inhuman — an impression enhanced later by reference to the nurse's "glass marble" eyes (62) and her skin "the color of spoiled cantaloupe" (64). When the nurse is (finally) described physically, she also seems rather grotesque: "so short as to seem almost dwarfish. Hardly five feet tall. But round-bodied, with a moon face, peculiar flushed skin that was smooth and shiny as scar tissue; small close-set damp eyes; a thin pursed mouth" (28). Complete with the references to her sweat-stained armpits, she seems a disgusting creature. There is also an implied malevolence to the way she appears in or leaves the room, seemingly from nowhere (see paragraphs 20, 23, 48, and 56). Grace's impressions of her early in their conversation also enhance this impression: *"She's mad, she's come to injure me"* (65). Much to our surprise, and Grace's as well, Harriet ultimately turns out to be something other than a monster. Just when she seems poised to attack Grace, hovering over her in anger, Harriet has her own epiphany: "her expression shifted suddenly, turned unexpectedly thoughtful. She said, with the air of one making a discovery, 'Yes, I can forgive you, Grace Burkhardt. I'm a Christian woman. In my heart I'm empowered to forgive'" (106). Students might initially interpret the tone of this passage as sanctimonious or self-righteous, but the exposition and the imagery suggest a more sincere interpretation. Harriet "spoke with such sudden pride, it was as if sunshine flooded the room" (106). In contrast with all the dark, night imagery, Harriet's forgiveness warms both characters like afternoon sun.

POSSIBLE CONNECTION TO ANOTHER SELECTION

Nathaniel Hawthorne, "Young Goodman Brown" (text p. 1246)

JOHN UPDIKE, *A & P* (p. 981)

John Updike is one of those rare writers who command both popular acclaim and critical respect. The prolific novelist, short story writer, and poet was born in Shillington, Pennsylvania, in 1932, completed a bachelor's degree at Harvard University (where he worked for a time as a cartoonist for the Harvard *Lampoon*), and spent a year at Oxford University studying at the Ruskin School of Drawing and Fine Arts. After returning from England in 1955, he worked at *The New Yorker*, where he began publishing his short fiction. He left the magazine in 1957 to write full time.

Updike's great subject is the relationship between men and women, especially in marriage. The Rabbit novels (*Rabbit, Run*, 1960; *Rabbit Redux*, 1971; *Rabbit Is Rich*, 1981; and *Rabbit at Rest*, 1990; named for their protagonist, Harry "Rabbit" Angstrom) constitute perhaps the best-known examples of this preoccupation. Updike has received numerous awards, including the National Book Award, the Pulitzer Prize, and the Creative Arts Medal for Lifetime Achievement from Brandeis University. His collections of stories include *Pigeon Feathers* (1962) and *Trust Me* (1987); his novels include *The Centaur* (1963), *The Coup* (1978), and most recently, *S.* (1988). His poetry collections include *The Carpentered Hen and Other Tame Creatures* (1958) and *Tossing and Turning* (1977); his nonfiction works include a collection of essays and criticism, *Hugging the Shore* (1983), and the memoir *Self-consciousness* (1989).

Sammy's voice is what pulls us into "A & P," thanks to his engaging first-person narration. Ask the class to describe his voice — the tone he uses, the things he thinks and says, the way he says them. What kind of a person is Sammy?

While Sammy is not exactly an all-American boy — he's too much of a smart aleck and somewhat disrespectful to his elders and to women (when he's not telling us about "sheep" or "houseslaves," he's focused on someone's belly or shoulders or "sweet broad soft-looking can") — he is funny, and we excuse most of his prejudices on the ground of youth. (He is young. It is difficult to imagine the more mature, responsible Stokesie, for example, quitting his job over this incident.) Updike's mastery of the vernacular makes Sammy all the more appealing: we enjoy hearing him talk and think, and his observations about protocol in the A & P and his small town are mercilessly accurate. At the same time Sammy is critical of this context, however, he is also a part of it: "We're [the A & P is] right in the middle of town, and the women generally put on a shirt or shorts or something before they get out of the car into the street. . . . Poor kids, I began to feel sorry for them, they couldn't help it" (paragraphs 10–11). He understands how the little world he lives in works, and he knows it is inappropriate for the girls to be wearing bathing suits in the A & P.

Ask the class to identify the climax of the story (Sammy quitting his job) and to discuss why Sammy quits.

Sammy hasn't given us any evidence that he hates his job. He has a friend there, and his wonderful description of using the cash register suggests he gets a certain amount of pleasure from his mastery of the machine. He is bored, however. (His descriptions of the store's regular clientele and the view from the front of the store demonstrate this.) And, without realizing it, he's probably looking for a cause, or at least something to react to. He does, after a while, feel bad for the girls, and quitting becomes a heroic gesture. In his mind, he isn't defending the honor and dignity of just these three embarrassed girls but of everyone, including himself, who feels humiliated or restricted by the narrow parameters of the silly, limited, limiting town or society in which they live.

Ask the class what Sammy gains from quitting. In acting on what has suddenly become principle, does he gain anything?

On the surface, he certainly loses more than he gains. The gesture is lost on the girls, who hightail it out of the store too fast even to hear him. And, of course, he loses his job. But for the moment, anyway, he retains his dignity — and the last line of the story suggests he has already gained some perspective.

Ask the class whether they think Sammy should have quit and whether they agree that "once you begin a gesture it's fatal not to go through with it" (31). How do they imagine Updike feels about this statement?

The relatively somber tone of the story's last three paragraphs, along with the narrator's dramatic last line, suggests that Updike does not agree with Sammy on this point. Sammy's going to learn from this experience, but he's learning the hard way. (This can lead to an interesting paper: exploring the roles and attitudes of the two minor characters, Stokesie and Lengel, by comparing them with Sammy.)

Another good writing assignment would be to compare this story with Bambara's "The Lesson" (p. 925), a story with a similarly humorous and personable first-person narrator. Both narrator-protagonists have many critical things to say about the people around them. Both are young, use slang, and come from a different social class than some of the people they encounter, or have to think about, during the course of their respective stories. Both learn something unpleasant about the way the world works and experience a certain initiation into maturity. In what ways are Sammy's and Sylvia's experiences different? Is one story more concerned with the issue of growing up, while the other focuses more on social and political issues? In what other ways are the stories similar or different?

Possible Connections to Other Selections

Colette, "The Hand" (text p. 163)

Ernest Hemingway, "Soldier's Home" (text p. 579)

Resources for Teaching

John Updike. 30 min., b/w, 1966. 16-mm film. Discusses Updike's beliefs and attitudes. The author reads selections from his works. Distributed by Indiana University Instructional Support Services.

Selected Stories by John Updike [recording]. 2 cassettes (2 hrs., 49 min.), 1985. Updike reads six unabridged stories: "A & P," "Pigeon Feathers," "The Family Meadow," "The Witnesses," "The Alligators," and "Separating." Distributed by Random Audiobooks.

What Makes Rabbit Run? 29 min., color, 1986. VHS, 16-mm film. Updike reads from his works and discusses his life. Distributed by Barr Entertainment.

Writers: John Updike. 30 min., b/w, 1966. ¾″ U-matic cassette, 16-mm film, special-order formats. An interview with the writer. Distributed by Indiana University Instructional Support Services. Available for rental from member institutions of the Consortium of College and University Media Centers.

POETRY

JULIA ALVAREZ, *Woman's Work* (p. 986)

This poem describes a woman whose mother tried to convince her that "woman's work" (i.e., domestic chores) is "high art." The speaker's mother is devoted to the perfection of her art, and she tries to convince the speaker to follow in her footsteps. While the mother argues that housework is an art, the speaker feels that it is a prison at the same time. The speaker rejects this life-style but still manages to become her "mother's child" (line 17) since she devotes herself wholeheartedly to her own art, writing.

The effect of the poem's departure from the villanelle form (it does not repeat line 1 exactly in lines 6, 12, and 18 but rather varies the theme in each of these lines) is to emphasize the poem's theme: redefining "woman's work" while elevating it as "high art." The speaker alters the original line each time she repeats it just as she alters her mother's definition of woman's work. The other departure from the villanelle form is that the rhymes are not always strict (tiles, outside, satisfied, pies, advised, child). How would the poem be different if the poet had kept the rhyme scheme strict, as Thomas does in "Do not go gentle . . ."? Comparisons of these poems may prove interesting, since each one may seem to exclude the other gender. Alvarez's poem is consciously a woman's poem. Is Thomas's consciously a man's poem? Would his poem change considerably if references to "men" became references to "people"? Are the traits he is lauding in others and encouraging in his father typically "masculine" traits?

POSSIBLE CONNECTIONS TO OTHER SELECTIONS

Jim Daniels, "Short-order Cook" (text p. 989)

Dylan Thomas, "Do not go gentle into that good night" (text p. 268)

WILLIAM BLAKE, *The Chimney Sweeper* (p. 987)

There is an ironic distance in this poem between the speaker, who seems to be too young to make judgments, and Blake, who through his ironic perspective underscores the harm that comes from too meekly doing one's duty, not to mention the evil of a society indifferent to the plight of "thousands of sweepers" whose only pleasure is in dreams. Needless to say, sacrificing one's hair for the sake of on-the-job cleanliness is not a principle Blake would endorse.

On the surface the poem could be interpreted as a dream of desire for some beneficent angel to release the boys from their "coffins of black" (the chimneys). More likely, the dream expresses a desire for release through death from the torturous and life-threatening trials of sweeping soot from chimneys. Here again, irony operates in that a dream of death makes it easier for the boy to face his life the next morning.

POSSIBLE CONNECTION TO ANOTHER SELECTION

Paul Laurence Dunbar, "We Wear the Mask" (text p. 1279)

ANN CHOI, *The Shower* (p. 988)

Many of your students may have a friend with whom they share a long history. For younger students, they may just be beginning to move in different directions from this friend. Older students can attest to the importance of seeing these friends through life's major milestones — graduation, marriage, parenthood. As a first response, ask your students to write a description of their longest-lasting friendship and to speculate about what the friendship will bring in the future. How do they feel about their friends moving on, experiencing lives of which they can only be a small part?

These are the types of questions invited by a reading of Ann Choi's "The Shower." The poem's tone is bittersweet: clearly, the speaker is happy to see her friend "marry and fill / a house with sounds of dishes / and of children," but there is a sense of loss as well, a sense of "time / quicken[ing]" and a certain dread in "the permanence of the ring / around your finger." Point out to your students the way Choi's opening and closing stanzas imply the continuity of life. Just as the speaker and her friend were once young girls learning music, so will the friend's children one day play "one brief note after another."

While this poem is about the speaker's friend, your students should be able to infer some characteristics of the speaker as well. She says nothing about her life, but the fact that she does not mention a ring around her own finger or children of her own implies that she is still single at the occasion of her best friend's wedding shower. Ask your students if they think the tone of the poem would be different if the speaker were referring to her own marriage and children as well as those of her friend. (You might note that "The Shower" was first published when its author was twenty-two years old; does this fact affect your students' reading in any way?)

POSSIBLE CONNECTIONS TO OTHER SELECTIONS

Mark Halliday, "Young Man on Sixth Avenue" (text p. 942)

E. B. White, "Once More to the Lake" (text p. 532)

JUDITH ORTIZ COFER, *Common Ground* (p. 989)

This poem has two seemingly distinct stanzas whose connection is not at first apparent. The first stanza, addressed to a vague "you," employs very specific bodily images to refer to "your" inevitable death. The second stanza is written in the first person, with the odd transitional phrase "these days" linking the two, although the speaker has not referred to any days besides "these." Ask your students what they make of this transition.

Nearly all people who know their relatives can relate to the experience of seeing their own physical traits in someone else. Many people's earliest memories consist of being told which parent they most resemble or which side of the family they take after. These connections are past of what provides us with our identity and creates ties to our past. If you ask your students, they will probably speak about these connections in a positive way. If invited, they may wish to share stories of their own physical resemblance to other family members.

Cofer's poem puts a different spin on this notion of common ground. If the past is painful, this "common ground" can be an unpleasant reminder of how difficult it is to escape the legacy and destiny of one's family members. Inheriting "stern lips," "disdainful brows," and "nervous hands" is a sad reminder of where one has been and (worse) where one is going. Ultimately, as the first stanza reminds us, these physical characteristics are the first manifestations of certain death, a return to "the stuff of your origin."

POSSIBLE CONNECTIONS TO OTHER SELECTIONS

Ann Choi, "The Shower" (text p. 988)
E. B. White, "Once More to the Lake" (text p. 532)

JIM DANIELS, *Short-order Cook* (p. 989)

Under the pressure of time and the scrutinizing gazes of the counter girls, the speaker of this poem, a short-order cook, rises to the challenge of an unusually large order. He summons all the grace he can and completes the order, celebrating the cycle of "pressure, responsibility, success" (line 27).

The poem's structure contributes to the rhythm of the speaker's situation: the breaks between the first and second stanzas act as pauses before the frenzied activity of the third stanza. The slashes between lines in the third stanza serve to contribute to the frenzied pace of the speaker's activity. Does anything else motivate this speaker besides "responsibility" (27)? The counter girls, not the "average joe," are his audience. How does their interaction alter his behavior?

Students may be quick to find the humor in this poem, because the speaker takes his job so seriously. You might want to begin a discussion by listing as many jobs as your students have had. Were/are there times when they have felt as seriously the "responsibility" associated with work? What other situations (that might evoke diction as elevated) arise at work? Does work, or attitudes toward work, ever have social implications? If so, what?

POSSIBLE CONNECTION TO ANOTHER SELECTION

Marge Piercy, "The Secretary Chant" (text p. 213)

EMILY DICKINSON, *From all the Jails the Boys and Girls* (p. 990)

Here is a perfect poem for the last day of the semester! Dickinson captures the joy and energy of children released from school by playing trios of images against one another. The "Jails" of the first line and the "Prison" and "keep" — a pun that evokes both a sense of being held and the medieval image of a castle dungeon — in the fourth express the confinement the children endure during the school day. The released prisoners "leap" (line 2), and "storm" and "stun" (5) the world into which they escape. The sense of attacking life to demand everything it has to give is unmistakable, especially when one considers the use of transcendent words such as "ecstatically" (2), "beloved" (3), and "bliss" (6). The triple alliteration of *F*s in the last two lines attempts to bring things back down to earth. You might ask your students whether or not the last two lines have the tempering effect that the bearers of the frowns hope to convey. With which feeling does the end of the poem leave students?

POSSIBLE CONNECTIONS TO OTHER SELECTIONS

Robert Frost, " 'Out, Out–' " (text p. 992)

Judy Page Heitzman, "The Schoolroom on the Second Floor of the Knitting Mill" (text p. 995)

ROBERT FROST, *After Apple-Picking* (p. 991)

The sense of things undone and the approach of "winter sleep" seem to betoken a symbolic use of apple picking in this poem. Moreover, the speaker has already had an experience this day — seeing the world through a skim of ice — that predisposes him to view things strangely or aslant. At any rate, he dreams, appropriately enough, of apple harvesting. Apples take on connotations of golden opportunity and inspire fear lest one should fall. As harvest, they represent a rich, fruitful life, but as the speaker admits, "I am overtired / Of the great harvest I myself desired" (lines 28–29).

Apples are symbolically rich, suggesting everything from temptation in the garden of Eden, with overtones of knowledge and desire, to the idea of a prize difficult to attain, as in the golden apples of Hesperides that Hercules had to obtain as his eleventh labor. Here they can be read as representing the fruit of experience.

POSSIBLE CONNECTION TO ANOTHER SELECTION

William Stafford, "Traveling through the Dark" (text p. 1175)

ROBERT FROST, " 'Out, Out —' " (p. 992)

So often when disaster strikes, we tend to notice the timing of events. Frost implies here that "they" might have given the boy an extra half-hour and thereby averted the disaster. This perspective, coupled with the final line, in which the family seems to go on with life and ordinary tasks, can appear callous. But compare the wife's chastisement of her husband in "Home Burial" (text p. 617). Is the attitude callousness, or is it, rather, the impulse of an earth-rooted sensibility that refuses pain its custom of breaking the routine of life-sustaining chores and rituals? Very little in this poem seems to be a criticism of the survivors; rather, like *Macbeth* and the famous speech that proclaims life's shadowy nature (text p. 239), it seems to acknowledge the tenuous hold we have on life.

POSSIBLE CONNECTIONS TO OTHER SELECTIONS

Emily Dickinson, "From all the Jails the Boys and Girls" (text p. 990)

William Shakespeare, From *Macbeth* (text p. 239)

NIKKI GIOVANNI, *Clouds* (p. 993)

In this short poem, Nikki Giovanni writes eloquently of the joys of joining nature in its everyday routines. The narrator's desire to "swim with hippos" and "jump with salmon" indicate a celebration of the here and now, but her final wish, to "ride off with the clouds / at the end," also implies an escape. What sorts of activities does the speaker long for? What is so appealing about her desires? Do your students share these wishes?

The poem is arranged in an unusual way. Ask your students why they think the poem's lines are centered the way they are. How does this choice combine with Giovanni's word choices to create the poem's total effect?

Gerard Manley Hopkins, "God's Grandeur" (text p. 258)

MARILYN HACKER, *Groves of Academe* (p. 993)

From the point of view of a weary poetry professor, this poem encompasses the various responses she receives when she asks, "Tell me about the poetry you're reading." All of the responses dodge the question, focusing instead on the budding poets themselves rather than on the seemingly nonexistent poetry they are reading.

As students of poetry themselves, your students may feel uncomfortable as the subjects of this poem. They may also tend to distance themselves from the student voices in the poem. They may characterize the speaker as cynical: why doesn't she include any of the brilliant responses from students who *do* take the initiative to read poetry that isn't required in class? You might ask them if it is necessary to read poetry if you are to be a poet. If so, how does one find the time to do so in college? This may spark a lively discussion about the undergraduate experience — how valuable a commodity time is, how professors have no sense that students are taking more than one course, and so forth.

Having flushed out the attitudes of the speaker and students in the poem, you may return the discussion to the topic of "Groves of Academe" as a poem. It has an elaborate rhyme scheme, for instance, which addresses the student's question in lines 12–13. How else do Hacker's techniques play with the content of the poem? While characterizing the speaker, it is also useful to characterize the poem: is it a satire? Is the poet exaggerating the voices that she represents? (She has fit them into a rhyme scheme, so it isn't likely that she's copied them verbatim from students.) Is the humor biting — the speaker wants to foster "perversity" in herself, after all — or is it light? Point out how each of the students emphasizes themselves in their responses. Is the speaker arguing that all young poets are egotistical?

Robert Browning, "My Last Duchess" (text p. 827)
Mark Halliday, "Graded Paper" (text p. 994)

MARK HALLIDAY, *Graded Paper* (p. 994)

Students may enjoy analyzing Halliday's characterization of this professor who soliloquizes about the merits and faults of his student's paper. Ask students to identify the professor's biggest objection to the paper. What pleases him about it? What displeases him? How much does the professor seem to have in common with the student, as far as we can tell from the comments included in "Graded Paper"?

The professor begins by noting those aspects of the student's paper that please him: "your main argument about the poet's ambivalence — / how he loves the very things he attacks — / is mostly persuasive and always engaging" (lines 2–4). The remainder of the poem incorporates the professor's criticisms of the work, and those criticisms are made in a highly organized fashion. First, the professor comments on the paper's thesis. He then moves on to the supporting ideas, the language, and the punctuation, winding up with some quasi-encouraging comments. The grade, an "A-", is a symbol of the grader's own ambivalence toward the student. What prompts the "minus"? A partial answer lies in the professor's acknowledgment that "You are not / me, finally" (35–36) as well as his comments on age — his own and his student's — throughout the poem.

POSSIBLE CONNECTIONS TO OTHER SELECTIONS

Robert Browning, "My Last Duchess" (text p. 827)
Marilyn Hacker, "Groves of Academe" (text p. 993)

JUDY PAGE HEITZMAN, *The Schoolroom on the Second Floor of the Knitting Mill* (p. 995)

The narrator comments in the opening lines of Heitzman's poem that she misses her teacher, Mrs. Lawrence. This establishes an impression of the teacher — that she has made an unforgettable, positive impact on the narrator — that the last stanza chillingly contradicts. Ask students to assess the initial description of Mrs. Lawrence, in which the narrator explains that "While most of us copied letters out of books, / Mrs. Lawrence carved and cleaned her nails" (lines 1–2). Clearly, the narrator is not in an interactive classroom — the task of copying letters seems less an effective pedagogical approach than drudgery. In addition, the teacher obviously withholds her attention from her students. Why, then, does Mrs. Lawrence's comment have such a dramatic impact on the narrator, not only in her memory of that day, but throughout her life?

Students may find themselves inspired by this poem to write about their own childhood memories, as well as the effect of the past on the present.

POSSIBLE CONNECTION TO ANOTHER SELECTION

Emily Dickinson, "From all the Jails the Boys and Girls" (text p. 990)

M. CARL HOLMAN, *Mr. Z* (p. 996)

Students will readily perceive the irony of this poem: the man who lived so that his racial identity was all but obliterated earned as his summary obituary the reductive, faint, and defaming praise "One of the most distinguished members of his race." His loss is a double loss, to be sure; not only did he fail finally to be judged according to white standards (those he aspired to) but in the process of living up to those standards he "flourish[ed] without [the] roots" of his own racial identity. Review the poem for its ironic phrases. You may have to explain that racial, religious, and ethnic differences were often suppressed in favor of assimilation and that the celebration of and return to these differences is a relatively recent tendency.

POSSIBLE CONNECTIONS TO OTHER SELECTIONS

Elizabeth Alexander, "Harlem Birthday Party" (text p. 612)
Paul Laurence Dunbar, "We Wear the Mask" (text p. 1279)

ANDREW HUDGINS, *Seventeen* (p. 997)

This brutal poem describes the experience of a teenaged speaker who watches a dog nearly die as it spills out of a pick-up truck ahead of him. After a brief confrontation with the truck driver, it is up to the speaker to put the dog out of its misery. He does so, methodically, and indicates that some time has passed between the event and the present, during which he has been able to contemplate the meaning of it.

Seventeen is not that long ago for many college students, and it may be productive to begin by asking them to describe any defining moments or events that they experienced at or around that age. The speaker cusses at an adult for the first time in his life and expects "a beating" (line 18) in return, which is the punishment a child would have received. What he undergoes is much more painful; you might want to ask students to describe the psychological or social differences between being beaten up and having to do away with a suffering animal.

The poem relies on verbs to communicate the scene; you might want to isolate some of these verbs and discuss why the speaker chose them to paint the picture. It is interesting to note how the speaker begins to rely on adjectives — consider "blue" (33), "loose" (35), and "orange and purple" (36) — in the final six lines of the poem. Does this event somehow change the way he thinks about the world? How does the preponderance of adjectives vs. verbs reflect the speaker's emotional or mental state? Why is it significant that he didn't know the words for "butterfly weed and vetch" at the time, but now, when he writes about the scene, he both uses these words and emphasizes that he didn't know the words before?

POSSIBLE CONNECTION TO ANOTHER SELECTION

William Stafford, "Traveling through the Dark" (text p. 1175)

LANGSTON HUGHES, *Johannesburg Mines* (p. 998)

Hughes creates a very stark and political poem out of the statistical fact that 240,000 native Africans work in the Johannesburg mines. The social implications of this poem about exploitation, victimization, and colonization are designed to force some level of consideration on the part of the reader. Ask your students why South Africa, even today, is such a highly suggestive setting. What sort of automatic response does South Africa elicit from readers? You might ask students to discuss what they know about South Africa, including recent political developments. How (if at all) do they believe that conditions there have changed since Hughes wrote this poem in 1925?

Ask students what they feel the tone of this poem is. It may be described, in part, as angry, serious, stunned, outraged, and sober. The fact that there are "240,000 natives / Working in the / Johannesburg mines" (lines 7–9) may lead students to question this exploitative social system. The mines are presumably owned by whites, and black Africans work in the mines because they have few employment opportunities. This subjugation of the natives by nonnative whites becomes at least part of the theme of this poem. Ask students how they see Hughes's radical political ideology evidenced in this brief poem. How would an American worker in 1925 relate to this poem? How would an American worker today react?

POSSIBLE CONNECTION TO ANOTHER SELECTION

William Blake, "The Chimney Sweeper" (text p. 987)

LANGSTON HUGHES, *Theme for English B* (p. 998)

This poem reads like a personal narrative, and indeed it does embody certain elements of Hughes's life. For example, "the college on the hill above Harlem" (line 9) is a reference to Columbia University, where Hughes was (briefly) a student. Therefore, asking a student to read this narrative to the class might make the speaker's story appear more poignant than if it were read in silence. You might ask students to pay particular attention to lines 21–26. The speaker defines himself in terms of the things he likes, which are nearly universal in their appeal, and recognizes that "being colored doesn't make [him] *not* like / the same things other folks like who are other races" (25–26). Ask students how this observation complicates the speaker's understanding of his relationship with the white college instructor and with whites in general.

You might also ask students how the double meaning of "theme" adds to the meaning of the poem. The speaker's assignment is to write a one-page "theme," that is, a brief composition. But the subject, or "theme," of that "theme" is far broader and more complicated: race relations and personal experiences. You might ask students if they noticed any other words with more than one interpretation in the context of this poem. One example might be the word *colored*, which means both that the writer is black and that he has been "colored," that is, affected, by the racial conditions into which he was born.

Ask your class to consider, in discussion or in a brief writing assignment, the importance of lines 31–33. How does the speaker understand himself and the white instructor to be part of each other? Why does he consider this to be particularly "American" (33)? How would your students describe Hughes's vision of America?

POSSIBLE CONNECTIONS TO OTHER SELECTIONS

Chitra Banerjee Divakaruni, "Indian Movie, New Jersey" (text p. 1277)
Mark Halliday, "Graded Paper" (text p. 994)

MAXINE HONG KINGSTON, *Restaurant* (p. 999)

You may wish to begin a discussion of this poem by noting the way Kingston has structured the lines — they are rhymed couplets (though often the rhymes are slant), and they have no regular rhythm or meter. Because there is no particular meter, the rhymes are subtle and unpredictable, and the line breaks take the reader by surprise. This irregular rhythm lends a sense of breathlessness to the poem — readers rarely get to relax as they move from one line to the next, since many of the lines are heavily enjambed as they adhere to the poem's rhyme scheme. To demonstrate this breathless pacing, you might ask students to read aloud the first eight lines, where only lines five and eight are end-stopped, and where all the rest of the lines create a strong sense of tension and resolution in the reader. The breathless quality of the poem captures the breathlessness of the scene the speaker is describing — the frantic pace of a restaurant kitchen.

Have your students consider lines 15–16, when the speaker admits, "In this basement / I lose my size." Students may have different interpretations of these lines. One possible interpretation is that the speaker loses her individual identity in the basement as she slaves away. Other students might intrepret these lines to mean that the speaker had imagined herself to be "too big" for this job — above it somehow — and as a result is diminished by the reality of her situation. Although the speaker may lose size, she still demonstrates a remarkable strength, lifting "a pot as big as a tub with both hands" (18).

The final lines of the poem contain a powerful image — one that students are not likely to miss for its unavoidable irony. After the exhausting ordeal in which so many workers expend so much energy to create a meal, the "clean diners" dine in luxury — "behind glass in candlelight" (25), blissfully unaware of the effort it took to create the meal they are enjoying. This is the first moment in the poem where the speaker moves from description into something more reflective, as the frantic pace of the kitchen slows to allow the workers to observe the fruits of their labor.

Student readings of this poem may be enriched by some understanding of Marxist literary theory (text p. 68), since Kingston presents a startling picture of difference based on privilege and wealth.

POSSIBLE CONNECTION TO ANOTHER SELECTION

Langston Hughes, "Dinner Guest: Me" (text p. 1286)

RESOURCES FOR TEACHING

Maxine Hong Kingston [recording]. 1 cassette, 1986. Interview. Distributed by American Prose Library.

The Stories of Maxine Hong Kingston. 54 min., color, 1990. VHS. Kingston discusses her perspective on the "Great American Melting Pot." Distributed by University of Washington Educational Media Collection.

KATHARYN HOWD MACHAN, *Hazel Tells LaVerne* (p. 1000)

You might begin discussing this poem by talking about names and how they too have connotative value. Would our expectations be the same if the poem were titled "Sybil Speaks with Jacqueline"? By and large this poem does a good job at getting across its meaning through denotative language. But the fact that Hazel does use language almost exclusively in denotative terms is in itself a sign of her personality. As in a dramatic monologue by Robert Browning, Hazel tells more about herself, her social class, and her impenetrably matter-of-fact outlook on life than she does about her encounter with the frog. We as readers then fill in the gaps of the speaker's perceptions as well as piece together her outlook and attitude.

You might ask students to respond to Hazel's personality. She is likable; her matter-of-factness cuts through any of the fairy tales the world might try to sell her, and she's funny. Students can probably provide examples of characters from TV shows who are like Hazel and whose humor derives from their plain-spoken concreteness. We all admire the survivor who cannot be duped.

POSSIBLE CONNECTION TO ANOTHER SELECTION

Robert Browning, "My Last Duchess" (text p. 827)

SAUNDRA SHARP, *It's the Law: A Rap Poem* (p. 1001)

Note this poem's title. It claims to be a "rap poem." What expectations does this claim set up? What do your students associate with rap music? Are any of them fans of rap? In what ways is this poem a rap poem? Does it read like it could be set to music? How does the author's use of rhyme, rhythm, and "filler" lines like "unh-hunh" and "Listen up!" contribute to our sense that this is rap poem?

The other part of the title indicates the poem's content, "It's the law." What does the speaker say about "laws" here? In how many different ways is she using the term?

The speaker seems to have an ambivalent attitude about laws, implying that there are too many laws on the books yet stating, that "The laws we make are what we do to each other." In other words, if we obeyed a single law — "Don't do to me what you don't want done to you"— there would be no need for the endless numbers of laws on the books that date back centuries. There is also a sense that many of the laws are unjust; the speaker reminds us, for example, that some go back to the days "when the Indians got kicked," but again she sees the larger problem as being a lack of self-respect in those who might break the laws. Her focus is more on convincing her readers to respect themselves, to "walk tall," than it is on praising or criticizing any specific law, just or unjust.

POSSIBLE CONNECTION TO OTHER SELECTIONS

K. C. Cole, "Calculated Risks" (text p. 538)
Langston Hughes, "Theme for English B" (text p. 998)

PATRICIA SMITH, *What It's Like to Be a Black Girl (For Those of You Who Aren't)* (p. 1003)

Students are likely to have strong reactions to this powerful poem. Race is sometimes a difficult issue to discuss, especially in racially mixed classes, and this poem asks us to look at the reality that racism and sexism are not things of the past, despite what some optimistic students like to think. The speaker asserts in unambivalent terms that life as a "black girl" involves self-loathing, insecurity, sadness, and violence. Ask your students to write a first response to this poem; do they think that Smith is accurately representing the experience of all or most black girls? Are the black girls in Smith's description representative of all social and economic classes? Does she seem to foreground the problems of race or gender in her description of a black girl's life?

Consider the parenthetical subtitle. How important is audience to this poem? Smith's intended audience could include white girls (and women) and black and white males. What specific messages is she sending these groups, and why do you think she addresses her poem to people who aren't like herself? How might this poem be different if it were addressed to other black girls?

With the exception of the initial letter, Smith chooses to write exclusively in lowercase letters. Ask your students what effect this alteration of standard English has on their reading. Smith's repetition of the word "it's" to describe life as a black girl has the relentless quality of life's trials being one thing after another.

Possible Connection to Another Selection

Saundra Sharp, "It's the Law: A Rap Poem" (text p. 1001)

JEAN TOOMER, Reapers (p. 1003)

"Reapers" is taken from Toomer's experimentalist novel *Cain* (1923), which combines poetry and prose and was one of the works that helped launch the Harlem Renaissance. The poem is ominous and grim in tone. Long before it was fashionable to call his people blacks, Toomer here stressed the dire nature of the scene by talking about black reapers and black horses. Scythes and mowers call to mind the image of death as a grim reaper, sometimes cutting down people in their prime. That symbolic association is enhanced by the death of the field rat, which seems to indicate also the vulnerability of the reapers to being cut down by some impersonal, indifferent force.

The sound of the rasping blade being honed to sharpness is suggested in lines 1 and 2 by the *s*-sounds. In question 4's version of line 6, certain alliterative and assonant sounds are linked by echoing sounds, as in "*fi*eld rat," "squ*ea*ling," "*b*l*ee*ds." A cause-effect relation is underscored by Toomer's version, which places "squealing" and "bleeds" together. Finally, the caesura provides rhythmic reinforcement of the action described.

Possible Connection to Another Selection

William Blake, "The Chimney Sweeper" (text p. 987)

D R A M A

JANE MARTIN, *Rodeo* (p. 1004)

Martin's brief monologue in the voice of Big Eight/Lurlene, a woman whose whole life has been involved in rodeo, hardly seems to be the stuff of engaging drama. However, the author's talent for drawing the audience into the lives of her characters soon makes her a sympathetic, then an empathetic character. By the time she utters her challenge — "[L]ook out, honey! They want to make them a dollar out of what you love. Dress *you* up

147

like Minnie Mouse. Sell your rodeo" (p. 1006) — the audience is more than ready to accept Big Eight as an individual and her plight as something that is a danger to us all.

CONSIDERATIONS FOR CRITICAL THINKING AND WRITING (p. 1006)

1. Martin presents Big Eight to the audience in such a way as to play into audience preconceptions about rodeo people. Consider the stage directions, which place her among horse equipment, dressed in jeans and a workshirt, drinking beer and listening to "Tanya Tucker . . . or some other female country-western vocalist" (p. 1004). Big Eight's later comments indicate that she probably chews tobacco, and her dialect stamps her as uneducated and crude. Martin allows, even encourages, the audience to prejudge her character, and the character of rodeo, then works to force us to see the other aspects of both the woman and the rodeo that exist beneath the stereotypical trappings. Big Eight turns out to be funny, touching, and wise, though uneducated. Audiences may be surprised to learn of the importance rodeo places on family life, as exemplified by the Tilsons and their five children on the circuit. By the time the audience learns that Big Eight has a real name — Lurlene — it is ready to accept her as a human being and lament the very human problem she exemplifies: that decent and caring people are pushed out of the way in the name of progress and the name of profit.

2. Rodeo is probably the most genuinely American of sports, having had its origin in the American West of the 1880s. Its events — saddle-bronc riding, bareback horse riding, bull riding, calf roping, steer dogging, and barrel racing — developed from skills necessary for cowboys on cattle drives. Rodeo probably began as an end-of-the-roundup celebration and competition. Rodeo has not historically been a "money" sport. Although six-time world champion Larry Mahan earned about $50,000 at the peak of his career, most rodeo participants only earn $15,000 to $20,000 per year, out of which they must pay all their living and traveling expenses. There is a certain lyricism in Big Eight's repeated lament of how the rodeo "used to be." According to Big Eight, the participants were cowboys and, more important, families of cowboys. The audiences were knowledgeable about and appreciative of rodeo skills — they "*knew* what they were lookin' at" because they "had a horse of their own back home" (p. 1005). As she sums it up at the end of the dialogue, "Rodeo used to be people ridin' horses for the pleasure of people who rode horses" (p. 1006). According to Big Eight, rodeo changed when business people realized they could make money from it: "they figure if ya love it, they can sell it" (p. 1006). But the investors who brought money into rodeo also brought a new set of rules, all meant to make the event marketable. They brought in clowns, costumes, and Astro-Turf. Largely through their efforts, Big Eight says, rodeo has become a group of hired performers playing to a crowd of "disco babies and dee-vorce lawyers."

3. Big Eight's language is full of slang and often crude. It helps to characterize her as tough and close to the earth. The colorful vocabulary she often employs enables the audience to feel the excitement and vitality of her character and her life. To emphasize this point, you might have students rewrite a few of her lines in standard English and compare their rewrites to the liveliness of the original. It is also interesting to note that Big Eight stereotypes businessmen and actors in cigarette commercials in much the same way as the new rodeo owners — and the audience — attempt to stereotype her.

4. Big Eight's sense of humor relies on crudity and exaggeration. Much of her humor is either sexual or scatological, but not mean. Audiences of the play are likely to

accept her as funny and likable. She probably expresses a lot of things members of the audience would love to say but wouldn't dare to.

5. As noted in the answer to Question 1, Martin initially presents Big Eight as a stereotype. However, the audience quickly gets to know her as a daughter, a hard worker, a funny woman, and an idealist whose dreams are being shattered. By the time she relates her story of being fired from the rodeo, the audience is ready to at least sympathize with her plight. Her final warning to her audience that the merchandisers will one day try to sell what *they* love serves to underscore the broader implications of her story.

    Two further considerations might develop in a discussion of this question. Do any of your students dislike Big Eight by the end of the play? Is it possible, once we realize that she has been fired from the rodeo, to consider this monologue as "sour grapes" on the part of a poor loser? Also, you might encourage your students to discuss other instances in modern life where business interests have entered into areas that are supposedly "off-limits." College basketball is one possible example. Another example is the Whittle Corporation's offer to equip American schools with high-tech video equipment on the condition that they be allowed to broadcast a daily newscast, including commercials, to the classrooms. Is any aspect of modern life "safe" from advertising? Should certain areas be kept free of such influences? Is business's entry into new areas always negative?

6. The aspect of rodeo that Big Eight mentions the most is the importance of family and community. The play opens with the story she tells about how she received her nickname from her father for staying on a bucking horse. The rodeo is "us" to Big Eight: "We'd jest git us to a bar and tell each other lies about how good we were" (p. 1005). The outsiders who come in and change the rodeo are "they." Significantly, one of the things the businessmen have done is to change the character of the people who participate in the rodeo. At the end of the monologue, we find out that neither Big Eight nor the Tilson family is involved any longer. The rodeo has been transformed from a closely-knit community to a business.

POSSIBLE CONNECTIONS TO OTHER SELECTIONS

Stephen Crane, "The Bride Comes to Yellow Sky" (text p. 1122)
Arthur Miller, *Death of a Salesman* (text p. 1007)
William Shakespeare, *Hamlet, Prince of Denmark* (text p. 345)
_____, *A Midsummer Night's Dream* (text p. 852)

ARTHUR MILLER, *Death of a Salesman* (p. 1007)

Willy Loman's intentions are the best; he wants what the "American Dream" of success promises: in addition to security, comfort, and possessions, he longs for love and respect. Unfortunately, he is all too willing to sacrifice the highest human values to achieve his dreams. He is a salesman who, ironically, sells himself; he fails to realize that he loses much more than he can possibly gain by lying, cheating, or stealing. His aspirations reflect everyone's longings, but his dream falls far short of the kind of idealism associated with his father's hard work and perseverance. He mistakes brand names for true values and in doing so earns the name of "Lo[w] man."

As you read and discuss this play with your class, consider its inclusion in an anthology chapter titled "Lessons from Life." Who are the recipients of the life lessons in this play? Is there any value in Willy's newfound understanding given his suicide? Does the promise of the next generation compensate for Willy's tragic mistakes? Are we,

149

the audience, the ones who should take Willy's lessons to heart? Although his specific situation is different, Willy resembles some other characters in this chapter who think they have life figured out but who have been going about things all wrong. Consider Mark Halliday's "Young Man on Sixth Avenue" or Marilyn Hacker's "Groves of Academe" in this light.

Ask your students if they feel the problems of Willy Loman and his family are typical problems faced by today's middle class. Does the pursuit of the American Dream still have the same romance? How has feminism altered the situation of the American family trying to achieve economic success? Do your students think a play like this could be written today?

POSSIBLE CONNECTIONS TO OTHER SELECTIONS

Lorraine Hansberry, *A Raisin in the Sun* (text p. 635)
Jane Martin, *Rodeo* (text p. 1004)
William Shakespeare, *Hamlet, Prince of Denmark* (text p. 345)
Tennessee Williams, *The Glass Menagerie* (text p. 448)

RESOURCES FOR TEACHING

Arthur Miller. 25 min., color, 1982. Beta, VHS, ³/₄" U-matic cassette. Explores themes in the works of Arthur Miller. Distributed by Films, Inc., Video.

Death of a Salesman [recording]. 2 cassettes, 2 hr., 16 min. Dramatization performed by Lee J. Cobb and Mildred Dunnock. Distributed by Caedmon/HarperAudio.

Death of a Salesman. 135 min., color, 1985. Beta, VHS. With Dustin Hoffman, John Malkovich, Charles Durning, and Stephen Lang. Directed by Volker Schlondorff. A made-for-TV adaptation of the play. Distributed by Orion Home Video, Facets Multimedia, Warner Home Video.

Private Conversations on the Set of *Death of a Salesman*. 82 min., color, 1985. Beta, VHS. With Arthur Miller, Dustin Hoffman, Volker Schlondorff, and John Malkovich. This PBS documentary presents heated discussions between actor, director, and playwright. Various interpretations of the play emerge and viewers gain insight into how each part contributed to the final production. See local retailer.

ESSAYS

REGINA BARRECA, *Envy* (p. 1073)

Even before reading Barreca's "Envy," most of your students will have something to say about the topic of this essay. Ask your students to freewrite in class about their experience with Envy: what types of people do they envy? Why? Do they consider themselves more or less envious than the average person? How deadly is Envy compared to the other deadly sins?

Look at this essay's opening. The tone is casual, almost as if the author were taking you into her confidence. In the second paragraph the author lists the things that she envies; there is a hint of shame, but also one of glee as Barreca unabashedly admits to being less than skinny, less than powerful, less than polished, less than graceful, and less than musically talented. This confession is an effective rhetorical strategy, eliminating the perceived distance between author and reader and winning the reader over to the author's side. Your students may not envy the same things Barreca does, but it is likely they share her feelings of wishing they possessed some of the desirable qualities of others.

Barreca uses other rhetorical strategies as well. She capitalizes the names of the seven deadly sins in order to personify them, making them sound almost like bickering siblings. Though she treats the subject humorously, it quickly becomes clear that the dark side of Envy is real as well and can lead one to "[grow] gaunt watching others eat" (p. 1074).

On p. 1074, Barreca distinguishes between Envy and jealousy. Ask your students to give other examples of this distinction. Do they agree that the two terms have different meanings? Unlike jealousy, Barreca implies, Envy can have a constructive as well as a destructive effect. Do your students see any benefits to Envy?

This essay might yield an interesting discussion about envious characters and speakers in this chapter. To what degree has Envy been a factor for the narrator in Melville's "Bartleby, the Scrivener," the speaker in Ann Choi's "The Shower," the teacher in Mark Halliday's "Graded Paper," or Willy Loman in *Death of a Salesman*?

POSSIBLE CONNECTIONS TO OTHER SELECTIONS

Katerina Angheláki-Rooke, "Jealousy" (text p. 826)
K. C. Cole, "Calculated Risks" (text p. 538)

GLORIA NAYLOR, *Taking Possession of a Word* (p. 1077)

In this essay Gloria Naylor expands on her thesis that "[w]ords themselves are innocuous; it is the consensus that gives them true power" (p. 1077). To illustrate her point, she discusses the painful and controversial word *nigger*. You and most of your students may have a knee-jerk repulsion to this word and may well be uncomfortable even saying it out loud in class. Confront this issue directly at the beginning of your discussion. What kinds of associations do your students have with the word *nigger*? Does the word have positive associations for any of them, as it does for Naylor? Why do your students think this is a such a powerful word? There are many other loaded words in our language. For example, the particular combination of letters that spell "Adolph" is harmless enough, but the word's association with history's most notorious mass murderer has made it synonymous with evil. Ask your students to think of other examples of the way consensus gives power to language.

Toward the end of her essay Naylor writes, "I don't agree with the argument that use of the word *nigger* at this social stratum of the black community was an internalization of racism" (p. 1078). What does Naylor mean by this statement? Do your students agree that by using the term, her community has rendered the word "impotent"? If so, why is it painful for black parents to explain the word to their children? Ask your students to write a brief passage in the voice of Naylor's mother explaining the meaning of the word *nigger* to her school-age daughter. Although Naylor does not include her mother's explanation or her own reaction to it, we can infer that this moment represented a turning point for a young black girl trying to "grow up in America" (p. 1079).

POSSIBLE CONNECTION TO ANOTHER SELECTION

Patricia Smith, "What It's Like to Be a Black Girl (for Those of You Who Aren't)" (text p. 1003)

GARY SOTO, *The Childhood Worries, or Why I Became a Writer* (p. 1079)

Most readers of this essay will recall the sensation of childhood worries: a sense of fear coupled with a lack of perspective and understanding. As you examine this essay, ask your students to describe the narrator's worries: Is there a pattern to the types of things he fears? Are these fears rational or irrational? You might look specifically at his fears of disease, using a bedpan in the hospital, roaches, his grandpa, church, being deformed, radiation, Communists, falling, and dying. Do your students think Soto was an unusually fearful child? The essay's final paragraphs address the narrator's emergence from this period of intense worry to the common childhood feeling of invincibility: "I knew that hurt and disease were way off, in another country, one that thanks to Jesus Almighty, I would never think to visit" (p. 1087).

This essay captures a sense of the universal insecurities of childhood, but it is also Soto's own story. To what degree do your students think Soto's story is universal, and to what degree are his experiences unique? Although everyone has childhood worries, not everyone becomes a writer. Consider how the essay's subtitle separates the narrator from the rest of us. He never directly discusses why he became a writer. Do your students see the answer to that question within the essay?

POSSIBLE CONNECTION TO ANOTHER SELECTION

K. C. Cole, "Calculated Risks" (text p. 538)

WRITING IN PROCESS: CRITICAL ANALYSIS

In this chapter's casebook, student writer Nancy Lager analyzes John Updike's short story "A & P" in light of the chapter's theme of "Lessons from Life." Point out to your students that Nancy begins with a first response that is more of a gut reaction than an analysis, a sense that the story is "strange." She also points out that it takes a second reading before she can really get a handle on the work (always a good idea for students, too). Although her analysis moves beyond this initial reaction, with a number of specific references to the text, another draft would improve it still. The essay relies a bit too much on summary and not enough on analysis. As you go through Nancy's writing as a class, discuss places where she could drive her thesis home more convincingly. Look also at her conclusion, which is abrupt. How might your students write a conclusion that gives this essay a greater sense of closure?

ALTERNATIVE ASSIGNMENTS

1. Nancy's analysis of the setting of "A & P" demonstrates the way an element of literature can contribute directly to our understanding of the work as a whole. Choose another text in this anthology and write a similar analysis of the way the setting of the work contributes to its meaning. There are a large number of stories, poems, plays, and essays that would work well with this assignment. Here are some suggestions from this chapter:

   Robert Frost, " 'Out, Out —' " (text p. 992)
   Arthur Miller, *Death of a Salesman* (text p. 1007)
   Gary Soto, "The Childhood Worries, or Why I Became a Writer" (text p. 1079)

2. Reread Nancy Lager's essay "The A & P as a State of Mind," this time in the persona of her teacher. Your job is to write a detailed response to her essay, commenting on what you think was successful in her work and what you think could be improved. Be very specific: as with any writing, you'll want to support your ideas with quotations from the text (in this case Lager's essay) and with thorough and detailed explanations of the essay's strengths and weaknesses. The more specific your suggestions for improvement are, the better.

12

The Natural and Unnatural

The first work in this chapter, Margaret Atwood's "Death by Landscape," sets up a number of important issues. These works of literature constitute more than just nature writing; they involve humankind's complicated and difficult relationship with nature. Like the main character in Atwood's story, many of us are both attracted to and repelled by nature. You might begin this unit with a class discussion about what determines people's relationship to the natural world. Part of it, of course, depends on where one is raised, although the connection is not always predictable. Sarah Orne Jewett's protagonist in "A White Heron" was raised in a manufacturing town but is identified strongly with farm and woodland life.

A number of works in this chapter are about animals and our place within and in relation to the animal kingdom. Mary Oliver's "The Black Snake" and William Stafford's "Traveling through the Dark" demonstrate how the death of an animal can lead us to consider our own death. Robert Frost's "Design" and William Blake's "The Lamb" and "The Tyger" all use an animal as a means of trying to understand God or the creator. A glance at some of the titles in this chapter reveals a number of other works about animals. Ask your students why they think so many writers use stories about and representations of animals to express their ideas about the natural world.

As Thomas Hardy's poem "The Convergence of the Twain" reveals, the will of humans and that of nature often clash. Yet this chapter demonstrates that though the force of the natural world is one human beings will never totally dominate, we can learn from it.

FICTION

MARGARET ATWOOD, Death by Landscape (p. 1095)

Like its title, this story is humorous and serious at the same time. Atwood's story about the disappearance of a teenage girl from summer camp lends itself well to a discussion about nature and Lois's ambivalent relationship with the natural world. Before learning about the literal loss of Lois's best friend at the age of thirteen, readers might find her attraction to and repulsion by nature perplexing. Paradoxically, Lois has filled her homes with paintings of landscapes but has taken great pains to avoid any confrontation with nature itself — glad that her new condominium exposes her only to potted plants. Ask your students why why Lois avoids nature itself while preferring representations of nature in her home.

This story works well when taught in terms of its elements; individually, they work together to create the rather haunted, sad effect of the story as a whole. The most important element to look at is probably setting; notice how Atwood describes Camp Manitou — a place where girls are removed from "civilization" in order to get closer to nature. Yet the camp leaders' attempts to make the experience more "natural" are laughably artificial: naming different groups of children after animals and imitating the cultural stereotypes of Native Americans. Even the choice of Canada is significant. Looking closely at character, notice how Atwood contrasts Canada and the United States in order to contrast Lois and Lucy. What do your students think of these characterizations? Do they think Atwood is stereotyping Americans or Canadians? If so, to what end?

In some ways, the friendship between Lois and Lucy seems an unlikely one. Ask your students why they think these two are drawn to one another. Do they think the two would be equally friendly outside of camp? Why or why not?

Although written in the third person, the story's point of view is almost exclusively Lois's. We learn the events of the Camp Manitou tragedy through Lois's memory. As a result, we never learn exactly what happens to Lucy. She probably jumped or fell over the lookout into the water below, but the mysterious tone Atwood creates in the latter part of the story allows us to speculate on a number of other possibilities: she ran away, or perhaps she vanished into some mysterious other world in which she still lives and from which she continues to haunt Lois. While we know this ghostly explanation is unlikely, it is nonetheless "true" for Lois and therefore it is "true" within the context of the story. Ask your students what they think happened to Lucy. As a writing exercise, consider having them write another scene in which Lucy's fate is revealed.

Possible Connection to Another Selection

Sarah Orne Jewett, "A White Heron" (text p. 1141)

T. CORAGHESSAN BOYLE, Carnal Knowledge (p. 1107)

Students might begin their analysis of this story by looking up a definition for the word *carnal*. *Webster's New Collegiate Dictionary* refers to "carnal" in part as "relating to or given to crude bodily pleasures and appetites," and in the *Oxford English Dictionary*, a prominent definition is "of the flesh." The question to be asked in connection with Boyle's title is, which flesh? The opening and concluding paragraphs depict Jim's thoughts about meat — from "[b]eef, mutton, pork, venison, dripping burgers and greasy ribs" (paragraph 1) to McDonald's hamburgers. While much of Jim's odyssey throughout this story involves the kind of meat he might find in a sandwich (pastrami, Thanksgiving turkey, a Big Mac), more of it focuses on his pursuit of Alena. Beginning in the first two paragraphs of "Carnal Knowledge," when Jim says, "I could never resist the veal scallopini. And then I met Alena Jorgensen," hunger is aligned with lust.

"Carnal Knowledge" is full of similar ironic parallels and *double entendres* playing Jim's participation in the Animal Liberation Front against his love affair with Alena. The connection is signified in the text by Jim's recognition that Alena's "eyes were ever so slightly mismatched, like the dog's" (11). Stunned as he might be about the way Alf was tortured by the shoe company, Jim is "moved even more by the sight of [Alena] bending over the box in her Gore-Tex bikini" (26): "'Tortured him?' I echoed, feeling the indignation rise in me — this beautiful girl, this innocent beast" (21). He calls in sick to work the next morning not because of a fierce personal commitment to fighting "species fascism" (18), but because he envisions himself spending "the rest of the day right there beside her, peeling grapes and dropping them one by one between her parted and expectant lips" (46). Later, considering his role as a liberator of turkeys, Jim thinks "about meat and jail and the heroic proportions to which I was about to swell in Alena's eyes and what I intended to do to her when we finally got to bed" (81). Thus the overall irony of the title. When Jim comforts himself at the end of the story — "'Meat,' and I spoke the word aloud, talking to calm myself as if I'd awakened from a bad dream, 'it's only meat'" (117) — he's talking about Alena as much as he is about his Big Mac.

There's also plentiful humor in Boyle's word choice throughout the story — word choice that foreshadows the end of the love affair, undermines Jim's attempt to be convincing in his commitment to the cause, and satirizes the animal rights movement along the way. Discovering that Alf has urinated on him, Jim is "glad to see that the thing was hobbled — it would simplify the task of running it down and beating it to death" (5). When Alena describes her work with the Animal Liberation Front, Jim "could only nod and exclaim, smile ruefully and whistle in a low 'holy cow!' sort of way" (32). Jim does begin to think more about the plight of animals — he admits that Alena "fascinated me, fixated me, made me feel like a tomcat leaping in and out of second-story windows" (55). And his ruminations at Rolfe's cabin reveal the limits of his allegiance to turkey liberation: "I was thinking of all the turkeys I'd sent to their doom, of the plucked wishbones, the pope's noses, and the crisp browned skin I used to relish as a kid. It brought a lump to my throat, and something more: I realized I was hungry" (72). From the name for the turkey farm ("Hedda Gabler's Range-Fed Turkey Ranch" [71]) to his depiction of the liberated turkeys' fate — "the road was coated in feathers, turkey feathers, . . . [a]nd more: there was flesh there too, slick and greasy, a red pulp ground into the surface of the road, thrown up like slush from the tires of the car ahead of me" (115) — Boyle never allows his reader to take Jim's odyssey seriously.

As a means of identifying the overall irony of "Carnal Knowledge," students might identify Jim's motivation. Encourage them to discuss Jim's situation. Certainly his age (and the fact that his adventure begins on his thirtieth birthday), his vocation (as a writer of advertisements), his aspirations (an evening of listening to his mother, aunt, and grandmother engage in "a spate of reminiscences," followed by "a divorced computer programmer in her midthirties with three kids and bad breath" [14]) all contribute to his participation in Alena's cause. As he admits, "I was giddy with the adolescent joy of it" (56). Some aspects of Jim's life may be all too realistic for some readers, but his career as a "liberator of turkeys" and his turn as "a turkey expressway" (97) resonate with humor, satire, and irony.

POSSIBLE CONNECTION TO ANOTHER SELECTION

Nathaniel Hawthorne, "Young Goodman Brown" (text p. 1246)

STEPHEN CRANE, The Bride Comes to Yellow Sky (p. 1122)

In this story Jack Potter is conflicted between the love and duty he feels toward his new wife and the love and duty he feels toward Yellow Sky. As town marshal, protector and defender of, and friend to, Yellow Sky, he feels he has betrayed the town not only by marrying a stranger but by marrying without the town's knowledge as well. Crane is playing with some traditional western myths here — most notably the idea of the lawman's loyalty to his territory above anything else, even personal happiness.

In fact, the title and first paragraph of this story set up our expectations for a typical western. The bride's coming to Yellow Sky supplies the element of adventure and a little bit of tension (how will she react to her new home, and how will the town react to her?). The train and the plains, with their mesquite, cactus, "little groups of frame houses," and the "sweeping" vista all provide the setting we associate with western adventures. But Crane is quick to let us know that he is playing off these traditions rather than adopting them conventionally. Notice that the bride is neither pretty nor young, and that while the newlywed couple is ostensibly very happy, they are practically tortured by embarrassment.

As far as traditional westerns go, something is definitely askew here. Marshals don't usually have brides because women only get in the way in the wild world of gunslingers and Indians. And if there is a wife, she is decidedly young and pretty. She is also in the house, where she belongs, rather than in San Antonio, dragging the marshal miles away from where he belongs, taking care of the local drunk bully. Finally, while we expect this story to end in a shoot-out (though because of the comic tone we don't really expect anyone to get killed), words are exchanged instead of bullets and Scratchy Wilson is "disarmed" by the incredible fact (and sight) of Jack Potter's bride. For all we know, if Mrs. Potter hadn't been standing there, Wilson might not have believed Potter's claim that he had just gotten married (which is also his explanation for why he doesn't have a gun). So Mrs. Potter actually serves as a weapon more powerful than a gun; Wilson takes one look at her and loses interest in shooting.

What kind of shoot-out is this, where no shots are fired? What kind of West is this, with a bride in a cashmere dress (attire we can't imagine women wearing, or even having access to, in that setting)? And we're explicitly told that Scratchy Wilson's gaudy outfit is inauthentic western garb; the shirt came from New York City and the inappropriate boots are, we learn in paragraph 63, "the kind beloved in winter by little sledding boys on the hillsides of New England." The suggestion is that the romantic West of the storybooks is dead, or at least dying fast. Edwin H. Cady, in *Stephen Crane* (New York: Twayne, 1962), notes that " 'The Bride Comes to Yellow Sky' is a hilariously funny parody of neo-romantic lamentations over 'The Passing of the West.' The last marshal is tamed by a prosaic marriage and exempted from playing The Game so absurdly romanticized. . . . His occupation gone, the last Bad Man, a part-time worker anyhow, shuffles off into the sunset dragging boot tracks through the dust like the tracks of the last dinosaur" (102). When Scratchy Wilson says, "I s'pose it's all off now" (88), the specific reference is to his rampage on the town, but the larger implication is that the whole myth of the West is over as well.

Scratchy's comic and ineffective qualities are meant to suggest those same qualities in Yellow Sky, and in any part or member of the West that still adheres to this myth. The drummer in the saloon reinforces this concept; as an outsider to Yellow Sky, he helps dramatize this episode. The fact that he has been many places but hasn't encountered such a situation before suggests how ridiculous this little scene really is; people just don't go around shooting up a town this way anymore (if they ever really did), and Yellow Sky seems to be one of the last places to find this out.

Crane creates suspense by delaying the inevitable meeting between Potter and Wilson; he alternates scenes of the bride and groom en route to Yellow Sky with scenes of what is going on in Yellow Sky at the same moment. But it is a teasing rather than a gripping suspense; Crane's tone is sufficiently mocking and ironic that we don't really believe Wilson, or anybody else, is actually going to kill anyone.

POSSIBLE CONNECTIONS TO OTHER SELECTIONS

Katherine Mansfield, "Miss Brill" (text p. 1270)
Jane Martin, *Rodeo* (text p. 1004)

RESOURCES FOR TEACHING

The Bride Comes to Yellow Sky [recording]. 1 cassette (50 min.), 1983. Read by Walter Zimmerman and Jim Killavey. Illustrates the contrasting sides of Crane's art — the humorous and the gruesome. Distributed by Jimcin Recordings.

The Red Badge of Courage and Other Stories [recording]. 6 cassettes (6 hrs., 39 min.), 1976. Includes title story, "The Mystery of Heroism," "The Open Boat," and "The Bride Comes to Yellow Sky." Distributed by Listening Library.

The Red Badge of Courage and Other Stories [recording]. 9 cassettes (1 hr. each). Read by Michael Pritchard. Includes "The Bride Comes to Yellow Sky," "The Blue Hotel," and "The Open Boat." Distributed by Books on Tape.

See also "American Story Classics" series in the appendix of Film, Video, and Audiocassette Resources.

NATHANIEL HAWTHORNE, *The Birthmark* (p. 1130)

Aylmer (a variant of Elmer, meaning "noble") in this story is neither evil nor mad. An eighteenth-century scientist, he embodies the period's devotion to science and reason. However, his studies supersede all else in his life; they are his first love — even before his wife. His choice of science over love identifies him as the kind of Hawthorne character who displays an imbalance of head and heart. His intellect usurps his common sense and feelings. He loses sight of Georgiana's humanity in his monomaniacal quest to achieve an ideal perfection in her person.

Aylmer is shocked by Georgiana's birthmark because he sees it as a "visible mark of earthly imperfection" (paragraph 5). To him the "crimson hand" (a sign perhaps that humankind's fallen nature is imprinted by the devil [original sin] on all human beings) symbolizes the "fatal flaw of humanity" and is a sign of mortality, "toil and pain" (8). This extreme perspective differs from the more normal views of the birthmark in paragraph 7.

Georgiana (whose name is appropriately associated with the earthy rather than the ideal) loves her husband so completely that she is willing to risk her life to win his approval. Her feelings serve as a foil to his obsessive efforts to perfect her; she loves him despite his willingness to dehumanize her. She is unaware of his blasphemous pride, which the reader sees clearly: "What will be my triumph when I shall have corrected what Nature left imperfect in her fairest work!" (19). Though the story is set in the 1700s, Georgiana can be seen as a prototype of many nineteenth-century female characters — passive and incapable of changing the course of events that will inevitably destroy her. She becomes a martyr to her love for Aylmer. Students are likely to see her as hopelessly weak rather than nearly perfect. When Georgiana reads Aylmer's journal and observes that "his most splendid successes were almost invariably failures, if compared with the ideal at which he aimed" (51), many readers wonder why this and other grim foreshadowings about the nature of his work (see 32–37) do not alarm her. Hawthorne, however, stresses her loyal devotion to her husband more as a virtue than as a weakness.

Aminadab is also an obvious foil to Aylmer. His name spelled backward is, interestingly enough, *bad anima* (bad soul or life principle). He represents the opposite of Aylmer's aspirations for the ideal: "He seemed to represent man's physical nature." His physical features — his grimy, shaggy, low stature and "indescribable earthiness" — are in stark contrast to Aylmer's "slender figure, and pale, intellectual face," which make him "a type of the spiritual element" (25). Aminadab's "smoky aspect" is the result of his tending Aylmer's "hot and feverish" furnace, which seems demonic and evokes the destructive nature of Aylmer's efforts to spiritualize matter (57).

Although Aylmer's motives are noble, his egotism blinds him to a central fact that his science ignores, for according to Hawthorne, there can be no such thing as mortal perfection. The story's theme argues that the nature of mortal existence necessarily means humanity's "liability to sin, sorrow, decay, and death" (8). For Hawthorne, no science can change that fact of life. As soon as the birthmark fades from Georgiana's face, her life fades because mortality and perfection do not coexist. Aylmer lacks the profound wisdom to embrace the human condition. Like Young Goodman Brown, he fails to accept the terms on which life offers itself.

Students may find provocative a discussion (or writing assignment) about this story as a modern version of our obsession with attaining physical perfection, through exercise, cosmetic surgery, or some other means. Hawthorne's theme of human imperfection is largely a philosophical issue, but it can also be addressed through psychological and sociological perspectives.

POSSIBLE CONNECTIONS TO OTHER SELECTIONS

Colette, "The Hand" (text p. 163)
Nathaniel Hawthorne, "Young Goodman Brown" (text p. 1246)
Fay Weldon, "IND AFF, or Out of Love in Sarajevo" (text p. 817)

RESOURCE FOR TEACHING

> **The Birthmark** [recording]. 1 cassette (63 min.). Read by Walter Zimmerman.
> Distributed by Jimcin Recordings.

SARAH ORNE JEWETT, *A White Heron* (p. 1141)

Sarah Orne Jewett is often classified as a regional writer, since she details the landscape and local color of her native Maine. Carefully go over this story's opening with your class and determine what kind of world Jewett is depicting. Jewett introduces us to a little girl named Sylvia (which means "of the woods"). Her life is somewhat isolated — a cow is her only playmate — but she is more than content at her grandmother's farm and says that "she should never wish to go home" (p. 1142) to the crowded manufacturing town in which she grew up. In this way Jewett sets up a dichotomy between the town, a place where children (and geraniums) do not thrive, and the country, a "beautiful place" (p. 1142) where people can come to life. This dichotomy structures the controlling conflict in the story — the conflict between humans and nature. Sylvia bridges these two categories: she is from the town but is also a part of nature. Her grandmother says that "the wild creatur's counts her as one o' themselves" (p. 1144). As the story progresses, Sylvia must make a choice between the destructive world of mankind or the life-giving world of the country.

Into this ideal pastoral comes the "somewhat aggressive" sound of a whistle. Despite the friendliness of the young man who approaches her, Sylvia views him as "the enemy" (p. 1143). Why does she consider this intruder to be such a threat? At this point in the story, did your students regard him as an enemy too? Why or why not? Despite the fact that Sylvia later comes to view him as a friend, does he turn out to be her enemy?

Ask your students how Jewett continues to elucidate the contrast between nature and human destruction. Note the details she associates with the man: his gun and his practice of stuffing and preserving birds. Why does Sylvia come to love this stranger despite the fact that "she could not understand why he killed the very birds he seemed to like so much" (p. 1145)? Why *does* he kill them?

Ask your students what they think of the story's end. While most readers will applaud Sylvia's refusal to locate the bird for the gunman, they should also be able to articulate the stranger's appeal. It is too simplistic a reading merely to assert that because Jewett links Sylvia with nature, Sylvia would automatically choose the heron over the man. Sylvia is truly torn, and it is a real choice she makes, not merely an intuitive response. Ask your students to discuss why Sylvia's choice is such a difficult one. Finally, what is at stake in the stranger's attempt to "preserve" nature by killing it and stuffing it?

POSSIBLE CONNECTIONS TO OTHER SELECTIONS

Robert Frost, "Mending Wall" (text p. 121)
Flannery O'Connor, "Good Country People" (p. 803)

TIM O'BRIEN, *How to Tell a True War Story* (p. 1149)

Tim O'Brien's work is heavily influenced by his service in Vietnam and by the "war writing" of Ernest Hemingway and Joseph Heller. His first book, *If I Die in a Combat Zone, Box Me Up and Ship Me Home* (1973) collects anecdotes of O'Brien's tour of duty, and *Going After Cacciato*, which won the National Book Award in 1978, revolves around a vision in which one of the characters decides to leave the war and walk to Paris.

O'Brien was born in 1946 in Austin, Minnesota, graduated *summa cum laude* from Macalester College, and did graduate work at Harvard University. He has written for the *Washington Post, Esquire,* and *Playboy,* among other publications, and his books include *Northern Lights* (1974) and *The Nuclear Age* (1985). His most recent novel, *In the Lake of the*

Woods, was published in 1994. "How To Tell a True War Story" appears in O'Brien's short story collection, *The Things They Carried* (1990).

In "How to Tell a True War Story," O'Brien establishes the pattern of his narrative in the first seven paragraphs. The vignette about Rat, his friend, and the sister who doesn't write back is a microcosm of the story as a whole. It establishes a sequence — introduction of characters, narration of details, topped by a punch line — that the following portions of the story closely parallel, incorporating specific terminology and black humor, as well as metanarration in which instructions about how to write and tell war stories are conveyed. In its inability to identify a single moral or a distinct meaning, this vignette, like the rest of "How to Tell a True War Story" parallels American reaction to the Vietnam War.

In the opening sequence, the narrator introduces his characters: Bob "Rat" Kiley, the friend who is killed, and the dead soldier's sister — the "dumb cooze" who "never writes back" (7). O'Brien's later amplifications of the story also rely on immediate characterization: "The dead guy's name was Curt Lemon" (11); "I heard this one, for example, from Mitchell Sanders" (21); and finally, affecting the narrator most directly, "this one wakes me up" (97). Even the commentaries about telling war stories focus most immediately on the people who listen to them and respond — "Now and then, when I tell this story, someone will come up to me afterward and say she liked it. It's always a woman. Usually it's an older woman of kindly temperament and humane politics" (106). Through his characters, O'Brien can reach his readers. More important, O'Brien reminds us that stories cannot exist without storytellers and audiences.

Within the narratives, O'Brien fills the readers' minds with graphic, brutal details and terminology appropriate to the war situation. In the opening section, Rat describes how his friend's courage caused him to "volunteer for stuff nobody else would volunteer for in a million years, dangerous stuff, like doing recon or going out on these really bad-ass night patrols" (3). In later sections, the details reveal the way Curt Lemon explodes in the sunlight, the bewilderment of the patrol on the mountain, or the gruesome horror of Rat's slow, deliberate destruction of the baby buffalo. Each of the sections builds on the trauma of previous ones: the buffalo sequence is far more tortuously laid out than the story about Rat's friend.

The final sentences of each portion of the story invariably build to punch lines. They either depend on black humor for their power or reveal the seeming meaninglessness of the war effort. The punch lines also indicate some buildup of power — some exaggeration — leading to ironic endings in which little is actually accomplished. The first section, told in a tone of incredulity and cynicism, involves silence on the part of a soldier's family. Later story lines end with the ominous silence of the mountain after the patrol has expanded its force to destroy sound, and with Rat's meaningless annihilation of a mute animal. Each narrative points to the soldiers' frustrations in a variety of different situations — frustrations that affect them not only during the war, but years later: "Often in a true war story there is not even a point, or else the point doesn't hit you until twenty years later, in your sleep, and you wake up and shake your wife and start telling the story to her, except when you get to the end you've forgotten the point again" (96). Like America's involvement in Vietnam, which its citizens are still questioning, the episodes in "How to Tell a True War Story" do not deliver any neatly packaged truisms.

Students should compare the sections of the story that contain the narratives with those that tell about the narratives. Why has O'Brien included both types of narrative in his story? Students might also trace the progression of each type of narration: to what point does each build? Finally, O'Brien's artistry should be recognized. His words are forceful, but they convey the beauty and grandeur of war as well. He writes that war "is grotesque. But in truth war is also beauty. For all its horror, you can't help but gape at the awful majesty of combat" (92). Like the war it describes, O'Brien's story combines the grotesque and the beautiful to create a powerful statement about conflict.

Ernest Hemingway, "Soldier's Home" (text p. 579)
William Shakespeare, *A Midsummer Night's Dream* (text p. 852)

POETRY

ELIZABETH BISHOP, *The Fish* (p. 1158)

Born in Worcester, Massachusetts, Elizabeth Bishop knew displacement early: her father died when she was an infant, and her mother was committed to an asylum when she was five. Bishop lived with relatives during her childhood and adolescence in Nova Scotia and New England; after completing a degree at Vassar College, she lived in New York City, Key West, and for sixteen years in Brazil. Travel and exile, as well as the insistent yet alien presence of the "things of the world," figure prominently in her work.

The most arresting feature of "The Fish" is its imagery. Consider, for example, the brown skin that "hung in strips / like ancient wall-paper" (lines 10–11), the ornamentation of "fine rosettes of lime" (17), or the pause to mention and comment again on "the frightening gills" (24). Not only does Bishop have an eye for the particular, even the minute, but in this poem she exhibits an ability to dissect imaginatively flesh, bones, bladder, the interior of the fish's eyes.

After you review the appearance of the fish, it might be a good idea to glance back at the syntax of the poem. Note, for example, the syntactic simplicity and parallelism of lines 5–7, conveying with their flat factuality the fish's implacable "thereness." The syntax becomes a little more complex later on, as Bishop's vision penetrates into the interior of the fish's anatomy and, eventually, into its being. The fish is no longer a mere member of its species but a kind of military hero and a survivor that has escaped at least five attempts on its life.

Bishop's skill transforms the fish into a thing of beauty and an object of admiration, almost without our realizing it. At this point in the discussion, though, it would be a good idea to step back and see what she is looking at. The scene is simply an old fish, brown and battle-scarred, with sullen jaw, staring back at the speaker (Bishop, we assume). Not an ideal setting for the epiphanic moment.

But that is, of course, what occurs — signaled to us by the repetition of the word *rainbow*. In a sense, both fish and poet have transcended themselves — the one by surviving, the other by seeing beyond the ugliness. Victory, indeed, fills up the boat.

Sarah Orne Jewett, "A White Heron" (text p. 1141)

WILLIAM BLAKE, *The Lamb* and *The Tyger* (pp. 1160–1161)

These two poems when paired make excellent examples of diction, rhythm, and sound and how these elements enhance tone. Ostensibly, each poem employs a four-stress pattern of trochaic feet, but the gliding *l*-sounds of the opening of "The Lamb" make the first stress on "Little" seem much lighter than the emphasis "Tyger" receives. The rhyme in the opening two lines of "The Lamb" is feminine, again unlike the stressed rhyme in "The Tyger." Only one question ("Who made Thee?") is asked of the lamb, and that question is repeated several times, giving the poem a sense of childlike simplicity and innocence. In this poem, moreover, there is a figural pattern of exchangeable identities between Lamb and Creator (Lamb of God), and speaker as child and Christ as God's child. Unlike the fearful symmetry of "The Tyger," this poem reflects a wholeness and innocence by the cohesiveness of these identities.

"The Tyger" poses far more questions about the creation of this powerful, regal beast, including the question in line 20: "Did he who made the Lamb make thee?" Ways of reading that question include the debate over the presence of evil in a God-created universe and the possibility of a second creator from whom darkness, evil, and fierce energy emanate. Could not the tiger stand for positive expressions of power? By and large, though, the questions in "The Tyger" go unanswered. Notice, for example, the substitution of *dare* in the final line for *could* in line 4.

As a writing assignment, you might ask students to examine several elements in each poem, including rhythm, patterns of consonance and assonance, pace, tone, even levels of ambiguity so that they are able on a fairly sophisticated level to articulate the differences between the two lyrics.

POSSIBLE CONNECTION TO ANOTHER SELECTION

William Wordworth, "My Heart Leaps Up" (text p. 263)

JAMES DICKEY, *Deer Among Cattle* (p. 1162)

The speaker of this poem, who observes a nighttime meadow scene with a flashlight, considers the contrasts between the herd of cattle grazing there and the lone deer who has joined them. He contemplates not only the differences between the "wild one" (line 5) and those "bred- / for-slaughter" (8–9), but also their subtle similarities: the deer is also "domesticated" (7) but "by darkness" (8) rather than by humankind. However, the differences far outweigh the similarities, and at the end of the poem the speaker is compelled to acknowledge the different way the "sparks from [his] hand" (19) reflect in the eyes of the deer as opposed to the cattle.

This relationship between the speaker and all of the animals together becomes more interesting than the relationship between the deer and the cattle as the poem concludes. The words "human" (4) and "inhuman" (16) set up a dichotomy in the poem that is not as easily recognizable as it might at first appear to be. The speaker's hand holds a "searing beam" (1) and "sparks" (19) — images of destruction — and he observes the scene behind a "paralyzed fence" (10) which contains "human grass" (6) and a wild animal "domesticated / by darkness" (7–8). The night becomes "the night of the hammer" in the penultimate line. Ask students to try to make sense of the speaker's attitude toward this scene by situating him within it: does he feel more part of the human realm or the animal realm? (Recall that the grass and the light in the cows' eyes are described as "human" [4] and that the grass enclosed by the fence is "a green frosted table" [12]). The speaker seems detached from the scene, but the poem begins and ends with the illumination from his flashlight, seen through his eyes.

POSSIBLE CONNECTION TO ANOTHER SELECTION

William Blake, "The Tyger" (text p. 1161)

RESOURCES FOR TEACHING

James Dickey [video]. Color, VHS (30 min.), 1989. A production of the University of South Carolina and the South Carolina ETV Network. Distributed by PBS Video.

James Dickey [recording]. 1 cassette (29 min.), 1987. Distributed by New Letters on the Air.

James Dickey [recording]. 1 cassette, 1976. Distributed by Tapes for Readers.

James Dickey Reads His Poetry & Prose [recording]. 1 cassette, 1972. Distributed by Caedmon/HarperAudio.

The Poems of James Dickey [recording]. 1 cassette (52 min.), 1967. Distributed by Spoken Arts.

EMILY DICKINSON, *A Light exists in Spring* (p. 1163)

This poem, like the light it describes, is frustratingly evasive. The first line makes it seem as though a scene is to be described, but in actuality the speaker only sketches the roughest outline. The "Light" (line 1), the "Color" (5), even the "Lawn" (9) and "Horizons" (13) are just suggestions of a landscape. Our attention is on the landscape, but the speaker's attention is elsewhere: on the mood she perceives.

There is something irrational and ineffable about the light, and the speaker admits it by acknowledging that "Science cannot overtake" (7) its color, yet "Human Nature feels" (8) it. The light seems always just beyond our reach; in line 12, "It almost speaks" to us, and by line 16 "It passes and we stay." You might begin discussion by having students color in the picture that the speaker has sketched: what do they see? How would they describe the light? Perhaps those students versed in the visual arts could compare it to the work of an artist (like Edward Hopper, perhaps, or Winslow Homer). They are likely to describe a scene void of people, even though the subject shifts from "you" (12) to "we" (16). The word "Solitary" (6) haunts the scene. Is it possible to feel such melancholy, such "A quality of loss" (17) in public, or is this type of perception limited to those times when we are alone with nature? Such a discussion might lead into an analysis of the final two lines, in which "Trade," something apparently base existing between people, interferes with "a Sacrament," something holy existing between an individual soul and God.

POSSIBLE CONNECTIONS TO OTHER SELECTIONS

Margaret Holley, "Peepers" (text p. 1165)
William Carlos Williams, "Spring and All" (text p. 1176)

ROBERT FROST, *Design* (p. 1163)

The opening octave of this sonnet is highly descriptive and imagistic in its presentation of spider, flower, and moth, all white. The sestet asks the question of design: who assembled all these elements in just such a way as to ensure that the moth would end up where the spider was — inside a "heal-all" (ironic name for this flower), its "dead wings carried like a paper kite"? Frost has in mind the old argument of design to prove the existence of God. There must be a prime mover and creator; otherwise, the world would not be as magnificent as it is. But what of the existence of evil in this design, Frost asks. The final two lines posit choices: either there is a malevolent mover (the "design of darkness to appall") or, on this small scale of moth and spider, evil occurs merely by chance ("If design govern . . ."). The rhyme scheme is *abba, abba, acaa, cc,* and its control provides a tight interlocking of ideas and the strong closure of the couplet.

Randall Jarrell's remarks on the imagery and ideas here are superb; he appreciates this poem with a poet's admiration (see his *Poetry and the Age* [New York: Farrar, 1953, 1972], pp. 45–49). He notes, for example, the babylike qualities of "dimpled . . . fat and white" (not pink) as applied to the spider. Note, too, how appropriate the word *appall* is since it indicates both the terror and the funereal darkness in this malevolently white trinity of images.

As a writing assignment, you might ask students to analyze the use of whiteness in "Design" and show how the associations with the idea of whiteness contrast with the usual suggestions of innocence and purity.

POSSIBLE CONNECTIONS TO OTHER SELECTIONS

William Blake, "The Tyger" (text p. 1161)
Thomas Hardy, "The Convergence of the Twain" (text p. 1164)

THOMAS HARDY, *The Convergence of the Twain* (p. 1164)

Between the ages of fifteen and twenty-one, Thomas Hardy was apprenticed to an architect in his native Dorchester, an area in southwest England that he was to transform into the "Wessex" of his novels. He went to London in 1862 to practice as an architect and pursue a growing interest in writing. Though he enjoyed a successful career as a novelist, Hardy stopped writing fiction after publishing *Jude the Obscure* in 1895, concentrating instead on the poetry that ranks him among the major English poets.

This poem ushers in an event that some consider to be the beginning of the modern era: the sinking of the *Titanic*. The final two stanzas support this idea. What is the true significance of the event, according to the speaker? What are the implications of a God who is described as both "The Immanent Will that stirs and urges everything" (line 18) and "the Spinner of the Years" (31)? On a superficial level, the "twain" of the title signifies the ship and the iceberg; what are some of the connotative meanings of the word?

The *Titanic* as described in this poem is "gaily great" (20) in its luxurious opulence, but Hardy also stresses the ship's "vaingloriousness" (15), planned by the "Pride of Life" (3). It is as though in this dramatic gesture of invention and design humanity became the tragic overreacher.

The "marriage" between ship and iceberg is suggested through the use of several words and phrases, such as "sinister mate," (19), "intimate welding," as in "wedding" (27), and "consummation" in the final line.

POSSIBLE CONNECTIONS TO OTHER SELECTIONS

William Blake, "The Tyger" (text p. 1161)
Robert Frost, "Design" (text p. 1163)

RESOURCES FOR TEACHING

The Poetry of Thomas Hardy [recording]. 1 cassette. Distributed by Caedmon/ HarperAudio.
See also "Introduction to English Poetry," "Romantics and Realists," and "Victorian Poetry" (recording) in the appendix of Film, Video, and Audiocassette Resources.

MARGARET HOLLEY, *Peepers* (p. 1165)

This poem begins by describing the sexual frenzy of young frogs in the springtime. The imagery is of the raucous, wet, unbridled sexuality that casts spring as a kind of orgy that threatens to "last forever." The poem shifts suddenly in line 40 from a description of these young peepers to a sleeping human subject who is surprised by an overwhelming sexual feeling, culminating in a striking utterance of ecstasy in the final line/stanza: "Oh."

Students may not have spent much time contemplating the mating rituals of young amphibians, so you may have to pull back initially to consider what such a motif might represent to a poet. Is it a return to nature, a reverence for the rebirth and transformation of spring, or is it simply a new way to regard the human subject in the final 12 lines of the poem? Much depends upon the way students read the tone of the first 40 lines. There is something frightening about all of this unrestrained sexuality, especially since it comes from such small creatures who are transformed without warning from innocent seeming "berry-eyed" (line 2) things with "fetal fingers" (4) into "flying bat-fish / ready to jump / full-tilt into anything" (10–12). The transformation is important, signalled by the allusion to Ovid in line 29. Mirroring the peepers' metamorphosis to "mature adults" in line 30, the sexual appetite of the creatures transforms into that of the human subject of the final lines. Note also the personification of the frogs beginning with line 22.

It might help at this point to list the transformations the poem suggests, then discuss how they relate to one another: infant into adult, winter into spring, animal into human, slumber into ecstasy. Once students have addressed these questions, they may be better prepared to take on some of the complexities of the final lines, such as the simile that compares the future to "a kind / but relentless scientist," or the meaning of the "immensity / that grips you." You may choose to compare this poem to others that play with the notion of spring's surprising transformations, such as Jane Kenyon's "Surprise" (text p. 835).

POSSIBLE CONNECTIONS TO OTHER SELECTIONS

E. E. Cummings, "in Just–" (text p. 269)
Walt Whitman, From "I Sing the Body Electric" (text p. 270)

GERARD MANLEY HOPKINS, *Pied Beauty* (p. 1167)

It seems appropriate for Hopkins to have used so many innovations in style, structure, and diction in a poem that glorifies God — the only entity "whose beauty is past change" (line 10) — by observing the great variety present in the earth and sky. Ask students to point out examples of poetic innovation in this poem and to suggest their effects on the poem.

In form, "Pied Beauty" is what Hopkins termed a "curtal [that is, shortened] sonnet." Not only is it shortened, but it is shortened to exactly three-fourths of a traditional sonnet: the "octet" is six lines, the "sestet" four and a half. Having compressed the sonnet structure to ten and a half lines, Hopkins must make careful word choices to convey meaning in fewer words. Note the hyphenated words, which are his own creations; is it possible to understand the meanings of these made-up compounds?

Students will need to know what *pied* means (patchy in color; splotched). How do the many synonyms for *pied* in the first few lines emphasize the theme of the poem? How does the repetition of the *le* sound (dappled, couple, stipple, tackle, fickle, freckled, adazzle) add a sense of rhythm and unity to this poem's untraditional metrics?

POSSIBLE CONNECTION TO ANOTHER SELECTION

Margaret Holley, "Peepers" (text p. 1165)

ALICE JONES, *The Foot* (p. 1167)

The anatomical terms make "The Foot" scholarly and intellectually precise. The speaker of the poem clearly knows a great deal about the foot — the scientific terminology communicates much more than most people know about their feet. Given that poems are scanned in metrical feet, you might suggest to your students that this poem can be read as a pun; the metrical feet of a poem, such as iambs, support the poem just as human feet support people. The scholarly and foreign terms used to describe the subject of the poem obscure the function of the foot, just as overly scholarly terminology about scansion can obscure the function (and enjoyment) of a poem.

Certainly, the poem can be read not only as a pun. The first line of the poem does reveal the speaker's surprise about the human foot — that it is our "improbable" support — and the ending of the poem returns to this sense of mystery when it alludes to our connection to "an ancestor" (line 22) with a "wild / and necessary claw" (24–25). It might be interesting to have students explore one or more of the following questions in writing: What effect does the poet achieve by using language the common reader does not understand? Likewise, why would a poet write about a familiar object and make it seem foreign? Does the poet intend to humble readers by suggesting that despite all our learning we still are rooted in a past that contains ancestors with claws rather than feet?

Elizabeth Bishop, "The Fish" (text p. 1158)

JOHN KEATS, *To Autumn* (p. 1168)

"To Autumn" was the last major lyric Keats wrote. But despite its tone and imagery, particularly in the last stanza, there is no indication that Keats had an exact foreknowledge of his impending death.

Personification is a major device in this poem. In stanza I, which suggests the early part of the day, autumn is the "bosom-friend" (line 2) of the sun and a ripener of growing things. In stanza II, which has a midday cast, autumn is a storekeeper and a harvester or gleaner. In the final stanza, which reflects "the soft-dying day" (25), the image of autumn is less directly named, but the idea of the contemplative is suggested. One sees things ripening in the opening stanza; in stanza II, autumn feels the wind and drowses in the "fume" (17) of poppies; in the final stanza, autumn and the reader both are invited to listen to the special music of the close of the day and of the year.

In his brief poetic career, Keats seems to have grown into a more serene acceptance of death, preferring the organic ebb and flow of life over the cool, unchanging fixity of the artifact.

POSSIBLE CONNECTION TO ANOTHER SELECTION

Robert Frost, "After Apple-Picking" (text p. 991)

GALWAY KINNELL, *Blackberry Eating* (p. 1169)

Some poems are memorable for their themes, while others are enjoyed not for what they say but for how they say it. This poem seems to fall into this second category, as Kinnell tries in lieu of the blackberries themselves to offer us a blackberry language. It would probably be a good idea to read this poem aloud in class. Kinnell plays with the kinesthesia of the sound in words such as *strengths* or *squinched*, which by their compacted consonance physically suggest to him the pressure of the tongue bursting open the berry's mysterious ("black art") icy sweetness. What other words are there (you might ask) that seem to touch the inside of the body before they are spoken? Look at some of the heavily consonantal words in lines 12 and 13, marking especially words like *splurge* and *language*. Lines 4–6, besides containing good examples of consonance patterns, also express a pathetic fallacy, with Kinnell's imaginative supposition that blackberry bushes are punished with nettles for knowing the art of blackberry making. You might ask what, if anything, this image adds to the poem. Probably it underscores Kinnell's whimsical sense of the black artistry of blackberry making.

The sound then moves from the hard *b* of *blackberry* to the softer *ss* of the final lines. Many assonant *os* occur in the first lines, *es* and *as* in the middle of the poem. The sounds attempt to capture the delectable berries, making the experience of reading the poem as sensuous as eating a berry.

More than providing a message of "truth" for its reader, this poem invites us into an experience of sound and image. The poem is about language in that it considers the difficulty of capturing an idea in words and communicating it effectively. Attempting to write a poem can be as much a learning experience about poetry as attempting to write about a poem. Perhaps some members of the class would like to try writing their own lyric beginning with the words *I love to*.

POSSIBLE CONNECTIONS TO OTHER SELECTIONS

Gerard Manley Hopkins, "Pied Beauty" (text p. 1167)
John Updike, "Player Piano" (text p. 252)

Galway Kinnell I & II [recording]. 1 cassette (60 min.), 1982, 1991. Distributed by New Letters on the Air.

The Poetry of Galway Kinnell [recording]. 1 cassette (33 min.), 1965. Part of the YM-YWHA Poetry Center Series. Distributed by Audio-Forum.

The Poetry & Voice of Galway Kinnell [recording]. 1 cassette. Distributed by Caedmón/HarperAudio.

See also "Moyers: The Power of the Word" in the appendix of Film, Video, and Audiocassette Resources.

HERMAN MELVILLE, *The Maldive Shark* (p. 1170)

The title of this poem leads us away from the pilot-fish, who could be considered the true subject of the poem. The poem begins by reinforcing the title, "About the Shark," and it also ends with a description of "the dotard lethargic and dull" (line 15). Yet the rest of the poem is about the "sleek little pilot-fish" (3) who serve as the shark's "Eyes and brains" (15). You might want to spend a few minutes discussing the effect of naming the poem after the shark rather than after the pilot-fish before moving into a broader interpretation of the poem. Are students likely to try to extract some human "truth" out of Melville's description of nature? Does the poem encourage us to do so at all? By using the distinctly human words "friends" and "friendly" (13), Melville personifies the relationship between the fish, and hints at an allegorical meaning. The pilot-fish "guide [the shark] to prey," giving the shark his food, but "never partake" (13–14). In return, the little fish are given safety, and clemency from his wrath. You may want to discuss Melville's take on the nature of friendships and how human relations mirror the fish in this poem.

Students who have read *Moby-Dick* are likely to notice that the shark is described as "Pale" twice and that his teeth are emphatically white; those same students might be encouraged to try to emphasize the philosophical nature of Melville's writing.

POSSIBLE CONNECTIONS TO OTHER SELECTIONS

Robert Frost, "Design" (text p. 1163)
N. Scott Momaday, "The Bear" (text p. 1171)

N. SCOTT MOMADAY, *The Bear* (p. 1171)

This poem investigates not only the character of the bear (who is only named as such in the title), but also the speaker's perception of him. The poem is largely about how we perceive nature, and how this perception changes according to rules that we do not expect or even understand. The poet leads us through a series of revelations about his subject, who is endowed with "old age" (line 6), "valor" (7), and "courage" (8), and then, as the speaker looks more closely, we see the effect of human hunting on the bear. It is as though we are there with the speaker, seeing the bear as he sees him, and losing sight of him as the speaker does. The bear is evasive, but the speaker is too; he does not paint himself into the picture. Sight is described in passive terms, first as a vague "ruse of vision" (1), and later the bear is "Seen" (9), then finally, "is gone . . . from sight" (17–18). What is the relationship between the speaker and the bear? And what is the speaker's relationship with us? Are we complicit in the bear's decline? If it's possible to establish these relationships, what is our relationship with the bear?

POSSIBLE CONNECTION TO ANOTHER SELECTION

James Dickey, "Deer among Cattle" (text p. 1162)

House Made of Dawn [recording]. 7 cassettes (7 hours). Distributed by Books on Tape.

N. Scott Momaday. 50 min., color. The author discusses the creative sources for his work. Distributed by Films for the Humanities and Sciences.

N. Scott Momaday: House Made of Dawn [recording]. 1 cassette (39 min.). Momaday reads excerpts from his stories. Distributed by the American Audio Prose Library.

N. Scott Momaday Reading [recording]. 2 cassettes (109 min.), 1983. Distributed by American Audio Prose Library.

MARY OLIVER, *The Black Snake* (p. 1171)

This is one of several poems in this anthology that confronts the death of an animal. The speaker describes the snake's death very matter-of-factly, yet seems to find herself surprised that this lowly animal's death should lead to some weighty musings about the shock and inevitability of death. Through death, we are connected to that unfortunate snake, "a dead brother."

In the last two stanzas the poem shifts in tone, from a pensive melancholy musing to "a brighter fire," which has little to do with reason. While we live, while the snake lived, we continue to believe in our ability to defy death. "Not me!" we think smugly when we hear of the death of another. Your students, many of whom are probably still in their teens or early twenties, will probably be willing to acknowledge the appeal of "not me!" and a belief in their own "endless good fortune."

After discussing the poem's message, look at its images: the second stanza's description of the snake as "looped and useless / as an old bicycle tire" contrasts sharply with the image of the living snake in the final stanza, "coiling and flowing forward / happily all spring through the green leaves." It is the tension created by the juxtaposition of these images that accounts for the poem's power.

POSSIBLE CONNECTIONS TO OTHER SELECTIONS

Mark Halliday, "Young Man on Sixth Avenue" (text p. 942)
William Stafford, "Traveling through the Dark" (text p. 1175)

WILFRED OWEN, *Dulce et Decorum Est* (p. 1172)

This poem is an argument against war, not against a country. So often war is an act surrounded by image-making words of glory and honor and flanked by the "nobility" of slogan sentiments. Here Owen has presented the actuality of battle and death by a particularly dehumanizing and agonizing weapon: poison gas. He wants his audience to know a little more exactly what war entails.

The famous indictment of war centers around the experiences and emotions of a disillusioned World War I soldier. It might be necessary to provide a little background about the nature of warfare during "the war to end all wars." The ground war was fought mostly in trenches, where not only did close and relentless combat last much longer than anyone initially expected, but the threat of illness from decomposing bodies and diseases that bred in the mud of the trenches was very real. You are likely to push some buttons by doing so, but you may want to try to discuss the final lines first.

Owen seems to want to collar and talk to each reader directly. After the vividness of his description, some of which is in the present tense, Owen's attitude toward the "lie" (line 27) that his "friend" (25) might tell is disdainful, and understandably so.

You may want to ask students where the notion that it is noble to fight for one's country comes from. Under what circumstances does such a notion break down? Is war still glamorized by way of songs, films, and poetry? (If students respond quickly, "No; all that ended with Vietnam," push the question a little further: what about movies that take on an abstract enemy, like the popular patriotic alien-fighting thriller *Independence Day*?)

POSSIBLE CONNECTION TO ANOTHER SELECTION

Matthew Arnold, "Dover Beach" (text p. 235)

RESOURCES FOR TEACHING

Wilfred Owen: The Pity of War. 58 min., color, 1987. Beta, VHS, ³/₄″ U-matic cassette. A documentary drawn from Owen's poems, diaries, and letters. Distributed by Films for the Humanities and Sciences.

War Requiem [video]. Color & b/w, VHS (92 min.), 1988. Written and directed by Derek Jarman, music by Benjamin Britten. Distributed by Mystic Fire Video.

War Requiem [recording]. 2 compact discs, 1993. Distributed by Deutsche Grammophone.

ALDEN NOWLAN, *The Bull Moose* (p. 1173)

This poem describes a conflict between man and nature, one in which man, through his actions, futilely attempts to make nature (that is, the moose) look ridiculous, but is rewarded only by appearing cowardly and cruel. The speaker, observing the interactions of a lost bull moose and the townspeople, succeeds in making the townspeople and not the moose look ridiculous. The people demonstrate a complete misunderstanding of the moose; they lack respect for creatures of the wild in general and this trapped moose in particular. They condescend to the moose, treating it like a sideshow freak by feeding it beer, opening its mouth, planting "a little purple cap / of thistles on his head." Their affection for the animal is utterly skewed; they don't realize the moral problems inherent in so amiably agreeing that "it was a shame / to shoot anything so shaggy and cuddlesome." The moose's last act was one of power, strength, and dignity — it refused to die with bottles in its mouth or thistles on its head. As "the bull moose gathered his strength / like a scaffolded king, straightened and lifted its horns," it terrified the onlookers, even the wardens. But the final act of the young men, the honking of the car horns as the moose is executed, serves as both a way to mask their guilt by drowning out the sounds of the screaming moose, and as a sort of victory cry upon winning a cruel, unfair, and dishonorable battle.

POSSIBLE CONNECTION TO ANOTHER SELECTION

William Stafford, "Traveling through the Dark" (text p. 1175)

MARGE PIERCY, *A Work of Artifice* (p. 1174)

Marge Piercy's bonsai tree in "A Work of Artifice" is an extended metaphor in which the pruning and domestication of nature is likened to the way women's nature is deformed by society's insistence on their need for delicacy and protection. The poem's meaning should become apparent as students read, but it is worth examining the metaphor in order to unpack its layers of meaning.

The tree is not being damaged by nature or even by a malevolent force or person. The gardener, like a woman's overly solicitous husband or father, takes great care of his plant, "crooning" at it lovingly and justifying his treatment of it with an honest belief that it is best for the tree to be dwarfed.

The final five lines make the comparison between the tree and the woman explicit rather than implicit. Ask your students to discuss the connection between the "bound feet," the "crippled brain," the "hair in curlers," and the "hands you love to touch." The first two of these images are more obviously abusive than the last two. What is your students' response to seeing hair in curlers likened to foot binding? How does Piercy take a positive image, loving hands, and render it negative, even dangerous, by its context? (Remind students that the last line is from a soap commercial. How have commercials and the media contributed to the "dwarfing" of woman's potential?)

POSSIBLE CONNECTION TO ANOTHER SELECTION

Henrik Ibsen, *A Doll House* (text p. 700)

WILLIAM STAFFORD, *Traveling through the Dark* (p. 1175)

This poem is a gut-wrenching narrative of a man who finds a deer by the side of the road who has been struck dead but whose unborn fawn is still alive. After hesitating a moment, he decides to pursue his original course of action and throw her over the edge of the road. Students might be taken aback by the speaker's reaction to this incident, especially the language he uses to describe the occurence: "It is usually best to roll them into the canyon" (line 3). Do we believe that he is emotionless or simply that he must suspend his emotions in order to accomplish his task? What is the effect of the truncated final stanza?

One of the surprising qualities about this poem is just how much time Stafford takes to describe his car. Given this description, with its glowing light, its "warm exhaust," the "steady" engine that "purred," the car acquires a stronger lifelike sense than anything else in this poem, which laments the death of something beautiful in the natural world. The car, "aimed ahead," seems symbolically to foreshadow a darker, more inhuman future, in which mechanization replaces old-fashioned Fate.

Providing every physical detail of his encounter with the deer, the speaker sounds like a news reporter, calmly telling his story to his listeners. But the final stanza suggests that he is meditative and brooding, that this incident means much more to him than its details imply, that his thinking involves the fate of the deer as well as that of the human race.

The short final stanza emphasizes its contemplative tone, setting it against the previous stanzas, moving the focus away from the deer, toward the speaker and his fellow human beings. It also suggests the finality of his decision.

POSSIBLE CONNECTIONS TO OTHER SELECTIONS

Andrew Hudgins, "Seventeen" (text p. 997)
Alden Nowlan, "The Bull Moose" (text p. 1173)
John Updike, "Dog's Death" (text p. 215)

WALT WHITMAN, *When I Heard the Learn'd Astronomer* (p. 1176)

Whitman's poem sets forth in verse the often-debated argument over the relative values of art and science; true to the traditions of American romanticism, art is the winner in Whitman's view. You might ask your students to recall other instances in which they have seen this issue debated. Which side seemed to have the stronger argument in each case? Is this necessarily an either/or debate? That is, are art and science ever interconnected? What about stanzaic and metrical patterns, in which art depends on numbers? (You might ask students why a poet like Whitman might not be impressed with this particular example.) Can your students think of any poet whose use of imagery or structures depends on scientific principles? Does science owe anything to the power of the artist's imagination?

Thomas Hardy, "The Converge of the Twain" (text p. 1164)

WILLIAM CARLOS WILLIAMS, *Spring and All* (p. 1176)

All sounds a good deal like *fall*, and indeed there is something autumnal about Williams's chill spring, with its "reddish/purplish" bushes and "dead, brown leaves." But these tokens of death actually bespeak a quickening life of the season that connotes rebirth. The images of human birth are not far from Williams's mind in this poem, as he talks about the nameless "They" who come into the world naked. Syntactically "They" (line 16) stands for the vegetation of grass, wild carrot leaf, and the rest (all), but we do not know this until after the pronoun appears. Williams can thus have it both ways and point to both a human and a nonhuman world.

Williams's spring, like so many of his subjects, is earth-rooted, literally. No surface change here; this profound "change" is "rooted" far down, so that life springs forth from its depths.

You might ask the class whether there is any significance in the setting of the poem — by the road to the contagious hospital.

POSSIBLE CONNECTION TO ANOTHER SELECTION

E. E. Cummings, "in Just–" (text p. 269)

D R A M A

WILLIAM SEEBRING, *The Original Last Wish Baby* (p. 1178)

Satirizing "a nation known for its thirst of spectacle" (p. 1182), William Seebring's *The Original Last Wish Baby* should resonate with students on a number of levels. Like many other contemporary dramas, this play eschews any semblance of realism by creating a series of ludicrous characters and situations. Yet the issues invoked by Seebring are ones that most students will recognize. Using irony and humor, Seebring creates an implausible situation, a live baby born without a heart, to demonstrate the opportunism prevalent in American culture. The hospital executive and his assistant focus exclusively on the liability and profit that the "miracle" baby represents. Even the baby's mother is complicitous in manipulating sentiment for commercial reward. The play contains a number of comical scenes, as when the baby's "heart was delivered separately by a surprised New Jersey woman on her way home" (p. 1180). Yet Seebring also addresses serious issues such as abortion and euthanasia with the play's "Right to Extended Life" movement.

POSSIBLE CONNECTION TO ANOTHER SELECTION

T. Coraghessan Boyle, "Carnal Knowledge" (text p. 1107)

E S S A Y S

HENRY DAVID THOREAU, *Life without Principle* (p. 1190)

Students reading "Life without Principle" for the first time may be astonished to note that it was written in 1854. Thoreau's descriptions of life and human interaction seem remarkably contemporary. Ask your students to note passages that struck them as being particularly relevant to today. They might point to any of the following: "This world is a place of business. . . . There is no sabbath. . . . It is nothing but work, work work" (p. 1191); "It is remarkable that among all the preachers there are so few moral teachers" (p. 1196); "I hardly know an *intellectual* man, even, who is so broad and truly liberal that you can think aloud in his society" (p. 1197); "Do we call this the land of the free? What is it to be free from King George and continue the slaves of King Prejudice?" (p. 1200). As these examples reveal, the challenge of teaching this essay is to address its many ideas. One way to accomplish this is to break your class into small groups, assigning each group a topic from Thoreau's essay. Alternatively you might ask your student to choose one of these topics and write about it in a brief essay. Potential topics include

1. Economics and work
2. Knowledge and understanding
3. Information and news
4. Freedom and politics

After your class has determined what Thoreau has to say on these subjects, ask them their own opinions. Do they agree that Americans are overly focused on work and money? That news is trivial? Do they agree with Thoreau that these problems amount to a life without principle?

This essay was originally given as a speech, and Thoreau's sense of his listening audience comes through vividly. Despite his serious topic, he uses humor effectively to keep his listeners interested and to drive his argument home. Consider this passage: "If a man was tossed out the window when an infant, and so made a cripple for life, or scared out of his wits by the Indians, it is regretted chiefly because he was thus incapacitated for — business!" (p. 1191). How does Thoreau's use of hyperbole reveal a truth about America's values? How do you think Thoreau's audience might have responded to this example? Ask your students to locate other examples of Thoreau's use of humor and discuss why or why not these examples work (or don't work) in the essay as a whole.

In general, do your students agree or disagree with the tone and content of this essay? If they were writing about life without principle today, how might their approach be different?

POSSIBLE CONNECTION TO ANOTHER SELECTION

Herman Melville, "Bartleby, the Scrivener" (text p. 944)

EDWARD HOAGLAND, *The Courage of Turtles* (p. 1203)

It is probable that most of your students have spent little time thinking about turtles before reading Hoagland's essay and certainly have never characterized them as courageous. By the essay's end, they may find themselves feeling strongly about the abuse of turtles due to individuals' thoughtlessness and communities' greed. Hoagland accomplishes this transformation by personifying his subjects. Ask your students to locate instances of this personification. Hoagland states that turtles "manage to contain the rest of the animal world" (p. 1205) and goes on to cite examples. In what way does Hoagland imply that they possess human characteristics as well?

When discussing the essay's tone, notice the combination of scientific and conversational language. What kind of speaker's voice does this juxtaposition create? Do your students trust this speaker? Are they convinced of "the courage of turtles" as well as their danger? Do your students think Hoagland manages to avoid sentimentalizing his subject?

Hoagland supports his ideas with a few specific memories of himself with turtles — his childhood and the drying up of Mud Pond, the painted turtles on Broadway, and the diamondback turtle he mistakenly tries to rescue by putting him in the Hudson. How do these examples work together to create the essay's overall effect? Which examples do your students find most compelling, and why?

John Updike, "Dog's Death" (text p. 215)

WRITING IN PROCESS: AN AUTHOR IN DEPTH

In addition to Emily Dickinson, this anthology provides several opportunities to write about an author in depth (see Alternative Assignments, question 1). This casebook on Dickinson provides some useful background material on the author, but more important, it provides a number of poems by Dickinson; this selection enables the student writer Michael Weitz to see connections between an author's works. Writing about any author in depth demands all the explication, analysis, and attention to the elements that writing about a single work requires, but it also calls for an ability to draw conclusions, make connections, and notice patterns, often in works that seem quite different from one another.

After they have gone through the poems themselves, ask your students to look for patterns and connections between the works. What do they notice about Dickinson's subject matter, style, and imagery that would enable them to come up with a thesis about her writing? Direct your students to Questions for Writing About an Author in Depth (p. 1216) to help them generate ideas. Michael's first response focuses on religion and continues to work with that topic as he proceeds through brainstorming, a rough outline, and then his final paper. Notice the way his essay cites lines from the poems that support his thesis. He draws connections between the text both in his transitions from one work to another and in his conclusion.

EMILY DICKINSON

If I can stop one Heart from breaking and *If I shouldn't be alive*
(pp. 1212, 1213)

You might wish to impress on your class the difference in quality between these two poems by means of a prereading experiment. Before your students have read the introductory text for this section, show them copies of the two poems with key words removed, and have them attempt to fill in the blanks. They will probably have no trouble with phrases like "in vain," "Robin," or "his Nest again" in the first poem, but do any of them anticipate "Granite lip" in the second?

You might begin discussion of "If I can stop" by asking students to consider the comments on sentimentality and the greeting-card tradition in the text (pp. 691–694). Dickinson's relation to such popular occasional verse is, after all, not so far-fetched, since she is reputed to have honored birthdays and other social occasions by composing poems. Ask students to speculate on why this poem was so popularly successful and then to explore its limitations. The poem's simplicity and the extent to which it recounts what we *think* it should are among its popular virtues. If students have trouble seeing the poem's limitations, ask them if it is possible to live life with only one rule of conduct. Would they consider their entire lives successful if they saved one robin? You might also speculate with students on why the least common denominator of a poet's work is so often what the popular mind accepts. Recall as a parallel Walt Whitman's poem on Lincoln, "O Captain! My Captain!" — a rhymed lyric that has found its way into many high-school anthologies and may be even more popular since its use in the film *Dead Poets Society*.

"If I shouldn't be alive" is much more in keeping with Dickinson's usual ironic mode. In what ways does this poem seem to be like the previous one? What emotions are evoked by the use of the Robin in each poem? Where does "If I shouldn't be alive" break away from the world of sentimentality evoked by "If I can stop one Heart . . ."? What does the speaker's concern that she might be thought ungrateful, suggested by the second stanza, say about her? How do the speakers of these two poems differ?

As a way of enabling students to appreciate the master stroke of the "Granite lip" in the last line, you might have them rewrite the line so that it steers the poem back toward a more conventional expression.

The Thought beneath so slight a film — (p. 1214)

Just as laces and mists (both light, partial coverings) reveal the wearer or the mountain range, so a veiled expression reveals the inner thought or opinion. Dickinson is here implying that the delicate covering makes the eye work harder to see the form behind the veil; therefore, misted objects appear in sharper outline.

Ask students to suggest other metaphors Dickinson might have used to describe the distinctness of things that are partially hidden. Depending on your class, you might be able to discuss one of the more obvious examples: whether or not seminudity is more erotic than complete nakedness. Why does Dickinson use such totally different metaphors — women's clothing and a mountain range — to make her point here? Is there any connection between the two? Do your students agree with Dickinson's premise? Are things more distinct, or simply more intriguing, when the imagination must become involved? Does one see another person's thoughts more clearly when a "film" necessitates working harder to understand, or is it just as likely that the "understanding" that results is a hybrid of two persons' thoughts?

To make a prairie it takes a clover and one bee (p. 1215)

"To make a prairie" reads like a recipe — add this to that and you will get the desired result. But it could just as well be a call for props in a theater production: take these items and add a little reflective imagination and the result will be a prairie, itself a symbol of open-endedness and freedom of spirit.

To enable students to understand the poem more clearly, you might ask them to explore the idea of essential ingredients by writing their own "recipe" poem: How do you make a family? A term paper? A painting? What happens to each of these entities as various ingredients are removed? What cannot be removed without destroying the entity or changing its character completely?

Possible Connection to Another Selection

Robert Frost, "Mending Wall" (text p. 121)

"Faith" is a fine invention (p. 1217)

This poem highlights a witty, even satirical side of Dickinson. Have students note the words that define each of the alternative ways of seeing. "Faith" is an "invention" (line 1), and microscopes are "prudent" (3). When examining Dickinson's diction, it is helpful to note the variety of possible definitions for ordinary words used in an unusual manner. *Invention* not only means a created or fabricated thing; it also carries the more archaic sense of an unusual discovery or a find. Likewise, while *prudence* has a rather stilted, utilitarian ring to it in the twentieth century, it once meant having the capacity to see divine truth. You might want to ask your class whether they feel the speaker favors religion or science. Since both faith and microscopes are meant to help people perceive directly rather than through a mist, is it possible that the poet favors neither side in this argument?

Ask your students what they think of Charles R. Anderson's comment on this poem in *Emily Dickinson's Poetry* (New York: Holt, 1960): "This is a word game, not a poem" (35).

I know that He exists (p. 1218)

Dickinson here seems to be at the cutting edge of modern sensibility and its dare-seeking fascination with death. The poem begins as a testimony of faith in the existence of a God who is clearly an Old Testament figure. If you ask students how the poem's speaker characterizes this deity, they may note the attributes of refinement, hiddenness, and removal from the gross affairs of earthly life. With this in mind, the tone of the next stanza, in which God seems to be the orchestrator of a cosmic game of hide-and-seek between Himself and whichever of His creatures will play, and in which the reward is "Bliss" (line 7), may be puzzling to students. The word *fond* in line 6 begins to sow a seed of doubt about the rules of this game. Does it mean "affectionate" or is it being used in its older sense of "foolish"?

In the third stanza, the speaker more fully comprehends the meaning of the game: finding God can mean finding oneself in God at the moment of death. Instead of death being a discovery that begins a condition of everlasting bliss, one may be confronted with an abrupt and everlasting ending. "Death's — stiff — stare" (12) caps three lines of halting verse, further emphasized by the hardness of the alliteration (you may wish to read these lines aloud so that students will appreciate their impact). By the third stanza, the ironic barb pierces through the texture of ordinary language. Instead of saying that the joke has gone too far, the speaker substitutes the verb *crawled,* which summons up the image of the serpent in the Garden of Eden in addition to bringing the lofty language of the first stanza down to earth.

This poem receives a brief but adequate discussion in Karl Keller's *The Only Kangaroo among the Beauty* (Baltimore: Johns Hopkins UP, 1979, p. 63). Keller observes that the "tone of voice moves from mouthed platitude to personal complaint." Ask your students if they agree with this assessment.

Possible Connection to Another Selection

Robert Frost, "Design" (text p. 1163)

I never saw a Moor — (p. 1218)

This straightforward profession of faith follows a pattern of expansion of imagery from the natural to the supernatural. Despite its simplicity, it reflects sound theology; one of the basic theological proofs of the existence of God is the existence of the universe. Ask your students if the poem would be as effective if the first stanza relied on images of man-made things such as the Pyramids. Why or why not? How would it change the impact of the poem if the stanzas were reversed?

Apparently with no surprise (p. 1218)

While a first reading of "Apparently with no surprise" seems to present the reader with a picture of death in an uncaring, mechanistic universe overseen by a callous God, a closer look reveals a more ambiguous attitude on the part of the speaker. Most of the poem deals with an ordinary natural process, an early-morning frost that kills a flower. Framing this event is the viewpoint of the speaker, who acknowledges by means of the word *apparently* that his or her perspective may not be correct. According to the speaker, God is not involved in the event, other than to observe and to approve, as the speaker apparently does not. An examination of the adjectives and adverbs used in the poem reinforces the uncertainty of tone for which we have been prepared by the opening word. "No surprise" (line 1), "accidental power" (4), and the Sun proceeding "unmoved" (6) suggest a vision of nature as devoid of feeling. However, how can anything proceed and at the same time be *un*moved? How can power be used forcefully, as "beheads" (3) and "Assassin" (5) imply, and yet be accidental? The description of the frost as a "blonde Assassin" in line 5 is particularly worth class discussion. Does the noun *Assassin* suggest that the frost is consciously evil? What about the adjective *blonde*? You may wish to have your students recall other images of whiteness in Dickinson's poetry. Can they come to any conclusions as to the connotations this color has for her?

ADDITIONAL RESOURCES FOR TEACHING DICKINSON

SELECTED BIBLIOGRAPHY

Anderson, Charles R. *Emily Dickinson's Poetry.* New York: Holt, 1960.

Bennett, Paula. *Emily Dickinson: Woman Poet.* Iowa City: U of Iowa P, 1990.

Bloom, Harold, ed. *Emily Dickinson.* New York: Chelsea, 1985.

Chase, Richard. *Emily Dickinson.* New York: William Sloane Assocs., 1951.

Dickinson, Emily. *The Complete Poems of Emily Dickinson.* Ed. Thomas H. Johnson. Boston: Little, 1955.

———. *The Letters of Emily Dickinson.* Ed. Thomas H. Johnson and Theodora Ward. Cambridge: Belknap Press of Harvard UP, 1958.

———. *The Master Letters of Emily Dickinson.* Ed. Ralph W. Franklin. Amherst: Amherst College P, 1986.

Diehl, Joanne Feit. *Dickinson and the Romantic Imagination.* Princeton: Princeton UP, 1981.

Farr, Judith. *The Passion of Emily Dickinson.* Cambridge: Harvard UP, 1992.

Ferlazzo, Paul J., ed. *Critical Essays on Emily Dickinson.* Boston: Hall, 1984.

Johnson, Thomas H. *Emily Dickinson: An Interpretive Biography.* New York: Atheneum, 1955.

Juhasz, Suzanne, ed. *Feminist Critics Read Emily Dickinson.* Bloomington: Indiana UP, 1983.

Leyda, Jay. *The Years and Hours of Emily Dickinson.* New Haven: Yale UP, 1960.

Orzeck, Martin and Robert Weisbuch, eds. *Dickinson and Audience.* Ann Arbor: University of Michigan Press, 1996.

Patterson, Rebecca. *Emily Dickinson's Imagery.* Amherst: U of Massachusetts P, 1979.

Porter, David. *Dickinson, the Modern Idiom.* Cambridge: Harvard UP, 1981.

Smith, Martha Nell. *Rowing in Eden: Rereading Emily Dickinson.* Austin: U of Texas P, 1992.

Stocks, Kenneth. *Emily Dickinson and the Modern Consciousness: A Poet of Our Time.* New York: St. Martin's, 1988.

Stonum, Gary Lee. *The Dickinson Sublime.* Madison: U of Wisconsin P, 1990.

Wardrop, Daneen. *Emily Dickinson's Gothic: Goblin with a Gauge.* Iowa City: University of Iowa Press, 1996.

AUDIOVISUAL RESOURCES

Emily Dickinson: The Belle of Amherst. 90 min., color, 1980. Beta, VHS, $^3/_4''$ U-matic cassette. With Julie Harris. Distributed by Cifex Corporation.

Emily Dickinson: A Brighter Garden [recording]. 1 cassette (15 min.). Distributed by Spoken Arts.

Emily Dickinson: A Certain Slant of Light. 29 min., color, 1978. Beta, VHS, $^3/_4''$ U-matic cassette, 16-mm film. Explores Dickinson's life and environment. Narrated by Julie Harris. Distributed by Pyramid Film and Video.

Emily Dickinson. 22 min., color, 1978. Beta, VHS, $^3/_4''$ U-matic cassette. A film about the poet and her poems. Part of the "Authors" series. Distributed by Journal Films Inc.

Emily Dickinson [recording]. 1 cassette. Distributed by Recorded Books.

Emily Dickinson: Poems and Letters [recording]. 2 cassettes. Distributed by Recorded Books.

Emily Dickinson Recalled in Song [recording]. 1 cassette (30 min.). Distributed by Audio-Forum.

Emily Dickinson: Magic Prison — A Dialogue Set to Music. 35 min., color, 1969. Beta, VHS, ³/₄″ U-matic cassette, 16-mm film. Dramatizes the letters between Dickinson and Colonel T. W. Higginson. With an introduction by Archibald MacLeish and music by Ezra Laderman. Distributed by Britannica Films.

Emily Dickinson: An Interpretation with Music. 18 min., color, VHS. A musical presentation of "Because I could not stop for Death —". Distributed by Films for the Humanities and Sciences.

Emily Dickinson: Selected Poems [recording]. 4 cassettes (360 min.), 1993. Read by Mary Woods. Distributed by Blackstone Audio Books.

Emily Dickinson: A Self-Portrait [recording]. 2 cassettes (90 min.). Distributed by Caedmon/HarperAudio, Filmic Archives.

Fifty Poems of Emily Dickinson [recording]. 1 cassette (45 min.). Distributed by Dove Audio.

Poems and Letters of Emily Dickinson [recording]. 1 cassette. Distributed by Caedmon/HarperAudio.

Poems by Emily Dickinson [recording]. 2 cassettes (236 min.), 1986. Distributed by Audio Book Contractors.

Poems of Emily Dickinson [recording]. 1 cassette. Distributed by Spoken Arts.

Poems of Emily Dickinson & Lizette Woodworth Reese [recording]. 1 cassette (60 min.), 1981. Unabridged edition. Part of the "Poetic Heritage Series." Distributed by Summer Stream.

Seventy-Five Poems [recording]. 2 cassettes (2 hrs., 15 min.), 1990. Distributed by Recorded Books.

See also "Inner Ear, Parts 3 and 4," "Introduction to English Poetry," "Voices and Vision," and "With a Feminine Touch" in the Appendix of Film, Video, and Audiocassette Resources.

TIP FROM THE FIELD

I have my students become "experts" on one of the poets treated in depth in the anthology. The students then work in pairs and "team-teach" their poet to two other students who are experts on another poet.

— KARLA WALTERS, *University of New Mexico*

ALTERNATIVE ASSIGNMENTS

1. Several authors in this book are represented by more than one work. Choose one of these authors to study in depth, using the selections in the text as a beginning. You may want to seek out some additional biographical or historical materials or other selections before getting too far into this project. Using the Questions for Writing About an Author in Depth (p. 0000) to help generate ideas, come up with a thesis about that author's works and write an essay that makes strong connections between the works you are studying. Here are some authors to consider:

William Blake
E. E. Cummings
Robert Frost
Nathaniel Hawthorne
Langston Hughes

Marge Piercy
John Updike

2.   Reread the poetry of Emily Dickinson presented in this chapter, as well as other works throughout this anthology. Although Michael Weitz chose to focus on religion, Dickinson's work invites a number of interpretations. Write your own in-depth study of Emily Dickinson's poetry, taking your writing through the same steps that Michael did his. You might choose to write about nature, the subject of this chapter; other topics include the self, love, relationships with others, or Dickinson's unique writing style.

13

Culture and Identity

Students probably will not be surprised to see Isabel Allende, Langston Hughes, or David Henry Hwang in a chapter on culture and identity, but they may not expect to see Nathaniel Hawthorne, Emily Dickinson, and T. S. Eliot represented in the same context. When we think of "culture" we often think of ethnicity, but we forget that white Americans are also writing out of and about their own culture. This chapter demonstrates the way culture — whether that of an ethnic minority or a powerful white overclass — shapes the lives and identities of everyone. Drawing connections between the problems of Eliot's J. Alfred Prufrock and Hughes's dinner guest can yield some surprising readings of familiar and unfamiliar texts.

ISABEL ALLENDE, *The Judge's Wife* (p. 1226)

Although the characters and the plot of this story have their parallels in every culture, there are many details in "The Judge's Wife" that are distinct cultural markers. The widespread acceptance of and reliance on superstitions, for instance, may surprise American readers. From the beginning of the story, when we are told that "Nicolas Vidal always knew he would lose his head over a woman. So it was foretold on the day of his birth, and later confirmed by the Turkish woman in the corner shop the one time he allowed her to read his fortune in the coffee grounds" (paragraph 1), Allende incorporates many folk customs and characteristics. Folk remedies are prominent: Nicolas's mother tries to "wrench him from her womb with sprigs of parsley, candle butts, douches of ashes, and other violent purgatives" (2). Some readers might scoff at and dismiss a superstition such as the fortune-teller's prediction, yet at the end of the story, it actually comes true.

The events in "The Judge's Wife" serve to underscore the rituals through which the community is maintained. Every character seems necessary to the community. Even a seemingly shy and retiring woman such as Doña Casilda makes a distinct contribution. She has such an effect on the Judge that his judgments in court alter dramatically (1), and she is the one person in town who will stand up to him and bring water and food to Juana (13). Though there are disagreements, and some of the citizens take advantage of others, there is a commitment to the community as a whole, and the community comes to the aid of its individuals. Frequently, there is a humorous aspect to events. For instance, when Juana the Forlorn is in the cage, we are told that "the Judge couldn't prevent a steady stream of people filing through the square to show their sympathy for the old woman, and was powerless to stop the prostitutes going on a sympathy strike just as the miners' fortnight holiday was beginning" (11). There's also something amusing about the game played by the Judge and Nicolas: "Whenever there was an outcry after a crime had been committed in the region, the police set out with dogs to track [Nicolas] down, but after scouring the hills invariably returned empty-handed. In all honesty they preferred it that way" (4). Although Nicolas as an outlaw is in danger of being captured whenever he has contact with the members of the community, he clearly maintains communication with them. The Turkish shopkeeper, for instance, sends him a message when the Judge and his family have left town (17).

A highly masculine "code of honor" is overtly emphasized in "The Judge's Wife." When the Judge attempts to trap Nicolas by torturing Nicolas's mother, Allende writes that "though for many years [Nicolas] had had no contact with Juana, and retained few happy childhood memories, this was a question of honor. No man can accept such an insult, his gang reasoned as they got guns and horses ready to rush into the ambush and, if need be, lay down their lives" (7). Nicolas himself says, "We'll see who's got more balls, the Judge or me" (10). His pursuit of the Judge is as a man, not as a leader of a gang. Such behavior is not only apparent but accepted and even expected by the other characters.

Ask students to compare the Judge's treatment of Juana with Nicolas's treatment of Doña Casilda. The Judge tries to capture Nicolas by assaulting his mother. We are told that her cries are heard by all of the members of the town and that only Doña Casilda will take a stand to help her. Nicolas and the town can endure Juana's cries, but the Judge gives in when he hears his own children's wails. At the end of the story, the Judge is beyond the reach of Nicolas's wrath. Paralleling the earlier incident, Nicolas decides to take revenge by "assaulting" Doña Casilda. She begs him to escape when the troops approach, but he refuses. How does his action compare with the Judge's? Who, in Nicolas's vernacular, has "got more balls"?

POSSIBLE CONNECTION TO ANOTHER SELECTION

Andre Dubus, "Killings" (text p. 566)

ALISON BAKER, *Better Be Ready 'Bout Half Past Eight* (p. 1232)

In "Better Be Ready 'Bout Half Past Eight," Byron Glass moves from being self-centered and determinedly oblivious toward an awakened sense of acceptance and a recognition of his place within his community. Along the way, he is forced to confront the limitations of his assumptions about friendship, family, and his professional identity.

The crisis that initiates Byron's new awareness is brought on by his lifelong friend Zach's announcement that he is going to become a woman. Near the beginning of the story, Byron sees a license plate — "IMAQT" — and automatically assumes that the car's owner is "a woman, of course" (paragraph 44). His assumptions about the nature of femininity are stereotypical and rigid, and his insistence on a similar interpretation of masculinity is also evident. He reflects this attitude in the scene where he changes his son's diaper: " 'You know what you are, don't you?' he said, leaning over and peering into Toby's face. 'A little man. No question about that' " (85). Yet by the end of the story, Byron has realized that his son, Toby, "could grow up to be anything!" (336). Byron reacts to Zach's announcement with disbelief and derision, followed by a number of attempts to come to terms with it. Ask students to identify the points at which Byron advances in his acceptance of Zach/Zoe. For instance, Byron's wife, Emily, clarifies the situation for him when she tells Byron, "We're talking about a human being who has suffered for forty years, and you're jealous because we're giving him some lacy underpants?" (169). Students might contrast a number of scenes in order to examine Byron's changing attitude. Possible scenes to contrast include the one near the beginning when Zach comes into the office wearing makeup and the scene where Byron first uses Emily's lipstick in the bathroom, concluding with the discussion of Byron's experience wearing makeup at the shopping mall. Or, contrast Byron's discussion in Terry Wu's office with his comments to his wife when they meet Terry at the shower. Because so much of the story consists of dialogue, the most effective way to identify characterization is through what the characters say to and about each other.

Through Zach/Zoe's transformation and Byron's resulting growth, Baker challenges readers' assumptions about gender roles. Byron is depicted throughout the story as an involved parent. He feeds Toby, changes him, sings and tells stories to him, carries him in a Snugli through stores, and cradles him as he moves through the crowd at the shower. In a number of instances, Baker's depiction of Byron carrying his son evokes images of pregnancy: "from his shoulders, like a newly discovered organ of delight, hung the little bag full of Toby Glass" (335). In contrast, Emily is often associated with stereotypically masculine qualities. She is seen putting together the Baby Bouncer for Toby; we also read that "Byron's mother used to say that Emily was built like a football player" (88). Emily sings a song to her son that implies a male voice: " 'I'll be Don Ameche in a taxi, honey,' she'd sing. 'Better be ready 'bout half-past eight' " (123). Yet Byron's and Emily's love and attraction to each other are depicted in a very traditional way. This couple's acceptance of and intimacy with each other's individuality prepares us to accept Byron's eventual understanding of Zach/Zoe's new identity. At the end of the story, we see Byron physically accept Zoe: "Byron put his arm through hers and squeezed it, and he could feel her breast against his triceps as she squeezed back, her muscles hardening briefly against his own" (334). Through Zach/Zoe's sexual development, Byron becomes more accepting and finally, at the end of the story, affirms his sense of community: "[Byron] felt a rush of pleasure. On his left Emily reached for a bacon-wrapped chicken liver; on his right his oldest friend in the world gently disengaged her arm from his to touch the hands of the dozens of people who had come to wish her well" (335). With the addition of his son, Byron's world is complete.

Ask students to draw connections between the scenes in which Byron struggles with his interests in science and poetry and the scenes that concern his relationship with Zach/Zoe. Some students might associate Byron's involvement with science with his masculine side; his poetry might seem more feminine. However, instructors might easily challenge these assumptions by pointing out that in Byron's first discussion with Emily, she sits at the kitchen table, "ostensibly editing a paper on the synthesis of mRNA at the transcriptional level in the Drosophila Per protein" (25). Byron hopes to achieve an understanding of "the meaning of life" (271) through his interest in both science and poetry. Is he ultimately successful?

POSSIBLE CONNECTIONS TO OTHER SELECTIONS

T. Coraghessan Boyle, "Carnal Knowledge" (text p. 1107)
Andre Dubus, "Killings" (text p. 566)
David Henry Hwang, *M. Butterfly* (text p. 1296)

NATHANIEL HAWTHORNE, *Young Goodman Brown* (p. 1246)

Brown's name conveys several meanings that can be determined after reading this story. This is a point worth stressing with students so they do not mistakenly assume that they should perceive the following meanings on a first reading. "Young" suggests the protagonist's innocent, simple nature at the beginning of the story, when he has an as yet untested, abstract faith in life. "Goodman," in addition to being a seventeenth-century honorific somewhat like "mister," takes on an ironic meaning when Brown meets the devil. "Brown" is a common name that perhaps serves to universalize this character's experience. If Hawthorne had chosen the name "White" or "Black," he would have cast the protagonist in too absolute a moral role. "Gray" would do, but "Brown" has the additional advantage of associating the protagonist with the forest, particularly in the fall, an appropriate season for the story's movement from innocence to experience.

The opening paragraphs provide important contrasts between the village and the forest. The village represents the safe, predictable landscape of home, associated with light, faith, goodness, and community. In paragraph 8 the forest is dreary, dark, gloomy, narrow, and threatening; it represents a moral wilderness in which skepticism and evil flourish. Brown journeys into the forest to meet the devil. No specific reason is given for the journey, but most of us can understand Eve's curiosity about biting into the apple. Brown assumes that he will be able to cling to "Faith" after his encounter with the devil (although students may never have heard of this story, most will grasp its allegorical nature very quickly). But of course Brown turns out to be wrong because when he sees that the rest of the community — from all the respectable deacons, selectmen, and religious leaders to his family and beloved Faith — share the impulses he has acted on, his faith is shattered.

We know that Brown's meeting is with a supernatural figure because the old man explains that he had been in Boston only fifteen minutes before his meeting in the forest outside Salem village. His devilish nature is conveyed by his serpentine staff; indeed, he even sits under "an old tree" (10) that suggests the tree of knowledge in Genesis. We don't have to believe, however, that Brown has a literal encounter with the devil. Hawthorne tells us that the staff's wriggling like a snake probably was only an "ocular deception" (13). This kind of calculated ambiguity is used a number of times in the story to accommodate readers who are wary of supernatural events and prefer "reality" in their fiction.

Students should be asked to locate other instances of ambiguity — such as Faith's ribbons and the question at the end concerning whether Brown simply dreamed the entire sequence of events. It seems that the answer to this question doesn't really matter because in the final paragraph Hawthorne dismisses such questions and instead emphasizes the terrible results of Brown's belief — that he has been betrayed by everyone in the community. Brown's life is ruined; he becomes as stern and dark as the moral wilderness he abhors. Because he turned away from life and lost faith, "his dying hour was gloom." There is no absolute evidence either to relieve the community of responsibility for its involvement with evil or to pronounce it innocent. (A reader can, however, draw on Hawthorne's other works to demonstrate that he viewed humankind as neither wholly corrupt nor perfect; see, for example, "The Birthmark," text p. 1130.)

Even if Faith has some knowledge of evil or is tempted by it, that does not mean that "evil is the nature of mankind" (65) as the devil (not Hawthorne) falsely claims. When she joyfully meets her husband on the village street, Hawthorne paints on Faith's face no ironic smile, which would indicate hypocrisy or deception. And she has her pink ribbons. There is no actual reason for Brown to shrink "from the bosom of Faith" (72). He does so because he refuses to tolerate any kind of ambiguity. He is a moral absolutist who mistakenly accepts the devil's view of humanity. In a psychological sense his rejection of the world may be seen as a projection of his own feelings of guilt, and so he repudiates all trust, love, and especially faith, because he now sees faith as a satanic joke.

Hawthorne's built-in ambiguities in "Young Goodman Brown" have encouraged many readings of the story. For a convenient sample of twelve different readings see *Nathaniel Hawthorne: Young Goodman Brown,* edited by Thomas E. Connolly (Columbus: Merrill, 1968). If a dozen students are asked to read and summarize varying interpretations, the class will have an opportunity to debate the story in detail and develop an idea of what makes one interpretation more valid than another. It's also useful for them to realize that critics can disagree.

POSSIBLE CONNECTIONS TO OTHER SELECTIONS

T. Coraghessan Boyle, "Carnal Knowledge" (text p. 1107)
Nathaniel Hawthorne "The Birthmark" (text p. 1130)
Herman Melville, "Bartleby, the Scrivener" (text p. 944)

RESOURCE FOR TEACHING

Young Goodman Brown. 30 min., color, 1972. Beta, VHS, ³/₄" U-matic cassette, 16-mm film. Distributed by Pyramid Film and Video. Available for rental from member institutions of the Consortium of College and University Media Centers.

RUTH PRAWER JHABVALA, *The Englishwoman* (p. 1256)

A good way to start discussion of this story is to ask students to contrast the two settings described in the final paragraph of "The Englishwoman." The first half of the paragraph depicts Sadie's Indian garden: "faint silver light," "the fountain with the stone statue, and the lime trees, and the great flowering bush of queen of the night" (paragraph 40). In addition, there is a reference to Chandralekha, the relative who eventually killed herself because her family disagreed with her choice of husband. The reference is of particular significance because Sadie had sympathized with Chandralekha, had not understood the family's objections concerning caste, and had "met the man, who struck her as intelligent and of a strong character" (34). At that time, Sadie had realized that "everything that went on in the house during those days was a mystery to her" and that "the passions that were aroused, the issues that were thought to be at stake, were beyond her comprehension" (34). The reference reminds readers that despite having lived in India for thirty years, Sadie remains an alien.

In contrast to that silver, ghostly Indian garden, Sadie imagines a green and golden English landscape. Where India has been dry, muggy, and heavy, England appears dewy, fresh, and full of life. Sadie envisions "mild soft rain coming down like a curtain," "a sun as mild and soft as that rain," and winds "as cold and fresh as the waters of a mountain torrent" (40). In her mind, England is open, empty, and strikingly free of people. Encourage students to discuss the images of England here and to contrast the description in the final paragraph with earlier descriptions of setting in the story. For instance, the cold English wind is strikingly different from the stifling Indian heat Sadie remembers in connection with the day her son was ill. Then, she longed only to escape the Indian air "thick as a swamp in which fevers breed" and to "be alone with her sick child in some cool place" (19).

Once students understand the nuances of the physical setting, encourage them to connect it with the characters. How does Sadie's demeanor remind readers of the English climate? How does Annapurna embody the characteristics of Indian climate? Throughout the story, there are numerous references to the women's bodies and personalities that ally them with England and India. Sadie is "a spare, stringent, high-bred English beauty" (16); Annapurna is "a very, very physical sort of person. She is stout, with a tight glowing skin, and shining eyes and teeth, and hair glossy with black dye. She loves clothes and jewelry and rich food" (6). During her son's illness, Sadie is scared and angry, and her psychological distress manifests itself in physical discomfort. In an attempt to sympathize with and soothe her, Annapurna holds Sadie close, but Sadie's reaction is a rejection of Annapurna and in effect of India: "It's so *hot!* " (28). "Hot" here might refer not only to the actual temperature, but to temperament as well. Sadie abhors highly emotional scenes such as her husband's demonstrations when he protests Chandralekha's lover or when he hears that Sadie is leaving. Conversely, Annapurna and the other Indian characters understand, participate in, and draw strength from such scenes. On the night before she leaves for England, Sadie visits with her husband and Annapurna during their card game. Sadie "lowers her eyes away from them: she sits there, silent, prim, showing no emotion" (37). Both her husband and Annapurna sit with tears flowing down their faces. It's not only the climate that Sadie rejects; it's also the passionate emotions that she has come to find suffocating in India.

The title of this story, "The Englishwoman," is a succinct, effective indication of Sadie's status as alien in India. Have your students discuss the significance of the title. We learn that she has lived in India for thirty years; her children are half Indian, and she doesn't have especially warm memories of her life in England. We also learn that she "knows almost no one there: a few distant relatives, one old school friend; she hasn't been there for thirty years, she has no contacts, no correspondence" (29). Yet she is referred to as "the Englishwoman" throughout the story. It is particularly striking that in the final section of the story, in which Sadie's husband and Annapurna resign themselves to her leaving, Sadie has literally become "like a guest" (37) in the house. Have students examine the story for the numerous references to Sadie as "the Englishwoman" — references that imply that characters such as Annapurna may never have seen Sadie as anything but alien.

POSSIBLE CONNECTIONS TO OTHER SELECTIONS

Gail Godwin, "A Sorrowful Woman" (text p. 189)
Ernest Hemingway, "Soldier's Home" (text p. 579)

CHARLES JOHNSON, *Exchange Value* (p. 1265)

Like Cooter, the story's character, students initially may wonder why Loftis decides not to spend Miss Bailey's money. In addition, they may notice the way the brothers begin to change after they discover their neighbor's treasure hoard. Both of them begin to behave like Miss Bailey after they steal her money. The brothers' curious reactions to sudden prosperity may be rooted to some extent in their family history and their racial identity.

Students should characterize each of the brothers prior to their discovery of Miss Bailey's cache. Loftis, the older brother, is (at thirty) a night watchman; however, he is "the kind of brother who buys *Esquire,* sews Hart, Schaffner & Marx labels in Robert Hall suits, talks properlike, packs his hair with Murray's; and he took classes in politics and stuff at the Black People's Topographical Library in the late 1960s. At thirty, he makes his bed military-style, reads *Black Scholar* on the bus he takes to the plant, and, come hell or high water, plans to make a Big Score" (paragraph 3). Students may not recognize all the references in this description; however, they can determine an accurate, general meaning through context clues. The most accessible detail may be the reference to *Esquire:* what kind of publication is *Esquire*? (How does it differ from, for instance, *Playboy*?) How does reading *Esquire* enhance Loftis's image of himself? (Students might even free-associate with his name.) They might also determine Loftis's characterization through comparison with his brother. Cooter, the first-person narrator, "can't keep no job and sorta stay close to home, watching TV, or reading World's Finest comic books, or maybe just laying dead, listening to music, imaging I see faces or foreign places in water stains on the wallpaper, 'cause some days, when I remember Papa, then Mama, killing theyselves for chump change — a pitiful li'l bowl of porridge — I get to thinking that even if I ain't had all I wanted, maybe I've had, you know, all I'm eve gonna get" (3). Loftis masterminds the break-in; he also decides that the brothers should move all Miss Bailey's goods into their apartment. He shows no qualms about seeing Miss Bailey's dead body. Cooter, on the other hand, is a follower and a dreamer who demonstrates an acquiescence to his poverty and lower-class standing. He interprets the world in a less ambitious or practical, more imaginative manner. (Students might study the numerous literary allusions embedded in his narrative, ranging from his description of the hoard as "so like picturebook scenes of plentifulness you could seal yourself off in here and settle forever" [5] to his self-characterization after stealing the money: "barricaded in by all that hope-made material, the Kid [a reference to the comic book protagonist, The Yellow Kid?] felt like a king in his counting room [a reference to the nursery rhyme]" [37].)

How do Loftis and Cooter react differently to their new-found wealth? Though Loftis first "inventories" the cache and then ponders its possibilities, Cooter is in favor of immediate gratification. He tells the reader, "Be like Miss Bailey's stuff is raw energy, and Loftis and me, like wizards, could transform her stuff into anything else at will. All we had to do, it seemed to me, was decide exactly what to exchange it for" (21). Cooter acts on his enthusiasm; he reports that he took a stack of "fifties, grabbed me a cab downtown to grease, yum, at one of them high-hat restaurants in the Loop. . . . But then I thought better of it, you know, like I'd be out of place — just another jig putting on airs — and scarfed instead at a ribjoint till both my eyes bubbled. . . . Then I copped a boss silk necktie, cashmere socks, and a whistle-slick maxi leather jacket on State Street, took cabs *everywhere*, . . ." (22). When he returns home, Loftis reproaches him, "As soon as you buy something you *lose* the power to buy something" (25). Loftis also tells Cooter a significant story: " 'Remember the time Mama give me that ring we had in the family for fifty years? And I took it to Merchandise Mart and sold it for a few pieces of candy?' He hitched his chair forward and sat with his elbows on his knees. 'That's what you did, Cooter. You crawled into a Clark bar' " (25). Loftis exchanged family heritage and history for something transitory; by hocking the ring, he squandered both its economic and sentimental value. Hence, he approaches Miss Bailey's hoard with more understanding for her eccentric behavior. He also begins to emulate her, booby-trapping the apartment and refusing to buy anything.

Cooter begins to act like Loftis (and Miss Bailey) after Loftis explains the concept of "exchange value" to him. He carefully wraps up his new jacket and adds it to "Miss Bailey's unsunned treasures" (36), he refuses to call the landlord when the toilet begins to malfunction, he begs Pookie White for food, and in the end, he stows the penny Loftis has labeled in the jar. In part, he modifies his behavior because Loftis is his big brother. In part, thinking back on his parents' experiences, he begins to understand some of Loftis's ideas. Though at the beginning he asks Loftis, " 'But why didn't she use it, huh? Tell me that?' " (20), at the end of the story he has a much clearer understanding of Miss Bailey's perspective. Claiming that it comes to him as he watches the fireman remove Miss Bailey from the building, Cooter thinks, "when Connors will her his wealth, it put her through changes, she be spellbound, possessed by the promise of life, panicky about depletion, and locked now in the past 'cause *every* purchase, you know, has to be a poor buy: a loss of life" (36). Students should discuss the economic theory embedded in this line.

Cooter's realization is also linked to race. As a black man living in a world where the white people control the wealth, he understands that his possibilities in life are limited. He remembers his father "always wanting the things white people had out in Hyde Park, where Mama did daywork sometimes" (3). When he first acquires the money, he thinks maybe it will bring him power in some way: he fantasizes about crowing about his windfall to the cook who reminds him of his old baby-sitter (22). However, he begins to realize in the course of the story that spending money means depleting the possibility for power as well. He demonstrates this realization as he muses about Miss Bailey: "maybe she'd been poor as Job's turkey for thirty years, suffering that special Negro fear of using up what little we get in this life — Loftis, he call that entropy — believing in her belly, and for all her faith, jim, that there just ain't no more coming tomorrow from grace, or the Lord, or from her own labor, like she can't kill nothing, and won't nothing die" (36).

In order for students to connect with this story, even though its diction might confuse them, they might compare it to the fairy tale of "Aladdin." Cooter invokes the comparison when he refers to "the power of that fellah Henry Conners trapped like a bottle spirit — which we could live off, so it was the future, too, pure potential"; he adds, "we had $879,543 worth of wishes, if you can deal with that" (21). Students should characterize the moment in "Aladdin" before the protagonist begins to make his wishes. What are his possibilities at that moment? Even if he gets what he desires, isn't his potential diminished after he has used up his wishes?

POSSIBLE CONNECTION TO ANOTHER SELECTION

Toni Cade Bambara, "The Lesson" (text p. 925)

KATHERINE MANSFIELD, Miss Brill (p. 1270)

Mansfield's characterization of Miss Brill is a portrait of an elderly woman alone. We never learn her first name because there is no one to address her familiarly. She carefully observes the crowds in the park because they are the only people in her life, aside from the students she tutors or the old gentleman for whom she reads the newspaper. She notices that the band conductor wears a new coat, and she looks forward to her special seat in the park, which is for "sitting in other people's lives just for a minute while they talked around her" (paragraph 3). By silent participation in other people's lives — even if they are only a husband and wife quarreling over whether one of them should wear spectacles — her life is enriched.

Miss Brill is content with her solitary life of observations. She is not merely a stock characterization of a frail old lady. She prides herself on her ability to hear and watch others. She sorts out the children, parents, lovers, and old people and vicariously participates in their lives, but she does not see herself in the same light as the other people who sit on the benches: "they were odd, silent, nearly all old, and from the way they stared they looked as though they'd just come from dark little rooms or even — even cupboards!" (5). Miss Brill believes she is more vital and alive than that.

Life in the park offers all the exciting variety of a theater production to Miss Brill. She regards herself as part of a large cast, every member of which plays an important role. She feels a sense of community with them that makes her want to sing with the band. The music seems to be a confirmation of her connection with people and a fitting expression of her abiding concern that kindnesses be observed: she wants to rebuke a complaining wife; she disapproves of the haughty woman who rejects the violets picked up for her by a little boy; and she regards the man who blows smoke in the face of the woman with the ermine toque as a brute. Her reactions to these minor characters reveal her decency and sensitivity.

At the climactic moment, when she feels elated by the band's music, she is suddenly and unexpectedly made to realize that the young "hero and heroine" (actually the story's antagonists) who sit nearby regard her as an unwelcome intrusion in their lives. She hears herself described as a "stupid old thing" and the fur that she so fondly wears is dismissed as merely "funny" (11–14). This insensitive slight produces the conflict in the story and changes Miss Brill because she is suddenly made aware of how she is like the other old people in the park. She returns home defeated, no longer able to delight in the simple pleasure of a honeycake. "Her room [is] like a cupboard," where she places her fur in a box. When "she put the lid on she thought she heard something crying" (18). Her fur — Miss Brill's sense of herself — expresses for her the painful, puzzled sense that she is less vitally a part of the world than she had assumed. Her life appears to be closed down — boxed up — at the end. Having denied herself the honeycake, it seems unlikely that she'll return to the park the following Sunday. If she does, her role in the "play" she imagined will have been significantly diminished because she no longer perceives herself as an astute observer of other characters but as one of them, "odd, silent," and "old."

As a writing assignment, you might ask students to discuss the function of the minor characters mentioned in the story. They can analyze the way Mansfield uses these characters to reveal Miss Brill's character.

There is almost no physical description of Miss Brill in the story. Another writing assignment might be to develop a detailed description that is consistent with Miss Brill's behavior.

POSSIBLE CONNECTIONS TO OTHER SELECTIONS

Stephen Crane, "The Bride Comes to Yellow Sky" (text p. 1122)
Fay Weldon, "IND AFF, or Out of Love in Sarajevo" (text p. 817)

POETRY

JIMMY SANTIAGO BACA, *Green Chile* (p. 1274)

You might begin a discussion of this poem by focusing on the way the differences between the red and green chiles reflect the differences between the speaker and his grandmother. Students may note that in the poem the red chiles function as decoration while the green chiles symbolize passion and tradition. For example, the speaker likes to have "red chile" (line 1) with his "eggs and potatoes for breakfast" (1, 2) and also uses them as decoration throughout his house (3, 4).

The speaker's use of red peppers could be seen as signs of the speaker's assimilation into mainstream United States culture, for the speaker eats a traditional breakfast of "eggs and potatoes" (2), whereas the grandmother prepares "green chile con carne / between soft warm leaves of corn tortillas / with beans and rice" (32–34). In contrast to the speaker, who uses red chile peppers as decoration, the grandmother views the green chile peppers as a "gentleman" (19) — more than a decoration, green chile peppers represent "passion" (31) and "ritual" (45). Considering the contrast in the function of the red and green chile peppers, ask your students to discuss what the speaker could be implying about the differences between his generation and his grandmother's generation. Is it possible that the speaker finds himself separated from the passion and intensity of the Hispanic community in which his grandmother lives? How does the image of the chile peppers work to reconcile the life-style of the speaker with the life-style of the grandmother? What could the speaker hope to convey in the sexual description of his grandmother's relationship with the green chile?

POSSIBLE CONNECTIONS TO OTHER SELECTIONS

Martín Espada, "Coca-Cola and Coco Frío" (text p. 1284)
Richard Wilbur, "A Late Aubade" (text p. 843)

RESOURCE FOR TEACHING

Jimmy Santiago Baca [recording]. 1 cassette (29 min.), 1991. Distributed by New Letters on the Air.

DIANE BURNS, *Sure You Can Ask Me a Personal Question* (p. 1275)

In this humorous poem, we see one side of a conversation between a Native American and a rudely inquisitive acquaintance or stranger. The person being addressed by the speaker has apparently inquired about the speaker's ethnic background and brings up every cultural and biological stereotype of Native Americans he or she can think of.

The speaker is asked questions that range from the merely curious (presumably what tribe she is descended from) to the ridiculous (whether Cher is Native American). Have your students go through the poem and see if they can fill in the questions the speaker is trying patiently to answer. On what cultural or biological assumptions are the questions based? Do your students recognize (or share) these stereotypes of Native Americans?

Burns repeats certain words to indicate the speaker's boredom with the conversation. How does Burns reveal the speaker's increasing exasperation as the poem progresses? It is clear that she has had conversations like this one in the past and is accustomed to being asked to speak for her entire race. You might ask your students why the speaker allows the conversation to go on as long as it does. To whom is she speaking? What situation — personal? business? — has brought them together? The final line, "This is my face," invites the questioner to really look at the person he or she is addressing, not as a Native American but as a human being.

POSSIBLE CONNECTION TO ANOTHER SELECTION

Wole Soyinka, "Telephone Conversation" (text p. 219)

EMILY DICKINSON, *Much Madness is divinest Sense* — (p. 1276)

This poem could be the epigram of the radical or the artist. For all its endorsement of "madness," however, its structure is extremely controlled — from the mirror-imaged paradoxes that open the poem to the balancing of "Assent" and "Demur" and the consonance of "Demur" and "dangerous." Try to explore with the class some applications of the paradoxes. One might think, for example, of the "divine sense" shown by the Shakespearean fool.

CHITRA BANERJEE DIVAKARUNI, *Indian Movie, New Jersey* (p. 1277)

The speaker in "Indian Movie, New Jersey" contrasts the safety and hope of the world inside the movie theater with the threats and disappointments of the world outside. The irony of the poem is that the movie theater itself underscores the thwarted possibilities and expectations that America represents — "the America that was supposed to be" (line 51).

You might begin a discussion of this poem by asking students to identify and describe a "world" they participate in, such as a university or college, that is different from the "real world" they know. One way to further the discussion is to focus on the idea of the "American Dream."

POSSIBLE CONNECTIONS TO OTHER SELECTIONS

Langston Hughes, "Theme for English B" (text p. 998)

GREGORY DJANIKIAN, *When I First Saw Snow* (p. 1278)

This is a poem of transformation — a moment that is much larger and more significant in the poet's life than the simple event it describes. Ask students to point to specific lines in the poem that describe in detail the feel of this moment. Students are likely to point out the red bows (line 13), the dusting of snow on the gray planks of the porch (17), the smell of the pine tree (6), the feel of the sticky sap on his fingers (5), and, most particularly, the sounds (the music, the sound of the Monopoly game in progress, his boot buckles, and the imagined whistling of the train).

These images are woven together to effectively recreate the speaker's first experience of snow, but they take on larger relevance within the context of the beginning and ending of the poem. After reading the poem in class, you may wish to ask students about the beginning and the end — what do they make of the "papers" the family is waiting for (3)? How does an understanding of that phrase affect an understanding of the final two lines of the poem?

POSSIBLE CONNECTIONS TO OTHER SELECTIONS

Elizabeth Alexander, "Harlem Birthday Party" (text p. 612)
John Keats, "On First Looking into Chapman's Homer" (text p. 267)

PAUL LAURENCE DUNBAR, We Wear the Mask (p. 1279)

Dunbar's racial heritage certainly provides one key to understanding "We Wear the Mask." The descriptions of the "tortured souls" (line 11) who "wear the mask that grins and lies" (1) remind us of the oppressive social conditions for African Americans in Dunbar's day, as well as the considerable and evident oppression in our own society. Dunbar allows insight into both the experience of suffering African Americans, "all our tears and sighs" (7), and the perception of the whites who enforce a particular kind of "acceptable," "civilized," or "happy" behavior. There are a number of allusions to the slave condition in Dunbar's poem. For instance, because they were prohibited from gathering together and "socializing," slaves became adept at singing — a subversive manner of communication that might contain news about the Underground Railroad or other issues of interest to slaves. Dunbar emphasizes this aspect of his heritage in lines such as "We sing, but oh the clay is vile / Beneath our feet, and long the mile" (12–13), even as he highlights the tendency of whites to perceive such singing as a sign that the slaves were happy.

For readers unaware that Dunbar was black, the poem may inspire a more general understanding of the behavior of the oppressed. This poem highlights the way individuals are expected to conform to societal expectations — a tendency students may be familiar with from their own experience. As a possible topic for discussion, ask students to consider whether such a "humanistic" interpretation of Dunbar's poem is a limited one. Is our understanding of the poem enriched by a knowledge of Dunbar's African American heritage?

POSSIBLE CONNECTIONS TO OTHER SELECTIONS

William Blake, "The Chimney Sweeper" (text p. 987)
Langston Hughes, "Dinner Guest: Me" (text p. 1286)

GEORGE ELIOT, *In a London Drawingroom* (p. 1280)

This poem could more accurately be titled "*From* a London Drawingroom" since the speaker's gaze seems to be directed entirely outward, through a window that makes London (or even the world) seem like a prison. The colors are drab, the people are lifeless, the architecture monotonous. Despite the monotony of the landscape, everyone is in constant motion, which is part of the problem; "No figure lingering / Pauses to feed the hunger of the eye / Or rest a little on the lap of life" (lines 9–11). Ask students to unpack these lines; what do they imply about these people and their surroundings, or about the relationship between this speaker and the rest of the world? What is meant by the phrase "multiplied identity" (16)? And in the last two lines, what do students suppose "men" are being punished for? By whom? The relationship between humankind and nature is also worth pursuing; we have presumably created the "smoke" of the first line, and the "solid fog" of the fourth line; yet the punishment seems to come from elsewhere. This poem is a good example of how an outward-looking description really reflects inward psychology.

POSSIBLE CONNECTIONS TO OTHER SELECTIONS

Matthew Arnold, "Dover Beach" (text p. 235)
T. S. Eliot, "The Love Song of J. Alfred Prufrock" (text p. 1280)

T. S. ELIOT, *The Love Song of J. Alfred Prufrock* (p. 1280)

This dramatic monologue is difficult but well worth the time spent analyzing the speaker, imagery, tone, and setting. Begin with the title — is the poem actually a love song? Is Eliot undercutting the promise of a love song with the name J. Alfred Prufrock? Names carry connotations and images; what does this name project?

The epigraph from Dante seems to ensure both the culpability and the sincerity of the speaker. After reading the poem, are we, too, to be counted among those who will never reveal what we know?

The organization of this monologue is easy enough to describe. Up until line 83, Prufrock tries to ask the overwhelming question. In lines 84–86, we learn that he has been afraid to ask it. From line 87 to the end, Prufrock tries to explain his failure by citing the likelihood that he would be misunderstood or by making the disclaimer that he is a minor character, certainly no Prince Hamlet. Notice how the idea of "dare" charts Prufrock's growing submissiveness in the poem from "Do I dare / Disturb the universe?" to "Have I the strength to force the moment to its crisis?" (which rhymes lamely with "tea and cakes and ices") and, finally, "Do I dare to eat a peach?"

You might ask students to select images they enjoy. Consider, for example, Prufrock's assertion that he has measured out his life in the shallowness of the ladies Prufrock associates with: "In the room the women come and go / Talking of Michelangelo" (lines 13–14). The poem offers many opportunities to explore the nuances of language and the suggestive power of image as a means of drawing a character portrait and suggesting something about a particular social milieu at a particular time in modern history.

Grover Smith, in his *T. S. Eliot's Poetry and Plays* (Chicago: U of Chicago P, 1960), provides extensive background and critical comment on this poem.

As a writing assignment, you might ask the class to explore a pattern of images in the poem — those of crustaceans near the end, for example — and how that pattern adds to the theme. You might also ask the class to give a close reading of a particular passage — the final three lines come to mind — for explication.

POSSIBLE CONNECTIONS TO OTHER SELECTIONS

John Keats, "La Belle Dame sans Merci" (text p. 834)
Alberto Ríos, "Seniors" (text p. 840)

MARTÍN ESPADA, *Coca-Cola and Coco Frío* (p. 1284)

The cultural dichotomy set up by this poem is implicit in the title; a child of Puerto Rican descent is surprised to find that Puerto Ricans are more likely to drink Coca-Cola than to drink coconut milk. The boy is ultimately confused as to why his culture has been overshadowed by one that seems to him shallow by comparison. The implication in the final line is that Puerto Rican culture — as shown through the metaphor of coconut milk — is ultimately more nourishing than the version of American culture that has oveshadowed the island. Besides the obvious analogy between coconut milk and mother's milk in the final lines, what other evidence is there in the poem that the two beverages are not to be taken at face value but rather as symbolic of broader issues?

POSSIBLE CONNECTIONS TO OTHER SELECTIONS

Langston Hughes, "Theme for English B" (text p. 998)
Gary Soto, "Mexicans Begin Jogging" (text p. 1293)

RUTH FAINLIGHT, *Flower Feet* (p. 1285)

Born in New York City, Ruth Fainlight now lives in England, where she writes many poems about women and their relationships with their families, children, pets, and others. Her interest in non-Western cultures is clear from her travel sketches of India as well as from this poem.

The terrible price of "beauty" is one consideration of this poem. Ask students to talk about the custom of binding feet. How do the speaker's descriptions of the process reveal the mentality of those who invented and sustained the custom? Notice how the speaker talks about the shoes as artifacts in the first stanza, painting their appearance in complimentary images, then, in the second stanza, undercuts their appealing exteriors by examining what they produced.

In a writing assignment, you might ask students to consider the speaker's attitude toward women. How does she feel about "nurse and mother" (line 15)? What are the larger implications of her perspective on sex discrimination sanctioned by cultural custom?

Robert Frost, "Mending Wall" (text p. 121)
Janice Mirikitani, "Recipe" (text p. 1288)

CAROLYN FORCHÉ, *The Colonel* (p. 1285)

It may be true ("What you have heard is true"), but is it poetry? Students will probably be surprised to find this paragraph of ostensible prose in the poetry section of the anthology, and you may want to bring in other examples of prose poetry by Charles Baudelaire or W. S. Merwin to illustrate the idea that this form is a continuing tradition.

In "The Colonel" the apocryphal (what you have heard to be true) becomes realized as apocalypse. Reality here knows a variegated texture in which the daily papers and pet dogs are conjoined offhandedly with the omnipresent pistol on the couch. As in poetry (and not prose), the real world and the fictional world, the natural and the fantastic, are placed alongside each other without the pointers of transition, causality, or connection. The effect is to merge the real and the surreal in an amalgam of potent horror that blurs the line between the two. An example of this merging occurs between the introduction of the "cop show" in sentence 7 and the reference to the broken bottles (used to scoop out kneecaps) in sentence 9. The arenas of violence shift back and forth between the TV screen and the living room, with the moon (sentence 6) arcing its ominous pendulum over the house like a swinging hangman's rope or the glare of the inquisitor-torturer's lamp.

This discussion is intended as an illustration of the suggestive power of prose poetry. Words, images, even patterns of speech and silence ricochet off one another to create meanings beyond themselves. The poem comes to an end when the forces of its own energy collide and cannot break apart again. The horrifying evidence of the actual killings (the bags of ears) metamorphoses into a surreal horror show as the ears ("like dried peach halves") become alive in water. Likewise, language as both damnation ("go fuck themselves") and salvation (poetry) meet head on in the colonel's taunt and the fact of the poem itself.

You might explore the close of the poem with students or ask them to describe in a brief essay the import and tone of the final two sentences. Is Forché intimating here that both poetry and a voice beyond the colonel's might someday be heard?

William Seebring, "The Original Last Wish Baby" (text p. 1178)

LANGSTON HUGHES, *Dinner Guest: Me* (p. 1286)

It is important for students to know that "the Negro Problem" was at one time a common term used by whites to refer to the complicated issues of civil rights and the social treatment of blacks in America. The speaker's immediate announcement that "I know I am / The Negro Problem" (lines 1–2) reveals both the speaker's understanding of this term and his keen sense of the irony of his situation, in which white guests at an elegant dinner party inquire of their single black companion the details of the black American experience. This scenario ridicules the white "quasi-liberalism" of the 1960s.

Ask your students to consider the white diners' statement, "I'm so ashamed of being white" (14), in the context of this luxurious lobster dinner on Park Avenue. Do they see humor in this remark? Empathy? Sarcasm? You might ask your students to discuss the speaker's impression of the white diners. Do they believe the speaker when he says "To be a Problem on / Park Avenue at eight / is not so bad" (18–20)? What does it cost the speaker to partake of this lavish dinner?

You might also ask your students to consider the way Langston Hughes uses setting in his poems, particularly his tendency to name actual streets in New York in order to set the scene for his readers. You might ask your students how Hughes incorporates these specific streets into his poetry so that even someone who has never been to New York understands these points of reference.

POSSIBLE CONNECTIONS TO OTHER SELECTIONS

M. Carl Holman, "Mr. Z" (text p. 996)

Maxine Hong Kingston, "Restaurant" (text p. 999)

JULIO MARZÁN, *Ethnic Poetry* (p. 1287)

The phrase, "The ethnic poet said" begins each of the poem's five stanzas, followed by a quotation and the response of the ethnic audience. In each case, the poet speaks in language or imagery that isn't "conventional" — it seems to disrupt conventions of typical Western poetry or thought. In each case, the audience responds by eating ethnic food or playing on ethnic instruments. In the final stanza, though, the poet quotes from Robert Frost's "Mending Wall" and the audience's response is to "deeply [understand] humanity" (line 20).

The poem invites us to consider the "proper" response to poetry as it satirizes the notion that poetry is a philosophical venture, that it is supposed to evoke in its listeners a deep understanding of human nature. The irony (and subtle humor) is made thicker by the fact that Frost's poem is about divisions between neighbors and that this poem begins with the assumption that there are differences between ethnic and other poetry. It might be interesting to apply the notion that poetry is meant to evoke a deep understanding about human nature to the poems excerpted within each stanza of "Ethnic Poetry." Is it possible to do so? Why does the "ethnic audience" choose to respond differently? What assumptions are made about the ethnicity of the poet and the audience in each stanza?

This poem may tend to touch off discussions of the "proper" response to poetry and the proper way to construct a poem. Has our perception of poetry made it an elitist form as much as the poet's conception that, as Hughes says, it "should treat / Of lofty things"? This is a good opportunity to get students to consider the nature of the barriers between "high" and "low" culture: where do they experience poetry in their lives besides in college courses? And what is their response to it? Do they ever *read* poetry "for fun," or do they know anyone who does? Have they ever been to a poetry reading? Is the emphasis in contemporary music on lyrics or on melody, instrumentation, etc.? Would their response to the lyrics of their favorite band be altered if those lyrics were presented in a classroom? (The general question: does our understanding of poetry depend more on the context in which we read it or on the nature of the poetry itself?)

POSSIBLE CONNECTION TO ANOTHER SELECTION

Robert Frost, "Mending Wall" (text p. 121)

JANICE MIRIKITANI, *Recipe* (p. 1288)

Before discussing this poem, be sure students understand the literal message of the poem — this is a recipe for "Round Eyes" (that is, caucasian eyes) written by a Japanese American poet. The poem is fairly straightforward, outlining the necessary equipment and the step-by-step process involved in making eyes that are not round into round eyes. However, a close examination shows that the poem is loaded with double meanings. For example, examine the final instruction of the recipe: "Do not cry" (line 16). Ask your students to consider the tone and stance of the speaker in light of line 16. What do the round eyes represent, and why does this speaker imply that round eyes might be desirable?

Discuss what the poem implies about cultural standards of beauty and the price individuals — particularly women and women of color — are required to pay to meet these standards.

This poem also serves as an excellent example of irony. Ask students how irony functions in the poem. In order to help students appreciate the difficulty of employing a successful ironic strategy, and in order to help them examine some cultural assumptions that are often taken for granted, you might ask students to write a similar cultural critique — to choose a cultural standard of beauty or success and to write an ironic piece describing how this cultural standard may be obtained or maintained, and at what cost.

POSSIBLE CONNECTIONS TO OTHER SELECTIONS

Ruth Fainlight, "Flower Feet" (text p. 1285)

Kenneth Fearing, "AD" (text p. 250)

PABLO NERUDA, *Sweetness, Always* (p. 1288)

In an essay on "impure poetry," Chilean-born Pablo Neruda defended the importance to the poet's craft of not-so-nice images and words. Neruda criticized American poets for ignoring politics to pursue their own, "loftier" pleasures. Art was life for Neruda; he believed that poetry must be kept near the bone, where it originates, and not elevated to irrelevancy. "Sweetness, Always" illustrates this point in delicious, sense-appealing imagery, which contrasts with the dullness of more abstract poetry. The speaker defends the poor, the politically oppressed, the mundane, and the earthy as the truly valuable subjects for poetry.

The poem appeals to the sense of taste, pointing out that even the builders of great monuments have to eat. Talking about the body makes Neruda's appeal appropriate for every man and woman. Poems do indeed feed the world, although clearly the poets Neruda distrusts claim that feeding is not their job: "We are not feeding the world." Working from the extremes of underground and sky, Neruda focuses on the earth — at the level of the people: "and the poor adults' also." He derides the typical monuments of human power in favor of the food that creates living monuments of joy and misery — human beings.

Neruda's poetry has been discussed in Manuel Duran and Margery Safir's *Earth Tones* (Bloomington: Indiana UP, 1980); Rene de Costa's *The Poetry of Pablo Neruda* (Cambridge: Harvard UP, 1979); and "Pablo Neruda, 1904–1973," *Modern Poetry Studies* 5.1 (1974).

POSSIBLE CONNECTION TO ANOTHER SELECTION

Galway Kinnell, "Blackberry Eating" (text p. 1169)

OCTAVIO PAZ, *The Street* (p. 1290)

A Mexican poet of metamorphic surrealism, Octavio Paz has influenced many writers, including William Carlos Williams, Denise Levertov, and Muriel Rukeyser, each of whom has translated him. He has served the Mexican diplomatic service in Paris, New Delhi, and New York.

Students may let this poem too easily defeat them or too easily collapse into platitudes: "OK, a guy becomes his own shadow or he can't tell whether he's real or not." The poem's simple diction, pleasing (and very frequent) rhymes, and skillful alliteration work in opposition to its mournful tone and shadowy imagery, a tension that mirrors the speaker's situation: the everyday world of streets, leaves, stones, and people is not at all everyday. Nothing has definition on "The Street" (note the references to night, blindness, and awkwardness and to the unstated reasons for the pursuit), yet the urgent certainty of the "narrative" is almost palpable.

You might ask students to change all the verbs in the poem to the past tense and comment on the resulting differences in tone. Other questions that would yield productive discussion or writing include: How would the poem's effect be altered if it ended with line 11? How does the speaker know the street is "long" if he walks "in blackness"? How can stones be anything but "silent"? To what extent could the poem's logic be considered dream logic?

POSSIBLE CONNECTION TO ANOTHER SELECTION

T. S. Eliot, "The Love Song of J. Alfred Prufrock" (text p. 1280)

WYATT PRUNTY, *Elderly Lady Crossing on Green* (p. 1290)

"Elderly Lady Crossing on Green" undercuts the reader's expectations; although unlike William Hathaway's "Oh, Oh" (text p. 217), this poem's surprise comes early on in the poem. The reader's expectations that an elderly woman crossing a street will be feeble, helpless, and aged, are blown away first by her rejection of all of the nice gestures young people offer, then by the vision that she was not only once young, but also vicious. The poem becomes a vision of a younger version of the woman behind the wheel, driving like a maniac, disregarding all pedestrians in her path.

That the poem begins *in medias res* adds to an invisible litany of the reader's expectations, set up by the title. Having students write a list of images that come to mind when they see or think about old women, then listing these images on the board may lead to an interesting discussion of stereotypes and expectations. Why is it relatively acceptable to harbor stereotypes about the elderly in our culture while it is taboo to harbor stereotypes about race, ethnicity, gender, etc.? The speaker begins by assuming that we all know (and perhaps share) these stereotypes, and the vision of his menacing subject as a young woman points up our prejudice. We are even denied the opportunity to romanticize her past, to dwell on the fact that she was once a "widow, wife, mother, or a bride" (line 14).

Is this poem meant to be funny, as "Oh, Oh" is? Does it play up our pity even as it confounds our expectations? Much of the interpretation hinges on the last two stanzas, and you may have to work hard to get students to transfer their attention from the relatively simple fantasy about the past to the somewhat philosophical ending. Is the poem entirely a fantasy based on a woman's anger? Is she feeling alienated, "a small tug on the tidal swell" (19)? Is her rejection of nice gestures in the first stanza motivated by fear rather than cantankerousness? While exploring these questions, you might want to ask students to examine the references to death in the poem, for example: "run you flat as paint" (6), "jaywalked to eternity" (12), "the other side" (16). Why do we sometimes treat death in such a cartoonish, ostensibly humorous way?

POSSIBLE CONNECTION TO ANOTHER SELECTION

William Hathaway, "Oh, Oh" (text p. 217)

MARY JO SALTER, *Welcome to Hiroshima* (p. 1291)

In the second person, this poem traces the speaker's reactions upon visiting Hiroshima (the site of the first atomic bomb dropped on Japan during World War II) by projecting the speaker's emotions onto the reader, the "you" who is ostensibly the subject of the poem. At first she is turned off by the crass commercialism that has taken over the town, then meditates on the irony of the eerie optimism of the place — the "mistaken cheer" (line 19) with which "humanity" has "erased its own erasure" (20). Her desire to drink in history leads her into the memorial museum, but she is struck initially by the bad taste with which the bombing is presented. Just as she is about to dismiss the experience, she is drawn in by a striking exhibit: the wristwatch of a child, jammed at the precise moment the bomb struck.

One way into the poem is to trace in detail the speaker's emotional development, paying careful attention to the imagery. You may have to coax students a little to recognize the difficulty of moving the reader from a comparison between the mushroom cloud of the A-bomb and a television advertisement for beer, to "the blood and scum afloat / on the Ohta River" (10), to the absurdity of a maraschino cherry garnishing a pizza. Getting from the town into the museum is equally jarring, and tracing the poet's use of imagery will help students to feel what the speaker is going through: from being able to compare "strings of flesh" (24) to "gloves / a mother clips to coatsleeves" (23–24) to being struck by the image of the stopped watch. Once you have established the specifics of her emotional journey, you can take on the question of why the watch is a particularly resonant symbol for this speaker.

It may also be beneficial to speculate about the motivations of the speaker. Why would a person make such a visit? It isn't likely that your students will have been to Hiroshima, but some may have visited another memorial site that recalls a historical tragedy: concentration camps in Eastern Europe or Holocaust monuments or museums in America, any number of Vietnam memorials, the site of a Native American massacre, etc. You may want to approach their experience by first asking what they hoped to feel, contrasted with what they actually did feel; but you might also want to emphasize the difference between individual memorials: how the memorial in Hiroshima is not exactly the same as the ones they might have seen. Such a discussion might branch out into considerations of how history should best be commemorated, particularly history that necessarily disturbs us. How can historical events best be felt in the present, and why might "bad taste" such as that described in the poem make itself felt?

POSSIBLE CONNECTION TO ANOTHER SELECTION

Carolyn Forché, "The Colonel" (text p. 1285)

GARY SOTO, *Mexicans Begin Jogging* (p. 1293)

Born in America but mistaken for a Mexican, the speaker of this poem is encouraged by his factory boss to run out the back door and across the Mexican border when the border patrol arrives. Rather than protest, the speaker runs along with a number of Mexicans, yelling *vivas* to the land of "baseball, milkshakes, and those sociologists" (line 18) who are apparently keeping track of demographics.

It is noteworthy that the speaker doesn't protest his boss's orders but joins the throng of jogging Mexicans because he is "on [the boss's] time" (11). Why wouldn't he simply stand his ground and show proof that he is a U.S. citizen? The key may lie in the word "wag" (12), which describes a comic person or wit in addition to its familiar associations with movement: to move from side to side (as in "tail"), or even to depart. The speaker's parting gesture, after all, is "a great silly grin" (21). The joke is on the boss, or the border patrol, or on America in general with its paranoid sociologists. Although the tone is somewhat comic, the subject is serious, whether students take it to be the exploitation of workers from developing nations, or prejudice based on appearance (i.e., the speaker is taken to be Mexican because he looks like he is). What effect does the tone have on a consideration of these subjects? Is there a "point" to his irony?

POSSIBLE CONNECTION TO ANOTHER SELECTION

Wole Soyinka, "Telephone Conversation" (text p. 219)

WILLIAM BUTLER YEATS, *The Lake Isle of Innisfree* (p. 1293)

The Irish writer William Butler Yeats depicts an ideal solitary world as an alternative to the speaker's current life. The poem says little about what it is Yeats is trying to escape or why the idea of escape is so attractive. Clues include the speaker's longing for peace, "for peace comes dropping slow." He also refers to the fact that in his current life "I stand on the roadway, or on pavements gray," indicating an urban existence.

Notice the poem's imagery as Yeats creates a dreamlike tone. His appeal is largely sensory: he mentions the "bee-loud glade," the songs of the cricket, and the "lake water lapping with low sounds by the shore." The visual description of the island where "midnight's all a glimmer, and noon a purple glow" gives the reader the opportunity to imagine the colors and lights of this ideal setting.

Ask your students whether they think the speaker is serious about leaving his gray pavements and moving to Innisfree. What do they make of the last stanza, in which the speaker asserts that he hears its sounds in the midst of his current life?

POSSIBLE CONNECTION TO ANOTHER SELECTION

Richard Wilbur, "A Late Aubade" (text p. 843)

D R A M A

DAVID HENRY HWANG, *M. Butterfly* (p. 1296)

M. Butterfly opened on Broadway in March 1988 with John Lithgow in the role of Gallimard and B. D. Wong (an actor whose name does not give away his gender) portraying Song Liling. Students may find themselves carried far into the play by the absurdity of the premise, a man in love with a man whom he believes to be a woman, before realizing the seriousness of Hwang's larger themes.

CONSIDERATIONS FOR CRITICAL THINKING AND WRITING (p. 1341)

1. Certainly we are meant to despise Gallimard's arrogance in cultural, sexual, and diplomatic matters; we cheer Song's assessment of his superficiality in Act I, Scene vi. Throughout the play, the audience has reasons to dislike him. Nevertheless, the self-deprecating sense of humor he displays in his speeches to the audience ("I've become a patron saint of the socially inept" [p. 1298]) and the vulnerability so obvious in his dealings with his old friend Marc make us sympathize and perhaps identify with him. Furthermore, he does eventually fall in love with Song and loses everything because of the relationship.

2. Nearly all the characters display at least one kind of prejudice. There is sexism on both sides of the bamboo curtain, as Marc and Song ("only a man knows how a woman is supposed to act" [p. 1327]) demonstrate. Helga is biased against Chinese culture, Chin against homosexuals, to name but a few examples.

3. Gallimard's reactions to Song's letters reveal his motivations at the beginning of their relationship. He will not respond to dignified begging, to the asexual (and therefore more equal) term *friend,* or to anger. Only complete submission and humiliation make him feel powerful enough to return. Gallimard does not want to exercise his power over Song (i.e., by tearing her clothes off); he does, however, want to be sure that he *can.*

4. Both are essentially foils who help to further define Gallimard. There is a point at which Marc and his friend have similar sexual attitudes, but Gallimard shows a greater capacity for growth. For instance, Marc considers Gallimard "crazy" when he feels ashamed of his behavior regarding Song's letters. Marc makes Gallimard seem much less despicable by comparison; it is Marc, not Gallimard, who finally fits the Pinkerton role.

Helga is slightly more sympathetic. Gallimard admits he married her for ambition, not love; this and his cold announcement that he wants a divorce display a side of him that counterbalances some of his positive qualities. On the other hand, the complete lack of feeling with which Hwang presents Helga helps the audience to comprehend what was missing in Gallimard's life when he became involved with Song.

5.   The real "Gallimard" claimed that his meetings with the actor always took place hastily and in the dark, a claim Hwang at least partially reinforces by the way he presents their first meetings and by the fact that Gallimard never sees Song naked. Chin suggests homosexuality as the explanation; the scene between the two toward the end of the play (Act III, Scene ii) gives credence to this interpretation. Song claims Gallimard believed because he wanted so much to believe and because his Western attitude toward the East dictated that "being an Oriental, I [Song] could never be completely a man" (p. 1337). Since this is the last explanation offered, and Gallimard essentially agrees with at least the first part of it, it is possibly the most convincing. However, the question is intended to provoke discussion rather than a definitive answer.

6.   Early in the play, Gallimard equates Asian women with centerfold models because both are "women who put their total worth at less than sixty-six cents" (p. 1301). Further, both appeal to his sense of power: the centerfold is a fantasy figure and will perform whatever Gallimard's imagination dictates. This provocative submissiveness is also an important part of Gallimard's fantasy about Asian women.

Later, Gallimard's centerfold reappears as Renee, with whom he has an "extra-extramarital" affair. At this point, he discovers that Renee's total lack of inhibition renders her almost "masculine" to him; nevertheless, he continues to see her to force Song into further submissiveness.

7.   By overlapping scenes from present and past, reality and fantasy, and even from two separate plays, Hwang reinforces the interconnectedness of his themes. The play is not merely an attempt to address separate problems — sexism, racism, and imperialism — within the confines of a single work. Hwang's contention is that these attitudes are all part of the same problem: the need to dominate another in order to feel complete — a need that has disastrous consequences.

Hwang has the characters move in and out of the various plays being enacted, with many of them taking on two or three roles and even stepping out of character to relate directly to the audience. This shifting of roles and direct address of the audience constantly remind the audience that it is watching a play; *M. Butterfly* thus becomes a metadrama, a drama about drama, about role-playing, about the illusions we are capable of creating — and believing in.

8.   The role reversal begins taking place gradually, before the final scene, once Gallimard falls in love with Song and wants to marry him/her. Prior to that time, Gallimard controls the relationship; afterward, Song assumes more and more power, so the final reversal is a culmination rather than a sudden reversal. Both Gallimard and the audience come to realize the depth of Madame Butterfly's love, a love that has little to do with a stereotypical vision of Oriental submissiveness. This love raises the play beyond all of its "isms" to a story of love and loss, which finally touches even Song.

9. The absurd situation upon which the play is based is enough to elicit embarrassed laughter from the outset. Hwang's quotations from the song lyrics of David Bowie and Iggy Pop further augment the light mood. Gallimard portrays himself as a clown in his first speech. Throughout the play, there are hilarious moments — Renee's discussion of Gallimard's "weenie," the revolutionary rhetoric of Chin's meetings with Song, Song's repartee with the trial judge. Nevertheless, the drama's themes and ultimate outcome are tragic. True to tragic form, Gallimard becomes enlightened only when it is too late for him to do anything about it except die. Perhaps the play should be considered a tragicomedy.

10. Despite the many awards *M. Butterfly* has garnered, the play has not received universal acclaim. Some critics have faulted it for the heavy-handed way in which Hwang links Western sexism to the events in Vietnam rather than letting the audience draw its own conclusions. Others claim that Hwang reinforces racial stereotypes: that his use of a Japanese character for a story based in China says that "all Orientals are alike" and that the play as a whole reinforces a "Mata Hari" image of Asian women — beautiful but dangerous. In a writing assignment, you might ask students to respond to these criticisms.

POSSIBLE CONNECTIONS TO OTHER SELECTIONS

Alison Baker, "Better Be Ready 'Bout Half Past Eight" (text p. 1232)

William Shakespeare, *Hamlet, Prince of Denmark* (text p. 345)

Sophocles, *Oedipus the King* (text p. 293)

Tennessee Williams, *The Glass Menagerie* (text p. 448)

ESSAYS

HELEN BAROLINI, *How I Learned to Speak Italian* (p. 1342)

This essay addresses the importance of food and language in creating a cultural identity. Instead of struggling to assimilate to American ways, as some ethnic Americans do, Barolini recalls, she made the transition from a "homogenized" standard American to a young woman more in touch with her Italian heritage. Of course, her Italian heritage had always been there, but it was her grandparents, not her parents, who represented that link to the past. Why are Barolini's parents unable (or unwilling) to inspire in their children a connection to their ethnic background? In what way is Barolini's grandmother both "a stranger" to her and "part of the most fundamental sense of who [she is]"? (p. 1344). Food plays a significant role in this essay, evoking memories of family and a connection to a homeland that Barolini does not know. What does Barolini mean — literally and metaphorically — when she says that her grandmother "founded the family well-being on food" (p. 1345)?

As she becomes an adult, Barolini seems to substitute her Italian instructor, Mr. Mascoli, for her grandmother and language for food, but this shift from the domestic to the academic is part of the process of moving closer to her heritage. Ironically, despite her efforts, her travels to Italy, and her marriage to an Italian poet, it is in the next generation — that of her daughters — that the affinity for the Italian language really takes hold.

POSSIBLE CONNECTION TO ANOTHER SELECTION

Judith Ortiz Cofer, "Advanced Biology" (text p. 1351)

JUDITH ORTIZ COFER, *Advanced Biology* (p. 1351)

Like many immigrants growing up in the United States, Judith Ortiz Cofer struggled to reconcile the values and customs of her native country with those of America. In "Advanced Biology," Cofer contrasts what she perceived at the age of thirteen to be an irreconcilable split between the religious faith of her Puerto Rican Catholicism (represented by her mother) and the scientific values of American education (represented by her Jewish tutor and "boyfriend"). As is often the case for adolescents, this conflict has a sexual component, as Cofer's questioning of her faith leads her to question the possibility of the virgin birth of Christ. This essay raises some issues that many of your younger students, away from home for the first time, may also be wrestling with. Do they identify with the essay's narrator? Do they feel that the conflict between faith and science is so clear-cut?

The essay has an unusual organization. The opening and closing paragraphs discuss the author's current life, career, and relationship with her mother. The internal paragraphs focus on her adolescent crush on Ira Nathan, her fascination with science (especially reproductive science), and finally her mother's response to discovering her daughter's relationship with Ira. What is the relationship between the author's focus on her present life and the incident she recalls from her past? Do your students feel she has come to terms with having a foot in both worlds by the essay's conclusion?

Ortiz draws a clear parallel between her developing crush on Ira Nathan and her movement away from Puerto Rican religious values. Ask your students to trace the progression of her feelings for Ira and note her changing feelings for her parents' values at the same time. Do your students think Ira is responsible for this change in Cofer, or do they think she would have developed these more "rational" views on her own? How significant is the fact that her tutor is Jewish?

By the end of the essay Ortiz seems satisfied with her relationship with her mother and her ability to briefly enter "the garden of faith" with her mother before she returns to "leading the examined life" (p. 1357). Do your students think Ortiz has really managed to bridge both worlds so smoothly? In her final paragraph, Ortiz implies that people with strong faith do not live examined lives. Do your students agree or disagree with that statement?

POSSIBLE CONNECTION TO ANOTHER SELECTION

Bernard Cooper, "A Clack of Tiny Sparks: Remembrances of a Gay Boyhood" (text p. 523)

GEORGE ORWELL, *Shooting an Elephant* (p. 1358)

Hopefully your students are familiar with the colonial history of India and are aware of the relationship between the British empire and its colonies. If not, they can probably infer a good amount of information from this essay, though you might direct them to do a bit of basic research before or after reading this work.

Orwell, as an English police officer in Burma, is in a difficult position — intellectually he is a liberal opposed to colonial oppression, but personally he is as susceptible to racism and stereotyping as any white imperialist. Ask your students how they feel about Orwell's characterization of himself during this phase of his career. What kind of attitude does he seem to have toward his younger self? Why do your students think that ambivalent feelings like those experienced by Orwell "are the normal by-products of imperialism" (p. 1358)? What is inherent in imperialism that produces such confusing and contradictory impulses?

Why does the incident with the elephant prove to be "enlightening" (p. 1358). How does Orwell feel about the shooting before the event and soon after it occurs? How has his attitude changed in the years since? Do your students understand why Orwell shot the elephant? Would they have done the same thing under the circumstances? How powerful is the human fear of being laughed at? Is Orwell's desperation to avoid looking like a fool unusual? Although your students are unlikely to have ever shot an elephant (especially under these circumstances!), they may have other stories to share about times they acted out of character in order to avoid being laughed at.

WRITING IN PROCESS: CULTURAL ANALYSIS

This section presents a poem along with various materials that will aid students in understanding the historical and cultural context of the poem. This may seem a great departure to students if the class has previously taken a more formalist approach, or even to students who have dealt with the poems more thematically, as it grounds discussion in a consideration of a specific historical moment. The poem could stand on its own, even based on the limited knowledge that most students have of recent history. However, the other materials can show students what can be added to the understanding of a poem by a careful investigation of its cultural context.

The poem "Queens, 1963" deals with issues of neighborliness, immigration, and racism. It is followed by an excerpt from an interview with Alvarez (the full text of which is available online — see Additional Resources for Teaching). The interview presents in a concise form many of the pressures that Alvarez felt as an immigrant and that have informed her poetry. It puts a human face on some of the events listed in the chronology, and can be useful to students in that capacity.

The other resources deal more with the wider cultural context of New York and America at the time. The ad for Gibson's Homes may initially be puzzling to the students. However, the picture in the ad can give them a sense of the physical environment in which the events of the poem took place. Students' experiences with "neighborhoods" can vary widely, from rural to suburban to urban, and this may help them more clearly understand the setting. The newspaper article provides a complementary picture of life in Queens. Students may or may not be cynical about such obvious public relations rhetoric; considering this article in relation to the poem may provide for an interesting discussion.

In stark contrast to these sanitized views of life in Queens, the photograph of the demonstrator and police reveals a hidden underside that is not all light and air. You might find it appropriate to point out that the picture was taken the same year as the events in the poem and the newspaper article; dissent was contemporaneous with images of the "good life," a fact that the poem also acknowledges, in its portrayal of the darker side of the "good neighborhood."

As an interesting exercise for this unit, you might have students do a similar cultural case study for one of the other poems in the text, or a cultural portfolio of a place familiar to them: either their hometown or where they are going to school. You may find that it is easier on students if you make this an assignment for small groups, which will enable them to cover more ground with less work.

JULIA ALVAREZ, *Queens, 1963* (p. 1365)

This poem deals with the childhood experience of an immigrant girl in Queens who discovers open racism for the first time. It contains an interesting meditation on immigration, assimilation into a culture, and racism.

When a black family moves into the neighborhood that the immigrants have only recently joined, the speaker sees racism covered over by a variety of guises: the Haralambides's desire to avoid trouble, Mr. Scott's separatism, Mrs. Bernstein's seemingly enlightened position undercut by her worry over property values. These are counterpointed by the presence of the police, which shows even official involvement in trying to maintain barriers between the races. The speaker tries for a connection, a welcoming wave, but fails to bridge the gap, one that she can bridge only through sympathy and imagination. The final image of the poem retreats to an idyllic moment before any immigration. This final affirmation of a land before immigrants of any sort serves to undercut the self-righteousness of the immigrants in the poem, and points out that all the property owners were, at one point, immigrants themselves.

The connections between immigrants wanting to assimilate themselves into America and the racism perpetrated against African Americans makes this a particularly fascinating poem. You might ask your students if they believe that the black family will be integrated into the neighborhood in a year, just the Alvarez family, or if they believe the dynamic will be fundamentally different this time. Lorraine Hansberry's play *A Raisin in the Sun* would be a particularly interesting parallel text to consider in this case.

Students may misunderstand the presence of the police car in line 68, and believe that the family is being arrested for some reason. A close reading provides no evidence of this however: merely that the police are performing a subtle kind of intimidation on the family, making them feel like criminals despite the fact that they have committed no crime. This may be a touchy point for students who have accepted the current police-heavy answers being offered for social problems.

This poem can be read as indicting American culture on many levels, from personal reactions to civil servants to supposedly impersonal property values. Students, however, may be uncomfortable with this kind of reading. You might want to take this into account in the class discussion, and use the analyses of the later cultural materials to present this idea in a less threatening manner, one that will enable productive discussion and disagreement.

If you have been following the previous chapters and dealing with formal issues in the course, you may find it interesting to have students apply their skills in these areas to this poem, particularly noting the use of significant detail and irony.

MARNY REQUA, *From an Interview with Julia Alvarez* (p. 1367)

The interview raises several themes that are important to a consideration of the poem: immigration, cultural identity, and belonging. Alvarez speaks of the old "model for the immigrant," which meant buying into the American melting-pot ideology, an ideology that has since come under fire from a variety of sources. She also speaks of being caught between two worlds, American and Caribbean. It is precisely this sense of not-quite-belonging that enables the sympathetic identification between Alvarez and the black girl across the street.

An Advertisement for Tudor Row Houses (p. 1369)

As mentioned above, this ad can be puzzling to students, who may be unsure why it was included. In addition to giving them a better sense of the scene of the poem, it can give insight into the rhetoric of American identity in the first part of the century. You might encourage students to examine the selling points: driveways, low pricing, ideal for children, sewers, and so on. What do these selling points say about the promise of "the good life" in America? It is no coincidence that the development is billed as "The Perfect Low Priced American Home," particularly given the immigrant populations that came to occupy it. It is also interesting that the establishments mentioned are schools, churches, stores, and amusements. You might ask students how these institutions relate to ideas about "the American Dream" and the idealized versions of America popular throughout the century.

Additionally, you might encourage students to make connections between this ad and the interview, to articulate how it might appeal to the kinds of immigrants Alvarez describes, people all too eager to become American. You might also draw some connections in terms of style and rhetoric to the newspaper article that follows: in forty-three years, the perceptions of "the good life" in Queens appear to have remained largely unchanged. Another approach would be to ask students to evaluate this ad for irony, particularly in light of the poem and the photograph of the demonstrator.

Queens: "The 'Fair' Borough" (p. 1370)

The questions given in the text can help anchor a discussion of this article, focusing on the ironies revealed by its juxtaposition with the poem and photograph. You might find it helpful to ask students why the brochure was produced in the first place. Why is there a need to " 'reacquaint our residents' with the borough's history and present stature"? What sort of function is this brochure actually performing? Another interesting detail worth comment is the historical note at the end of the article: how does this fact about religious freedom mesh with the story America tells about itself, and how does the poem call this story into question?

NORMAN LEAR, *Meet the Bunkers* (p. 1371)

Though presumably taking place in Queens in 1971, eight years after Julia Alvarez's "Queens, 1963," this episode of the popular *All in the Family* sitcom highlights similar racial tensions that existed for Alvarez's speaker. For one thing, even before Lionel's entrance, the conversation focuses largely on race. In the scene presented here, the issue remains in the forefront of the characters' consciousness — and as the centerpiece of conversation. You may want to have students look for specific lingual clues that present each character's view on race. When the class has characterized the overall racial climate of Queens in 1971 that Lear shows us, have them do the same thing with "Queens, 1963." What climate changes seem to have taken place in the eight years between these selections? How would your students characterize these changes? Is one view more hopeful? More cynical?

A Civil Rights Demonstration (photograph) (p. 1374)

This photograph stands in stark contrast to the happy pictures of Queens life offered in the previous two entries. You might have students note the visual composition of the photograph: the dark wall of police cutting off the protestors, and the one protestor's face clearly visible in the center of the photo, staring at the camera. You might want to talk as a class about the power of such images, and similar images of demonstrations in civil rights protests and at Kent State. You might also have the class draw connections between the presence and function of police in this photograph and in the poem.

ADDITIONAL RESOURCES FOR TEACHING

SELECTED BIBLIOGRAPHY

Alvarez, Julia. *The Other Side/El Otro Lado: Poems.* New York: Dutton, 1995. The collection from which this poem is taken.

———. *Something to Declare: Essays.* Chapel Hill: Algonquin, 1998.

Requa, Marny. The Politics of Fiction." *Frontera* 5 (29 Jan. 1997). <http://www.fronteramag.com/issue5/Alvarez>. The magazine itself might be an interesting resource for students to explore.

AUDIOVISUAL SOURCES

Julia Alvarez. 60 min., 1997, videocassette. Alvarez reads new poems and prose. Available through interlibrary loan from Appalachian State University.

Julia Alvarez Reads from *How the Garcia Girls Lost Their Accents* and Talks about the Dominican American Immigrant Experience. [recording]. 1 cassette. Newport Beach: Moveable Feast, 1990.

ALTERNATIVE ASSIGNMENTS

1. Julia Alvarez's poem "Queens, 1963" can be enjoyed on its own, but our understanding of the work is enhanced by a greater knowledge of the cultural atmosphere and history of Queens during the 1960s. Choose another work in this text that is dependent on a certain place and time for its meaning and do some cultural research on this setting. You might look at magazine articles, photos, interviews with residents, or any artifact that might shed light on the place itself, as well as its people and culture. After you have located some interesting material, write an essay modeled after Holly Furdyna's cultural analysis that demonstrates how cultural material can lead to a greater understanding of a literary work. Here are some texts with prominent settings you might consider:

    Elizabeth Alexander, "Harlem Birthday Party"
    William Blake, "London"
    William Faulkner, "Barn Burning"
    Susan Glaspell, *Trifles*
    Ernest Hemingway, "Soldier's Home"
    William Seebring, *The Original Last Wish Baby*

2. This is a creative assignment: "Queens, 1963" is written from the perspective of a young immigrant girl who partially identifies with the black family moving into the neighborhood because of her own feelings of not belonging. Write a poem (or monologue or short story) telling about life in Queens and the new neighbors from the perspective of one of the characters Alvarez introduces in her poem. Alvarez gives brief glimpses of characters like the the Haralambides, the Scotts, and Mrs. Bernstein. What would they say if they were given more space to tell their own story? (Alternatively, you might write this assignment from the perspective of the new black neighbors as well.)

Film, Video, and Audiocassette Resources

The following list of resources is organized by genre (Fiction, Poetry, and Drama), and within each genre section the listings are alphabetically arranged by author. Resources include films and videos of theatrical performances, tapes of poets reading their own work, videos of short stories adapted for film and for the stage, interviews with authors, and films and videos that provide biographical information on an author or general information on a particular period or genre. This list is not intended to be exhaustive; rather, it is meant to provide a number of exciting possibilities for supplementing and provoking class discussion

Many of the films and videos in this list will be most readily available from a local retailer. If not, you may contact the distributor by using the addresses and phone numbers provided at the end of the list. The films and videos marked with an asterisk (*) are available for rental from member institutions of the Consortium of College and University Media Centers. For further information, consult *The Educational Film & Video Locater,* published by R. R. Bowker.

FICTION

Isabel Allende

Giving Birth, Finding Form [recording].
1 cassette (90 min.), 1993.
Authors Isabel Allende, Alice Walker, and Jean Shinoda Bolen discuss their lives and work.
Distributed by Sounds True.

Isabel Allende: The Woman's Voice in Latin American Literature.
56 min., color, 1991.
VHS.
The author discusses the emotions that inform her fiction and the events that set them in motion.
Distributed by Films for the Humanities and Sciences.

Margaret Atwood

*Atwood and Family.
30 min., color, 1989.
Beta, VHS, ¾" U-matic cassette, 16-mm film.

Atwood talks about her life and work.
Distributed by the National Film Board of Canada.

Interview with Margaret Atwood [recording].
1 cassette (56 min.).
Covers Atwood's feminism, nationalism, themes, and craft.
Distributed by American Audio Prose Library.

Toni Cade Bambara

Interview with Toni Cade Bambara [recording].
1 cassette (58 min.).
Discussion of Bambara's origins, work habits, publishing, and writing.
Distributed by American Audio Prose Library.

Edgar Rice Burroughs

Tarzan of the Apes [recording].
6 cassettes (90 min. each).

Read by Walter Costello.
Distributed by Books on Tape.

Raymond Carver

Interview with Raymond Carver [recording]
1 cassette (51 min.).
Stimulating introduction to Carver's life
and work.
Distributed by American Audio Prose
Library.

Raymond Carver.
50 min., color, 1996.
VHS.
Fellow writers, Carver's wife, and others
discuss his lower-middle-class roots in
the Northwest as the source of
inspiration for his characters and
stories. A BBC Production. From the
"Great Writers of the 20th Century"
Series.
Distributed by Films for the Humanities
and Sciences.

Readings [recording].
1 cassette (51 min.).
Distributed by American Audio Prose
Library.

Short Cuts.
189 min., color, 1993.
Cast: Jennifer Jason Leigh, Tim Robbins,
Madeleine Stowe, Frances
McDormand, Peter Gallagher, Lily
Tomlin, Andie MacDowell, Jack
Lemmon, Lyle Lovett, Huey Lewis,
Matthew Modine, Lili Taylor,
Christopher Penn, Robert Downey Jr.
Directed by Robert Altman.
Distributed by Columbia Tristar Home
Video.

Anton Chekhov

*Anton Chekhov: A Writer's Life.
37 min., color and b/w, 1983.
Beta, VHS, $^3/_4$" U-matic cassette.
A biographical portrait of the writer.
Distributed by Films for the Humanities
and Sciences.

The Lady with the Dog.
86 min., b/w, 1960.
Beta, VHS.
In Russian, with English subtitles.
Distributed by White Star, Facets
Multimedia, Inc., Tapeworm Video
Distributors.

Kate Chopin

Kate Chopin's "The Story of an Hour."
24 min., color, 1982.
$^1/_2$" open reel (EIAJ), 16-mm film.
A dramatization of the story, with an
examination of Chopin's life.
Distributed by Ishtar.

Colette [Sidonie-Gabrielle Colette]

*Colette.
30 min., b/w, 1950.
16-mm film.
Still photos and live footage provide the
background for Colette's own
narration. In French with English
subtitles.
Out of print.

Stephen Crane

The Bride Comes to Yellow Sky [recording].
1 cassette (50 min.), 1983.
Read by Walter Zimmerman and Jim
Killavey. Illustrates the contrasting
sides of Crane's art — the humorous
and the gruesome.
Distributed by Jimcin Recordings.

*The Red Badge of Courage and Other Stories
[recording].*
6 cassettes (6 hrs., 39 min.), 1976.
Includes title story, "The Mystery of
Heroism," "The Open Boat," and "The
Bride Comes to Yellow Sky."
Distributed by Listening Library.

*The Red Badge of Courage and Other Stories
[recording].*
9 cassettes (60 min. each).
Read by Michael Pritchard. Includes "The
Bride Comes to Yellow Sky," "The Blue
Hotel," and "The Open Boat."
Distributed by Books on Tape.

Charles Dickens

Charles Dickens: An Introduction to His Life and Work.
27 min., color, 1979.
Beta, VHS, ³/₄" U-matic cassette, special-order formats.
An introduction to Dickens's life and work.
Distributed by the International Film Bureau.

The Charles Dickens Show.
52 min., color, 1973.
Beta, VHS, ³/₄" U-matic cassette, 16-mm film.
Deals with the writer and his times. Includes dramatization from his life and works.
Distributed by the International Film Bureau.

Hard Times.
240 min., color, 1977.
Beta, VHS, ³/₄" U-matic cassette.
A TV adaptation of the novel.
Distributed by WNET/Thirteen Non-Broadcast.

Hard Times [recording].
16 hrs., 8 cassettes.
Read by Frederick Davison.
Distributed by Blackstone Audio.

Andre Dubus

Andre Dubus: Reading [recording].
1 cassette (51 min.).
The writer reads his work and discusses the writing process.
Distributed by American Audio Prose Library.

Andre Dubus: Interview [recording].
1 cassette (50 min.).
The writer reads his works and discusses the writing process.
Distributed by American Audio Prose Library.

William Faulkner

Barn Burning.
41 min., color, 1980.
Beta, VHS, 16-mm film.

With Tommy Lee Jones.
Same program available in *"The American Short Story Series II"* on manual p. 209. See local retailer.

Collected Short Stories of William Faulkner, Volumes 1 and 2 [recording].
Volume 1, 11 90-min. cassettes; Volume 2, 11 90-min. cassettes.
Read by Wolfram Kandinsky and Michael Kramer. (Volume 2 includes "A Rose for Emily.")
Distributed by Books on Tape.

The Long Hot Summer.
118 min., color, 1958.
Beta, VHS.
A film adaptation of "Barn Burning." Directed by Martin Ritt. With Paul Newman, Orson Welles, Joanne Woodward, Lee Remick, Anthony Franciosa, Angela Lansbury, and Richard Anderson.
See local retailer.

The Long Hot Summer.
172 min., color, 1986.
Beta, VHS.
A made-for-TV version of "Barn Burning." Directed by Stuart Cooper. With Don Johnson, Cybill Shepherd, Judith Ivey, Jason Robards, and Ava Gardner.
See local retailer.

*A Rose for Emily.
27 min., color, 1983.
Beta, VHS, ³/₄" U-matic cassette, 16-mm film.
Distributed by Pyramid Film and Video.

A Rose for Emily (William Faulkner).
27 min., color, 1983.
VHS.
Cast: Anjelica Huston. Narrated by John Houseman.
Distributed by Pyramid Film & Video.

William Faulkner: A Life on Paper.
120 min., color, 1980.
Beta, VHS, ³/₄" U-matic cassette.
A documentary biography. With Lauren Bacall, Howard Hawks, Anita Loos,

George Plimpton, Tennessee Williams, and Jill Faulkner Summers (the author's daughter).
Distributed by Films, Inc.

William Faulkner's Mississippi.
49 min., color and b/w, 1965.
Beta, VHS, ³/₄" U-matic cassette.
Deals with Faulkner's life and works.
Distributed by Benchmark Films.

Gail Godwin

Interview [recording].
1 cassette (56 min.).
Godwin discusses the recurring themes and concerns in her fiction.
Distributed by American Audio Prose Library.

Nathaniel Hawthorne

The Birthmark [recording].
1 cassette (63 min.). Read by Walter Zimmerman.
Distributed by Jimcin Recordings.

Favorite Stories by Nathaniel Hawthorne, Vol. 1 [recording].
2 cassettes (2 hrs., 30 min.).
Read by Walter Zimmerman and John Chatty. Includes "Dr. Heidegger's Experiment" and "The Minister's Black Veil."
Distributed by Jimcin Recordings.

The Minister's Black Veil [recording].
1 cassette (82 min.).
Read by Walter Zimmerman and John Chatty. Includes "Young Goodman Brown."
Distributed by Jimcin Recordings.

The Minister's Black Veil [recording].
1 cassette.
Distributed by Spoken Arts.

Nathaniel Hawthorne: Light in the Shadows.
23 min., color, 1982.
Beta, VHS, ³/₄" U-matic cassette, 16-mm film, special-order formats.
A background of the author's life and

works, especially *The Scarlet Letter* and *The House of the Seven Gables*.
Distributed by the International Film Bureau.

Young Goodman Brown.
30 min., color, 1972.
Beta, VHS, ³/₄" U-matic cassette, 16-mm film.
Distributed by Pyramid Film and Video.

Ernest Hemingway

Ernest Hemingway.
53 min., color, 1983.
VHS.
This program explores Hemingway's life and literary psyche through the eyes of those who knew him. A BBC Production. Part of the "Great Writers of the 20th Century" series.
Distributed by Films for the Humanities and Sciences.

Ernest Hemingway: A Life Story [recording].
Part 1, 11 cassettes, Part 2, 10 cassettes (1 hr., 30 min. per cassette).
Read by Christopher Hunt. Draws from Hemingway's diaries, letters, and unpublished writing as well as personal testimony from the people who played a part in the author's life.
Distributed by Blackstone Audio Books

Hemingway.
18 min., b/w, 1993.
Beta, VHS, ³/₄" U-matic cassette, 16-mm film.
A biography using rare stills and motion-picture footage. Narrated by Chet Huntley.
Distributed by Thomas Klise Company.

Hemingway: Up in Michigan, the Early Years.
28 min., color, 1986.
Beta, VHS, ³/₄" U-matic cassette.
A literary biography of the writer.
Distributed by Centre Communications.

Soldier's Home. See ***"The American Short Story Series I"*** on manual p. 209.

Charles Johnson

Charles Johnson.
29 min., color, 1993.
VHS.
This program shows how Charles Johnson blends black folk tales, Zen parables, eighteenth-century picaresque novels, and twentieth-century philosophy into his storytelling.
Distributed by Films for the Humanities and Sciences.

In Black and White: Charles Johnson.
27 min., color, 1992.
VHS.
Johnson describes his literary objective: to explore classic metaphysical questions from East and West against the backdrop of American life and history.
Distributed by California Newsreel.

See *"In Black and White: Conversations with African American Writers"* on manual p. 209.

Herman Melville

*Herman Melville.
22 min., color, 1978.
Beta, VHS, ³/₄" U-matic cassette, 16-mm film.
Ancillary materials available. Part of the "Authors" series of biographies.
Distributed by Journal Films, Inc.

*Herman Melville: Consider the Sea.
28 min., color, 1982.
Beta, VHS, ³/₄" U-matic cassette, 16-mm film, special-order formats.
Deals with the author and his relationship with the sea. Major works discussed include *Moby-Dick, Billy Budd,* and "Bartleby, the Scrivener."
Distributed by the International Film Bureau.

Melville: Six Short Novels [recording].
8 cassettes (60 min. each).
Read by Dan Lazar. Includes "Bartleby, the Scrivener," "The Apple Tree Table,"
"My Chimney," and "The Happy Failure."
Distributed by Books on Tape.

*Herman Melville: Damned in Paradise.
90 min., color, 1986.
Beta, VHS, ³/₄" U-matic cassette.
Documents Melville's personal and intellectual history.
Distributed by Pyramid Film and Video.

Bartleby.
79 min., color, 1970.
VHS.
Cast: Paul Scofield, John McEnery. Directed by Anthony Friedman.
Distributed by White Star.

Bartleby.
60 min., color, 197?.
VHS.
Distributed by Maryland Public Television.

Bartleby.
28 min., color, 1969.
VHS.
Distributed by Britannica Films.

Bartleby.
29 min., b&w, 1965.
VHS.
Videotape from the "American Story Classics" series.
Distributed by Film Video Library.

Bartleby, the Scrivener [recording].
1 cassette (90 min.).
Read by Walter Zimmerman.
Distributed by Jimcin Recordings.

Bharati Mukherjee

Bharati Mukherjee: Conquering America.
30 min., color, 1994.
VHS.
In this interview with Bill Moyers, Mukherjee discusses America's newest immigrants and the building resentment and tensions between our country's various cultures.
Distributed by Films for the Humanities and Sciences.

Alice Munro

Interview with Alice Munro [recording].
1 cassette (72 min.).
Munro discusses influences, feminism, and Canadian literature.
Distributed by American Audio Prose Library.

Joyce Carol Oates

Joyce Carol Oates [recording].
1 cassette (29 min.), 1989.
The author talks about her writing habits.
Distributed by Letters on the Air.

Joyce Carol Oates.
28 min., color, 1994.
VHS.
Oates discusses her work as both a writer and teacher, her craft and methods, and the major themes of her novels, short stories, and poems.
Distributed by Films for the Humanities and Sciences.

Edgar Allan Poe

Edgar Allan Poe: Terror of the Soul.
60 min., color, 1995.
Beta, VHS.
A biography revealing Poe's creative genius and personal experiences through dramatic re-creations of important scenes from his work and life. Includes dramatizations of Poe classics such as "The Tell-Tale Heart" performed by Treat Williams, John Heard, and Rene Auberjonois.
Distributed by PBS Video.

Edgar Allan Poe Stories [recording].
2 cassettes (2 hrs., 5 min.).
Six stories performed by Basil Rathbone.
Distributed by Caedmon/HarperAudio.

"The Fall of the House of Usher": And Other Poems and Tales [recording].
1 cassette (44 min.).
Abridged. Performed by Basil Rathbone. Includes "The Fall of the House of Usher," "The Tell-Tale Heart," "The Haunted Palace," and "The Bells."
Distributed by Caedmon/Harper.

The Purloined Letter and Poems [recording].
1 cassette (60 min.).
Abridged. Performed by Anthony Quayle. Includes "The Purloined Letter," "The Valley of Unrest," and "A Dream within a Dream."
Distributed by Books on Tape.

John Updike

John Updike.
30 min., b/w, 1966.
16-mm film.
Discusses Updike's beliefs and attitudes. The author reads selections from his works.
Distributed by Indiana University Instructional Support Services.

Selected Stories by John Updike [recording].
2 cassettes (2 hrs., 49 min.), 1985.
Updike reads six unabridged stories: "A & P," "Pigeon Feathers," "The Family Meadow," "The Witnesses," "The Alligators," and "Separating."
Distributed by Random Audiobooks.

What Makes Rabbit Run?
29 min., color, 1986.
VHS, 16-mm film.
Updike reads from his works and discusses his life.
Distributed by Barr Entertainment.

*Writers: John Updike.
30 min., b/w, 1966.
3/4" U-matic cassette, 16-mm film, special order formats.
An interview with the writer.
Distributed by Indiana University Instructional Support Services.

Tobias Wolff

Interview [recording].
1 cassette (56 min.).
Discussion of stories and storytelling.
Distributed by American Audio Prose Library.

GENERAL

The American Short Story Series I.

45 min./program, color, 1978.

Beta, VHS, ³/₄" U-matic cassette, 16-mm film.

Ancillary materials available. Includes nine film adaptations of short stories that appeared on PBS: "Parker Adderson, Philosopher," "The Jolly Corner," "The Blue Hotel," "I'm a Fool," "Soldier's Home," "Bernice Bobs Her Hair," "Almos' a Man," "The Displaced Person," and "The Music School."

Distributed by Coronet/MTI Film & Video.

The American Short Story Series II.

50 min./program, color, 1980.

Beta, VHS, ³/₄" U-matic cassette, 16-mm film.

Eight programs: "The Golden Honeymoon," "Paul's Case," "The Greatest Man in the World," "Rappaccini's Daughter," "The Jilting of Granny Weatherall," "The Sky Is Grey," "The Man That Corrupted Hadleyburg," and "Barn Burning." With Geraldine Fitzgerald, Brad Davis, and Tommy Lee Jones.

Distributed by Coronet/MTI Film & Video.

The Authors Series.

22 min./program, color, 1978.

Beta, VHS, ³/₄" U-matic cassette, 16-mm film.

Programs deal with biographical information as related to the creative process. Five programs: James Fenimore Cooper, Stephen Crane, Emily Dickinson, Henry James, and Herman Melville.

Distributed by Journal Films.

Dialogue.

20 min., b/w, 1974.

Beta, VHS, ³/₄" U-matic cassette.

Mr. and Mrs. Alfred A. Knopf remember the authors they worked with, including John Updike and Albert Camus.

Distributed by Phoenix/BFA Films.

Exploring the Short Story: For Entertainment and Comprehension.

37 min., color, 1976.

Beta, VHS, ³/₄"U-matic cassette.

Ancillary materials available. Deals with character, plot, setting, style, theme, and point of view.

Distributed by the Center for Humanities, Inc.

Great American Short Stories, Vol. I [recording].

7 cassettes (90 min. each), 1981.

Includes "Bartleby, the Scrivener," "The Minister's Black Veil," and fourteen others.

Distributed by Jimcin Recordings and Books on Tape.

Great American Short Stories, Vol. II [recording].

7 cassettes (90 min. each), 1984.

Includes "The Bride Comes to Yellow Sky," "The Birthmark," and fifteen others.

Distributed by Jimcin Recordings and Books on Tape.

In Black and White: Conversations with African American Writers.

Approx. 30 min./program, color, 1992.

VHS.

Interviews with African American writers Alice Walker, August Wilson, Charles Johnson, Gloria Naylor, John Wideman, and Toni Morrison.

Distributed by California Newsreel.

A Movable Feast.

30 min./program, color, 1991.

VHS.

Hosted by Tom Vitale. Profiles eight contemporary writers: (1) Allen Ginsberg; (2) Joyce Carol Oates; (3) Li-Young Lee; (4) Sonia Sanchez; (5) T. Coraghessan Boyle; (6) T. R. Pearson; (7) Trey Ellis; (8) W. S. Merwin.

Distributed by Acorn Media.

The Short Story.

20 min., color, 1962.

16-mm film.

A history of the American short story.

Women in Literature, The Short Story: A Collection [recording].
5 cassettes (7 hrs., 30 min.), 1984.
Various readers. Includes "The Story of an Hour" by Kate Chopin and other works by Edith Wharton, Willa Cather, Mary E. Wilkins Freeman, Sarah Orne Jewett, George Sand, Frances Gilchrist Wood, and Selma Laerloff.
Distributed by Jimcin Recordings and Books on Tape.

*The Writer in America.
29 min./program, color, 1979.
Beta, VHS, ³/₄" U-matic cassette, 16-mm film.
Interviews with eight contemporary writers: (1) Eudora Welty; (2) Ross MacDonald; (3) Janet Flanner; (4) John Gardner; (5) Toni Morrison; (6) Wright Morris; (7) Robert Duncan; (8) Muriel Rukeyser.
Distributed by Coronet/MTI Film & Video.

POETRY

Matthew Arnold

Treasury of Matthew Arnold [recording].
1 cassette.
Distributed by Spoken Arts.

See also **"Literature: The Synthesis of Poetry," "Palgrave's Golden Treasury of English Poetry,"** and **"Victorian Poetry"** (film and recording) on manual pp. 227–230.

Magaret Atwood

The Poetry and Voice of Margaret Atwood [recording].
1 cassette (59 min.), 1977.
Distributed by Caedmon/HarperAudio.

Margaret Atwood Reads [recording].
1 cassette (36 min.).
Distributed by Caedmon/HarperAudio

Jimmy Santiago Baca

Jimmy Santiago Baca [recording].
1 cassette (29 min.), 1991.
Distributed by New Letters on the Air.

Elizabeth Bishop

Delmore Schwartz, Richard Blackmur, Stephen Spender, and Elizabeth Bishop.
1 cassette.
Distributed by the Library of Congress.

See also **"Voices and Vision"** on manual p. 230.

William Blake

*Essay on William Blake.
52 min., color, 1969.
³/₄" U-matic cassette, 16-mm film, special-order formats.
A profile of the poet.
Distributed by Indiana University Instructional Support Services.

The Poetry of William Blake [recording].
1 cassette.
Distributed by Caedmon/HarperAudio.

Poetry of William Blake [recording].
1 cassette.
Distributed by Spoken Arts.

*William Blake.
26 min., color, 1973.
16-mm film.
Hosted by Kenneth Clark. Focuses on Blake's drawings and engravings.
Distributed by Pyramid Film and Video.

William Blake.
30 min.
VHS.
A dramatization of Blake's inner world.
Distributed by Insight Media.

William Blake.
57 min., color, 1976.
Beta, VHS, ³/₄" U-matic cassette, special-order formats.
A biographical portrait.
Distributed by Time-Life Video.

William Blake: The Book of Thel [recording].
1 cassette.
Distributed by Audio-Forum.

William Blake: Selected Poems [recording].
2 cassettes (180 min.), 1992.
Includes "Tyger! Tyger!" and "A Poison Tree."
Distributed by Blackstone Audio Books.

William Blake: The Marriage of Heaven and Hell.
30 min., color, 1984.
³/₄" U-matic cassette.
Dramatizes the life of Blake and his wife Catherine. With Anne Baxter and George Rose.
Distributed by Modern Talking Picture Service.

William Blake: Something About Poetry [recording].
1 cassette (22 min.), 1969.
Distributed by Audio-Forum.

See also *"Introduction to English Poetry"* and *"Romantic Pioneers"* on manual pp. 227, 229.

*William Blake: Poems [recording].
1 cassette (80 min.).
Distributed by HighBridge.

Robert Bly

The Poetry of Robert Bly [recording].
1 cassette (38 min.), 1966.
Part of the YM-YWHA Poetry Series.
Distributed by Audio-Forum.

Robert Bly I & II [recording].
1 cassette (60 min.), 1979, 1991.
Distributed by New Letters on the Air.

Robert Bly: Booth and Bly, Poets.
30 min., color, 1978.
¹/₂" open reel (EIAJ), ³/₄" U-matic cassette.
A four-part series of workshops and readings by the poets.
Distributed by Nebraska Educational Television Network.

Robert Bly: An Evening of Poetry [recording].
2 cassettes.
Distributed by Sound Horizons.

Robert Bly: Fairy Tales for Men and Women [recording].
90 min., 1987.
Bly applies psychoanalytical analysis to poetry.
Distributed by Ally Press.

Robert Bly: For the Stomach — Selected Poems, 1974 [recording].
64 min.
Bly reads his poetry.
Distributed by Watershed Tapes.

Robert Bly: The Human Shadow [recording].
2 cassettes.
Distributed by Mystic Fire.

Robert Bly: A Man Writes to a Part of Himself.
57 min., color, 1978.
³/₄" U-matic cassette, special-order formats.
Poetry and conversation with the writer.
Distributed by Intermedia Arts of Minnesota.

Robert Bly: Poetry East and West [recording].
140 min., 1983.
Bly gives a poetry lecture, accompanied by the dulcimer.
Distributed by Dolphin Tapes.

Robert Bly: Poetry in Motion.
30 min., color, 1981.
Beta, VHS, ³/₄" U-matic cassette.
Video biographies of three poets: Robert Bly, Frederick Marfred, and Thomas McGrath.
Distributed by Intermedia Arts of Minnesota.

Robert Bly: Poetry Reading — An Ancient Tradition [recording].
2 cassettes (150 min.), 1983.
Bly talks about the oral tradition in poetry.
Distributed by Dolphin Tapes.

Robert Bly — A Home in the Dark Grass:

Poems & Meditations on Solitudes, Families, Disciplines *[recording].*
2 cassettes (131 min.), 1991.
Distributed by Ally Press Audio.

Robert Bly: Poems of Kabir *[recording].*
2 cassettes (1 hr., 59 min.), 1977,1995.
Distributed by Audio Literature.

Robert Bly: Poems of Kabir *[recording].*
1 cassette.
Distributed by Ally Press.

Robert Bly: Selected Poems *[recording].*
2 cassettes (131 min.), 1987.
Distributed by Ally Press.

Robert Bly: The Six Powers of Poetry *[recording].*
1 cassette (90 min.), 1983.
A lecture from the San Jose Poetry Center.
Distributed by Dolphin Tapes.

See also ***"Moyers: The Power of the Word"*** on manual p. 228.

Gwendolyn Brooks

*Gwendolyn Brooks.
30 min., b/w, 1966.
³/₄″ U-matic cassette, 16-mm film, special-order formats.
Brooks talks about her life and poetry.
Distributed by Indiana University Instructional Support Services.

Gwendolyn Brooks I & II *[recording].*
1 cassette (60 min.), 1988, 1989.
Distributed by New Letters on the Air.

Gwendolyn Brooks Reading Her Poetry *[recording].*
1 cassette.
Distributed by Caedmon/HarperAudio.

See also ***"The Harlem Renaissance and Beyond"*** on manual p. 227.

Robert Browning

Robert Browning: "My Last Duchess" & Other Poems *[recording].*
1 cassette.
Distributed by Caedmon/HarperAudio.

Robert Browning: Selected Poems *[recording].*
4 cassettes (360 min.).
Read by Frederick Davidson.
Distributed by Blackstone Audio Books.

The Poetry of Browning *[recording].*
1 cassette.
Distributed by Caedmon/HarperAudio.

*Robert Browning — His Life and Poetry.
21 min., color, 1972.
Beta, VHS, ³/₄″ U-matic cassette, 16-mm film, special-order format.
A dramatization of Browning's life and several of his poems, including "My Last Duchess."
Distributed by International Film Bureau.

Treasury of Robert Browning *[recording].*
1 cassette.
Distributed by Spoken Arts.

See also ***"Victorian Poetry"*** (recording) on manual p. 230.

E. E. Cummings

E. E. Cummings Reading His Poetry *[recording].*
1 cassette.
Distributed by Caedmon/HarperAudio.

E. E. Cummings Reads *[recording].*
1 cassette (60 min.), 1987.
From The Poet Anniversary Series.
Distributed by Caedmon/HarperAudio.

E. E. Cummings Reads His Collected Poetry, 1920 — 1940, & Prose *[recording].*
2 cassettes (79 min.).
Distributed by Caedmon/HarperAudio.

E. E. Cummings Reads His Collected Poetry, 1943–1958 *[recording].*
2 cassettes.
Distributed by Caedmon/HarperAudio.

*E. E. Cummings: The Making of a Poet.
24 min., 1978.
Beta, VHS, ³/₄″ U-matic cassette.
A profile of Cummings told in his own words.
Distributed by Films for the Humanities and Sciences.

E. E. Cummings: Nonlectures [recordings].
6 cassettes.
(1) I & My Parents; (2) I & Their Son; (3) I & Self-discovery; (4) I & You & Is; (5) I & Now & Him; (6) I & Am & Santa Claus.
Distributed by Caedmon/HarperAudio.

Poems of E. E. Cummings [recording].
1 cassette (60 min.), 1981.
Part of the Poetic Heritage Series.
Distributed by Summer Stream.

E. E. Cummings: Twentieth-Century Poetry in English: Recordings of Poets Reading Their Own Poetry, No. 5 [recording].
Distributed by the Library of Congress.

See also *"Caedmon Treasury of Modern Poets Reading Their Own Poetry," "Inner Ear, Parts 5 and 6,"* and *"Poetry for People Who Hate Poetry"* on manual pp. 226–228.

James Dickey

James Dickey.
Color, VHS (30 min.), 1989.
A production of the University of South Carolina and the South Carolina ETV Network.
Distributed by PBS Video.

James Dickey [recording].
1 cassette (29 min.), 1987.
Distributed by New Letters on the Air.

James Dickey [recording].
1 cassette, 1976.
Distributed by Tapes for Readers.

James Dickey Reads His Poetry & Prose [recording].
1 cassette, 1972.
Distributed by Caedmon/HarperAudio.

The Poems of James Dickey [recording].
1 cassette (52 min.), 1967.
Distributed by Spoken Arts.

Emily Dickinson

Emily Dickinson: A Brighter Garden [recording].
1 cassette (15 min.).
Distributed by Spoken Arts.

Emily Dickinson: A Self-Portrait [recording].
2 cassettes (90 min.).
Distributed by Caedmon/HarperAudio, Filmic Archives.

Fifty Poems of Emily Dickinson [recording].
1 cassette (45 min.).
Distributed by Dove Audio.

Emily Dickinson: Seventy-Five Poems [recording].
2 cassettes (2 hours, 15 min.), 1990.
Distributed by Recorded Books.

*Emily Dickinson: The Belle of Amherst.
90 min., color, 1980.
Beta, VHS, ¾" U-matic cassette.
With Julie Harris.
Distributed by Cifex Corporation.

*Emily Dickinson: A Certain Slant of Light.
29 min., color, 1978.
Beta, VHS, ¾" U-matic cassette, 16-mm film.
Explores Dickinson's life and environment. Narrated by Julie Harris.
Distributed by Pyramid Film and Video.

Emily Dickinson: Magic Prison — A Dialogue Set to Music.
35 min., color, 1969.
Beta, VHS, ¾" U-matic cassette, 16-mm film.
Dramatizes the letters between Dickinson and Colonel T. W. Higginson. With an introduction by Archibald MacLeish and music by Ezra Laderman.
Distributed by Britannica Films.

Emily Dickinson: Poems and Letters [recording].
2 cassettes.
Distributed by Recorded Books.

Emily Dickinson: Selected Poems [recording].
4 cassettes (360 min.), 1993.
Read by Mary Woods.
Distributed by Blackstone Audio Books.

Poems and Letters of Emily Dickinson [recording].
1 cassette.
Distributed by Caedmon/HarperAudio.

*Emily Dickinson.
22 min., color, 1978.
Beta, VHS, ¾″ U-matic cassette.
A film about the poet and her poems. Part of the "Authors" series.
Distributed by Journal Films Inc.

Emily Dickinson [recording].
1 cassette.
Distributed by Recorded Books.

Emily Dickinson Recalled in Song [recording].
1 cassette (30 min.).
Distributed by Audio-Forum.

Poems by Emily Dickinson [recording].
2 cassettes (236 min.), 1986.
Distributed by Audio Book Contractors.

Poems of Emily Dickinson [recording].
1 cassette.
Distributed by Spoken Arts.

Poems of Emily Dickinson & Lizette Woodworth Reese [recording].
1 cassette (60 min.), 1981.
Unabridged edition. Part of the "Poetic Heritage Series."
Distributed by Summer Stream.

See also *"Inner Ear, Parts 3 and 4," "Introduction to English Poetry," "Voices and Vision,"* and *"With a Feminine Touch"* on manual pp. 227 and 230.

John Donne

Essential Donne [recording].
From the Essential Poets Series.
Distributed by Listening Library.

John Donne.
40 min., color.
VHS.
Discusses the poet's life and works.
Distributed by Insight Media.

John Donne: Love Poems [recording].
1 cassette.
Distributed by Recorded Books.

John Donne: Selected Poems [recording].
2 cassettes (180 min.), 1992.
Read by Frederick Davidson.
Distributed by Blackstone Audio Books.

The Love Poems of John Donne [recording].
1 cassette.
Distributed by Caedmon/HarperAudio.

Treasury of John Donne [recording].
1 cassette.
Distributed by Spoken Arts.

See also *"Metaphysical and Devotional Poetry"* and *"Palgrave's Golden Treasury of English Poetry"* on manual pp. 227–228.

Paul Laurence Dunbar

*Paul Laurence Dunbar: American Poet.
14 min., color, 1966.
Beta, VHS, ¾″ U-matic cassette, 16-mm film, open-captioned.
A biographical sketch of the poet.
Distributed by Phoenix/BFA Films.

*Paul Laurence Dunbar.
22 min., color, 1973.
Beta, VHS, ¾″ U-matic cassette.
A biographical tribute to the poet. Directed by Carlton Moss.
Distributed by Pyramid Film and Video.

T. S. Eliot

*The Mysterious Mr. Eliot.
62 min., color, 1973.
Beta, VHS, ¾″ U-matic cassette, 16-mm film.
A biographical film about the poet.
Distributed by Insight Media and CRM Films.

T. S. Eliot: Selected Poems *[recording].*
1 cassette (49 min.), 1971.
The author reads his poetry, including "The Waste Land."
Distributed by Caedmon/HarperAudio.

T. S. Eliot: Four Quartets *[recording].*
1 cassette.
Distributed by Caedmon/HarperAudio.

T. S. Eliot: Twentieth-Century Poetry in English: Recordings of Poets Reading Their Own Poetry, No. 3 *[recording].*
Distributed by the Library of Congress.

T. S. Eliot and George Orwell *[recording].*
1 cassette (41 min.), 1953.
Read by Stephen Spender.
Distributed by Caedmon/HarperAudio.

T. S. Eliot Reading "The Love Song of J. Alfred Prufrock" *[recording].*
1 cassette.
Distributed by Caedmon/HarperAudio.

T. S. Eliot Reading "The Waste Land" & Other Poems *[recording].*
1 cassette.
Distributed by Caedmon/HarperAudio.

See also ***"Caedmon Treasury of Modern Poets Reading Their Own Poetry," "Modern American Poetry," "The Poet's Voice,"*** and ***"Voices and Vision"*** on manual pp. 226, 228, and 230.

Carolyn Forché

Carolyn Forché *[recording].*
1 cassette (29 min.), 1989.
Distributed by New Letters on the Air.

Carolyn Forché: Ourselves or Nothing *[recording].*
1 cassette (58 min.), 1983.
Distributed by Watershed Tapes.

Robert Frost

Afterglow: A Tribute to Robert Frost.
35 min., color, 1989.
Beta, VHS, $3/4''$ U-matic cassette.
Starring and directed by Burgess Meredith.
Distributed by Pyramid Film and Video.

Robert Frost *[recording].*
1 cassette, 1981.
Includes "The Pasture" and "Stopping by Woods on a Snowy Evening."
Distributed by the Library of Congress

*Robert Frost: A First Acquaintance.
16 min., color, 1974.
Beta, VHS, $3/4''$ U-matic cassette, 16-mm film.
An examination of Frost's life through his poems.
Distributed by Films for the Humanities and Sciences.

Frost and Whitman.
30 min., b/w, 1963.
Beta, VHS, $1/2''$ open reel (EIAJ), $3/4''$ U-matic cassette, 2" quadraplex open reel.
Will Geer performs excerpts from the two poets' works.
Distributed by New York State Education Department.

An Interview with Robert Frost.
30 min., b/w, 1952.
Beta, VHS, $3/4''$ U-matic cassette.
Bela Kornitzer interviews Frost, who reads from his poetry.
Distributed by Social Studies School Service.

*Robert Frost: A Lover's Quarrel with the World.
40 min., b/w, 1970.
Beta, VHS, $3/4''$ U-matic cassette, 16-mm film.
A documentary film on Frost's philosophic and artistic ideas.
Distributed by Phoenix/BFA Films.

*Robert Frost.
10 min., color, 1972.
Beta, VHS, $3/4''$ U-matic cassette, 16-mm film.
A biographical sketch of the poet.
Distributed by AIMS Media Inc.

Robert Frost in Recital *[recording].*
1 cassette.
Distributed by Caedmon/HarperAudio.

Robert Frost Reads [recording].
1 cassette (60 min.), 1987.
From The Poet Anniversary Series.
Distributed by Caedmon/HarperAudio.

Robert Frost Reads His Poems [recording].
1 cassette (55 min.), 1965.
Distributed by Audio-Forum.

Robert Frost Reads His Poetry [recording].
1 cassette (48 min.).
Distributed by Recorded Books.

Robert Frost Reads "The Road Not Taken" & Other Poems [recording].
1 cassette.
Distributed by Caedmon/HarperAudio.

*Robert Frost's New England.
22 min., color, 1976.
Beta, VHS, ³/₄″ U-matic cassette, 16-mm film, special-order formats. Ancillary materials available.
Explores some of Frost's poetry relating to New England and its seasons.
Distributed by Churchill Media.

Robert Frost: Twentieth-Century Poetry in English: Recordings of Poets Reading Their Own Poetry, No. 6 [recording].
Distributed by the Library of Congress.

See also *"Caedmon Treasury of Modern Poets Reading Their Own Poetry," "Literature: The Synthesis of Poetry," "Modern American Poetry," "Poetry by Americans," "The Poet's Voice,"* and *"Voices and Vision"* on manual pp. 226–228, and 230.

Marilyn Hacker

Marilyn Hacker: The Poetry and Voice of Marilyn Hacker [recording].
1 cassette.
Distributed by Caedmon/HarperAudio.

Donald Hall

Donald Hall: Prose and Poetry [recording].
2 cassettes (93 min.), 1997.
Distributed by Audio Bookshelf.

Donald Hall [recording].
1 cassette (29 min.), 1987.
Distributed by New Letters on the Air.

Donald Hall [recording].
1 cassette (29 min.), 1987.
Distributed by Spoken Arts.

Donald Hall and Jane Kenyon: A Life Together.
60 min., color.
VHS.
Bill Moyers interviews these husband-and-wife poets at their home in New Hampshire.
Distributed by Films for the Humanities and Sciences.

Donald Hall: Names of Horses [recording].
1 cassette (53 min.), 1986.
Distributed by Watershed Tapes.

The Poetry of Donald Hall [recording].
1 cassette (26 min.), 1964.
Part of the YM-YWHA Poetry Center Series.
Distributed by Audio-Forum.

Thomas Hardy

The Poetry of Thomas Hardy [recording].
1 cassette.
Distributed by Caedmon/HarperAudio.

See also *"Introduction to English Poetry," "Romantics and Realists,"* and *"Victorian Poetry"* (recording) on manual pp. 227 and 230.

Robert Hass

Robert Hass: A Story About the Body [recording].
1 cassette, 1988.
Distributed by Watershed Tapes.

William Hathaway

William Hathaway [recording].
1 cassette (29 min.), 1984.
Distributed by New Letters on the Air.

Robert Herrick

See *"Palgrave's Golden Treasury of English Poetry"* on manual p. 228.

Gerard Manley Hopkins

The Poetry of Gerard Manley Hopkins
   [recording].
1 cassette.
Distributed by Caedmon/HarperAudio.

Gerard Manley Hopkins: The Wreck of the
   Deutschland [recording].
1 cassette.
Distributed by Audio-Forum.

See also *"Romantics and Realists"* and
   "Victorian Poetry" (recording) on
   manual pp. 229–230.

Langston Hughes

*Langston Hughes.
24 min., color, 1971.
Beta, VHS, ³/₄″ U-matic cassette, 16-mm
   film.
A biographical sketch of the poet.
Distributed by Carousel Film & Video.

Langston Hughes: The Dream Keeper.
Color, VHS (60 min.), 1988.
Distributed by the Annenberg/CPB
   Collection.

Langston Hughes: Looking for Langston.
Color, VHS (45 min.), 1992. Produced by
   Isaac Julien.
Distributed by Water Bearer Films.

Langston Hughes Reads [recording].
1 cassette (50 min.).
Distributed by Caedmon/HarperAudio,
   Filmic Archives.

Langston Hughes Reads and Talks about His
   Poems [recording].
1 cassette. (42 min.).
Distributed by Dove Audio.

Langston Hughes: Dream Keeper and Other
   Poems [recording].
1 cassette, 1955.
Distributed by Smithsonian/Folkways
   Recordings.

Langston Hughes: The Making of a Poet
   [recording].
1 cassette (30 min.).

Read by the poet.
Distributed by National Public Radio.

Langston Hughes: Poetry & Reflection
   [recording].
1 cassette.
Performed by the author.
Distributed by Caedmon/HarperAudio.

Langston Hughes Reads and Talks about His
   Poems [recording].
1 cassette.
Includes "The Negro Speaks of Rivers" and
   "Dream Boogie."
Distributed by Spoken Arts.

The Poetry of Langston Hughes [recording].
2 cassettes.
Performed by Ruby Dee and Ossie Davis.
Distributed by Caedmon/HarperAudio.

The Voice of Langston Hughes: Selected
   Poetry and Prose [recording].
1 cassette or CD (38 min.).
Selections from the years 1925–1932. The
   author reads poetry from *"The Dream*
   Keeper" and Other Poems and *Simple*
   Speaks His Mind, and he narrates his
   text from *The Story of Jazz, Rhythms of*
   the World, and *The Glory of Negro History.*
Distributed by Smithsonian/Folkways
   Recordings.

Langston Hughes: Simple Stories [recording].
1 cassette.
Performed by Ossie Davis.
Distributed by Caedmon/HarperAudio.

See also *"Harlem Renaissance: The Black*
   Poets," "The Harlem Renaissance and
   Beyond," "Modern American Poetry,"
   "Twentieth-Century Poets Reading
   Their Work," and *"Voices and Vision"*
   on manual pp. 227, 228, and 230.

Randall Jarrell

Randall Jarrell: The Bat Poet [recording].
1 cassette.
Distributed by Caedmon/HarperAudio.

The Poetry of Randall Jarrell [recording].
1 cassette (67 min.), 1963.

Part of the YM-YWHA Poetry Center Series. Distributed by Audio-Forum.

Randall Jarrell Reads and Discusses His Poems against War *[recording].*
1 cassette.
Distributed by Caedmon/HarperAudio.

See also *"The Poet's Voice"* on manual p. 228.

John Keats

John Keats — His Life and Death.
55 min., color, 1973.
Beta, VHS, ³/₄" U-matic cassette, 16-mm film.
Extended version of *"John Keats — Poet"* (see below). Explores the poet's affair with Fanny Browne and the events surrounding his death. Written by Archibald MacLeish.
Distributed by Britannica Films.

John Keats — Poet.
31 min., color, 1973.
Beta, VHS, ³/₄" U-matic cassette, 16-mm film.
A biography of the poet, with excerpts from his letters and poems. Written by Archibald MacLeish.
Distributed by Britannica Films.

John Keats: Selected Poems *[recording].*
2 cassettes (180 min.), 1993.
Read by Frederick Davidson.
Distributed by Blackstone Audio Books.

John Keats: Odes *[recording].*
1 cassette.
Distributed by Audio-Forum.

The Poetry of Keats *[recording].*
1 cassette.
Distributed by Caedmon/HarperAudio.

Treasury of John Keats *[recording].*
1 cassette.
Distributed by Spoken Arts.

See also *"English Literature: Romantic Period,"* *"Palgrave's Golden Treasury of English Poetry,"* and *"The Young Romantics"* on manual pp. 226, 228, and 230.

Jane Kenyon

Jane Kenyon *[recording].*
1 cassette, 1987.
Distributed by New Letters on the Air.

Maxine Hong Kingston

Maxine Hong Kingston *[recording].*
1 cassette, 1986.
Interview.
Distributed by American Audio Prose Library.

The Stories of Maxine Hong Kingston.
54 min., color, 1990.
VHS.
Kingston discusses her perspective of the "Great American Melting Pot."
Distributed by University of Washington Educational Media Collection.

Galway Kinnell

Galway Kinnell I & II *[recording].*
1 cassette (60 min.), 1982, 1991.
Distributed by New Letters on the Air.

The Poetry of Galway Kinnell *[recording].*
1 cassette (33 min.), 1965.
Part of the YM-YWHA Poetry Center Series.
Distributed by Audio-Forum.

The Poetry & Voice of Galway Kinnell *[recording].*
1 cassette.
Distributed by Caedmon/HarperAudio.

See also *"Moyers: The Power of the Word"* on manual p. 228.

Christopher Marlowe

Christopher Marlowe: Elizabethan Love Poems *[recording].*
1 cassette (50 min.).
Unabridged edition.
Distributed by Spoken Arts.

See also *"Medieval and Elizabethan Poetry"* and *"Palgrave's Golden Treasury of*

English Poetry" on manual pp. 227–
228.

Andrew Marvell

*Andrew Marvell: Ralph Richardson Reads
Andrew Marvell [recording].*
1 cassette.
Distributed by Audio-Forum.

See also *"Metaphysical and Devotional
Poetry"* on manual p. 227.

N. Scott Momaday

N. Scott Momaday.
50 min., color.
The author discusses the creative sources
of his work.
Distributed by Films for the Humanities
and Sciences.

*N. Scott Momaday: House Made of Dawn
[recording].*
1 cassette (39 min.).
Momaday reads excerpts from his stories.
Distributed by the American Audio Prose
Library.

*N. Scott Momaday: House Made of Dawn
[recording].*
7 cassettes (7 hours).
Distributed by Books on Tape.

N. Scott Momaday Reading [recording].
2 cassettes (109 min.), 1983.
Distributed by American Audio Prose
Library.

Pablo Neruda

Pablo Neruda: Poet.
30 min., b/w, 1972.
Beta, VHS, $^3/_4$" U-matic cassette.
A profile of the poet.
Distributed by Cinema Guild.

Pablo Neruda: Selected Poems [recording].
1 cassette.
In Spanish.
Distributed by Applause Productions.

*Yo Soy Pablo Neruda.
29 min., b/w, 1967.

Beta, VHS, $^3/_4$" U-matic, 16-mm film.
A profile of the poet. Narrated by Sir
Anthony Quayle.
Distributed by Films for the Humanities
and Sciences.

Sharon Olds

Sharon Olds [recording].
1 cassette (29 min.), 1992.
Distributed by New Letters on the Air

*Sharon Olds: Coming Back to Life [re-
cording].*
1 cassette (60 min.).
Distibuted by Audio-Forum.

Michael O'Brien & Sharon Olds [recording].
1 cassette (29 min.).
Distributed by New Letters on the Air.

See also *"Moyers: The Power of the Word"*
on manual p. 228.

Wilfred Owen

Wilfred Owen: War Requiem.
Color & b/w, VHS (92 min.), 1988.
Written and directed by Derek Jarman,
music by Benjamin Britten.
Distributed by Mystic Fire Video.

Wilfred Owen: War Requiem [recording].
2 compact discs, 1993.
Distributed by Deutsche Grammophone.

*The Pity of War: From the Works of Wilfred
Owen.*
58 min., color, 1987.
Beta, VHS, $^3/_4$" U-matic cassette.
A documentary drawn from Owen's poems,
diaries, and letters.
Distributed by Films for the Humanities
and Sciences.

Octavio Paz

*Octavio Paz: An Uncommon Poet.
28 min., color, 198?.
Beta, VHS, $^3/_4$" U-matic cassette, 16-mm
film.
The poet talks about the distinctions
between his two careers: poet and
political activist.

Distributed by Films for the Humanities and Sciences.

See also *"Moyers: The Power of the Word"* on manual p. 228.

Marge Piercy

Marge Piercy: At the Core [recording].
1 cassette (58 min.), 1977.
Distributed by Watershed Tapes.

Sylvia Plath

Sylvia Plath: The Bell Jar.
113 min., color, 1979.
Beta, VHS.
Based on Plath's semiautobiographical novel.
See local retailer.

Sylvia Plath.
Color, VHS (1988).
Distributed by Annenberg/CPB Collection and Mystic Fire.

Sylvia Plath.
4 programs (30 min. each), color, 1974.
VHS, ½" open reel (EIAJ), ¾" U-matic cassette, 2" quadraplex open reel.
A biographical examination of the poet and her work.
Distributed by New York State Education Department.

Sylvia Plath [recording].
1 cassette (48 min.), 1962.
A historic reading of fifteen poems recorded the month before the poet's suicide.
Distributed by Poet's Audio Center.

Sylvia Plath: Letters Home.
90 min., color, 1985.
Beta, VHS, ¾" U-matic cassette.
Staged version of Plath's letters to her mother.
Distributed by Films for the Humanities and Sciences.

Sylvia Plath, Part I: The Struggle.
30 min., color, 1974.
Beta, VHS, ½" open reel (EIAJ), ¾" U-matic cassette, 2" quadraplex open reel.

A dramatization of Plath's poetry by The Royal Shakespeare Company.
Distributed by New York State Education Department.

Sylvia Plath, Part II: Getting There.
30 min., color, 1974.
Beta, VHS, ½" open reel (EIAJ), ¾" U-matic cassette, 2" quadraplex open reel.
Plath's poems are set to music by Elizabeth Swados and performed by Michele Collison.
Distributed by New York State Education Department.

Sylvia Plath Reading Her Poetry [recording].
1 cassette.
Distributed by Caedmon/HarperAudio.

Sylvia Plath Reads [recording].
1 cassette (60 min.), 1987.
From The Poet Anniversary Series.
Distributed by Caedmon/HarperAudio.

See also *"The Poet's Voice," "Voices and Vision,"* and *"With a Feminine Touch"* on manual pp. 228 and 230.

Edgar Allan Poe

Edgar Allan Poe: "The Raven," "The Bells," and Other Poems [recording].
1 cassette.
Distributed by Spoken Arts.

Edgar Allan Poe [recording].
2 cassettes (2 hours).
Distributed by Dove Audio.

See also *"Poetry by Americans"* on manual p. 228.

Alberto A. Ríos

Alberto A. Ríos: Reading His Poetry [recording].
1 cassette.
Distributed by Sound Photosynthesis.

See also *"Birthright: Growing Up Hispanic"* on manual p. 226.

Theodore Roethke

The Poetry of Theodore Roethke [recording].
1 cassette (36 min.).
Part of the YM-YWHA Poetry Center Series.
Distributed by Audio-Forum.

Theodore Roethke [recording].
1 cassette (48 min.), 1972.
A posthumous collection of Roethke
    reading his poetry.
Distributed by Caedmon/HarperAudio.

*Theodore Roethke: Twentieth-Century
    Poetry in English: Recordings of Poets
    Reading Their Own Poetry, No. 10
    [recording].*
Distributed by the Library of Congress.

*Words for the Wind: Read by Theodore
    Roethke [recording].*
1 cassette, 1962.
Distributed by Smithsonian/Folkways
    Recordings.

See *"The Poet's Voice"* on manual p. 228.

William Shakespeare

**William Shakespeare: Poetry and Hidden
    Poetry.*
53 min., color, 1984.
A microexamination of Shakespeare's
    poetry and its hidden meanings.
    Produced by the Royal Shakespeare
    Company.
Distributed by Films for the Humanities
    and Sciences.

Selected Sonnets by Shakespeare.
40 min., color, 1984.
Beta, VHS, $^3/_4''$ U-matic cassette.
Features readings by Ben Kingsley and Jane
    Lapotaire.
Distributed by Films for the Humanities
    and Sciences.

Selected Sonnets of Shakespeare [recording].
1 cassette.
Distributed by Spoken Arts.

*William Shakespeare: The Sonnets [re-
    cording].*
1 cassette.
Distributed by Recorded Books.

William Shakespeare Sonnets [recording].
2 cassettes (120 min.).
Distributed by Caedmon/HarperAudio.

William Shakespeare's Sonnets.
150 min., color, 1984.
Beta, VHS, $^3/_4''$ U-matic cassette.
An in-depth look at fifteen of Shakes-
    peare's sonnets. With Ben Kingsley,
    Roger Reese, Claire Bloom, Jane
    Lapotaire, A. L. Rowse, and Stephen
    Spender.
Distributed by Films for the Humanities
    and Sciences.

See also *"England: Background of Liter-
    ature," "Introduction to English
    Poetry," "Medieval and Elizabethan
    Poetry," "Palgrave's Golden Treasury
    of English Poetry,"* and *"Poetry for
    People Who Hate Poetry"* on manual
    pp. 226–228.

Gary Soto

Gary Soto I & II [recording].
1 cassette (60 min.), 1982, 1992.
The author reads his work and talks about
    the recent rise of Chicano literature.
Distributed by New Letters on the Air.

See also *"Poets in Person, No. 7"* on manual
    p. 229.

William Stafford

William Stafford I & II [recording].
1 cassette (60 min.), 1983, 1984.
The author reads his poetry and discusses
    politics, poetry, and the writing
    process.
Distributed by New Letters on the Air.

*William   Stafford: Troubleshooting
    [recording].*
1 cassette (50 min.), 1984.
Distributed by Watershed Tapes.

See also *"Moyers: The Power of the Word"* on manual p. 228.

Dylan Thomas

The Days of Dylan Thomas.
21 min., b/w, 1965.
Beta, VHS, ³/₄" U-matic cassette, 16-mm film.
A biography of the poet.
Distributed by CRM Films.

Dylan Thomas [recording].
4 cassettes.
Distributed by Caedmon/HarperAudio.

Dylan Thomas.
25 min., color, 1982.
Beta, VHS, ³/₄" U-matic cassette.
A portrait of the poet.
Distributed by Films, Inc.

A Dylan Thomas Memoir.
28 min., color, 1972.
Beta, VHS, ³/₄" U-matic cassette, 16-mm film.
A character study of the poet.
Distributed by Pyramid Film and Video.

Dylan Thomas Soundbook [recording].
4 cassettes.
Read by the author.
Distributed by Caedmon/HarperAudio.

Dylan Thomas Reading "And Death Shall Have No Dominion" & Other Poems [recording].
1 cassette.
Distributed by Caedmon/HarperAudio.

Dylan Thomas Reading His Poetry [recording].
2 cassettes.
Distributed by Caedmon/HarperAudio.

Dylan Thomas Reading "Quite Early One Morning" & Other Poems [recording].
1 cassette.
Distributed by Caedmon/HarperAudio.

Dylan Thomas Reading "Over Sir John's Hill" & Other Poems [recording].
1 cassette.
Distributed by Caedmon/HarperAudio.

Dylan Thomas Reads a Personal Anthology [recording].
1 cassette.
Distributed by Caedmon/HarperAudio.

An Evening with Dylan Thomas [recording].
1 cassette.
Distributed by Caedmon/HarperAudio.

Dylan Thomas: In Country Heaven — The Evolution of a Poem [recording].
1 cassette.
Distributed by Caedmon/HarperAudio.

Dylan Thomas: A Portrait.
26 min., color, 1989.
Beta, VHS, ³/₄" U-matic cassette.
A biographical film.
Distributed by Films for the Humanities and Sciences.

Dylan Thomas: An Appreciation [recording].
1 cassette.
Distributed by Audio-Forum.

Dylan Thomas: Under Milkwood [recording].
2 cassettes (90 min.).
Distributed by S & S Audio.

The Wales of Dylan Thomas.
Color, 1989.
Images of Wales in Thomas's poetry, prose, and drama.
Distributed by Films for the Humanities and Sciences.

See also *"Caedmon Treasury of Modern Poets Reading Their Own Poetry"* on manual p. 226.

John Updike

John Updike, I and II [recording].
2 cassettes (58 min.), 1987.
Distributed by New Letters on the Air.

The Poetry of John Updike [recording].
1 cassette (47 min.), 1967.
Part of the YM-YWHA Poetry Center Series.
Distributed by Audio-Forum.

Walt Whitman

Walt Whitman: "Crossing Brooklyn Ferry" & Other Poems *[recording]*.
1 cassette.
Distributed by Caedmon/HarperAudio.

Walt Whitman: American Poet, 1819–1892 *[recording]*.
Color, VHS (30 min.), 1994
Distributed by Kultur.

The Democratic Vistas of Walt Whitman *[recording]*.
1 cassette (22 min.), 1968.
By Louis Untermeyer. Part of the Makers of the Modern World Series.
Distributed by Audio-Forum.

Walt Whitman: Endlessly Rocking.
21 min., color, 1986.
Beta, VHS, ³/₄″ U-matic cassette.
Shows a teacher's unsuccessful attempts to interest her students in Whitman.
Distributed by Centre Communications.

Walt Whitman: Frost and Whitman.
30 min., b/w, 1963.
Beta, VHS, ¹/₂″ open reel (EIAJ), ³/₄″ U-matic cassette, 2″ quadraplex open reel.
Will Geer performs excerpts from the two poets' works.
Distributed by New York State Education Department.

Walt Whitman: Galway Kinnell Reads Walt Whitman *[recording]*.
1 cassette (59 min.).
Kinnell reads excerpts from "Song of Myself," "I Sing the Body Electric," and several shorter poems.
Distributed by Sound Rx.

Walt Whitman: The Living Tradition.
20 min., color, 1983.
Beta, VHS, ³/₄″ U-matic cassette.
Allen Ginsberg reads Whitman's poetry.
Distributed by Centre Communications.

Walt Whitman: Memoranda during the War: From Specimen Days *[recording]*.
240 min.
Distributed by Recorded Books.

Walt Whitman: Orson Welles Reads "Song of Myself" *[recording]*.
1 cassette.
Distributed by Audio-Forum.

Walt Whitman: Poet for a New Age.
29 min., color, 1972.
Beta, VHS, ³/₄″ U-matic cassette, 16-mm film.
A study of the poet.
Distributed by Britannica Films.

Readings of Walt Whitman *[recording]*.
1 cassette, 1957.
Distributed by Smithsonian/Folkways Recordings.

Treasury of Walt Whitman: Leaves of Grass, I & II *[recording]*.
2 cassettes (92 min.).
Unabridged edition.
Distributed by Spoken Arts.

Walt Whitman: Twentieth-Century Poetry in English, Nos. 13–17 *[recording]*.
From the Leaves of Grass Centennial Series.
Distributed by the Library of Congress.

Walt Whitman.
10 min., color, 1972.
Beta, VHS, ³/₄″ U-matic cassette, 16-mm film, open captioned.
Readings and a discussion of Whitman's life. Hosted by Efrem Zimbalist Jr.
Distributed by AIMS Media Inc.

Walt Whitman.
12 min., color, 1989.
Beta, VHS, ³/₄″ U-matic cassette.
Examines Whitman's poetic language.
Distributed by Films for the Humanities and Sciences.

Walt Whitman's Civil War.
15 min., color, 1988.
Beta, VHS, ³/₄″ U-matic cassette.
Discusses Whitman's perspective on the war.
Distributed by Churchill Media.

See also ***"Poetry by Americans"*** and ***"Voices and Vision"*** on manual pp. 228 and 230.

Richard Wilbur

Richard Wilbur [recording].
1 cassette (29 min.), 1990.
The author reads his poems and talks about early influences and censorship.
Distributed by New Letters on the Air.

Poems of Richard Wilbur [recording].
1 cassette.
Distributed by Spoken Arts.

*Poetry — Richard Wilbur and Robert Lowell.
30 min., b/w, 1966.
³/₄" U-matic cassette, 16-mm film, special-order formats.
Interviews with the two poets.
Distributed by Indiana University Instructional Support Services.

Richard Wilbur Reading His Poetry [recording].
1 cassette.
Distributed by Caedmon/HarperAudio.

See also *"Caedmon Treasury of Modern Poets Reading Their Own Poetry"* and *"Twentieth-Century Poets Reading Their Work"* on manual pp. 226 and 230.

William Carlos Williams

William Carlos Williams Reads His Poetry [recording].
1 cassette.
Distributed by Caedmon/HarperAudio.

William Carlos Williams: People and the Stones: Selected Poems [recording].
1 cassette (60 min.).
Distributed by Watershed Tapes.

See also *"Caedmon Treasury of Modern Poets Reading Their Own Poetry," "Inner Ear, Part 1," "The Poet's Voice,"* and *"Voices and Vision"* on manual pp. 226–228 and 230.

William Wordsworth

William Wordsworth: Selected Poems [recording].
2 cassettes (180 min.).
Read by Frederick Davidson.
Distributed by Blackstone Audio Books.

The Poetry of Wordsworth [recording].
1 cassette.
Distributed by Caedmon/HarperAudio.

Treasury of William Wordsworth [recording].
1 cassette.
Distributed by Spoken Arts.

William Wordsworth: William and Dorothy.
52 min., color, 1989.
Beta, VHS, ³/₄" U-matic cassette.
Explores Wordsworth's poetry and his troubled relationship with his sister. Directed by Ken Russell.
Distributed by Films for the Humanities and Sciences.

*William Wordsworth.
28 min., color, 1989.
Beta, VHS, ³/₄" U-matic cassette.
An examination of the poet's work set against the Lake District, subject for many of the poems.
Distributed by Films for the Humanities and Sciences.

William Wordsworth and the English Lakes.
15 min., color, 1989.
Beta, VHS, ³/₄" U-matic cassette.
Looks at Wordsworth's use of language.
Distributed by Films for the Humanities and Sciences.

See also *"English Literature: Romantic Period," "English Romantic Poetry," "Introduction to English Poetry," "Palgrave's Golden Treasury of English Poetry," "Romantic Pioneers,"* and *"The Young Romantics"* on manual pp. 226–230

William Butler Yeats

Dylan Thomas Reads the Poetry of W. B. Yeats & Others [recording].
1 cassette.
Includes readings of Yeats, Louis MacNeice, George Barker, Walter de la Mare, W. H. Davies, D. H. Lawrence, and W. H. Auden.
Distributed by Caedmon/HarperAudio.

The Love Poems of William Butler Yeats.
30 min., b/w, 1967.
Beta, VHS, 1/2" open reel (EIAJ), 3/4" U-matic cassette, 2" quadraplex open reel.
Selections from the poet's works.
Distributed by New York State Education Department.

Poems by W. B. Yeats and Poems for Several Voices.
1 cassette, 1973.
Includes "Sailing to Byzantium" and features poems by Thomas Hardy, Robert Graves, and Gerard Manley Hopkins. Read by V. C. Clinton-Baddeley, Jill Balcon, and M. Westbury.
Distributed by Smithsonian/Folkways Recordings.

Poems of William Butler Yeats [recording].
1 cassette.
Distributed by Spoken Arts.

The Poetry of William Butler Yeats [recording].
1 cassette.
Distributed by Caedmon/HarperAudio.

William Butler Yeats, et al.: Treasury of Irish Verse, Folk Tales, & Ballads [recording].
6 cassettes (294 min.), 1986.
Distributed by Spoken Arts.

William Butler Yeats: Twentieth-Century Poets Read Their Works [recording].
6 cassettes (270 min.), 1986.
Distributed by Spoken Arts.

W. B. Yeats [recording].
1 cassette (49 min.), 1953.
Read by Stephen Spender.
Distributed by Audio-Forum.

*Yeats Country.
19 min., color, 1965.
VHS, 3/4" U-matic cassette, 16-mm film.
Juxtaposes Yeats's poetry with scenes of the Ireland he wrote about.
Distributed by International Film Bureau.

Yeats Remembered.
30 min.
VHS.
Biographical film using period photographs and interviews with the poet and his family.
Distributed by Insight Media.

See also "Caedmon Treasury of Modern Poets Reading Their Own Poetry," "Introduction to English Poetry," and "Twentieth-Century Poets Reading Their Own Work" on manual pp. 226, 227, and 230.

GENERAL

Anthology of Nineteenth Century American Poets [recording].
1 cassette.
Includes Longfellow, Holmes, Whittier, Lowell, Emerson, Poe, and Whitman.
Distributed by Spoken Arts.

Anthology of Contemporary American Poetry [recording].
1 cassette, 1961.
Includes poems by John Ciardi, Richard Ebhardt, Theodore Roethke, Howard Nemerov, Galway Kinnell, Donald Justice, May Swenson, Richard Wilbur, Karl Shapiro, and others.
Distributed by Smithsonian/Folkways Recordings.

Anthology of Negro Poets [recording].
1 cassette, 1954.
Includes the poetry of Langston Hughes, Sterling Brown, Claude McKay, Countee Cullen, Margaret Walter, and Gwendolyn Brooks.
Distributed by Smithsonian/Folkways Recordings.

Archive of Recorded Poetry and Literature.
Library of Congress.

Birthright: Growing Up Hispanic.
59 min., color, 1989.
VHS, Beta, ³/₄" U-matic cassette.
Focuses on the achievements of Hispanic American writers. Includes the work of Alberto Ríos and Judith Ortiz Cofer.
Distributed by Cinema Guild.

Caedmon Treasury of Modern Poets Reading Their Own Poetry [recording].
2 cassettes (95 min.).
Includes T. S. Eliot, W. B. Yeats, W. H. Auden, Edith Sitwell, Dylan Thomas, Robert Graves, Gertrude Stein, Archibald MacLeish, E. E. Cummings, Marianne Moore, Stephen Spender, Conrad Aiken, Robert Frost, William Carlos Williams, Wallace Stevens, Ezra Pound, Richard Wilbur, and others.
Distributed by Caedmon/HarperCollins.

Conversation Pieces: Short Poems by Thomas, Hardy, Housman, Auden, Keats, and Others [recording].
1 cassette, 1964.
Distributed by Smithsonian/Folkways Recordings.

*England: Background of Literature.
11 min., color, 1962.
Beta, VHS, ³/₄" U-matic cassette, 16-mm film, special-order formats.
Presents the works of English writers Shakespeare, Dickens, and Tennyson against the backgrounds that inspired them.
Distributed by Coronet/MTI Film & Video.

*English Literature: Eighteenth Century.
14 min., color, 1958.
Beta, VHS, ³/₄" U-matic cassette, 16-mm film, special-order formats.
Treats the work of Addison and Steele, Pope, Swift, and others.
Distributed by Coronet/MTI Film & Video.

*English Literature: Romantic Period.
13 min., color, 1957.
Beta, VHS, ³/₄" U-matic cassette, 16-mm film, special-order formats.

Includes selections from Wordsworth, Byron, Shelley, Keats, and others.
Distributed by Coronet/MTI Film & Video.

*English Literature: Seventeenth Century.
13 min., color, 1958.
Beta, VHS, ³/₄" U-matic cassette, 16-mm film, special-order formats.
Examines works by Jonson, Pepys, and others.
Distributed by Coronet/MTI Film & Video.

English Romantic Poetry: Coleridge, Shelley, Byron, Wordsworth [recording].
3 cassettes.
Distributed by Recorded Books.

*Fried Shoes, Cooked Diamonds.
55 min., color, 1982.
Beta, VHS, ³/₄" U-matic cassette.
Documents a summer at the Jack Kerouac School of Poetics at the Naropa Institute in Boulder, Colorado. Features such poets from the Beat generation as Allen Ginsberg, Gregory Corso, William S. Burroughs, Peter Orlovsky, and Timothy Leary.
Distributed by Centre Communications, Inc. and Mystic Fire.

Great Poets of the Romantic Age [recording].
6 cassettes (270 min.), 1986.
Distributed by Spoken Arts.

*Haiku.
19 min., color, 1974.
Beta, VHS, ³/₄" U-matic cassette, 16-mm film.
An overview of this poetic form.
Distributed by AIMS Media Inc.

*Harlem Renaissance: The Black Poets.
20 min., color, 198?.
Beta, VHS, ³/₄" U-matic cassette, 16-mm film.
Discusses this era, including an examination of Georgia Douglas Johnson, Fenton Johnson, W. E. B. Du Bois, and Langston Hughes.
Distributed by Carousel Film & Video.

The Harlem Renaissance and Beyond.
31 min., 1989.
VHS.
A still-image program with excerpts from Countee Cullen, Langston Hughes, Claude McKay, Gwendolyn Brooks, Alice Walker, and Richard Wright.
Distributed by Insight Media.

Inner Ear, Part 1 [recording].
1 cassette (60 min.).
Includes the poetry of Carl Sandburg and William Carlos Williams.
Distributed by National Public Radio.

Inner Ear, Parts 3 and 4 [recording].
1 cassette (60 min.).
Emily Dickinson, Marianne Moore, and Wallace Stevens.
Distributed by National Public Radio.

Inner Ear, Parts 5 and 6 [recording].
1 cassette (60 min.).
E. E. Cummings and Gary Snyder.
Distributed by National Public Radio.

In Their Own Voices: A Century of Recorded Poetry [recording].
4 compact discs.
Distributed by Rhino Records.

*Introduction to English Poetry.
28 min., color, 1989.
Beta, VHS, ³/₄″ U-matic cassette.
Introduces students to English verse, with readings from Chaucer, Shakespeare, Herbert, Milton, Swift, Blake, Wordsworth, Shelley, Emily Brontë, Dickinson, Hardy, Yeats, and Ted Hughes.
Distributed by Films for the Humanities and Sciences.

*Lannan Literary Series
26 cassettes (60 min. each), color, VHS, 1989–1991.
Carolyn Forché, Allen Ginsberg, Louise Glück, Galway Kinnell, W. S. Merwin, Lucille Clifton, Czeslaw Milosz, Octavio Paz, Yehuda Amichai, Joy Harjo, Victor Hernandez Cruz, Kay Boyle, Alice Walker, Ishmael Reed, Richard Wilbur, Carlos Fuentes, Robert Creeley, Larry Heinemann, Sonya Sanchez, Andrei Voznesensky, Ernesto Cardenal, Anne Waldman, Sharon Olds, Amiri Baraka, Gary Snyder.
Distributed by The Lannan Foundation/Metropolitan Pictures/EZTV.

Literature: The Synthesis of Poetry.
30 min.
VHS.
Hosted by Maya Angelou, who reads some of her own work, as well as the poetry of Frost, Sandburg, and Arnold.
Distributed by Insight Media.

Medieval and Elizabethan Poetry.
28 min., color, 1989.
Beta, VHS, ³/₄″ U-matic cassette.
Examines trends of the period, focusing on John Skelton, Thomas Wyatt, Tichborne, Nashe, Walter Raleigh, Marlowe, Drayton, and Shakespeare.
Distributed by Films for the Humanities and Sciences.

*Metaphysical and Devotional Poetry.
28 min., color, 1989.
Beta, VHS, ³/₄″ U-matic cassette.
Looks at the works of John Donne, George Herbert, and Andrew Marvell.
Distributed by Films for the Humanities and Sciences.

Modern American Poetry.
45 min., 1989.
VHS.
Hosted by Helen Vendler. Deals with poets from between the World Wars: Eliot, Pound, Stevens, Cullen, Hughes, Frost, Moore, and Crane. Focuses on development of an American, as distinct from European, voice.
Distributed by Insight Media.

A Movable Feast.
8 programs (30 min. each), color, 1991.
VHS.
Hosted by Tom Vitale. Profiles eight contemporary writers: (1) Allen Ginsberg; (2) Joyce Carol Oates; (3) Li-

Young Lee; (4) Sonia Sanchez; (5) T. Coraghessan Boyle; (6) T. R. Pearson; (7) Trey Ellis; (8) W. S. Merwin.
Distributed by Acorn Media.

Moyers: The Power of the Word.
6 programs (60 min. each), color, 1989.
Beta, VHS, ³/₄" U-matic cassette.
Bill Moyers talks with modern poets: James Autry, Quincy Troupe, Joy Harjo, Mary Tallmountain, Gerald Stern, Li-Young Lee, Stanley Kunitz, Sharon Olds, William Stafford, W. S. Merwin, Galway Kinnell, Robert Bly, and Octavio Paz.
Distributed by PBS Video.

Palgrave's Golden Treasury of English Poetry [recording].
2 cassettes.
Includes Marlowe, Shakespeare, Barnefield, Wyatt, Lyly, Donne, Herrick, Dryden, Waller, Lovelace, Milton, Gray, Rogers, Burns, Goldsmith, Keats, Wordsworth, Byron, Shelley, Coleridge, Tennyson, Arnold, and Crashaw.
Distributed by Caedmon/HarperAudio.

Poems from Black Africa [recording].
1 cassette.
Many poets and poems from Africa, including oral traditions from various parts of the continent (Nigeria, South Africa, Ghana, and others).
Distributed by Caedmon/HarperAudio.

Poetic Forms [recording].
5 cassettes (5 hours), 1988.
Includes the list poem, the ode, the prose poem, the sonnet, the haiku, the blues poem, the villanelle, the ballad, the acrostic, and free verse.
Distributed by Teachers & Writers Collaborative.

*Poetry: A Beginner's Guide.
26 min., color, 1986.
Beta, VHS, ³/₄" U-matic cassette.
Interviews contemporary poets and examines the tools they use.
Distributed by Coronet/MTI Film & Video.

*Poetry by Americans.
4 programs (10 min. each), color, 1988.
Beta, VHS, ³/₄" U-matic cassette, 16-mm film.
Robert Frost, Edgar Allan Poe, James Weldon Johnson, and Walt Whitman. Narrated by Leonard Nimoy, Lorne Greene, Raymond St. Jacques, and Efrem Zimbalist Jr.
Distributed by AIMS Media Inc.

*Poetry for People Who Hate Poetry.
3 programs (15 min. each), color, 1980.
Beta, VHS, ³/₄" U-matic cassette, special-order formats.
Roger Steffens makes poetry accessible to students. Three programs: (1) About words; (2) E. E. Cummings; (3) Shakespeare.
Distributed by Churchill Media.

Poetry in Motion.
90 min., color, 1982.
Laser optical videodisc.
A performance anthology of twenty-four North American poets, including Ntozake Shange, Amiri Baraka, Anne Waldman, William Burroughs, Ted Berrigan, John Cage, and Tom Waits. Performed by Ntozake Shange, Amiri Baraka, and Anne Waldman.
Distributed by Voyager Company.

The Poet's Voice [recording].
6 cassettes.
From the tape archive of the Poetry Room, Harvard University. Includes John Ashbery, W. H. Auden, John Berryman, T. S. Eliot, Robert Frost, Allen Ginsberg, Randall Jarrell, Robinson Jeffers, Marianne Moore, Sylvia Plath, Ezra Pound, Theodore Roethke, Wallace Stevens, and William Carlos Williams.
Distributed by Watershed Tapes.

Poets in Person: A Series on American Poets & Their Art [recording].
7 programs (30 min. each), 1991.
Thirteen poets in conversation, reading their poems, discussing their lives, their work, and the changing styles in

contemporary American poetry: (1) Allen Ginsberg; (2) Karl Shapiro, Maxine Kumin; (3) W. S. Merwin, Gwendolyn Brooks; (4) James Merrill, Adrienne Rich; (5) John Ashbery, Sharon Olds; (6) Charles Wright, Rita Dove; (7) Gary Soto, A. R. Ammons.
Distributed by Modern Poetry.

Potpourri of Poetry — from the Jack Kerouac School of Disembodied Poetics, Summer 1975 [recording].
1 cassette (60 min.), 1975.
Allen Ginsberg, Dianne DiPrima, John Ashbery, Ted Berrigan, Philip Whalen, and others.
Distributed by Watershed Tapes.

*Restoration and Augustan Poetry.
28 min., color, 1989.
Beta, VHS, ³/₄" U-matic cassette.
Discusses the age of satire in England, including the Earl of Rochester, John Dryden, Jonathan Swift, and Alexander Pope.
Distributed by Films for the Humanities and Sciences.

*Romantic Pioneers.
28 min., color, 1989.
Beta, VHS, ³/₄" U-matic cassette.
Readings of poems by Christopher Smart, William Blake, William Wordsworth, and Samuel Taylor Coleridge.
Distributed by Films for the Humanities and Sciences.

*Romantics and Realists.
28 min., color, 1989.
Beta, VHS, ³/₄" U-matic cassette.
Discusses Thomas Hardy, Gerard Manley Hopkins, A. E. Housman, and Rudyard Kipling.
Distributed by Films for the Humanities and Sciences.

Serenade: Poets of New York [recording].
1 cassette, 1957.
Read by Aaron Kramer, Maxwell Maxwell, and Bodenheim.
Distributed by Smithsonian/Folkways Recordings.

Spoken Arts Treasury of American Jewish Poets Reading Their Poems [recording].
7 cassettes.
Includes the work of Dorothy Parker, Phillip Levine, Anthony Hecht, Denise Levertov, Allen Ginsberg, and John Hollander.
Distributed by Spoken Arts.

The Spoken Arts Treasury of 100 Modern American Poets Reading Their Poems [recording].
1985.
Distributed by Spoken Arts.

A Survey of English and American Poetry.
16 programs (28 min. each), color, 1987.
Beta, VHS, ³/₄" U-matic cassette.
A history and anthology of English-language poetry. Programs include: (1) Introduction to English Poetry; (2) Old English Poetry; (3) Chaucer; (4) Medieval to Elizabethan Poetry; (5) The Maturing Shakespeare; (6) Metaphysical and Devotional Poetry; (7) Milton; (8) Restoration and Augustan Poetry; (9) Romantic Pioneers; (10) William Wordsworth; (11) The Younger Romantics; (12) Victorian Poetry; (13) American Pioneers; (14) Romantics and Realists; (15) The Earlier Twentieth Century; (16) The Later Twentieth Century.
Distributed by Films for the Humanities and Sciences.

Teaching Poetry.
30 min., color, 1990.
VHS.
A new approach to teaching poetry. Includes discussion questions and homework assignments.
Distributed by Video Aided Instruction.

Twentieth-Century Poets in English: Recordings of Poets Reading Their Own Poetry [recording].
33 volumes.
Distributed by the Library of Congress.

Twentieth-Century Poets Reading Their Work [recording].

6 cassettes.

Includes William Butler Yeats, Stephen Spender, Langston Hughes, W. H. Auden, Richard Wilbur, and James Dickey.

Distributed by Spoken Arts.

*Victorian Poetry.

28 min., color, 1989.

Beta, VHS, ³/₄″ U-matic cassette.

An examination of works by Alfred Tennyson, Emily Brontë, Christina Rossetti, Elizabeth Barrett Browning, Matthew Arnold, and Algernon Swinburne.

Distributed by Films for the Humanities and Sciences.

Victorian Poetry [recording].

3 cassettes.

Includes John Henry; E. B. Browning; Edward Fitzgerald; Alfred, Lord Tennyson; W. M. Thackeray; Robert Browning; Edward Lear; Charlotte Brontë; Emily Brontë; A. H. Clough; Charles Kingsley; George Eliot; Matthew Arnold; George Meredith; Dante Gabriel Rossetti; Christina Rossetti; Lewis Carroll; James Thomson; Algernon Charles Swinburne; Thomas Hardy; Gerard Manley Hopkins; Coventry Patmore; Robert Bridges; William Ernest Henley; R. L. Stevenson; Oscar Wilde; A. E. Housman; Francis Thompson; George Santayana; Arthur Symons; and Rudyard Kipling.

Distributed by Caedmon/HarperAudio.

*Voices and Vision.

13 programs (60 min. each), color, 1988.

Beta, VHS, ³/₄″ U-matic cassette.

A series exploring the lives of some of America's best poets. Hosted by Joseph Brodsky, Mary McCarthy, James Baldwin, and Adrienne Rich. Programs include: (1) Elizabeth Bishop; (2) Hart Crane; (3) Emily Dickinson; (4) T. S. Eliot; (5) Robert Frost; (6) Langston Hughes; (7) Robert Lowell; (8) Marianne Moore; (9) Sylvia Plath; (10) Ezra Pound; (11) Wallace Stevens; (12) Walt Whitman; (13) William Carlos Williams.

Distributed by the Annenberg/CPB Collection.

With a Feminine Touch.

45 min., color, 1990.

VHS.

Readings from Emily Dickinson, Anne Brontë, Charlotte Brontë, Emily Brontë, Sylvia Plath, and Edna St. Vincent Millay. Read by Valerie Harper and Claire Bloom.

Distributed by Monterey Home Video.

The Young Romantics.

28 min., color, 1989.

Beta, VHS, ³/₄″ U-matic cassette.

Features the work of John Keats, William Wordsworth, and Lord Byron.

Distributed by Films for the Humanities and Sciences.

DRAMA

Anton Chekhov

*Anton Chekhov: A Writer's Life.

37 min., b/w, 1974.

Beta, VHS, ³/₄″ U-matic cassette.

A biographical portrait of the playwright.

Distributed by Films for the Humanities and Sciences.

Chekhov [recording].

12 cassettes (90 min. each), 1989.

By Henri Troyat, read by Wolfram Kandinsky. A biography of the writer.

Distributed by Books on Tape.

Chekhov: Humanity's Advocate [recording].
1 cassette (46 min.), 1968.
By Ernest J. Simmons. Explores various facets of Chekhov's works and his artistic principles. Classics of Russian Literature Series.
Distributed by Audio-Forum.

*Chekhov and the Moscow Art Theatre.
13 min., color.
Beta, VHS, 16-mm film. Yuri Zavadsky uses the Stanislavsky method in directing scenes from *The Cherry Orchard*. Program is set in the context of the Moscow Art Theatre and the Russian countryside.
Distributed by IASTA.

Susan Glaspell

Trifles.
21 min., color, 1979.
Beta, VHS.
Distributed by Phoenix/BFA Films.

Trifles.
22 min., b/w, 1981.
Beta, VHS, 3/4" U-matic cassette.
Distributed by Centre Communications.

Lorraine Hansberry

*A Raisin in the Sun.
128 min., b/w, 1961.
Beta, VHS.
With Sidney Poitier, Claudia McNeil, and Ruby Dee. Directed by Daniel Petrie.
See local retailer.

A Raisin in the Sun.
171 min., color, 1989.
Beta, VHS.
With Danny Glover, Esther Rolle, and Starletta DuPois. Directed by Bill Duke. An "American Playhouse" made-for-television production.
See local retailer.

A Raisin in the Sun [recording].
2 cassettes, (2 hours, 21 min.)
Dramatization performed by Ossie Davis and Ruby Dee.
Distributed by Caedmon/HarperAudio.

*Black Theatre Movement from A Raisin in the Sun to the Present.
130 min., color, 1979.
16-mm film.
Traces the Black Theatre Movement from its roots in Hansberry's play to the current black plays and musicals on Broadway. Includes interviews with performers, writers, and directors, as well as footage from plays and theatre pieces from around the country.

Lorraine Hansberry: The Black Experience in the Creation of Drama.
35 min., color, 1975.
Beta, VHS, 3/4" U-matic cassette.
With Sidney Poitier, Ruby Dee, and Al Freeman Jr. Narrated by Claudia McNeil. A profile of the playwright's life and work.
Distributed by Films for the Humanities and Sciences.

Lorraine Hansberry Speaks Out: Art and the Black Revolution [recording].
1 cassette.
By Lorraine Hansberry, edited by Robert Nemiroff.
Distributed by Caedmon/HarperAudio.

*To Be Young, Gifted, and Black.
90 min., color, 1981.
Beta, VHS, 1/2" open reel (EIAJ), 3/4" U-matic cassette, 16-mm film.
With Ruby Dee, Al Freeman Jr., Claudia McNeil, Barbara Barrie, Lauren Jones, Roy Scheider, and Blythe Danner. A play about the life of Lorraine Hansberry.
Distributed by Monterey Home Video.

David Henry Hwang

M. Butterfly [recording].
2 cassettes (118 min.).
Starring John Lithgow and B. D. Wong.
Distributed by L.A. Theatre Works.

M. Butterfly.
101 min., color, 1993.
Beta, VHS.
A film adaptation of Hwang's acclaimed
   play starring Jeremy Irons.
Distributed by Warner Home Video.

Henrik Ibsen

A Doll's House.
89 min., b/w, 1959.
Beta, VHS, ³/₄" U-matic cassette.
With Julie Harris, Christopher Plummer,
   Jason Robards, Hume Cronyn, Eileen
   Heckart, and Richard Thomas. An
   original television production.
See local retailer.

***A Doll's House.**
98 min., color, 1973.
VHS, 16-mm film.
With Jane Fonda, Edward Fox, Trevor
   Howard, and David Warner.
   Screenplay by Christopher Hampton.
Video: See local retailer.
Distributed by Prism Entertainment.

A Doll's House.
39 min., color, 1977.
Beta, VHS, ³/₄" U-matic cassette.
With Claire Bloom.
Distributed by AIMS Multimedia.

A Doll's House.
96 min., color, 1989.
Beta, VHS.
With Claire Bloom, Anthony Hopkins,
   Ralph Richardson, Denholm Elliott,
   Anna Massey, and Edith Evans.
   Directed by Patrick Garland.
Distributed by Hemdale Home Video.

A Doll's House [recording].
3 cassettes (180 min.), 1993.
Read by Flo Gibson.
Distributed by Audio Book Contractors.

A Doll's House [recording].
3 cassettes.
Translated by Christopher Hampton.
Dramatization performed by Claire Bloom
   and Donald Madden.
Distributed by Caedmon/HarperAudio.

***A Doll's House, Part I.**
34 min., color, 1968.
Beta, VHS, ³/₄" U-matic cassette, 16-mm
   film.
"The Destruction of Illusion." Norris
   Houghton discusses the subsurface
   tensions that make up the play.
Distributed by Britannica Films.

***A Doll's House, Part II.**
29 min., color, 1968.
Beta, VHS, ³/₄" U-matic cassette, 16-mm
   film.
"Ibsen's Themes." Norris Houghton
   examines the cast of characters and the
   themes in the play.
Distributed by Britannica Films.

*Ibsen's Life and Times, Part I: Youth and
   Self-Imposed Exile.*
28 min., color. VHS.
The conflict between individual and society
   is illustrated in scenes from *Ghosts,*
   featuring Beatrice Straight as Mrs.
   Alving. Includes a biographical
   segment on the playwright.
Distributed by Insight Media.

*Ibsen's Life and Times, Part II: The Later
   Years.*
24 min., color. VHS.
Includes scenes from *The Master Builder* and
   Lady from the Sea, emphasizing the
   realism in Ibsen's plays. A biographical
   segment includes on-location footage.
Distributed by Insight Media.

Arthur Miller

Arthur Miller.
25 min., color, 1982.
Beta, VHS, ³/₄" U-matic cassette.
Explores themes in the works of Arthur
   Miller.
Distributed by Films, Inc., Video.

Death of a Salesman [recording].
2 cassettes (2 hrs., 16 min.), unabridged.
Dramatization performed by Lee J. Cobb
   and Mildred Dunnock.
Distributed by Caedmon/HarperAudio.

Death of a Salesman.
135 min., color, 1985.
Beta, VHS.
With Dustin Hoffman, John Malkovich, Charles Durning, and Stephen Lang. Directed by Volker Schlondorff. A made-for-television adaptation of the play.
Distributed by Orion Home Video, Facets Multimedia, Warner Home Video.

Private Conversations on the Set of Death of a Salesman.
82 min., color, 1985.
Beta, VHS.
With Arthur Miller, Dustin Hoffman, Volker Schlondorff, and John Malkovich. This PBS documentary presents heated discussion between actor, director, and playwright. Various interpretations of the play emerge and viewers gain insight into how each part contributed to the final production.
See local retailer.

William Shakespeare

Hamlet

Hamlet.
242 min., color, 1996.
VHS.
Directed by Kenneth Branagh. Starring Kenneth Branagh, Kate Winslet, John Gielgud, Jack Lemmon, Julie Christie, Gerard Depardieu, Judy Dench, and others.
Distributed by Columbia Tristar Home Video.

*Hamlet.
153 min., b/w, 1948.
VHS and 16-mm film.
With Laurence Olivier, Basil Sydney, Felix Aylmer, Jean Simmons, Stanley Holloway, Peter Cushing, and Christopher Lee. Voice of John Gielgud. Directed by Olivier. Photographed in Denmark. Cut scenes include all of Rosencrantz and Guildenstern. Emphasizes Oedipal implications in the play.
Video: see local retailer.
Film: Learning Corporation of America.

*Hamlet.
115 min., color, 1969.
Beta, VHS, 16-mm film.
With Nicol Williamson. Directed by Tony Richardson.
Distributed by Learning Corporation of America.

Hamlet.
150 min., color, 1979.
Beta, VHS, 3/4" U-matic cassette, other formats by special arrangement.
Directed by Derek Jacobi.
Distributed by Time-Life Video.

Hamlet.
135 min., color, 1990.
VHS.
With Mel Gibson, Glenn Close, Alan Bates, Paul Scofield, Ian Holm, and Helena Bonham Carter. Directed by Franco Zeffirelli.
See local retailer.

Hamlet [recording].
3 cassettes (210 min.), 1993.
Performed by Kenneth Branagh.
Distributed by Bantam Audio Publishers.

Hamlet [recording].
4 cassettes.
Dramatization performed by Paul Scofield and Diana Wynyard.
Distributed by Caedmon/HarperAudio.

Hamlet [recording].
1 cassette (60 min.), 1985.
Dramatization performed by Michael Redgrave. Part of the Living Shakespeare Series.
Distributed by Crown Publishers.

Hamlet [recording].
2 cassettes (120 min.).
With John Gielgud and Old Vic Company.
Distributed by Durkin Hayes Publishing.

Hamlet [recording].
1 cassette (51 min.).
Performed by Dublin Gate Theatre. Using key scenes and bridges, a complete telling of Hamlet.
Distributed by Spoken Arts.

*Approaches to Hamlet.
45 min., color, 1979.
Beta, VHS, ³/₄" U-matic cassette, 16-mm film.
Includes footage of the four greatest Hamlets of this century: John Barrymore, Laurence Olivier, John Gielgud, and Nicol Williamson. Shows a young actor learning the role. Narrated by Gielgud.
Distributed by Films for the Humanities and Sciences.

Discovering Hamlet.
53 min., color, 1990.
VHS, ³/₄" U-matic cassette.
An exposition of the play, hosted by Patrick Stewart, including a behind-the-scenes look at a production by the Birmingham Repertory Theatre.
Distributed by PBS Video.

*Hamlet: The Age of Elizabeth, I.
30 min., color, 1959.
Beta, VHS, ³/₄" U-matic cassette, 16-mm film.
An introduction to Elizabethan theater.
Distributed by Britannica Films.

*Hamlet: What Happens in Hamlet, II.
30 min., color and b/w, 1959.
Beta, VHS, ³/₄" U-matic cassette, 16-mm film.
Analyzes the play as a ghost story, a detective story, and a revenge story. Uses scenes from Acts I, III, and V to introduce the principal characters and present the structure of each substory.
Distributed by Britannica Films.

*Hamlet: The Poisoned Kingdom, III.
30 min., color, 1959.
Beta, VHS, ³/₄" U-matic cassette, 16-mm film.

Observes that poisoning in the play, both literal and figurative, affects all the characters.
Distributed by Britannica Films.

*Hamlet: The Readiness is All, IV.
30 min., color, 1959.
Beta, VHS, ³/₄" U-matic cassette, 16-mm film.
Hamlet is presented as a coming-of-age story.
Distributed by Britannica Films.

*Hamlet: The Trouble with Hamlet.
23 min., color, 1969.
16-mm film.
Emphasizes Hamlet's existentialist dilemma.
Distributed by the National Broadcasting Company.

*The Tragedy of Hamlet: Prince of Denmark.
22 min., color, 1988.
VHS.
Actors depict Shakespeare and his contemporary, Richard Burbage, rehearsing the play. "Shakespeare" gives a line-by-line analysis of scenes from the play, along with insight into plot and character. Part of the Shakespeare in Rehearsal Series.
Distributed by Coronet/MTI Film & Video.

A Midsummer Night's Dream

A Midsummer Night's Dream.
117 min., b/w, 1935.
VHS.
With James Cagney, Mickey Rooney, Olivia de Havilland, Dick Powell, and Joe E. Brown. Directed by William Dieterle and Max Reinhardt.
See local retailer.

A Midsummer Night's Dream.
111 min., b/w, 1963.
Beta, VHS.
With Patrick Allen, Eira Heath, Cyril Luckham, Tony Bateman, Jill Bennett. A live BBC-TV performance, with Mendelssohn's incidental music.
Distributed by Video Yesteryear.

A Midsummer Night's Dream.
120 min., 1968.
Beta, VHS, 16-mm film.
With Diana Rigg and David Warner. Directed by Peter Hall. A Royal Shakespeare Company performance.
Distributed by Drama Classics Video.

A Midsummer Night's Dream.
120 min., color, 1982.
Beta, VHS.
With Helen Mirren, Peter McEnry, and Brian Clover.
See local retailer.

A Midsummer Night's Dream.
165 min., color, 1983.
Beta, VHS, ³/₄″ U-matic cassette.
With William Hurt and Michelle Shay. A lively interpretation by Joseph Papp.
Distributed by Films for the Humanities and Sciences.

A Midsummer Night's Dream.
194 min., color, 1987.
Beta, VHS.
With Ileana Cotrubas, James Bowman, and Curt Appelgren. Directed by Peter Hall. A performance of the Benjamin Britten opera, taped at the Glyndebourne Festival Opera.
Distributed by Films, Inc.

A Midsummer Night's Dream [recording].
1 cassette.
Dramatization performed by the Folio Theatre Players.
Distributed by Spoken Arts.

A Midsummer Night's Dream [recording].
3 cassettes (text included).
Dramatization performed by Paul Scofield and Joy Parker.
Distributed by Caedmon/HarperAudio.

A Midsummer Night's Dream [recording].
1 cassette (60 min.), 1985.
Dramatization performed by Stanley Holloway and Sarah Churchill. Part of the Living in Shakespeare Series.
Distributed by Crown Publishers.

A Midsummer Night's Dream [recording].
2 cassettes (120 min.).
Performed by Robert Helpmann and Moira Shearer. An Old Vic production.
Distributed by Durkin Hayes Publishing.

A Midsummer Night's Dream: Introduction to the Play.
26 min., color, 1970.
Introduction to famous scenes and characters.
Distributed by Phoenix/BFA Films and Video.

The Tempest

The Tempest.
76 min., color, 1963.
Beta, VHS, ³/₄″ U-matic cassette.
With Maurice Evans, Richard Burton, Roddy McDowall, Lee Remick, and Tom Poston. Directed by George Schaefer.
Distributed by Films for the Humanities and Sciences.

The Tempest.
150 min., color, 1980.
Beta, VHS, ³/₄″ U-matic cassette, other formats by special arrangement.
Distributed by Time-Life Video.

Tempest.
140 min., color, 1982.
Beta, VHS (stereo).
With John Cassavetes, Gena Rowlands, Susan Sarandon, Vittorio Gassman, and Raul Julia. Directed by Paul Mazursky. A York architect abandons city life to live on a barren Greek island with his daughter.
See local retailer.

The Tempest.
2 cassettes (126 min.), color, 1983.
Beta, VHS, ³/₄″ U-matic cassette.
With Efrem Zimbalist, William H. Basset, Ted Sorrel, Kay E. Kuter, Edward Edwards, Nicholas Hammond, and Ron Palillo. Directed by William Woodman. Puts American actors on

an artist's re-creation of the Globe Theatre stage.
Distributed by Kultur and Britannica Films.

The Tempest [*recording*].
1 cassette.
Dramatization performed by the Folio Theatre Players.
Distributed by Spoken Arts.

The Tempest [*recording*].
3 cassettes (text included).
Dramatization performed by Michael Redgrave and Vanessa Redgrave.
Distributed by Caedmon/HarperAudio.

Prospero's Books.
1992.
Directed by Peter Greenaway. With John Gielgud, Erland Josephson, Michael Clark, Tom Bell, and Kenneth Cranham.
See local retailer.

*The Tempest: O Brave World.
23 min., color, 1969.
16-mm film.
Explores the problem of evil in the play.
Distributed by the National Broadcasting Company.

GENERAL

Behind-the-Scenes Views of Shakespeare: Shakespeare and His Theatre [*recording*].
1 cassette (60 min.).
Read by Daniel Seltzer. Explores Shakespeare and the characteristics of his works suggesting how to watch a play.
Distributed by National Public Radio.

Behind-the-Scenes Views of Shakespeare: Shakespeare in Our Time [*recording*].
1 cassette (60 min.).
Read by Maynard Mack Jr. Discusses Shakespeare from a modern perspective, and addresses the issue of to what extent he is and is not our contemporary.
Distributed by National Public Radio.

Behind-the-Scenes Views of Shakespeare: Shakespeare the Man [*recording*].
1 cassette (60 min.).
Portrays Shakespeare as reflected in his work and in the facts and myths about his life that have survived.
Distributed by National Public Radio.

*The Life and Times of William Shakespeare 1: The Historical Setting.
25 min., color, 1978.
VHS.
An overview of Elizabethan England.
Distributed by the University of Wyoming Audio-Visual Services.

*The Life and Times of William Shakespeare 2: English Drama.
20 min., color, 1978.
VHS.
History of drama from that of the Greeks to that of Shakespeare's time.
Distributed by the University of Wyoming Audio-Visual Services.

*The Life and Times of William Shakespeare 3: Stratford Years.
18 min., color, 1978.
VHS.
Deals with Shakespeare's early life.
Distributed by the University of Wyoming Audio-Visual Services.

*The Life and Times of William Shakespeare 4: London Years.
33 min., color, 1978.
VHS.
A history of the center of the English-speaking world.
Distributed by the University of Wyoming Audio-Visual Services.

*The Life and Times of William Shakespeare 5: Globe Theatre.
27 min., color, 1978.
VHS.
A study of the Globe and English theatre.
Distributed by the University of Wyoming Audio-Visual Services.

Shakespeare and His Stage.
47 min., color, 1975.
VHS.
16-mm film.
Provides a montage of Shakespearean background, including scenes from *Hamlet* and the preparation of various actors for the role.
Distributed by Films for the Humanities and Sciences.

Shakespeare and His Theatre: The Gentle Shakespeare.
28 min., color.
VHS.
A history of Shakespeare's life in the theatre and an examination of his work.
Distributed by Films for the Humanities and Sciences.

Shakespeare and the Globe.
31 min., color, 1985.
VHS.
A survey of Shakespeare's life, work, and cultural milieu.
Distributed by Films for the Humanities and Sciences.

Shakespearean Tragedy.
40 min., color, 1984.
Beta, VHS, $^{3}/_{4}$" U-matic cassette.
Focuses on *Hamlet* and *Macbeth*.
Distributed by Films for the Humanities and Sciences.

Shakespeare's Heritage.
29 min., color, 1988.
16-mm film.
Narrated by Anthony Quayle. Explores the life of the playwright and his hometown of Stratford.
Distributed by Britannica Films.

Shakespeare's Theater.
13 min., color, 1946.
16-mm film.
Re-creates the experience of going to a play at the Globe Theatre in Shakespeare's time.
Distributed by the Indiana University Instructional Support Services.

Shakespeare's Theater.
28 min., b/w, 1952.
16-mm film.
Hosted by Frank Baxter. A discussion of the evolution of Elizabethan theater and the original staging of Shakespeare's plays.

Shakespeare's Theater: The Globe Playhouse.
18 min., b/w, 1953.
VHS.
Provides a model of the Globe Theater and a discussion of the original staging of some of Shakespeare's plays.
Distributed by the University of California Extension Media Center.

Shakespeare's World and Shakespeare's London.
29 min., b/w, 1952.
16-mm film.
Hosted by Frank Baxter. Re-creates the climate of Renaissance England that allowed Shakespeare's genius to flourish.
Distributed by Films, Inc.

The Two Traditions.
50 min., color, 1983.
VHS.
Deals with the problem of overcoming barriers of time and culture to make Shakespeare relevant today. Examples from *Hamlet, Coriolanus, The Merchant of Venice,* and *Othello.* Part of the Playing Shakespeare Series.
Distributed by Films for the Humanities and Sciences.

Understanding Shakespeare: His Sources.
20 min., color, 1972.
Beta, VHS, $^{3}/_{4}$" U-matic cassette, 16-mm film, other formats by special arrangement. Examines how Shakespeare's plays grew out of sources available to him, and how he enhanced the material with his own imagination.
Distributed by Coronet/MTI Film & Video.

Sophocles

Antigone

Antigone.
88 min., b/w, 1962.
16-mm film.
With Irene Papas. Directed by George Tzavellas. In Greek, with subtitles.
Distributed by Films, Inc.

*Antigone.
120 min., 1987.
Beta, VHS, ¾" U-matic cassette. With Juliet Stevenson, John Shrapnel, and John Gielgud. Staged version.
Distributed by Films for the Humanities and Sciences.

Antigone [recording].
2 cassettes.
Dramatization of the Fitts and Fitzerald translation. Performed by Dorothy Tutin and Max Adrian.
Distributed by Caedmon/HarperAudio.

Oedipus Rex

Oedipus Rex.
20 min., color, 1957.
Beta, VHS, ¾" U-matic cassette.
A performance by deaf actors.
Distributed by Gallaudet University Library.

*Oedipus Rex.
87 min., color, 1957.
VHS, 16-mm film.
With Douglas Campbell, Douglas Rain, Eric House, and Eleanor Stuart. Based on William Yeats's translation. Directed by Tyrone Guthrie. Contained and highly structured rendering by the Stratford (Ontario) Festival Players.
Distributed by Water Bearer Films.

Oedipus the King.
97 min., color, 1967.
VHS.
With Donald Sutherland, Christopher Plummer, Lilli Palmer, Orson Welles, Cyril Cusack, Richard Johnson, and Roger Livesey. Directed by Philip Saville. Simplified film version of the play, filmed in Greece using an old amphitheater to serve as the background for much of the action.
Distributed by Crossroads Video.

*Oedipus the King.
45 min., color, 1975.
Beta, VHS, ¾" U-matic cassette, 16-mm film.
With Anthony Quayle, James Mason, Claire Bloom, and Ian Richardson. A production by the Athens Classical Theatre Company, with an English soundtrack.
Distributed by Films for the Humanities and Sciences.

Oedipus Tyrannus.
60 min., color, 1978.
Beta, VHS, ¾" U-matic cassette.
Hosted by Jose Ferrer. Shown from the point where Oedipus is informed of the death of his father. Expository portion shows scenes of Greek theaters and recounts Aristotle's definition of tragedy.
Distributed by Films, Inc.

Oedipus the King.
120 min., color, 1987.
VHS.
With John Gielgud, Michael Pennington, and Claire Bloom.
Distributed by Films for the Humanities and Sciences.

Oedipus Rex [recording].
2 cassettes.
Translated by William Butler Yeats. Performed by Douglas Campbell and Eric House. Dramatization.
Distributed by Caedmon/HarperAudio.

*Oedipus Rex: Age of Sophocles, I.
31 min., color and b/w, 1959.
Beta, VHS, ¾" U-matic cassette, 16-mm film.
Discusses Greek civilization, the classic Greek theater, and the theme of man's fundamental nature.
Distributed by Britannica Films.

*Oedipus Rex: The Character of Oedipus, II.
31 min., color and b/w, 1959.
Beta, VHS, ³/₄" U-matic cassette, 16-mm film.
Debates whether Oedipus's trouble is a result of character flaws or of fate.
Distributed by Britannica Films.

*Oedipus Rex: Man and God, III.
30 min., color and b/w, 1959.
Beta, VHS, ³/₄" U-matic cassette, 16-mm film.
  Deals with the idea that Oedipus, although a worldly ruler, cannot overcome the gods and his destiny.
Distributed by Britannica Films.

*Oedipus Rex: Recovery of Oedipus, IV.
30 min., color and b/w, 1959.
Beta, VHS, ³/₄" U-matic cassette, 16-mm film.
Deals with man's existence in between God and beast.
Distributed by Britannica Films.

*The Rise of Greek Tragedy, Sophocles: Oedipus the King.
45 min., color, 198?.
Beta, VHS, ³/₄" U-matic cassette, 16-mm film.
With James Mason, Claire Bloom, and Ian Richardson. Narrated by Anthony Quayle. The play is photographed in the ancient Greek theater of Amphiaraion and uses tragic masks.
Distributed by Films for the Humanities and Sciences.

Wole Soyinka

Wole Soyinka.
50 min., color, 1985.
VHS, ³/₄" U-matic cassette.
An interview with the playwright, who discusses political and cultural life in Africa and the United States and what it means to be an artist.
Distributed by The Roland Collection.

Tennessee Williams

The Glass Menagerie.
134 min., color, 1987.
Beta, VHS.
With Joanne Woodward, Karen Allen, John Malkovich, and James Naughton. Directed by Paul Newman.
See local retailer.

The Glass Menagerie [recording].
2 cassettes.
1 hr., 49 min., unabridged.
Dramatization performed by Montgomery Clift and Julie Harris.
Distributed by Caedmon/HarperAudio.

The Glass Menagerie [recording].
Read by Tennessee Williams.
Includes "The Yellow Bird" (short story) and poems.
Distributed by the American Audio Prose Library.

Tennessee Williams Reads The Glass Menagerie and Others [recording].
1 cassette. (45 min.).
Complete selections. Read by Tennessee Williams. Includes *The Glass Menagerie* (opening monologue and closing scene), "Cried the Fox," "The Eyes," "The Summer Belvedere," "Some Poems Meant for Music: Little Horse," "Which Is My Little Boy," "Little One," "Gold-Tooth Blues," "Kitchen-Door Blues," "Heavenly Grass," and "The Yellow Bird."
Distributed by Caedmon/HarperAudio.

In the Country of Tennessee Williams.
30 min., color, 1977.
Beta, VHS, ¹/₂" reel, ³/₄" U-matic cassette 2" Quad.
A one-act play about how Williams developed as a writer.
Distributed by the York State Education Department.

GENERAL

Black Theatre: The Making of a Movement.
113 min., color, 1978.
VHS.
A look at black theatre born from the civil rights movement of the fifties, sixties, and seventies. Recollections from Ossie Davis, James Earl Jones, Amiri Baraka, and Ntozake Shange.
Distributed by California Newsreel.

A Day at the Globe.
30 min., color.
VHS.
Starts with a brief overview of early drama and of seventeenth-century England, then discusses the Globe Theatre, using still images. Explains how actors, artisans, and other company members prepared for performances, and pre sents dramatic readings, period costumes, music, and sound effects in order to help students envision how Shakespearean drama actually looked.
Distributed by Insight Media.

*Drama Comes of Age.
30 min., b/w, 1957.
16-mm film.
Discusses the Shakespearean theater and neoclassic drama. Demonstrates early realism with a scene from *Hedda Gabler.*
Distributed by the Indiana University Instructional Support Services.

*Drama: How It Began.
30 min., b/w, 1957.
16-mm film.
Discusses the beginnings of the theater. Explains the techniques of the Greek theater and how playwriting developed. Illustrates the chorus technique with a scene from *Oedipus the King.*
Distributed by the Indiana University Instructional Support Services.

Echoes of Jacobean England.
45 min., color.
VHS.
Re-creates the liberal arts in seventeenth-century England. Features authentically performed music, contemporary literature, scenes of daily life, and period setting to provide a background for the works of Shakespeare, Dryden, John Donne, and John Dowland.
Distributed by Films for the Humanities and Sciences.

The Elizabethan Age.
30 min., color.
VHS.
A discussion of the resurgence of enthusiasm for the arts and letters that swept seventeenth-century England. Uses original sources.
Distributed by Insight Media.

Greek Tragedy [recording].
1 cassette.
Works of Euripides and Sophocles, performed by Katina Paxinou and Alexis Minotis.
Distributed by Caedmon/HarperAudio.

The Theatre in Ancient Greece.
26 min., color, 1989.
Beta, VHS, ³/₄" U-matic cassette.
Program explores ancient theatre design, the origins of tragedy, the audience, the comparative roles of the writer/director and actors, and the use of landscape in many plays. Examines the theaters of Herodus, Atticus, Epidauros, Corinth, and numerous others.
Distributed by Films for the Humanities and Sciences.

DIRECTORY OF DISTRIBUTORS

Acorn Media
7910 Woodmont Avenue
Suite 350
Bethesda, MD 20814
(301) 907-0030
(800) 999-0212

AIMS Media Inc.
9710 DeSoto Ave.
Chatsworth, CA 91311-9409
(818) 773-4300
(800) 367-2467

Ally Press
524 Orleans St.
St. Paul, MN 55107
(612) 291-2652

American Audio Prose Library
P.O. Box 842
Columbia, MO 65205
(573) 443-0361
(800) 447-2275

Annenberg/CPB Collection
P.O. Box 2345
South Burlington, VT 05407-2345

Applause Productions
85-A Fernwood Lane
Roslyn, NY 11576
(516) 365-1259
(800) 253-5351

Audio Alternatives
P.O. Box 405
Chappaqua, NY 10514
(914) 238-5943

Audio Book Contractors
P.O. Box 40115
Washington, DC 20016
(202) 363-3429

Audio Bookshelf
174 Prescott Hill Road
Northport, ME 04849
(800) 234-1713

Audio Brandon Films
See *Films, Inc.*

Audio-Forum
Jeffrey Norton Publishers
96 Broad St.
Guilford, CT 06437
(203) 453-9794
(800) 243-1234

Audio Literature
P.O. Box 7123
Berkeley, CA 94707
(800) 841-2665

Audio Partners
1700 4th Street
Berkeley, CA 94710
(510) 528-1444
(800) 788-3123

Bantam Audio Publishers
A division of Bantam Doubleday Dell
2451 South Wolf Road
Des Plaines, IL 60018
(800) 323-9872

Barr Entertainment
12801 Schabarum Ave.
P.O. Box 7878
Irwindale, CA 91706
(818) 338-7878

Benchmark Films
569 North State Road
Briarcliff Manor, NY 10510
(914) 762-3838

Blackstone Audio Books
P.O. Box 969
Ashland, OR 97520
(541) 482-9239
(800) 729-2665

Books in Motion
E. 9212 Montgomery
Suite 501
Spokane, WA 99206
(509) 922-1646
(800) 752-3199

Books on Tape
P.O. Box 7900
Newport Beach, CA 92658
(714) 548-5525
(800) 626-3333

Britannica Films
310 South Michigan Ave.
Chicago, IL 60604
(800) 747-8503

Caedmon/HarperAudio
P.O. Box 588
Dunmore, PA 18512
(717) 343-4761
(800) 242-7737
(800) 982-4377 (in Pennsylvania)

California Newsreel
149 Ninth Street
Suite 420
San Francisco, CA 94103
(415) 621-6196
(800) 621-6196

Carousel Film & Video
260 Fifth Ave.
Suite 405
New York, NY 10001
(212) 683-1660
(800) 683-1660

Cassette Works
125 North Aspen
Azusa, CA 91702
(818) 969-6699
(800) 423-8273

Center for Humanities, Inc.
Box 1000
Mount Kisco, NY 10549
(914) 666-4100
(800) 431-1242

Centre Communications
1800 30th St.
Suite 207
Boulder, CO 80301
(800) 886-1166

Chelsea House Publishers
Division of Main Line Book Co.
P.O. Box 914
Brommall, PA 19008
(610) 353-5166
(800) 848-2665

Churchill Media
6901 Woodley Ave.
Van Nuys, CA 91406-4844
(818) 778-1978
(800) 334-7830

Cifex Corporation
1 Teconic Hills Center
Southampton, NY 11968
(516) 283-4795

Cinema Guild
1697 Broadway
Suite 506
New York, NY 10019
(212) 246-5522
(800) 723-5522

Columbia Records
550 Madison Avenue
New York, NY 10022-3211
(212) 833-8000

Columbia Tristar Home Video
Sony Pictures Plaza
10202 West Washington Boulevard
Culver City, CA 90232
(310) 244-4000

Coronet/MTI Film & Video
P.O. Box 2649
Columbus, OH 43216
(800) 221-1274

CRM Films
2215 Faraday Ave.
Carlsbad, CA 92008-7295
(619) 431-9800
(800) 421-0833

Crossroads Video
15 Buckminster Lane
Manhasset, NY 11030
(516) 741-2155

Crown Publishers
See **Random Audiobooks**

Direct Cinema Limited, Inc.
P.O. Box 10003
Santa Monica, CA 90410
(310) 396-4774
(800) 345-6748

Dolphin Tapes
P.O. Box 71
Esalen Hot Springs
Big Sur, CA 93920
(408) 667-2252

Dove Audio
301 North Canon Drive
Beverly Hills, CA 90210

Drama Classics Video
P.O. Box 2128
Manorhaven, NY 11050
(516) 767-7576
(800) 892-0860

Durkin Hayes Publishing
1 Colomba Drive
Niagara Falls, NY 14305
(716) 298-5150
(800) 962-5200
Canadian address:
3375 North Service Road
Unit B7
Burlington, ON
CANADA L79 3G2
(905) 335-0393
(800) 263-5224

Facets Multimedia, Inc.
1517 W. Fullerton Ave.
Chicago, IL 60614
(800) 331-6197

Films for the Humanities and Sciences
P.O. Box 2053
Princeton, NJ 08543-2053
(609) 275-1400
(800) 257-5126

Films, Inc.
5547 North Ravenswood Ave.
Chicago, IL 60640-1199
(800) 323-4312

First Run/Icarus Films
153 Waverly Place
New York, NY 10014
(212) 727-1711
(800) 876-1710

Gallaudet University Library
Gallaudet Media Distribution
800 Florida Avenue, NE
Washington, DC 20002
(202) 651-5579
(202) 651-5440

Home Vision Cinema
5547 North Ravenswood Avenue
Chicago, IL 60640-1199
(773) 878-2600
(800) 826-3456

IASTA
310 West 56th Street, #1B
New York, NY 10019
(212) 581-3133

Indiana University Instructional Support Services
Franklin Hall, Room 0001
Bloomington, IN 47405-5901
(812) 855-2853

Insight Media
2162 Broadway
New York, NY 10024
(212) 721-6316
(800) 233-9910

Interlingua VA
2615 Columbia Pike
P.O. Box 4132
Arlington, VA 22204
(703) 920-6644

Intermedia Arts of Minnesota
425 Ontario St. SE
Minneapolis, MN 55414
(612) 627-4444

International Film Bureau
332 S. Michigan Ave.
Suite 450
Chicago, IL 60604-4382
(312) 427-4545
(800) 432-2241

Ishtar
15030 Ventura Blvd.
Suite 766
Sherman Oaks, CA 91403
(800) 428-7136

Jimcin Recordings
P.O. Box 536
Portsmouth, RI 02871
(401) 847-5148
(800) 538-3034

Journal Films, Inc.
1560 Sherman Avenue, Suite 100
Evanston, IL 60201
(312) 328-6700
(800) 323-5448

Thomas S. Klise Company
P.O. Box 317
Waterford, CT 06385
(860) 442-4449
(800) 937-0092

Kultur
195 Highway #36
West Long Branch, NJ 07764
(908) 229-2343
(800) 458-5887

L.A. Theatre Works
681 Venice Boulevard
Venice, CA 90291
(800) 708-8863

Learning Corporation of America
See *Coronet/MTI Film & Video*

Library of Congress
orders to:
Superintendent of Documents
P.O. Box 371954
Pittsburgh, PA 15250-7954
(202) 783-3238

Listening Library
1 Park Ave.
Old Greenwich, CT 06870
(203) 637-3616
(800) 243-4504

Maryland Public Television
11767 Owings Mills Blvd.
Owings Mills, MD 21117
(410) 356-5600

Media Concepts Press
331 North Broad St.
Philadelphia, PA 19107
(215) 923-2545

Media Guild
11722 Sorrento Valley Rd., Suite E
San Diego, CA 92121
(619) 755-9191
(800) 886-9191

Modern Poetry
60 W. Walton Street
Chicago, IL 60610
(312) 255-3703

Modern Talking Picture Service
4707 140th Avenue North
Suite 105
Clearwater, FL 34622
(813) 541-7571
(800) 243-6877

Monterey Home Video
28038 Dorothy Drive
Suite 1
Agoura Hills, CA 91301
(818) 597-0047
(800) 424-2593

Mystic Fire
P.O. Box 9323
South Burlington, VT 05407
(800) 292-9001

National Broadcasting Company
30 Rockefeller Plaza
New York, NY 10112
(212) 664-4444

National Film Board of Canada
16th Floor
1251 Avenue of the Americas
New York, NY 10020-1173
(212) 586-5131

National Public Radio
Audience Services
635 Massachusetts Avenue NW
Washington, DC 20001
(202) 414-3232

Nebraska Educational Television Network
Public Affairs Unit
1800 N. 33 St.
Lincoln, NE 68583
(402) 472-3611

New Dimensions Radio
P.O. Box 569
Ukiah, CA 95482
(707) 468-5215
(800) 935-8273

New Letters on the Air
University of Missouri at Kansas City
5100 Rockhill Rd.
Kansas City, MO 64110
(816) 235-1168

New York State Education Department
Media Distribution Network
Room C-7, Concourse Level
Cultural Education Center
Albany, NY 12230
(518) 474-1265

PBS Video
1320 Braddock Place
Alexandria, VA 22314-1698
(703) 739-5380

Phoenix/BFA Films
2349 Chaffee Drive
St. Louis, MO 63146
(314) 569-0211
(800) 421-2304

Poet's Audio Center
P.O. Box 50145
Washington, DC 20091-0145
(202) 722-9105

Pyramid Film & Video
P.O. Box 1048
Santa Monica, CA 90406-1048
(310) 828-7577
(800) 221-1274

Random Audiobooks
400 Hahn Rd.
Westminster, MD 21157
(800) 733-3000

Recorded Books
270 Skipjack Rd.
Prince Frederick, MD 20678
(301) 535-5590
(800) 638-1304

Rhino Records
10635 Santa Monica Boulevard
Los Angeles, CA 90025-4900

The Roland Collection
22D Hollywood Avenue
Hohokus, NJ 07423
(201) 251-8200

S & S Audio
795 Abbot Blvd.
Fort Lee, NJ 07024
(201) 224-3100
(800) 734-4758

Smithsonian/Folkways Recordings
Office of Folklife Programs
955 L'Enfant Plaza, Suite 2600
Smithsonian Institution
Washington, DC 20560
(202) 287-3262

Sound Horizons
250 W. 57th St.
Suite 1517
New York, NY 10107
(212) 956-6235
(800) 524-8355

Sound Photosynthesis
P.O. Box 2111
Mill Valley, CA 94942-2111
(415) 383-6712

Sound Rx
See *Audio Alternatives*

Sounds True
P.O. Box 8010
Boulder, CO 80306-8010
(303) 663-3151
(800) 333-9185

Spoken Arts
P.O. Box 100
New Rochelle, NY 10801
(800) 326-4090

Summer Stream
P.O. Box 6056
Santa Barbara, CA 93160
(805) 962-6540

Tapes for Readers
4410 Lingan Road
Washington, DC 20007
(202) 338-1215

Tapeworm Video Distributors
27833 Avenue Hopkins
Unit 6
Valencia, CA 91355
(805) 257-4904

Teachers & Writers Collaborative
5 Union Square W.
New York, NY 10003
(212) 691-6590

Time-Life Video
Customer Service
1450 East Parham Rd.
Richmond, VA 23280
(703) 838-7000
(800) 621-7026

**University of California Extension
Media Center**
2000 Center Street
Suite 400
Berkeley, CA 94704
(510) 642-0460

**University of Washington Educational
Media Collection**
Kane Hall, DG-10
Seattle, WA 98195
(206) 543-9909

**University of Wyoming Audiovisual
Services**
Box 3273
Laramie, WY 82071
(307) 766-3184

Video Aided Instruction
P.O. Box 332
Roslyn Heights, NY 11577
(800) 238-1512

The Video Catalog
1000 Westgate Drive
Saint Paul, MN 55114
(612) 659-3700
(212) 334-0340

Video Yesteryear
Box C
Sandy Hook, CT 06482
(203) 426-2574
(800) 243-0987

Voyager Company
1 Bridge Street
Irvington, NY 10533
(914) 591-5500
(800) 446-2001

Water Bearer Films
205 West End Ave.
Suite 24H
New York, NY 10023
(212) 580-8185
(800) 551-8304

Watershed Tapes
Dist. by Inland Book Co.
P.O. Box 120261
East Haven, CT 06512
(203) 467-4257
(800) 243-0138

White Star
195 Highway 36
West Long Branch, NJ 07764
(732) 229-2343

WNET/Thirteen Non-Broadcast
356 West 58th St.
New York, NY 10019
(212) 560-2000
(800) 367-2467

A List of Selections on *Literature Aloud: Classic and Contemporary Stories, Poems, and Selected Scenes*

Available on both compact disc and audiotape, *Literature Aloud* offers a range of classic and contemporary short stories, poems, and excerpted plays from Michael Meyer's anthologies — *The Bedford Introduction to Literature, The Compact Bedford Introduction to Literature, Thinking and Writing about lityerature,* and *Poetry.* All selections are read either by the authors themselves or by other celebrated writers or actors. With its selections from all three genres and its focus on the voice of the writer, *Literature Aloud* provides students with the unique opportunity to hear the literature that they study.

FICTION

James Joyce, *Eveline* (read by Gabriel Byrne)
Jamaica Kincaid, *Girl* (read by Jamaica Kincaid)
John Updike, *A & P* (read by John Updike) (Chapter 11, p. 981)

POETRY

Regina Barreca, *Nighttime Fires* (read by Regina Barreca) (Chapter 17, p. 614)
Elizabeth Bishop, *The Fish* (read by Randall Jarrell) (Chapter 12, p. 1158)
Robert Bly, *Snowbanks North of the House* (read by Robert Bly)
GwendolynBrooks, *The Mother* (read by Gwendolyn Brooks) (Chapter 9, p. 616)
Gwendolyn Brooks, *We Real Cool* (read by Gwendolyn Brooks)
E. E. Cummings, *next to of course god america i*(read by E. E. Cummings)
Emily Dickinson, *I heard a Fly buzz — when I died —* (read by Glenda Jackson)
Emily Dickinson, I heard a Fly buzz — when I died — (read by Robert Pinsky)
Emily Dickinson, *Presentiment — is that long Shadow — on the lawn* (read by Meryl Streep)
    (Chapter 6, p. 240)
Emily Dickinson, *The Soul selects her own Society* (read by Julie Harris)
Emily Dickinson, *There's a certain Slant of light* (read by Sharon Stone)
Emily Dickinson, *There's a certain Slant of light* (read by Julie Harris)
Emily Dickinson, *What Soft — Cherubic Creatures —* (read by Robert Pinsky)
Emily Dickinson, *What Soft — Cherubic Creatures —* (read by Julie Harris) (Chapter 24, p.
    940)
Emily Dickinson, *Wild Nights — Wild Nights!* (read by Robert Pinsky) (Chapter 24, p. 939)
John Donne, *The Flea* (read by Richard Burton) (Chapter 10, p. 831)
John Donne, *Song: Sweetest love, I do not go* (read by Richard Burton)
John Donne, *The Sun Rising* (read by Richard Burton)
T. S. Eliot, *The Love Song of J. Alfred Prufrock* (read by T. S. Eliot) (Chapter 13, p. 1280)
Carolyn Forché, *The Colonel* (read by Carolyn Forché) (Chapter 13, p. 1285)
Robert Frost, *Acquainted with the Night* (read by Robert Frost) (Chapter 6, p. 245)

Robert Frost, *After Apple-Picking* (read by Robert Frost) (Chapter 11, p. 991)

Robert Frost, *Birches* (read by Robert Frost)

Robert Frost, *Mending Wall* (read by Robert Frost) (Chapter 4, p. 121)

Donald Hall, *Letter with No Address* (read by Donald Hall) (Chapter 9, p. 621)

Anthony Hecht, *The Dover Bitch* (read by Anthony Hecht)

Judy Page Heitzman, *The Schoolroom on the Second Floor of the Knitting Mill* (read by Judy Page Heitzman) (Chapter 11, p. 995)

Langston Hughes, *Dream Boogie* (read by Langston Hughes)

Langston Hughes, *Dream Variations* (read by Langston Hughes)

Langston Hughes, *Harlem* (read by Langston Hughes)

Langston Hughes, *Negro* (read by Langston Hughes)

Langston Hughes, *The Negro Speaks of Rivers* (read by Langston Hughes)

Langston Hughes, *The Weary Blues* (read by Langston Hughes)

John Keats, *La Belle Dame sans Merci* (read by Sir Ralph Richardson) (Chapter 10, p. 834)

John Keats, *Ode on a Grecian Urn* (read by Sir Ralph Richardson)

John Keats, *When I have fears that I may cease to be* (read by Sir Ralph Richardson)

Aron Keesbury, *Song to a Waitress* (read by Aron Keesbury)

X. J. Kennedy, *A Visit from St. Sigmund* (read by X. J. Kennedy)

Jane Kenyon, *The Blue Bowl* (read by Donald Hall)

Galway Kinnell, *After Making Love We Hear Footsteps* (read by Galway Kinnell) (Chapter 9, p. 625)

Galway Kinnell, *Blackberry Eating* (read by Galway Kinnell) (Chapter 12, p. 1169)

Etheridge Knight, *A Watts Mother Mourns While Boiling Beans* (read by Etheridge Knight)

Maxine Kumin, *Woodchucks* (read by Maxine Kumin)

Denise Levertov, *Gathered at the River* (read by Denise Levertov)

Katharyn Howd Machan, *Hazel Tells LaVerne* (read by Katharyn Howd Machan) (Chapter 9, p. 1000)

Sharon Olds, *Rite of Passage* (read by Sharon Olds) (Chapter 9, p. 627)

Dorothy Parker, *One Perfect Rose* (read by Dorothy Parker)

Linda Pastan, *Marks* (read by Linda Pastan)

Sylvia Plath, *Daddy* (read by Sylvia Plath) (Chapter 9, p. 628)

Theodore Roethke, *My Papa's Waltz* (read by Theodore Roethke) (Chapter 9, p. 630)

William Shakespeare, *My mistress' eyes are nothing like the sun* (read by Sir John Gielgud) (Chapter 10, p. 841)

William Shakespeare, *Not marble, nor the gilded monuments* (read by Sir John Gielgud)

William Shakespeare, *Shall I compare thee to a summer's day?* (read by Sir John Gielgud)

William Shakespeare, *When forty winters shall besiege thy brow* (read by Sir John Gielgud)

Gary Soto, *Black Hair* (read by Gary Soto)

Dylan Thomas, *Do not go gentle into that good night* (read by Dylan Thomas) (Chapter 6, p. 268)

Richard Wilbur, *Love Calls Us to the Things of This World* (read by Richard Wilbur)

William Carlos Williams, *The Red Wheelbarrow* (read by William Carlos Williams)

James Wright, *A Blessing* (read by James Wright)

William Butler Yeats, *That the Night Come* (read by Samantha Eggar)

William Butler Yeats, *Adam's Curse* (read by Julie Sands)

DRAMA

Ingmar Bergman, Scene from *Nora,* a stage adaptation of Henrik Ibsen's *A Doll House* (performed by Linda Purl, David Dukes, Robert Foxworth, Natalija Nogulich, and John Vickery) From Act III (Chapter 9, p. 700)

David Henry Hwang, A Scene from *M. Butterfly* (performed by John Lithgow and B. D. Wong) Act III, Scene 1 (Chapter 13, p. 296)

William Shakespeare, A Scene from *Hamlet* (performed by Sir John Gielgud) From Act III, Scene 1 ("To be or not to be . . .") (Chapter 00, p. 000)

William Shakespeare, Two Scenes from *Hamlet* (performed by Kenneth Branagh) From Act III, Scene 1 ("To be or not to be . . .") (Chapter 7, p. 000); Act III, Scene 4 ("The Queen's Closet") (Chapter 7, p. 000)

ORDERING INFORMATION

Literature Aloud is available to adopters of *Thinking and Writing about Literature,* Second Edition. To obtain a compact disc or cassette, please contact your local Bedford/St. Martin's sales representative, or call Bedford/St. Martin's at 1-800-446-8923.

Index